*The Cornish
in America*

Some books by A. L. Rowse

CORNISH

A CORNISH CHILDHOOD
A CORNISHMAN AT OXFORD
CORNISH STORIES
TUDOR CORNWALL
POEMS CHIEFLY CORNISH
POEMS OF CORNWALL AND AMERICA
ST AUSTELL: CHURCH, TOWN, PARISH
A CORNISH ANTHOLOGY: CHOSEN

ENGLISH

THE ENGLAND OF ELIZABETH
THE EXPANSION OF ELIZABETHAN ENGLAND
THE ELIZABETHANS AND AMERICA
RALEGH AND THE THROCKMORTONS
SIR RICHARD GRENVILLE OF THE *Revenge*
THE EARLY CHURCHILLS
THE LATER CHURCHILLS
THE CHURCHILLS
THE ENGLISH SPIRIT (*Revised edition*)
TIMES, PERSONS, PLACES
WILLIAM SHAKESPEARE: A BIOGRAPHY
SHAKESPEARE'S SONNETS
(*Edited with an Introduction and Notes*)
CHRISTOPHER MARLOWE: A BIOGRAPHY
SHAKESPEARE'S SOUTHAMPTON: PATRON OF VIRGINIA
POEMS PARTLY AMERICAN

THE CORNISH IN AMERICA

A. L. ROWSE

Macmillan

© A. L. ROWSE 1969

First published in the United States of America 1969

First published in the U.K. 1969 by
MACMILLAN AND CO LTD
Little Essex Street London W C 2
and also at Bombay Calcutta and Madras
Macmillan South Africa (Publishers) Pty Ltd Johannesburg
The Macmillan Company of Australia Pty Ltd Melbourne
The Macmillan Company of Canada Ltd Toronto
Gill and Macmillan Ltd Dublin

Printed in Great Britain by
LOWE AND BRYDONE (PRINTERS) LIMITED
London

To
a great historian
SAMUEL ELIOT MORISON
this tribute
to his genius

PREFACE

The Cornish people have always had a sense of their own distinctiveness, even of their separateness, but it is only today—perhaps paradoxically, if understandably—that the outside world is becoming aware of it. Even so, even in the United States, to which the Cornish have emigrated in larger numbers than anywhere else—so that there may well be seven or eight times the number of people of Cornish name and descent there than there are in Cornwall—Americans are hardly at all aware of the contributions made by Cornish folk to the making of the greatest of modern nations. That is, with the exception of the work of the Cornish miners, the Cousin Jacks, in the predominantly mining areas. Much has been written of other elements entering into the makeup of America—the Scandinavians, the Dutch, the Italians, the French Huguenots, the Irish, the Jews, the Germans of Pennsylvania who have a whole society devoted to them—but no one has written about the Cornish in general. Perhaps this is partly because they have not been much of a writing folk.

For a small people the Cornish have been a great emigrating folk, and have left their mark, and their distinctive names, in many parts of the world. Hence the story of the Cornish emigration overseas is the biggest and most significant of

Cornish themes. In this volume I have attempted to portray their presence in, depict their contribution to, the United States—representatively, since one cannot compass the subject completely. I hope that others may follow me with volumes on the Cornish in Australia, in New Zealand, South Africa, Canada, and then we shall have a fairly complete portrait of the Cornish diaspora. Within America, I hope too that the admirable state historical societies will pursue the subject within their boundaries, and fill out the picture I have drawn. To this end I have suggested at various points topics to pursue, studies yet to be written.

Working at this subject off and on for a number of years, I have incurred more obligations than I can particularize—some of them are specified in the course of the book. My prime obligations are to All Souls College and to the Huntington Library in California, but for the resources and amenities of which I could never have written the book. There the former Director, Dr. John E. Pomfret, spurred me on to the formidable task, encouraging me in a new and unfamiliar field; it has been an immense help to have two eminent (and veteran) American historians at hand, Allan Nevins and Ray Billington, to answer the questions of a beginner. The latter has most generously read the whole book in manuscript, making valuable corrections and suggestions, for which I am most grateful. Other fellow-workers in that congenial workshop have been very helpful. Professor Andrew Rolle and Mr. David Lavender read my chapters on California and Colorado, with comments and suggestions of value; Mrs. John Balderston, Mrs. Thomas Kimber, Professor R. W. Paul, Mr. Carey Bliss, Mr. Doyce B. Nunes, Jr., Miss Mary Isabel Fry, Miss Janet Hawkins helped me in various ways.

In Pennsylvania I have received much help from Mr. Boies Penrose, Mr. James F. Dallett and the late Mr. James Rawle; in California, from Dr. Robert O. Johns who took me to Grass Valley, Captain Richard Bennett and Mr. D. C. Clinch who showed me round, Mr. Harry M. Rowe, Jr., and Mr. James De

T. Abajian of the California Historical Society; in Arizona, from Bishop Restarick's daughter, Mrs. Withington and her son, and from the late Mr. John M. Foote, who introduced me to the ghost-towns; in Oregon, from Professor Earl Pomeroy, Mrs. Keith Powell, and from my boyhood friend, Mr. Ernest Brokenshire; in Vermont, from the late John Spargo; in Wisconsin, from Professor William B. Sachse, Mr. Kitto of Beloit, and Mr. Robert Neal who took care of me at Mineral Point and introduced me to the Blue Mounds country; in Michigan, to Professor Anthony Forbes, to whom I owe my acquaintance with the Upper Peninsula; in Chicago, from the late Thomas K. Davey, engineer at the Palmer House, as a young man a miner at Calstock; in Minnesota, the late Dr. Donald Cowling, my Oxford friend Mr. Louis J. Hill and Miss Robina Kneebone; for Colorado, Mr. Harry Clarke and Mr. and Mrs. G. R. Mackenzie; for South Dakota, Mr. Philip Dyer of the Homestake Mine; for Oklahoma, Mrs. Norman Penhall; in New York, Miss Charlotte Seymour Day; in New Hampshire, Mr. Donald S. Rickard, long ago on my first visit to the United States in 1951. I have received much help and information from various correspondents, whom I can only thank here generally.

I have been much indebted to a number of libraries in the United States, which have generously sent books to the Huntington for my use, and to others where I have worked. I am much indebted to the State Historical Library at Madison, Wisconsin, where I worked through the winter of 1958–59; to the Marquette Historical Society Library in Michigan, the Los Angeles Public Library, the University of Illinois Library, and a number of university and college libraries where I have visited.

At Oxford I am most indebted to Professor Idris Foster, without whose help I could not have tackled the thorny subject of Cornish surnames. In Cornwall my old friend, the late Claude Berry, editor of the *West Briton*, helped with early extracts from the paper; I am also obliged to Sir Geoffrey

x   *Preface*

Harmsworth and the present editor for allowing me to use its files. I am most grateful to Mr. R. R. Blewett of St. Day, for the generous help he has given me from his immense store of knowledge regarding Cornish surnames. Mr. Alfred Jenkin supplied me with a most useful account of his family's mining in California. At home it has been a particular pleasure to be helped by my old friends Mr. Jack Blake, and Mr. F. L. Harris, the latter of whom has read my typescript and made valuable criticisms and suggestions.

A. L. ROWSE

The Huntington Library
San Marino, California
March 1967

CONTENTS

PREFACE vii

1 · Cornish Folk in the United States   3
2 · Cornish Names in America   24
3 · Early Folk in Virginia and New England   37
4 · New Jersey and New York   59
5 · Pennsylvania   85
6 · The Old South   117
7 · Stepping Westward   140
8 · The First Wave of Miners: Michigan   161
9 · Wisconsin and Illinois: the Lead Region   196
10 · California: Gold and Otherwise   241
11 · Nevada, Idaho, Utah: Miners and Mormons   287
12 · Colorado: Gold and Silver   322
13 · Montana, Oregon, Washington, Dakota   351
14 · Arizona   384
15 · From Nineteenth to Twentieth Century   400

APPENDIX: Cornish Surnames   427

INDEX   439

The Cornish in America

1 CORNISH FOLK AND THE UNITED STATES

The inhabitants of the United States today are in large part, in President Kennedy's phrase, "a nation of immigrants." They are, in varying degrees, an extrapolation of the whole of Europe, with others added —though the contributions of some elements to the common stock are not significant. After all, by far the most significant contributions—the ones that shaped the country, transported their customs, traditions, institutions, with their stocks—were those from the British Isles.

These were not wholly English-speaking, though people think of them, wrongly, as simply Anglo-Saxons. There were those who spoke Celtic languages—the Highland Scots and Irish, from the northern group speaking Gaelic and Erse, the Welsh-speaking from the southern group, which includes also the languages spoken by the Cornish and the Bretons. For within the British Isles these older peoples were there before the Angles and Saxons crossed the North Sea to conquer and colonize the Lowland zone of Britain and make it England.

The Highland zone of Britain—roughly the territories north and west of a line drawn from Exeter in the Southwest to Newcastle in the Northeast—is still occupied dominantly by these earlier peoples. In addition to the four main groups that have emerged out of the pressures of history—English, Welsh, Scots, Irish—there is a fifth: the Cornish.

Americans are, for the most part, quite unaware of the Cornish people in their midst, and of the contribution these have made to the nation. The exception is with regard to mining: the mining areas have always been aware of the notable contribution made, especially in the nineteenth century, by the Cousin Jacks and there is a spreading consciousness about them and what they did, which I hope this book will help to advance. The Cornish, as Allan Nevins reminds me, have never produced a popular poet:* they have no Burns, or other peoples outside the British Isles would be more aware of them. Their genius has been for mining, so that their leading figures have been scientists, inventors and mining engineers, along with seamen, like Sir Richard Grenville of the *Revenge*, Admirals Hawke and Boscawen, or Bligh of the *Bounty*.

Within the United States there must be seven or eight times the number of Cornish folk that there are in Cornwall—it depends on how you reckon them. There are the old Cornish who came in from the first along with the English, but whose distinctive names marked them off from ordinary English and continue to carry their origins and where they came from through all the generations to this day. Such names are Chenoweth, Trevillian, Penrose, Argall, Bonython, Treffry— we find these quite early: they are, and can only be, Cornish. But the majority of Cornish people have names that do not distinguish them from the English—Williams, Thomas, Harris, Rowe—and this makes for difficulty in the subject. They are apt to get merged and lost in the mass as time goes on. One has to know, from records or from family tradition, whether they are Cornish or not. Names like Foote, Fox, Moyle, Nicholls, Peter, Rickard—each of whom made his

---

* Keats, however, was of Cornish descent, as were the Brontës and Matthew Arnold on the female side.

contribution—do not immediately tell one. A Penrose or a Rawle, a Chenoweth or a Trevillian, remembers his ancestry to the present generation. Then there are the newer immigrants—especially of the mass-emigration in the nineteenth century—who, whatever their names, can still retain the sense of their Cornishry and their origins, as I know, to the fourth and fifth generations. For, perhaps the deepest characteristic they have in common is their particular loyalty to Cornwall, and their sense of it, overt or latent, conscious or unconscious. There is plenty of evidence that Cornwall has a quite exceptional capacity to draw and retain the hearts of its children, wherever they may be. It is a power of attraction so strong that it is hardly accountable, certainly not definable; but we shall come across plenty of examples of it all through this book.

The Cornish are a small people, but a quite distinctive one. They have inhabited from prehistoric times the little peninsula at the extreme southwestern end of Britain, running from the frontier of the Tamar River out into the Atlantic with Land's End and the Scilly Isles beyond.* It is a very beautiful land, with half-a-dozen different landscapes within its narrow boundaries, and two contrasting coasts—the quiet southern coast on the English Channel opposite Brittany, and the stormy north coast with its great cliffs confronting the Atlantic and taking the beat of it. Standing on one of those cliffs—such as Beeny Cliff, sung in the poems of Thomas Hardy—one looks out across the waste of waters with nothing between one and the coasts of Newfoundland and Maine. Thither went the first emigrants, fishing folk, from the little land. By a pleasant return, all Americans who come to Cornwall respond to its beauty and feel its separateness from England, its difference.

* It will be remembered that it was on a reef between these two that the tanker, *Torrey Canyon*, owned by Barracuda Tankers Corporation and under charter to Union Oil of California, was lost in March, 1967.

With such narrow boundaries and such restricted resources —except for its wealth in minerals—the Cornish have been a great people for emigrating. In their much smaller, and humbler, way they have been as good at it as the Scots. Dr. Johnson said that the finest high road a Scot ever sees is the high road that leads from Edinburgh into England: much the same might be said of the Cornish and the high road across the Tamar into England. But in earlier times, we must remember, transit by water was easier than transit by land. With a situation like Cornwall, almost entirely surrounded by water, emigration to other parts of Britain—to London, to South Wales or Tyneside to work in the mines—was often by ship from the Cornish ports. In emigrating to America they often went, from early days, direct from the ports at hand, Plymouth, Fowey, Falmouth, Padstow; or, later, by ship from one of these to Southampton, London, or Liverpool first, as we shall see.

Thus the Cornish—distinguished as both an emigrating and a mining people—have left their mark upon Great Britain and the United States alike. And not only these: their mark is strong upon South Africa and Australia (particularly South Australia), and is observable in Canada and New Zealand.

There is an old saying, "wherever there is a hole in the earth, you will find a Cornishman at the bottom of it." This refers to the Cornish genius for mining, a skill inherited from many generations of forebears, for mining goes back to prehistoric times within the peninsula. They have been a marvellous mining people, and it is chiefly as such that they have left their mark upon the world—though they have been distinguished too, for such a small people, in the allied fields of mine-engineering, technical and scientific inventions. It was a Cornishman, Richard Trevithick, who first got a steam-locomotive to go; it was another, the brilliant scientist, Sir Humphry Davy, who invented the miner's safety-lamp; a third, Henry Trengrouse, who spent life and fortune on developing the rocket life-saving apparatus for ships at sea.

They have been rather undistinguished in the arts—perhaps, a poor hardworking folk, they had little time for the amenities of life. William Saroyan has written of himself as the one Armenian writer for his people of some 300,000. There are several times that number of Cornish folk scattered round the world and I am their voice today: *Lef a Gwernow*.

For, wherever they may be, they are conscious of themselves as Cornish folk—or a great many of them are. For one thing, they are reminded where they came from by their surnames:

> By Tre, Pol or Pen
> Ye may know most Cornishmen.

This means such names as Trelawny, Polglase or Penrose. There are, besides, many names, with other prefixes, which are specifically, unmistakably Cornish—stemming from the old Cornish language, which was ceasing to be spoken in the seventeenth and eighteenth centuries, so that people may no longer know what they mean.

There are several thousand people called Chenoweth in the United States, many times more than in all Britain, let alone in Cornwall by itself. The name is a pure Cornish name, meaning Newhouse, and could be nothing else. The Chenoweths are mostly old stock, who came into Virginia early and fanned out from there. So most of them will have become merged into the mass of the population, and probably few of them know the meaning of their name, though more may know its origin. Or take the name of Trevillian in its various forms. It is more usually spelt Trevelyan in Britain—the form preserved in the famous family to which the historians, Sir George Otto and George Macaulay Trevelyan, belonged. The name is a place-name; the old medieval house—still owned after seven hundred years by a Trevelyan—stands high up in the parish of St. Veep in a windy spot above the green waters of the River Fowey. The interesting thing is that the more common American spelling, Trevillian, represents the correct

Cornish pronunciation. There are several hundred times more of the name in America than there are in Britain. In central Virginia there is a village called Trevilians, with a station on the railroad where there was a scuffle during the Civil War.

There are so many names that have made their mark all round the world, which are and could only be Cornish. Such are Wilfred Grenfell, of Labrador, the heroic doctor who gave up his life to serving the Eskimos; or George Grenfell, explorer of the Congo. In the life of South Australia a Bonython has an honorable place, in South Africa a Colenso. In the history of New Zealand another Colenso, a cousin of the celebrated bishop of Natal, was a no less controversial figure, and the country's first botanist; a Tregear was one of its prime authorities on the Maori and the Polynesian languages, a Curnow—which means the Cornishman—is New Zealand's leading poet today. These are all recognizable Cornish surnames.

Similarly in America with names like Penhallow, the old New Hampshire family going back to the colonial Chief Justice, the two families of Penrose and Rawle, both famous in the history of Pennsylvania; the Pendarvis name which preceded the Pinckneys in possession of their delectable estate on the river at Charleston in South Carolina. A Pearce, a Penrose, a Vivian in the life of Colorado, a Richard Trevellick or a John Spargo in the story of the labor movement, a Trelease in the botanical history of Missouri, creator of the famous garden at St. Louis, for whom Mount Trelease in Colorado is named, a Tregaskis to the fore in journalism today, a Coon in the academic field of anthropology, a Trebilcock eminent as a portrait-painter: these are all Cornish names. Tremaine is a fairly common name in Cornwall: the well-known New York family must be of Cornish descent. There are some other, better known figures in American history—like General Francis T. Nicholls, who had an heroic career in the Civil War and became the first governor of Louisiana after Reconstruction—that we know to be Cornish but whose names are not specific, not recognizable as such. After all, in Cornwall today most people have ordinary English names. Similarly in America the great majority of Cornish folk are not distinguishable by their names: they are lost among the people with English names. There are many times more people of Cornish descent than are recognizable from having specific Cornish names which could be no other.

The miners brought over with them their inherited skill, their nose for minerals, their instinct for mining them. A fine old mining engineer of the third generation up in Grass Valley, in the foothills of the Sierra above Sacramento—Captain Dick Bennett—reminded me of the familiar phrase, " 'e d'knaw tin," i.e. he knows tin when he sees it. (They have known it at home in Cornwall since the Phoenicians.) When men were wanted for the mines, or a job was going, they always knew somebody at home for it: Cousin Jack. So they became known all over the world as "Cousin Jacks"; "Cousin Jennies" for the womenfolk seems to be a later addition. All Cornishmen the world over recognize themselves as Cousin Jacks. I am a Cousin Jack. The rhythm I keep between Cornwall and California—where I mine away in the basement of the Huntington Library for much of my material—is very much the rhythm of the miners, my forebears.

With their womenfolk they brought over with them also their way of life, their customs, traditions and folk-lore; their adherence to Methodism, with its chapels, Sunday schools, choir-outings and "tea-treats"—just as at home; their cooking, their utensils, their cherished objects, their little bits of china—always the most imperishable of objects—what archaeologists have accustomed us to call their "artifacts"; their nursery rhymes, their hymns and songs.

All this relates to the later mass-emigration, dominantly of miners, in the nineteenth century. It naturally applies much less to the earlier migration, of individuals, families, small groups—such as the Cornish Quakers who went to Pennsylvania. These merge more rapidly into the surrounding population, become absorbed—even if something remains over in the temperament, in conscious or unconscious memory. It is only where a group is large enough that it can impose its ways and remain distinctive for a longer period, and that means in the mining settlements. Such places as the Upper Peninsula of Michigan, the coppery shores of Lake Superior; Mineral Point in the southwest corner of Wisconsin, lead country to which they came across country from the Great Lakes, or up the Mississippi and Fever rivers; beautiful Grass Valley and Nevada City, neighboring towns in California; over the Sierra to Virginia City, Nevada, not far from lovely Lake Tahoe; Central City, Colorado, in the mountains not far from Pike's Peak; Butte, Montana, with its lurid reputation, still producing copper, with a cloud of dust hanging over it; or remote Bisbee in Arizona, right down on the Mexican frontier. (Or beyond it, for at Pachuca, north of Mexico City, is another Cornish community.)

In these places they have not forgotten the old home. Once I spent a bright Sunday morning in the graveyard at Mineral Point reading the names on the simple stones. A very old fellow, with one foot in the grave, told me that his grandparents had come from a place called Tuckingmill: "that's in Cornwall, isn't it?" It is indeed, plumb in the mining country of West Cornwall, between Redruth and Camborne, its center. What was no less characteristic was that the old fellow knew the run of the disused adits and levels under the graveyard, the slope—the whole town was honeycombed underneath with them. That afternoon a strapping farmer called Sawle said to me that he had "never been back"—the phrase itself was touching—but "we have called a strain of our wheat 'Trezise': that's Cornish isn't it?" It is, indeed. When the lead-mines gave out, the men went further afield—many of them to gold-mining in California and back again to buy a farm: from miners to farmers and so into the professions, a good sprinkling of them into education. Such is a fairly regular pattern.

At Beloit, Wisconsin, I recognized the name Kitto over the leading printing-shop in the town. I went in: there was Mr. Kitto, the second generation over from Mineral Point, where his people had been miners; his father had set up the printing press. He pointed out across the way the establishment of Mr. Penberthy, the dentist, apparently something of a humorous Cornish character. At Grass Valley one golden autumn day I was given a proper Cornish picnic, of pasties and saffron buns, in the grounds of the great Empire Mine—the grumbling machinery now stilled, hundreds of miles of levels tunnelled out beneath that countryside. Never were pasties better made than by the old Cornishwoman of the third generation in the town. As for saffron buns—rich, brightly colored, aromatic—they offer a test of Cornishry: if you are not Cornish, you are apt not to like them; if you are a true Cornishman, you do.

As for the artifacts, the traces of those vanished miners, they are still to be seen across the wasteland of the mining settlements and elsewhere. At Central City, Colorado, are fine "examples of Cornish dry-stone walling, built by miners to terrace their cabins on the mountain side, that have successfully withstood the ravages of the summer heat and the winter snow for more than a century. These same gold miners in their spare time built the opera-house which, like the one at Shullsburg, was open to wind and rain until the University of Colorado restored it for their summer drama and opera festivals, thus keeping alive the tradition of singing first begun by the Cornish choirs there. Across the street still stand in good condition the old livery stables erected for the theatre patrons and owned by Richard B. Williams, Cousin Jack and Sheriff of Gilpin County, who was killed by a gunslinger."[1] On another note, I am told that St. James's Church in that town was also built by the miners in their spare time, and that there they keep up a good tradition with their choir. The Grass Valley choir has been famous all through our time for its performances, many of them on the radio, especially of carols at

Christmas time. At Shullsburg in Wisconsin "an opera-house, given by a Copeland who married a Richards from Treswithian Downs near Camborne, awaits the demolition gangs as it lives out its last days as a hardware store."

At nearby Mineral Point a remarkable work of reconstruction has been effected by Robert Neal, whose grandmother was brought over as a child in 1847. In the 1930's he came back to find the good old stone-cottages in Shake-Rag Street going to rack and ruin—"Shake-Rag" from the miners' wives shaking their dusters out of the window to call their menfolk in to dinner from their diggings out on the hillside. (There is a New Diggings not far away.) The houses are of good workmanship, "perfect examples of the cottage on a Cornish moor adapted to the Wisconsin landscape, built on rock and into rock where they excavated a cellar for their root vegetables to protect them against the severe frosts, a hazard not met with in Cornwall." Robert Neal restored and rehabilitated them with excellent taste, and filled them with the good pieces of furniture, the knick-knacks, the Staffordshire figures the old folk brought over with them. There they stand behind their Victorian street-lamp—Pendarvis, Polperro, Trelawny and a fourth to be called Newlyn—like any such group of early Victorian houses to be found in Cornwall. An enduring monument, for they are now scheduled as historic buildings by the Department of the Interior. The local historical society—another product of the same devotion—is housed in a larger, but more American-style red-brick building that belonged to a family of the name of Gundry.

Further afield, at San José in California, another work of reclamation is going forward. Nearby was New Almadén, greatest of quicksilver-mines, much worked by the Cornish. In the museum at San José the local historical society has brought together from the mine "Cornish candlesticks, organ stops from the Methodist church that has now disappeared, parts of a Cornish wheelbarrow slenderly designed to work in the narrowest of stopes, lengths of tramway the Cornish introduced . . . and, most impressive of all, the working beam from the Cornish pump that was set up at the Cora Blanca shaft in 1873 . . . In 1961 the Cornish school-house was just standing, leaning on the wind, a home for wild bees and rattlers, but since then the bulldozer has levelled it, and the laths and plaster have been carried away like those of the church and the Cornish boarding-houses and the neat company cottages before them."

At Sonora, in California, the museum displays "a Cornish wooden cradle brought over in 1867 by Mrs. Edwina Carne when she came to join her husband who was the engineer at the Soulsby gold mine, one of the oldest in California." It was first worked by Cornish miners. Or on the way out west, the last lap, "at Wadsworth on the Nevada desert in a clump of trees and a tangle of undergrowth by the side of the Truckee river you can fork up, just beneath the surface of the sand, buttons, crockery, old glass bottles turned violet by the heat of the sun, the shoes of oxen and horses, wheel-ties and handwrought square-headed nails dropped by Cornish lead-miners from Wisconsin as they rested after their forty-mile dry drive from the Humboldt Sink, counted their losses and calculated their chances of scaling the razor-edge of the Sierras." Or there is the ghost-town of Pearce near Tombstone in Arizona, "where the Cornishman James Pearce discovered the Commonwealth Mine that yielded $15,000,000 in gold"—we shall learn its story when we reach Arizona at the end of our trail —now "a beautiful waste of adobes, mills and winding gear."

And so one might go on, across the enormous land.

They brought their melodies with them too. Helen Howe tells us that in her Pennsylvania childhood a friend of the family used to sing to them the long religious lyric, with its mystical meanings, that had been sung in antiphony by man and woman for generations in the long winter evenings in Cornwall. He had learned it from the miners on Lake Superior. My grandfather and grandmother could sing it all the way from the first verse, "What is your One-O?"—this refers to God Almighty—to the Twelve Apostles at the end, with its recapitulation in reverse. It is really a dialogue between male and female voice.

> Come and I will sing you.
>   What will you sing me?
> I will sing you One-O.
>   What is your One-O?
> One of them is All Alone
>   and ever will remain so.

When the interminable song is at an end, it is recapitulated thus, though I am unable to elucidate all the meanings:

> Come and I will sing you.
>   What will you sing me?
> I will sing you Twelve-O.
>   What is your Twelve-O?
> Twelve is the Twelve Apostles,
>   Eleven of them is gone to heaven,
> Ten is the Ten Commandments,
>   Nine is the moonshine bright and clear,
> Eight is the Eight Archangels,
>   Seven is the Seven Stars in the sky,
> Six is the Charmèd Watchers,
>   Five are the Ferrymen in the boats,
> Four is the Gospel Makers,
>   Three of them are Strangers,
> Two of them are Lily-White Babes,
>   Clothèd all in green-O,
> One of them is All Alone,
>   And ever will remain so.

One recognizes the Three Strangers as the three Magi, but who are the Charmèd Watchers, and the Lily-White Babes, and who are the Five Ferrymen in the boats?

This song penetrated into the Appalachians, for Cecil

Sharp heard it sung to its ancient pentatonic plainchant in North Carolina. By the time it came to my mother and father's generation they could not remember it all, or sing it through. But, by now, there was a reverse traffic, with all the miners coming to and fro, and my father in distant Cornwall could sing the Plantation melodies of the Christy Minstrels:

> O Susanna, don't you cry for me,
> I've come from Alabama
> With my banjo on my knee.

We come to the more elusive question of temperament, for there is such a thing as a Cornish temperament. Some people find it peculiar, difficult to deal with. Perhaps it is not altogether easy, but it seems quite natural to us. And why should Irish, Highland Scots, Welsh, Cornish, be expected to conform to English standards, be cut down to Anglo-Saxon patterns? One doesn't want everyone standardized, reduced to a boring monochrome—there is too much of that in the modern world already. The more variety of pattern, the more interesting. The Cornish are certainly an interesting people, and they are not quite like anyone else.

Let me illustrate their difference by a story. Three men of Cornish stock were in a room together: Boies Penrose, of the present generation of that famous family, Carleton S. Coon, famous in his own right as an anthropologist, and I. I happened to say that I was conscious of a defect of the Cornish temperament in myself—that I wasn't any good at teamwork. Coon, third generation in America, said "That goes for me too"; Penrose, eighth generation, added "And for me, too."

The truth is that the Cornish are exceedingly individualistic. Coming into a larger society, however, they stick together and are markedly clannish—there are Cornish Societies in London and Oxford, as there have been in New York and Detroit. Cornishmen are apt to have the sensitiveness not to say, the touchiness—of Celts, the one skin too few, the intuitiveness along with the rawness. They are easy to wound, but good fighters. Bob FitzSimmons, the famous blacksmith-pugilist, whose punch was like a hammer on an anvil —he was a great hero to my father's generation—was a Cornishman, whose career in America was proudly followed at home. So too were the celebrated champion, Polkinghorne, a Regency heavyweight, and the excellent Len Harvey of my own generation. Wrestling, however, has always been the historic Cornish sport—as with the Bretons; at home I have watched Cornish-Breton wrestling matches, with all the ill-feeling engendered by their slightly differing rules of the game. (Celts never have been able to unite—one reason why the Anglo-Saxons always get the better of them.) The miners brought their favorite sport to the mining camps.

The Cornish are a hard-working little people, forever burrowing and tunnelling underground, not much emerging into the light of day. Not for them the great fortunes of Rockefellers, Fords, Mellons, Carnegies—though there have been some rare exceptions with the Penroses in Colorado, the Bonythons in South Australia; not for them Presidencies or vice-royalties, dukedoms or Orders of Merit. It is characteristic that George Stephenson got all the profit, and most of the credit, for the steam-locomotive that Trevithick invented; Richard Pearce brought in the new smelting process that made the fortune of Colorado gold-mining, but he did not make the big money out of it. Only two or three men of Cornish blood have become United States Senators, as only one has ever become Prime Minister in England—that was a long time ago, with Lord Treasurer Godolphin in Queen Anne's reign. The Cornish have always been a poor and hard-working people, like the Scots; they bear the burden and the heat of the day, they do not get the laurels.

Nevertheless, they are on the whole a contented people, not given to making trouble, forever striking for more pay and less work, shirking their dues and obligations: ca'canny is not a Cornish word or a Cornish concept. In all the days of my youth I never heard my china-clay worker father—from tin-mining to china-clay was the social pattern—even mention the subject of wages, and that at eighteen shillings a week to raise a family on, in the end rising to the magnificent sum of just over £2 a week. He just set up a little grocery store to help himself. I have noticed that that is a regular pattern in the Cornish settlements in the United States. It is instinctive among the Cornish to be fairly independent, to make themselves so, by taking another part-time occupation on, if necessary. This goes back to the dominant social pattern in Cornwall for centuries: a small holding of one's own, with tin-streaming or tin-mining on the side. A man might be poor, but he had an essential independence of spirit.

So, in coming to America, they immediately made good citizens. Coming from the democratic society of their mining towns and villages, where they called no one lord and master and rarely saw a squire, they took to the democratic tone of American society like ducks to water. In any case there was the raw, primitive equality of mining camps and settlements. So one watches a fairly general social configuration emerge from the mid-nineteenth century: the Cornish, Methodist in religion, become Republican in politics, are mainly Oddfellows or to a lesser extent Masons in their club-affiliations. (Actually, the well-known Order of Elks was founded in America by a Cornishman, Charles A. S. Vivian.) In the Civil War the sympathies of the democratic Cornish—monarchy and aristocracy meant little to them, unlike the more conservative English—were naturally with the North against slavery. Not many people of Cornish descent fought on the Southern side. A regiment of Cornish miners from Illinois was badly cut up at Chickamauga.

But the Cornish took little part in politics, none whatever in the corruptions of city-life: Tammany and the Mafia-style Chicago Syndicate are Irish and Italian contributions to American life. The Cornish are much more to the fore today in education and the Methodist ministry in addition to their old-time genius for mechanical engineering and mining.

There goes with their independence of mind a certain

smugness—I have observed that flavoring, like a streak of saffron in their cake again and again—and, not unnaturally, a distinct tendency to boast. If not a proud people, like the Scots, the Cornish are proud of themselves. And why not? It may be that this characteristic goes with being a small people (they are small physically, for the most part): if a small people does not speak up for itself, nobody else is going to do it for them. And isn't this more in keeping with the pioneering spirit, the good hearty boasting that was so characteristic of nineteenth-century Americans, which everybody noticed in them long before Dickens and up to the First World War —the rugged, authentic America of Mark Twain, Bret Harte and Jack London?

—A far more exciting America than the middle-class America of today, with its sense of guilt, its professed lack of confidence, its apologetics, its habit of standing superfluously in a white sheet for sins it has not committed (really the obverse of a superiority-complex); above all, the habit of understatement, of not stating things too crisply for fear of offending someone. The Anglo-Saxons, without the Celts to help them out, do themselves an injustice: they are more intelligent than they make themselves appear, nor are they really so uninteresting as they make out. In any case, this inflection of under-emphasis is very recent with English-speaking people: it is quite un-Elizabethan, nor does it hold good of Georgian or Victorian England, any more than of New England or the Old South or the Western Frontier. It is quite foreign to the spirit of Shakespeare and Dickens, as it is to Mark Twain, or Walt Whitman or William Faulkner.

The curious thing is that the Cornish have not much written themselves up—in fact, quite insufficiently so, or this book would not have been necessary. This is partly because they have not been much of a writing folk—more expert with pick and shovel than with the pen. The mining folk who came to America were largely illiterate—one reason for the difficulty in writing about them: they left little in the way of written evidence. They produced no writers like a Mari Sandoz or a Rölvaag, let alone a novelist of genius like Willa Cather. My own parents at home in Cornwall could not read or write with any ease—perhaps I have somewhat over-compensated them in that. That too represents a social pattern: the third generation from a Cornish miner in America is apt to produce a professor.

There is the question of humor, always a subtle matter, very characteristic of a people, yet hardly describable. Some persons think that the Cornish have no sense of humor—and many of them have not. Speaking generally, other people certainly find it peculiar, an odd sense of humor. It may be primitive, that of a simple state of society, for it relates in essence to the practical joke: it is the practical joke carried over into an attitude of mind. It is hard to describe, though I have often observed it at work. The Cornish may be keeping a straight face, but they are really laughing at you; they are keeping it to themselves, but they are laughing *at*, rather than *with*. Taking in the "foreigner"—i.e. an Englishman—is always fair game. It may be that this is something that people don't like about them: people prefer the laugh to be with them, rather than against them. In overt expression, Cornish people prefer the old-fashioned outright humor of exaggeration—something more in keeping with Dickens or Mark Twain or Lincoln's favorite Artemus Ward. Anything rather than the supercilious snigger of the suburban intellectual!

Perhaps the odd-man-out, rather teasing and bantering sense of humor of the Cornish goes with their superstitiousness, for they are certainly a superstitious folk. They brought their underground superstitions to America with them, all the folklore of the mines—the "knockers" that forebode ill events, the caving in of the "burden" upon the men, the sudden inrush of water, the flame of gas leaping upon a level, the crash of a "skip." They had hard lives, these poor fellows: it was thus that a first cousin of mine died, a young man, in a mine in Arizona. Or one stands in a country cemetery by the shores of Lake Superior, the noise of the lake mingling with the wind in the pines, beside the grave of two Berryman brothers killed together in their twenties in an accident in Central Mine, so far away from home: April 29, 1872, "They fought the good fight." Or one comes upon an affecting entry in a Southern diary: at Charlotte, North Carolina, July 26, 1835, the Reverend M. A. Curtis "attended the funeral of a deceased miner, by name Trewartha, and about twenty-five years of age. He had come out from Cornwall, England, but a few weeks previous, and went to his grave unwept by a single relative or friend. He is said to have left a mother in England."[2]

If the Cornish are a somewhat secret people, living their life to themselves, is it any wonder, considering the many centuries they lived, shut away within the cocoon of their own language, in the narrow confines of that peninsula surrounded by the sea?

In all this it is evident that I have had the later, nineteenth-century mass-emigration in mind. The earlier immigrants, arriving in ones or twos, as a family or even as a group, were not numerous enough to impose themselves. They merged well, though often their specific names still identify them, and many of them remembered their origins, where they came from, kept a tincture of Cornishry. To begin with, one sees them coming in along with other folk from the old country, especially in West Country ships. Since in the original Jacobean plantation movement the Plymouth Company, backed by Sir Ferdinando Gorges and his associates, was based upon the West Country, it was natural that Cornishmen should trickle into Maine along with the others.[3] Considering that Robert Trelawny, the well-known Plymouth merchant trading to New England, was a Cornishman it is surprising that there were not more.

The most interesting earlier migration is into Pennsylvania. There we have not only the famous family of Penrose, going back to Bartholomew Penrose who arrived from building ships at Bristol to build ships on the Delaware in 1700, but a much more numerous clan of Quaker Penroses (Bartholomew's progeny, coming down to Senator Boies Penrose, were decidedly not Quakers). The Rawles, who occupied such a place in the legal and public life of the state for a quarter of a millennium, were Quakers. Lawrence Growden, the Quaker pewterer from Cornwall, built up the largest estate in Pennsylvania around his country place, Trevose; his heiress carried the estate to Joseph Galloway, who had it confiscated from him by the Revolution as a Loyalist. There were many others in Pennsylvania to diversify the picture, not only Quakers but workers in the slate quarries, the iron-mines and, to some extent, coal. For the Cornish worked mainly at hard minerals, not soft.

And so we come to the mass-emigration of the nineteenth century. For the first decades of that century Cornwall was the copper-kingdom *par excellence*, producing more copper than all the rest of the world. In the 1860's copper production collapsed and some thousands of miners, mainly from West Cornwall, were forced to leave home to make a living. These were the people who came to the copper shores of the Keweenaw Peninsula of Michigan, to other settlements such as Ironwood (to which my father's sister went), and thence fanned out. Others went to the lead-mines of southwest Wisconsin and northwest Illinois. Hence it is that three generations afterwards they are so thick on the ground in Chicago and Detroit, two of the chief centers of Cornish population in the United States. Some thousands became Forty-Niners and went to California, either directly from Cornwall or from Michigan and the upper Mississippi Valley. From the California gold-country they spread out into the mining territories of Nevada, Utah, Idaho, South Dakota and Montana. Thus it is that there is a strong Cornish element in the population of California: from the original settlements they have moved heavily into San Francisco and into the Los Angeles area. In

Pasadena alone, for example, there are not merely scores but hundreds of people with specific Cornish names; that must mean that there are many times more people of Cornish descent, but of ordinary English names, there besides. The Cornish take to California.

A later wave of Cornish mining immigration brought them notably to Colorado and Arizona; in consequence, in addition to what is left of the mining settlements, there is a marked Cornish element in the populations of Denver and of Phoenix.

This, then, is the predominant picture. One does not find them in any number in the Old South—the South had its own slaves; though one does find them fetching up in larger urban centers, like New Orleans. The same holds good for New York and Philadelphia, where there are many hundreds of Cornish names and one should multiply by ten or twelve to get nearer an estimate of the Cornish element as a whole. If one thinks of a colored map, one might see the Cornish contribution to the American population extending in a sickle-shape from the Old East, based on Philadelphia and New York, around by Detroit and Chicago, then across to the Far West to Butte, Montana, broadening out in a wider swathe through the mining country of the West—California, Nevada, Arizona—to touch with its tip the Mexican border at San Diego, which has a very fair sprinkling of them.

With many Cornish families one half of the family is overseas—it is the case with my own family. So that in Cornwall one has the natural sense of being in constant contact with America. In the village of my youth, Tregonissey near the town of St. Austell, the goings-on in Butte, Montana, were more familiar to us than those of London. In one road in a village near my home the cottages are named in succession, Calumet, Butte, Montana—proudly for their menfolk have returned thence. Cornish speech, with its short *a*'s as in "grass" and "father"—not "grahss" and "fahther" as in the London dialect that has submerged the south of England—is closer to American speech. I think Americans feel a closer sense of affinity when they come to Cornwall. Some sense of this may have transpired in the remarkable episode of the war, when for six months before D-Day Cornwall was occupied by a hundred thousand American troops practicing their invasion exercises on West Country beaches for the liberation of Europe—and without an incident, with nothing but mutual goodwill. Of how many "occupations" could this be expected?

From a lengthening experience and a fairly wide correspondence, I know that many of the American Cornish have a deep feeling for their original home. Some of them have a fixation on it, and come back again and again; some have an unappeasable nostalgia who cannot make it. For Cornwall has a strange power to draw, like no other part of the British Isles—as to that there is plenty of evidence, and not only from Cornish folk either.

In the cathedral at Truro a register is kept of Cornish exiles all over the world, and there they are always remembered, as in the hearts of their kinsfolk.

NOTES

1. A. C. Todd, "Some Cornish Industrial Artifacts in the United States of America," *The Journal of Industrial Archaeology*, vol. 1, 154ff.
2. *Devon and Cornwall Notes and Queries*, July 1962, 60.
3. cf. my book, *The Elizabethans and America*, chapter V.

2 CORNISH NAMES IN AMERICA

The majority of Cornish people in America, as in Britain, have ordinary English names. They are called such names as Williams, Thomas, Richards, Johns, Pearce, Edwards, Davies, Harris, Harvey, Jenkins, Phillips, Roberts, Rogers, Stephens, Hicks, Martin, Mitchell, James, Nicholls, Bennetts. Matthews, Julian, Walters, and so on. Those are among the English surnames that are most common among us, and they belong to the largest class of surnames—those formed from a Christian name or first name, usually with an *s*, to denote William's child, or Richard's. Pearce comes from Piers, for Peter; Mitchell is a softened form of Michael; Rickard seems to be a hardened form of Richard; Hicks a diminutive of Richard. Sometimes there are variants of these names: Jones is a far more common form of Johns; Davey is a Cornish form of Davies, more common in West Cornwall, where the Cornish language (a form of Welsh) lasted longest; so too with Harry as a surname; while Toms is quite frequent with us, as well as the more common Thomas and Thompson or Thomson.

The next largest class of English name that is also common with us is that of occupation names: Smith, Baker, Taylor, Tucker and Dyer (both from the woollen industry), Cook,

Carpenter, Carter, Brewer, Clark (i.e. Clerk), Chapman (meaning merchant or trader), Hooper, Wright and such. A third class of names is personally descriptive, frequently of coloring: Brown, Black (more common with us is the form Blake), White, Gray. Others in this class describe personal characteristics: Broad, Long, Short, Bone, Foot; or personal status, such as Bond—which means descended from a bondman, or serf; Parsons, from a parson or cleric. A fourth class is that of place-names, telling us where the original person or family dwelt: Green, at or near the village green; Hall, at the hall; and so with Wood, Warren, Hill, Rowe, which means dweller in the row or street.[1] Naturally, since most of the specific place-names in Cornwall come from the old language, nearly all our surnames coming from specific places follow suit—names like Penrosc, Lanyon, Polglase, Trewartha.

Thus there is a greater variety of surnames among Cornish people than those of any other county, for there are those of the majority having English names, and those of a considerable minority with pure Cornish names. Since the language went on longest in West Cornwall—it died out in popular use in the eighteenth century and has been revived only by individuals in our time—pure Cornish names are thicker on the ground in the West. In a sense surnames are almost doubled with us: all those four classes of English names can be paralleled with pure Cornish names, though in different proportions.

Let us give some examples from each class. I repeat that most Cornish people with names formed from Christian or first names will have English names, like Williams or Richards. But some will follow Cornish forms, with the plural ending in o or ow, indicating the "children of"; for example, Bennetto—the children of Bennett; Kitto—Kitt's children; Jago—James's. Notice that these are doubled again, for we also have the English forms, Bennetts, Kitson, Jacobs. Bennetto is very rare in the United States, but there are many more Kittos there than in Cornwall. Jago is rather rare in the

United States, and with Jacobs we have to be careful: it will be far more frequently German or Jewish. We should need to know the family record and where it came from; though if the name crops up in a Cornish area, like the Upper Peninsula of Michigan, or Butte, Montana, and especially if the first name is Wesley, say Wesley T. Jacobs, we can be fairly sure that it is Cornish. This already illustrates something of the difficulties of the subject, as well of the methods of inquiry.

Again, most of the occupation-names with the Cornish are English names, Smith, Cook, Taylor, etc. Only very occasionally are they doubled: in West Cornwall we find Angove, meaning the smith; the fairly common name Cock means cook, so Cocks (or Cox) means cook's son. In the class of personally descriptive names we find some doubles: some Cornish people are called White, others are called Angwin, meaning the white, or fair, man; some are called Black or Blake, but a few are called Dew, which means black or dark. A more common descriptive name with us is Couch, (properly pronounced Cooch), which means red-face or red-head. It is interesting that the most famous bearer of this name, Quiller-Couch, first of Cornish writers, was both red-faced and red-headed. This name is a fairly common one in the United States, but you have to know where the family comes from—for it can be an Americanized form of German Koch, or other foreign name. Fortunately there is no doubt with such people as the celebrated mine captain Thomas Couch of Butte, Montana. Moyle comes from the Cornish word for bald; it is the name of an eminent Mormon family in Salt Lake City. When we come to status-names, such as the English Bond or Parsons, we find a parallel in the name Uglow (pronounced Yóuglo), which means the upper people, yeomen farmers as against peasants. This is not a common name, and it is to be found, perhaps naturally, in East Cornwall; it is not a rare name in the United States, but quite well represented.

The great majority of specifically Cornish surnames are

place-names: they come from the places where the original person or family lived. These fall into two classes, general and particular. The first class will be names descriptive of the character of the place: Treffry means the house on the hill or slope; Polglase means the green pool; Penrose, the head of the heath. All these names are fairly common in America. Treffry came into New England from the beginning, into Maine and Massachusetts—the famous seventeenth-century Puritan, Hugh Peter, was a Treffry on his mother's side; Polglase is not uncommon in mining areas; Penrose is the name of a leading Mormon hymn-writer, Charles William Penrose, as well as of several thousand Cornish-Americans all over the country.

The second class, of particular place-names, afford more difficulty. Where it is nearly always possible to interpret the first, from the Cornish language, the second, particular names, often contain a personal name of which we have lost the sense or mislaid the key. Treworgy was a well-known name in early New England; it contains a personal name and means the house of a person with a name that has become rubbed down to Worgy—one does not know the original. No wonder people of this name in New England, or some of them, began to call themselves Trueworthy. That gave a certain Puritan flavoring, but the sense of the name and its origin were both lost. Names such as Tregidgo, Tregonning, Treneer, Trenerry, Treseder, Trevanion, Trevorrow, all appear to be compounds of Tre-, meaning house or place or hamlet with personal names that are not recognizable to us, have been lost in the mists of time.

There is an expanded form of the familiar distich that will serve as introduction to these names:

> By Tre, Ros, Car, Lan, Pol and Pen,
> Ye may know most Cornishmen.

We have already seen that the prefix Tre- means house or homestead, place or hamlet. This is the most common prefix for Cornish names; there are scores of thousands of people in the United States with names of this formation. They are not all Cornish names—Trezevant, for example, is not: it is a French Huguenot name, probably Breton in origin. But most of them are. One of the most numerous names of this type in the United States is Tremaine, or Tremain, meaning the place of rocks. In some instances, this name may descend from French stock of Breton origin, but in the vast majority of cases it will be Cornish. There are several places of the name in Cornwall, from which specific families may descend in addition to the generic origin. The prefix Ros- means heath: we have already met the element in Penrose. Rosevear, a beautiful name, is fairly common: it means the big heath. Car- means a hill fort or camp. Thus Cardew means dark fort; the romantic name Carlyon is more frequent in the United States than in Britain: it means the slate fort, or camp with an outcrop of slate. Lan- means a sacred enclosure, or churchyard; so Lanyon means the bleak or cold church place, unless it is a variant of Lyn-, meaning pool, the cold, bleak pool. Pol-, we have seen, means pool: a not uncommon name in America is Polkinghorne; this is pool with a personal name, like Welsh Cynhaern (meaning Iron Chief).

Pen- is the most common prefix after Tre-, meaning the head. There are a fair number of names with this prefix, and many thousands of people called by them. They are not all of them Cornish; for instance, Pendleton is not. But many of them are. Pendarvis is a rare aristocratic name in Cornwall, which has almost died out; it is not uncommon in America, having fanned outwards from South Carolina across the country. It means the head of the oak-trees. Penhale means the head of the marsh; the plural, head of the marshes, is Penhallow. Far more common names of this type are Pender, end of the village; Pengelly, head of the groves; Penberthy, head of the bushes. America has them all, and more besides.

There are other fairly common prefixes that give us a key to the meaning of other names. An- means the, as we have seen with Angove, meaning the smith. Take the interesting name Andrewartha: nothing to do with Andrew: it is an (the) - dre (house or place) - wartha (upper). So it means the upper homestead; its English equivalent would be Upton. Some people of this inconveniently long name will have shortened it to Andrew, and so have lost its meaning. This rare name is still to be found in Cornish areas, like the Upper Peninsula of Michigan or southwest Wisconsin. A few more prefixes provide useful keys. Bo- or Bos- means the abode or dwelling; thus Bonython means the dwelling in the furse. Bolitho—the name of a banking family in West Cornwall and of a New Zealand writer, Hector Bolitho—is more common in America: it means the dwelling in the damp place. Boscawen is the name of an historic Cornish family, which contributed famous Admiral Boscawen—"wry-necked Dick" —to the eighteenth-century sea-saga. A place in New Hampshire is called after him. The name means the dwelling by the elder tree.

A much more frequent prefix is Chy-, meaning house. This is the element that comes into Chenoweth, Newhouse, one of the most common Cornish names in America. It has spread enormously since it first came into Virginia; it has been reinforced by many recruits coming in later, and some of these have the spelling Chynoweth. Hen- means old; Hender means the old homestead, Henwood—an East Cornish name, with its mixture of Cornish and English—means the old wood. Men- means rock or stone; we have seen this element in the quite common name, Tremaine. The name Menhennick or Menhennett, in various forms, is not rare in America; it may come from the large moorland and quarrying parish of Menheniot, or it may mean little old rocks. Minear is met with more frequently: it means long stone, indeed the form menhir is one of the few Cornish contributions to the English language. I suspect that in America this name has sometimes become disguised as Miner—very understandably, if so.

Nan-, meaning valley, is much more frequently found. The

romantic name of Nancarrow means the valley of the stag; kervis is the plural for carrow, meaning stags or deer. Nankervis is the more common form in America as in Cornwall; there are many more of them in the former. I remember from childhood days a Nancarrow who was emigrating from St. Austell going down on the *Titanic*. Nankivell means the valley of the horse; Nancollas, of the hazel trees; Nanscawen, of the elder tree. Nance is not a common name in Cornwall, but very common in America; perhaps the English name is a pet-form for Nancy—certainly the great majority of American Nances will not be of Cornish descent.

We now come to an important general point: the accenting of Cornish names. The tendency of English and Americans alike—it is a phonological law of the language—is to shift the accent forward to the first syllable. This is even stronger in America than in England, with the result that many Cornish names are differently pronounced in America, and sometimes the sense is lost. In Cornwall we say Penróse and Chenóweth; in America people say Pénrose and Chénoweth, with the result that the latter name, with people losing the sense of it as they certainly do not know what it means, often becomes deformed into Chenworth or Chinworth, which means nothing. Just as Trewórgy became Trúeworthy. Here are a few examples of the way the meaning gets lost by shifting the accent. Tre-wín is a West Cornish name meaning the fair or pleasant place; English and Americans alike constantly mispronounce this name as Tréw-in. Even in Cornwall the Treseders are apt to mispronounce their name as Trés-eder. This is wrong: it has nothing to do with English "tress," it is the ordinary Cornish Tre- with an ancient Cornish name Seder or Sider. And it is pronounced quite simply—minatorily—to rhyme with consider, i.e. Tresídder. Tre-wéek means the homestead in the wood; by shifting the accent forward some Americans of this name have arrived at Tráwick, which means nothing. Similarly Americans say Tréffry for Treffrý; Réstarick for Restárick; Pénberthy, which I should find hard to say, for Penbérthy, which is easy.

The same thing has happened to at least two place-names. When the original Lawrence Growden bought an estate, then on the outskirts of Philadelphia, he called it Tre-vóse, after his home in Cornwall. It came ultimately to an heiress, who married Joseph Galloway, and was confiscated in the American Revolution. It is now a district in Philadelphia, with a railroad station, known to millions of Philadelphians as Trévos, which means nothing. Boscáwen in New Hampshire is pronounced Bóscwin, which again means nothing.

There are other deformations of Cornish names, carrying them away from sense or meaning. Trebílcock is a good old name that is not at all uncommon. In America it is the name of a distinguished painter in New York; at home, of a well known footballer who was a member of Plymouth Argyle team. If people mispronounce their name by shifting the accent forward it becomes Trébil-cock, and they are apt then not to like it. So some of them have taken to dropping the *ck* and becoming Trébilco—you might think they were Italians; others have become Trebílcott, as if they came out of a Devonshire cot; yet others have dropped the *cock* altogether—I can't think why—and become Trébil. All very silly and superfluous. The footballer, on finding himself famous, gave a radio interview in which he blissfully said that the original name was Trébilco; but he wouldn't know.

It is very frequent in America, and increasingly so in Britain, for people with the excellent old name of Uren to uglify themselves as U'Rén. The well-known political leader in Oregon, William S. U'Rén, did so; his father was simply a Uren, innocent of an apostrophe. This name is properly pronounced "Your'n"; it comes from the good Celtic—even Arthurian—Christian name, Urien. Quite romantic, in fact; it is simply because of people's inability to pronounce the word "urine" outright, to rhyme with "saline", that they sigh for, and shortly insert, an apostrophe.

One deformation of a Cornish name is curious and presented me with a puzzle. The president of a college in upper New York State has the rare name Palamountain and assured me that it was Cornish. I was able to assure him that there is no such Cornish name. He reassured me that he was of Cornish descent, and that this was reinforced by the second name he was given—Cornwall. In the still watches of the night I thought of the explanation: it is a deformation of the regular Cornish name Pelleymounter, or Polmounter. It is a placename, but I am not sure of the meaning: it may mean the still pool or, more probably, the pool by the mineral land. Evidently when the original immigrant was coming in at New York, the officials couldn't catch his name properly or he couldn't spell it. The result is that there is this romantic-sounding creation, Palamountain, in the United States—one of the name is a well-known Californian football-player.

The English are apt to entertain the illusion that the Cornish names ending in o, or ow, are foreign, as certainly they sound so to an English ear: Bennetto, Bolitho, Bosanko, Bosustow, Clemo, Daddow, Gummow, Jago, Kitto, Pascoe, Santo, Spargo. And they are apt to link this with the popular delusion that these people are descended from Spaniards who landed from the Spanish Armada. No Spaniards landed in Cornwall from the Spanish Armada. A good many of our names end with open vowels, particularly those representing Cornish plurals in o or ow. We have seen that Bennetto means Bennett's children; Clemo, Clemmow, Clymo, Clyma similarly mean Clement's or Clem's children. Here we may utter a warning for the benefit of American readers. If one comes across such names as Santo, Jago, Jose in the Spanish Southwest or, say, in the Puerto-Rican quarter of New York, one may be fairly sure that these people are Spanish-Americans. Only in the colder climes of Upper Michigan or Wisconsin, or in Cornish districts elsewhere, are they likely to belong to Cornish-Americans.

There are historic surnames that have completely died out in Cornwall, such names as Carminow, Cardynham, Nansladron, Killigrew—though these place-names remain. It is pleasant to notice how many of the rarest Cornish names continue in America, and often in greater number. Hardly any of the historic name Godolphin remain at home—that family that contributed a Lord Treasurer, a Cavalier poet, an ambassador, a Dean of St. Paul's, soldiers, sailors, lawyers, to English history. But the name is well represented in America by the family of Professor Francis Godolphin, professor of classics at Princeton. The name is usually taken to mean little hill, but its older form Gotholgan may connect with the little tin-stream from which their wealth originally flowed.

The Killigrews were an even more fascinating family of seamen and buccaneers, admirals and ambassadors, dramatists, court-wits, poets and rakes. They have died out, but I have come across the name in America—I do not know whether a true descendant. I am glad that the rare Penzance name, Colenso—held by the famous bishop of Natal and his cousin, the New Zealand missionary and botanist—occurs in the United States. The Mousehole name, Keigwin, meaning the white enclosure, is now very rare, but I have come across it in New York and Indiana. The rare name Baragwanath, meaning white bread (English form, Whitbread), occurs outside Cornwall: William Baragwanath, Jr., was a leading authority on Australian mines, and wrote a dozen books about them. In the United States John Baragwanath is the author of a very characteristic volume of mining stories, *Pay Streak*.[2] He tells us, with recognizable spirit, that "as a young man I tramped and rode the western Cordilleras from Alaska to Chile"; and that his uncle's discourses on geology "went straight to my Cornish instincts," and fixed his life. He began mining in the famous Cerro de Pasco mines in Peru which the great Richard Trevithick helped to develop. Baragwanath informs us that the vocabulary of mining, even in the Spanish countries, is full of Cornish words. The name Daddow has died out in the St. Austell district and is very rare in Cornwall, but goes on in America; so do such infrequent names as Trewavas, Trezona, Bosustow, Dowrick, Dungey, Restarick,

Hobba, Trerice, Carbis, Carkeek, Roskruge, Roscrow, Skewes. There are many more.

What, briefly, are the specific Cornish names most frequently to be found in the United States?

I repeat once more that the bulk of Cornish people are called by English names—Williams, Richards, Harris, Pearce and so on—and so are not immediately recognizable: they melt easily into the rest of the English-named population. This creates the prime difficulty of the subject. Of specific Cornish names I should say that the most commonly to be found are the following: Pascoe, which means Easter-child, Penrose, Chenoweth, Trevilian, Tremaine, Vivian, Treloar. That is the first and most numerous class. Next to these would be such names as Curnow, meaning the Cornishman, Coon, Goldsworthy, Grenfell, Penberthy, Pengelly, Treglown, Trembath, Trevithick, Trewartha, Trewhella, Trelease, Trudgeon. There are many more people of these names in America than in Britain. And some names that are fairly rare in Britain—such as Spargo, Trevorrow, Trezona—are not uncommon in the United States. The reader will get some idea of the proportions for himself.

For the rest, we shall come upon them all in the course of this book: they are all across the Atlantic and in America. But, for the reader who wants to learn their meanings, perhaps find out that of his own, it will be more convenient to look up the Appendix at the end.

Cornish place-names in the United States are few, and do not indicate Cornish settlement there: they were mostly chosen by the settlers according to fancy. The parish of Truro, Virginia, was established in 1732; its inhabitants were not Cornish, but grandees like the Fairfaxes, Masons and Washingtons.[3] A better known Truro—the name means the place on the hill—is the town near the tip of Cape Cod in Massachusetts. There is another town of the name in southern Iowa. Several Falmouths exist, the earliest and best known being that which included Portland, Maine, until 1786; now it is relegated to the northeastern district, with Falmouth Foreside. Another Falmouth is appropriately not far from Truro on Cape Cod, settled in 1660, formerly a ship-building and whaling harbor. Other places of the name exist in northern Virginia, at the falls of Rappahannock, in northern Kentucky, in Pennsylvania, and in Michigan. The grand maritime expansion of the eighteenth century carried the name to Jamaica, Antigua and Nova Scotia.

It is in Virginia that Cornish settlers mostly left evidences in place-names: Trevethans in Princess Anne County, Trevilians in Albemarle, Travilian in York. Virginia has a Blisland parish; early on there was an Edgcumbe precinct on the Pamlico River; there is an Edgecombe County in North Carolina. We have seen that there is Trevose in Philadelphia, Boscawen in New Hampshire. In upper New York State Trumansburg was originally Tremaine's Village, but the combination of misspelling and change of accent proved too much for it.

Several places are called after Cornwall itself. There is the small town in Connecticut whence Americans derive the delectable "Cornish hen," so frequent on their menus. There are others in Pennsylvania, New York and Vermont. The name Cornish appears in Maine, and Cornish Flat in New Hampshire. We have noticed Chenoweth Flats in Kentucky. We find Pengilly on the Mesabi iron range in Minnesota, now a resort village at the end of a lake—but there would have been miners there. There are Mount Trelease in Colorado, named for the botanist, Truscott in Texas, Pearce in Arizona after the family that discovered the Commonwealth Mine.

It is a pity that, in a country so vast that it has been hard put to it to find enough names to go round and has had to use many of them over and over again, they should not have drawn upon the extraordinary variety of names to be found in Cornwall. Many of them are beautiful, all of them memorable. There are such straightforward names as Redruth and Camborne, St. Austell and St. Just, Liskeard, Calstock and Callington, whence so many miners came; or Penzance, Padstow,

Fowey, whence they sailed. We have plenty of saints' names to dispose of: St. Ives or St. Juliot (beloved of Thomas Hardy), St. Winnow or St. Mabyn, St. Anthony-in-Roseland, St. Anthony-in-Meneague, St. Mawgan-in-Pydar. Or, even more musical, Lanreath or Lansallos, Talland and Pelynt, Lamorran, Merther or Malpas, Ruan Lanihorne or Lanteglos-by-Fowey.

They are hard to forget.

NOTES

1. P. H. Reaney, A *Dictionary of British Surnames,* 277.
2. Doubleday, 1936.
3. P. Slaughter, *The History of Truro Parish in Virginia,* 2.

3 EARLY FOLK IN VIRGINIA AND NEW ENGLAND

The open door into North America was a main issue for which the Elizabethans fought their twenty-year-long struggle with the world-empire of Spain and Portugal under Philip II. The determination of the English maritime interests to effect an opening into the New World, of which Spain claimed a monopoly, was a factor in bringing on the war. The Spaniards had ended by massacre the French attempts to found a colony in Florida. They had overthrown by the treachery of San Juan de Ulloa (now Vera Cruz) Hawkins's attempt to initiate a trade with the West Indies by agreement with Spain. Of the many scores of prisoners captured there few ever saw England again; the young—including a brother of Francis Drake—were forcibly converted and lived out their lives in Mexico, others languished in the prisons of the Inquisition, many were lashed within an inch of their lives, some were burned. Hawkins's right-hand man, Robert Barrett of Saltash—who would have been one of the great Elizabethan seamen if he had lived—was reserved for a more spectacular fate: he was taken back to Seville to be burned in the market-place, right by the Casa de Contratación of the Indies. The lesson was not lost upon the West Country seamen: they were all imbued with hatred of Spain and determined to go forward with the good work of opening up at least North America for the English.

In the first famous Roanoke colony of 1585–86, which garnered the experience as to life and conditions in America upon which the subsequent permanent colonies leaned, there was a Cornish element. This was natural, since the colony had been organized by Ralegh, who was Lord Lieutenant of Cornwall, and planted by Sir Richard Grenville. Among the West Country gentlemen accompanying Grenville was his cousin, John Arundell of Trerice; and among the ships' captains was Captain Bonython. Three Cornish gentlemen were among those who remained that first whole year on Roanoke gathering knowledge of America with Thomas Hariot and John White, the cartographer who painted the exquisite maps of the coast and the celebrated water-colors of fishes, animals, Indian villages and characters, illustrating their way of life. It is not known for certain, but this first of English water-colorists seems to have come from Truro. Then there were Master Kendall, of the Lostwithiel family, Master Prideaux, of the Padstow clan, and Master Anthony Rowse or Rous, Drake's friend and first executor, of that Puritan family that lived at Halton looking down upon the River Tamar before it opens out into the broad estuary and the sea.[1]

After twenty years of war with Spain peace was made in 1604, and the tacit assumption was that England was now free to go forward with her colonizing efforts in North America—though for long Spain regarded them with a jealous eye and did all she could to hamper them. At once, in 1606, a body chiefly of West Countrymen came together to petition James I for license to plant a colony—Ralegh's patent having lapsed by his condemnation for treason. In the event two companies emerged: the southern company, backed mainly from London with much larger resources ultimately, to plant between 34° and 41° N; the northern company, based mainly upon Plymouth, to plant between 38° and 45° N. It is convenient, if somewhat premature at the time, to refer to one as the Virginia Company and the other, which came to concern itself with New England, as the Plymouth Company.

In the tremendous roll-call of Jacobean society that rolled up behind the second charter for Virginia, of 1609—from which the main effort for planting Jamestown flowed—we find three Cornish knights. These were Sir William Godolphin, Sir Robert Killigrew, friend of Ralegh and shortly to be made Captain of Pendennis Castle at Falmouth, and Sir John Borlase, the Low Countries commander.[2] These became Virginia adventurers, i.e. subscribers to the Virginia Company. Among the adventurers under the third charter, of 1612, we find these additional names: William Roscarrock, another cousin of Grenville's, of Roscarrock hard by Padstow haven, Peter and John Arundell, Edward Carne and Richard Connock, of the Liskeard family.[3]

It is not my purpose to tell the story of the Virginia colony or indeed any of the colonies—that would be impossible here. But I doubt if people realize the immense efforts, the sacrifices made, the losses incurred with no return, before Virginia got going. Up to 1622 some ten thousand people were sent out; of these only some two thousand were alive. Then there occurred the fearful Indian massacre of that year, in which some hundreds perished and more hundreds died in consequence in the second "starving-time." Of those who survived, at any rate for a bit, we find Thomas Spilman of Truro, who came over in the good ship *Bona Nova* in 1620—when he was nineteen. He had some property, for, after the massacre, he was still able to muster four servants. At twenty-six he died, leaving his Virginia property to his widow, his property in England to a daughter. Later, another Spilman or Spelman followed, who left descendants; it is not, however, a Cornish name.[4]

Richard and Elizabeth Arundell came over in the *Abigail* in 1620 as servants to the governor, Sir George Yardley.[5] We learn in a witch-craft case, in which goodwife Wright was accused, that when someone was tying up a couple of hens to send over to Elizabeth Arundell, the witch said, "Why keep them tied up? The maid you send them to will be dead before they get there." Dorothy Behethlen testified that goodwife Wright was accounted a witch by all at Kehowtan.—We see that Massachusetts had no monopoly of this nonsense. Robert Behethlen, gentleman, came over in the first ship to Jamestown in 1607 and survived to be quite active in the affairs of the colony as Beheathland.[6] One doesn't know if this is a deformation of the name Behenna—later on we find Behennas in Virginia. The Arundells continued, for in 1632 John Arundell, gentleman, of Elizabeth City got a grant of one hundred acres on the Hampton River, due for part of a bill of adventure in 1617.[7] Peter Arundell was now dead, but he left a son and heir, John, who inherited one share in the same bill of adventure.

John Penrice was at Elizabeth City in 1623: he was a tenant of the Company, evidently one of those allotted fifty acres, under the system that ultimately prevailed. He witnessed someone's will in 1632; but this forlorn fellow did not continue the stock.[8] John Treherne came over in the *True Love* in 1622 and lived in Charles City. In 1625 he shipped a hogshead of tobacco to his brother in London; the master of the ship reported that Treherne was dead and sold the tobacco for his own benefit. But Trehernes continued in Virginia.[9] In 1625 John Penrose and four others were bound over in £20 for the offense of going aboard contrary to the proclamation —each was to pay a fine of 20 lb. of good tobacco towards building the bridges of Elizabeth City.[10] What had they been up to?—probably trying to stow away tobacco over and above their allotted quota.

In the 1630's we find William Berryman petitioning for land due to him for the transportation of John Treherne and three other servants—that would be at the regular rate of fifty acres for each person sent over.[11] William Berryman was active as vestryman and churchwarden, and was nominated for sheriff. In 1636 Richard Cock, gentleman, patented three thousand acres in Henrico, near John Pearce and Thomas Harris.[12] This sounds like a small clutch of Cornish settlers; and later we shall find an interesting group of kinsmen, Cock, Bolitho and Trevethan, settled at Lynnhaven on the lower James, where the excellent oysters grew. The result is that Bolithos are fairly common in Virginia, though infrequent in Cornwall.

These are the ventures of individuals. For a corporate venture we may turn to New England, where Sir Ferdinando Gorges, governor of Plymouth, struggled for the better part of a lifetime to plant settlements—spending his own and his wives' substance, meeting every kind of hindrance and setback, only to have a march stolen on him in the end by the imperious Puritans of Massachusetts. However, in the end the old man emerged as founder of Maine, while his friend Captain Mason became founder of New Hampshire.

In 1631 Gorges' fellow-townsman, Robert Trelawny, got a grant, under Gorges' patent, of Cape Elizabeth—the grant included the site of the present town of Cape Elizabeth—and Richmond's Isle, a bleak tip off the Cape. It was good, however, for sturgeon, salmon, bass, in addition to the ubiquitous, benevolent cod, which still served as "dry-fish" for staple winter-diet in the Cornwall of my youth. The mainland provided beaver, from which seventeenth-century persons got their tall felt hats. Robert Trelawny's father had settled in Plymouth in the reign of Queen Elizabeth, a younger sprig of the old family, and done well in trade. The son, another Robert, did even better: he became a rich, and therefore much respected, merchant. He went back to Cornwall for a wife, Ann Voga of Caerhays, whom he married at Mevagissey.[13]

In 1635 Robert Trelawny sent out his younger brother Edward—of Bake, in the parish of St. Germans—to survey things and speed them forward. He came in the *Speedwell* (Narias Hawkins, master) in April, along with a number of others from in and around Plymouth. We recognize the names of Alexander and William Freethy, from the Freethy farm in St. John's parish; Nicholas Edgcumbe, a poor relation of the great family, no gentleman; William Herle, Archilaus Hunkin, Sampson Jope, Christopher Jose, John Libby, Henry Hancock, Benjamin Stephens, Paul Mitchell, William Mellin.[14] Then there are Captain Richard Bonython and his son John; James and John Treworgy. In addition to these Cornish names there is John Billings at Kittery Point in 1639, who was granted land by Gorges in 1645.[15] He had descendants: there is a Billings family in Maine. Altogether, early Maine had quite a Cornish element.

John Winter was Trelawny's factor, and some sixty men were employed in the fur and fisheries trade. In 1636 John Vivian arrived, who returned in 1641; at the same time came John Treworgy as agent for Alexander Shapleigh. In this year 1636 James Treworgy purchased a grant on the eastern bank of the Piscataqua; he married Shapleigh's daughter, the sister of Nicholas Shapleigh, the Devonshireman prominent in the colony's affairs. James and John Treworgy were probably brothers, so all was in the family. The Treworgys, along with a Champernoun, John Edgcumbe and others, were the founders of Piscataqua, now the towns of Kittery, Eliot and Berwick. James Treworgy went off to Newfoundland, where he disappears into the mists; but he had a son Samuel, who had a son James, to whom his grandmother bequeathed a silver beaker. So the Treworgys were people of standing, and the name went on. John Treworgy married and had children, lived at Sturgeon Creek in Kittery, until he too went to Newfoundland, as commissioner for the Commonwealth, where the fog swallowed him up. In that year, 1651, Nicholas Treworgy of Piscataqua, a sailor of twenty-two gave evidence about two French men-of-war seizing a Boston ship and putting the crew ashore on an uninhabited island off Cape Sable in Newfoundland—so this Treworgy would have been born 1639–40.[16] There are Treworgy descendants in Maine today, under the name of Trewargy; while there are still three Treworgie families in Portland, Maine, and one in Boston. Among the first settlers of Ellsworth, there are two who had families, under the old form of the name: Mark and Daniel Treworgy.[17]

In 1637 Robert Trelawny sent out the Reverend Richard Gibson to look after the spiritual wants of his colony, and there followed the inevitable squabbles over religion. When Trelawny then expedited the Reverend Robert Jordan, the poor man was censured by the censorious Massachusetts Puritans for using the Prayer Book.[18] With Massachusetts one couldn't win anyway. In 1643 Nicholas Edgcumbe married a maid-servant before her time of service was up, and paid the fine of £5 for the pleasure. He then settled on a farm at Blue Point, which he leased of Captain Richard Bonython, until 1660, when he moved to Saco. He had four sons and two daughters—so the Edgcumbes go on in New England. Not, however, in the main line of that eminent family. In 1637 the head of the family, Sir Richard, purchased a large grant of eight thousand acres from Gorges, between Sagadahock and Casco Bay. Owing to the troubles of the Civil War Sir Richard could not go forward with it, and the grant lapsed. A century later, in 1756, the ennobled Edgcumbes tried to revive their claim: in vain. However, in 1774 a township was incorporated after the name of Lord Mount Edgcumbe, a Whig sympathizer with the colonists in their revolt against the old country.[19]

Captain Richard Bonython, who was baptized at St. Columb Major in 1580, was a respected senior of over fifty when he came with a son and two daughters.[20] He became joint proprietor, with Thomas Lewis, of the land embracing the present town of Saco. He was a leading member of the little colony, becoming a member of the first court in 1640, and a councillor to the deputy governor, Thomas Gorges. A subsequent deputy governor and Captain Bonython were both loyal Anglicans and were much troubled "to hear our mother church questioned for her impurity upon every occasion" by the Puritan bore of a minister at Saco. However, the poor captain had a worse thorn in the flesh in son John, who lived a life of outlawry for some twenty years. The first court held at his father's house brought him up as the father of an illegitimate child, by one of the servant-maids. The minister he insulted as "base priest, base knave, base fellow," and slandered his wife. In 1645 he threatened to kill anyone who laid hand on him, and the court, in which his father sat, outlawed him. When Massachusetts took over Maine in 1652—these imperialist Puritans were always out to take Maine, when nobody was looking—John still held out and refused to submit. At length in 1658 he was driven to do so; but only two years later, the Restoration of the king gave him a chance to insult the Saints. In the years 1668–71 he was once more in opposition to Massachusetts. Then, in the Indian hostilities of 1675, his house was burned and the family fled to Marblehead for safety. Next year he made his will; but in popular folklore:

> Here lies Bonython,
> The Sagamore of Saco:
> He lived a rogue and died a knave,
> And went to Hobbowocko (i.e. the Devil).

He was buried near the river on the boundary of his large estate, which was not settled until 1732, when five thousand acres at 18s. per acre were divided up among his heirs. John, his eldest son, moved to New Hampshire. A daughter, Eleanor, inherited the family temperament, had a bastard child, and her father paid the fine. The fate of the male line in New England could hardly have been worse than that in Old England, where it came to an end in madness and suicide. Yet the name has been rehabilitated in our time with distinction in Australia. The Bonython flagon of stoneware—presumably a greybeard—turned up among the possessions of an old lady near St. Austell, and was acquired by the Australian Sir Langdon Bonython. In New England Whittier used the name of John Bonython in "Mogg Megone"; while among his descendants on the female side was the blameless Longfellow.

The troubles of the times in England fell hard upon Robert Trelawny, and put an end to his particular venture; nevertheless the folk were across the Atlantic to proliferate in New England. Trelawny was imprisoned for his loyalism by Parliament in 1641, spent the last years of his life in prison and died there in 1644. No word of complaint passed his lips, merely, "I commit my funeral to the discretion of my executors, as a prisoner and according to the sadness of the times." In New England John Winter remained on as factor for Robert's heir, a minor, until hostilities broke out with the Casco Indians. The General Assembly took the opportunity to award the plantation unjustly to Winter's son-in-law, Jordan. Efforts were made by the Trelawnys for a century, and as late as 1758, to regain their right. But in vain. At length it was their descendant who gave Robert Trelawny's papers to the state of Maine, from which we derive the story.

The dominant elements in the great migration that made Massachusetts were East Anglian and from the East Midlands, though the governor before they began to arrive, from 1630, was a Devonshire man, John Endicott. But in 1635 there came a Cornishman, whose contribution, during the six years that he spent there, was second only to Governor Winthrop himself in building up the colony. This was the celebrated, the notorious, the controversial Hugh Peter.[21]

Hugh Peter was born at Fowey in 1598, the third generation there of Protestant refugees from Antwerp of the name of Dickwood (or Dyckvelt). These were prosperous merchants, who owned ships, houses and quays along the harbor, and in two generations married Treffrys, of the leading family of the town, living at Place, the fine castle overlooking that noble estuary. Hugh Peter's mother was a Treffry, his grandmother a Penhale. The mixture produced in him a marked "character," very individualist, energetic and pushing, temperamental and exhibitionist, excitable, with a talent for putting himself across to an audience, a famous preacher with a taste for low jests appealing to the gallery, public-spirited and avid of public notice, coarse-grained, though not without tact or goodwill. He certainly had more than his share of Cornish temperament. Brought up in comfort and affluence, at Cambridge he imbibed Puritan convictions, was ordained and went abroad to the Netherlands, where he adhered to the non-separatist Congregational tenets of the English churches there that were to prevail in New England. At some point he made the acquaintance of John White of Dorchester and joined him in promoting the Massachusetts Bay Company. But when Archbishop Laud's long arm began to reach out to impose order on the exiles in the Netherlands, Peter skedaddled across the Atlantic as agent for the new plantation of Saybrook in the lower valley of the Connecticut.

When Peter arrived the Massachusetts colony was in a precarious state, "builded upon rocks, sands, and salt marshes." Having yet no pastoral charge, Peter threw himself with all his exceptional energy into public affairs, "to quiet my own conscience about the state with what speed I can, who have made it my wife, my life."[22] (Fortunately he had left his wife behind him.) He urged upon the colony—he was nothing if not a promoter—the plan of raising funds for a public fishing company, to buy equipment, materials and force its way into the market. Governor Winthrop is our best witness to Peter's success: "Mr. Hugh Peter went from place to place labouring, both publicly and privately, to raise men to a public frame of spirit, and so prevailed as he procured a good sum of money to be raised to set on foot the fishing business . . . he wrote into England to raise as much more." In four years' time Winthrop was able to report, "men followed the fishing so well that there was about 300,000 dry fish sent to market." Peter, we may conclude, "had been a prime mover in forwarding one of Massachusetts' greatest enterprises," upon which her subsequent maritime achievement was founded.

When a Dartmouth ship put into the Bay in April, 1636, Peter was able to relieve the colony by himself purchasing the remnant of the cargo—of meal, peas, malt, prunes and the indispensable aqua vitae—at half price. "Which saved the country £200," said Winthrop. Peter put forward practical proposals, both religious and economic, to remedy the state the colony had fallen into. An orthodox Congregationalist, he proposed an association of the churches to heal the endemic fissiparousness of such fragmented sects. Most usefully, Peter advocated measures to give people employment, especially women and children in winter. He urged the import of cotton from the West Indies, for household manufacture, in return for fish, pipe-staves and lumber. He helped to set on foot the fishing settlement at Marblehead, then known as Foy—the proper pronunciation, and sensible spelling, of Fowey—and induced some Cornish fishermen to come over and settle there. He encouraged shipbuilding, helping with his capital to launch Salem's first ship, the *Desire*, which sold off a number of Pequot captives as slaves to Bermuda, and returned from Providence with a cargo of cotton, tobacco, salt and Negroes. Thus was the trade with the West Indies opened which led to the ultimate wealth of Massachusetts. Again it is Governor Winthrop who pays tribute to Peter's part as promoter: "Mr. Peter, being a man of a very public spirit and singular activity for all occasions, procured some to join for building a ship at Salem of 300 tons, and the inhabitants of Boston, stirred up by his example, set upon the building of another at Boston of 150 tons."[23] At Salem Peter helped to construct a water-mill, and encouraged the town to set up a glass-works, sending to Holland for the skilled men to operate it.

He was no less interested in education, and took a leading part in the founding of Harvard College. He got the selectmen of Salem to set aside a tract of land for the college, though he was disappointed when the General Court decided that it should be located at Cambridge. Nevertheless, he became a member of the first Board of Overseers; later, he and his co-agents raised £150 privately in England for books for the college. Never one for under-emphasis, he described himself as having "begged over all England" on its behalf.

In December 1636 Peter had succeeded Roger Williams as the pastor of Salem—since sooner or later, Williams got out of step with everybody, and in the end succeeded in getting out of step with himself. We are not much interested in the religious activities that took up so much of Peter's time and take up so much space in the books. Suffice it to say that, at least in New England terms, he took a regular orthodox line. He had to take a part in suppressing the holy, and tiresome, Mrs. Hutchinson, a very conceited woman who was creating dissension in the colony. No doubt he was willing to give a helping hand in getting her out of it. He himself preached and worked with tireless energy—indeed overworked, for he suffered from strain and periodic breakdowns. He was evidently a manic-depressive type. His name is commemorated by a hill—Peters Hill—where he preached the first sermon in Wenham. He was a Christian according to his lights, and, though involved with the colony in hostilities with the Pequots, he opposed the seizing of their corn. He was entirely trusted by the colony in all its affairs—served on committees to draft the laws, was sent to Piscataqua to settle disputes and push the interests of Massachusetts; he was sent in to the Connecticut Valley to regulate boundaries, and delegated by the colony to purchase arms for it. His services were much appreciated by his congregation in Salem, which grew rapidly, not only by incoming immigrants but by those attracted by his preaching and the ardor of his personality. The congregation was loath to lose him, when he was nominated, at a crisis in the colony's affairs, to go back to England as one of its agents, in 1641. His biographer concludes that "as a promoter of the public interest he was unsurpassed in New England at the time."[24] This is no more than the truth.

In England, in the turbulence of the Civil War, a larger sphere soon opened up for him; but he did not neglect the interests of Massachusetts, until the colony went bad on him. Altogether he and his fellow-agents raised "nearly £2000 in money and supplies for the languishing Bible Commonwealth." In the winter of 1642–43 Peter assisted the younger Winthrop to raise money for an iron-works there. It is probable that his growing influence with the Parliamentary forces helped. When the Royalist forces took over Cornwall in 1643, Peter's elder brother, Thomas—a quieter man—was driven from his living at Mylor and took refuge in New England, where he joined John Winthrop the younger in Connecticut and became the first minister of New London. But with the victory of Parliament Thomas Peter was called back to Mylor.[25]

Meanwhile, Hugh Peter had become the leading chaplain of Cromwell's Army, and under Cromwell's personal rule the first Independent cleric in the kingdom, with official apartments at Whitehall. He supported Cromwell's policy of toleration among the Protestant sects—again a sensible line in the circumstances. This was much disapproved of by censorious Massachusetts, which also excommunicated poor Mrs. Peter, who had been left behind, when she was merely off her head. The colony proceeded to lay the blame for its own dishonest dealings upon Peter and its agents, who had done their best, and then confiscated his property there. Characteristically for a Cornishman, Peter thereupon broke off all official relations with Massachusetts, having done so much for it and been rewarded so ill. In England he went on his own way, a kind of Independent Primate so long as Cromwell lived. Some New England visitors finding his apartments thronged with suitors hailed him as Archbishop of Canterbury—which was received with some complacency. He had, however, advocated the execution of the king in 1648–49, and for this, detested by the fickle populace, he was executed at Charing Cross at the Restoration. He met his death with dignity and fortitude.

Why was Hugh Peter so much execrated?

The judicious historian, Sir Charles Firth, says, "the popular hatred was hardly deserved. Peter had earned it by what he said rather than by what he did. His public-spirited exertions for the general good and his kindnesses to individual royalists were forgotten." It seems that among his kindnesses we must count his saving Place at Fowey—the ancestral castle of the Royalist Treffrys—from destruction when Cromwell won. Firth concludes, "an examination of the career and the writings of Peter show him to have been an honest, upright, and genial man, whose defects of taste and judgment explain much of the odium which he occurred, but do not justify it."[26]

But is that all? He was vilified in life, and traduced after death. Why? No doubt he had the defects of his qualities—but perhaps if he had not had the defects he would not have had the qualities. I think the explanation is that he was too much himself, that he was not afraid to be himself, with little regard for what others thought—and that is always an offense to some. Though intemperate in speech, he does not seem to have done an ill deed—of how many can that be said? In the end, we may conclude that he was a good man; people in condemning him merely condemn themselves.

Neither of the Peter brothers left progeny in New England, so far as we know—it was Hugh Peter's step-daughter, Elizabeth Reade, whom the younger John Winthrop married. But it may have been due to Hugh Peter that some of his Treffry kin became domesticated in New England. One finds a Thomas Treffry (or Turfrey) among the inhabitants of Marblehead in 1674.[27] The brothers Thomas and John Treffry, like their family always loyal to the Crown, were supporters of Sir Edmund Andros, appointed by James II as governor to consolidate the separate, and conflicting, colonies into one Dominion of New England, showing a firm front to the French without and subordinating the Puritan oligarchies within. Andros proclaimed liberty of conscience, which was very far from the intentions of Massachusetts. In April, 1689, encouraged by the Glorious Revolution in England, the people of Boston imprisoned the governor and the Treffrys with him.[28] However, when Andros was sent to England, they were released.

The Treffry stock proliferated in the bracing climate of New England, far more than in Cornwall. In Boston alone today one finds a score of Treffry families, whence they have spread across New England and into Canada.[29] Boston today has a considerable Cornish element in its variegated population, comparatively few going back to these early settlers. Of those early names we find no less than ten families of Vivian listed in the telephone directory, so there may well be more. There are eleven Pascoe families, though these came over later. Among names of earlier settlers we find Treweek, Tremaine, Trescott, Trerice, Rouse (or Rowse). Among others: Trebilcock, Tredennick, Trenouth (or Trenoweth), Trethewey, Tregonning, Tremaine (or Tremayne), Tregurtha, Trewhella; several families of Penrose, Nankervis, Uglow, Pengilly, Penketh, Penhallow, Pendarvis, Petherick, Hender, Clemo, Coon. There are no less than a hundred families of Hicks, a number of which will be Cornish: pretty certainly the one whose first name is Wesley. And there are many others—nine Pearce families, Nance, Oates, Hocking, Hunkins, Rundle, Trenholm, Rowe, Pomeroy—who will include some Cornish.

Let us take the Trerice name for an example: there are few enough left in Cornwall. Nicholas Trerice, captain of the *Planter*, brought many immigrants to New England—among them the Peabodys: think of that![30] He was a much trusted sea-captain, who made a good many voyages over the years, upon whom the Winthrops regularly relied to forward their correspondence and goods—on occasion, vinegar to pickle sturgeon in.[31] Nicholas was admitted a freeman of Charlestown in 1636 and had children there; fined for contempt of court in 1641, he removed to Woburn and, twice married, had another family there.[32] Nicholas was still sending a ship to and fro as late as 1648, for in that year Prince Rupert—in command of a Royalist squadron—captured her: Roger Williams reported that £2000 was offered for her in Holland.[33] Nicholas Trerice died not long after, in 1652; a son John, of Charlestown, married in 1663 and had a family.[34] His name sometimes appears as Trarise. Anyhow the Trerices were over, and so were the Pengillys. John Pengilly served as a corporal in King Philip's Indian War in 1675 and 1676, was made a freeman of Ipswich in 1678, whence he moved to Springfield.[35] (The name is sometimes given as Bengilley!) A Nicholas Pengelly was in Staten Island by 1664. It seems that a Nicholas Rouse came early to Casco; certainly the name has proliferated, usually in that form, though sometimes as Rowse, the form more common in Cornwall.[36] Among other early pioneers of Massachusetts we find such likely names as Trescott, Carwithen, Corrington (or Coryton).[37] A Richard Cornish arrived in 1634, but in 1644 was drowned at Agamenticus.[38] The Trescotts multiplied like the sands of the sea.

In July 1686 there arrived together in Massachusetts two persons, the Reverend Charles Morton and his pupil Samuel Penhallow, the first of whom was to play a part in the public life of the province, the second to be a commanding figure in New Hampshire, founder of an eminent family that still continues.

Charles Morton was born at Egloshayle in 1627, his mother a small heiress, Frances Kestle of Pendavy. At Oxford he did well academically but, a serious youth, became a Puritan—at Wadham, of all colleges—and during the Protectorate was intruded into the rectory of Blisland. At the Restoration he was ejected and went to London, where he founded the celebrated Newington Academy—a highly esteemed school for Dissenters, which included Defoe and Samuel Wesley among its pupils and many of the principal Dissenting ministers. Calamy says of him that "he had indeed a peculiar talent of winning youth to the love of virtue and learning, both by his pleasant conversation and by a familiar way of making difficult subjects easily intelligible."[39]

Harassed by the bishop of London's courts, Morton decided to leave for New England with young Penhallow and a nephew, another Charles Morton who, as a doctor, was a useful recruit to the colony. Another nephew had preceded them—so among the Massachusetts Mortons there is Cornish blood. Morton had been given an expectation of becoming president of Harvard but, for fear of offending the authorities, was disappointed of it. He set on a school which, with his talents, threatened to become successful; so the Harvard authorities, no better than the bishop of London, made him give it up. Instead, he became minister of Charlestown, where his preaching was highly esteemed and where he was the first minister to perform marriages, hitherto regarded as a civil rite. A kind man, without resentment, Morton made himself useful to Harvard, became a Fellow and eventually vice-president. He exerted himself actively for the college, and lectured on scientific subjects. His manuals on science and logic were used as text-books at Harvard far into the eighteenth century, and he left the college a bequest in his will.[40] In the politics of the commonwealth he followed the dominant line of the Mathers. It is to be regretted that he did not know better than to follow them into the odious prosecutions for witchcraft at Salem, but religion misled him into this. He founded an association of the leading ministers of the province to meet at Harvard every six weeks for spiritual counsel and mutual support. A prolific writer on religious and biblical themes— expounding, for example, the text from Jeremiah on "the stork in heaven knoweth her appointed times"—he wrote more usefully on the improvement of Cornish agriculture by the use of sea-sand.*

Samuel Penhallow, born at St. Mabyn July 2, 1665, was

---

* There is no biography of Morton; there is plenty of material for a short one: someone should write it.

the son of Chamond Penhallow and Ann Tamblyn. Of good family, he bore a coat of arms: vert, a hare argent; for crest, a goat argent, horned or.[41] He was also a virtuous youth: the Society for the Propagation of the Gospel proposed to support him for three years while he learned the language of the Narragansetts to become a missionary to the Indians.[42] Moving to Portsmouth, New Hampshire, he had a better—at any rate, a more paying—idea: he married the daughter of the president of the colony, Mary Cutt, who was an heiress, and made a fortune out of trade with the Indians. He became the largest landowner in the colony, for his wife "inherited from her father a valuable patrimony, part of which was land whereon a large portion of the town is built." By 1722 he had acquired the largest estate in Barrington, some 750 acres.[43] With his wife's money he was enabled to engage successfully in trade; and encouraged by the sexual prowess of hare and goat, so prominent in his coat of arms, he knocked up a family of thirteen by his wife before she died, fairly young—when he married again, a widow by whom he had another son. So the Penhallows have increased in New England, whereas they have come to an end in Cornwall.

This energetic man proceeded to play a leading part in the public affairs of New Hampshire for the rest of his life. His father-in-law, President John Cutt, the wealthiest man in the province, welcomed the reliable Penhallow into the charmed circle of the Great House and from the first leaned upon him in matters public and private. Penhallow's entry into the colony's governing class—he came from as good family as they —opened the way for his trading ventures. He had come with the idea that the setbacks from which the colonists suffered were punishments for their not caring for the spiritual welfare of the Indians; he soon found that trade was better. After making a success of that he proceeded, with firm and confident step, to occupy nearly every important office in the state.

In August 1699 he was made justice of the peace, in September speaker of the General Assembly, in December treasurer of the province—an office which he held for the rest of his life, except for a year's absence in England. In 1702 he became recorder of the province and a member of the council; in 1714 a judge of the Superior Court, in 1717 Chief Justice, while from 1719-22 he was also recorder again. His career proceeded without *contretemps* except for a moment when the governor was absent and the lieutenant-governor took on himself his powers. Penhallow objected and was suspended; shortly after the governor re-appeared and restored the faithful Samuel. As recorder he kept a careful record of the colony's troubles with the Indians, and in 1726 he published *The History of the Wars of New England with the Eastern Indians*. It is largely a harrowing recital of Indian atrocities—no conception that the Indians were being inexorably pushed out of their own lands; but then, when did Puritans ever see anybody else's point of view? The book has its small authentic place in early American historical writing, and Samuel Penhallow his as an historian. His public career, involved in all the actions of those times, coincided with the history of the province—which it is not my purpose to write.*

His first wife, by whom his good fortune came, died in 1713. He pays her a tribute of modest pride: "her attire was always neat and handsome, an utter enemy to anything gay or fashionable; as she was not so modish as to be first in fashion, neither was she so singular as to be the last out of it."[44] He himself died, aged sixty-one, in 1726. He left to his "well-beloved wife £150, with free liberty of carrying away with her whatever she brought." To the six surviving younger children he left £300 each, the eldest son, John, to maintain them out of the estate until they were twenty-one. He had already provided several lots of land for these children. There were small bequests to the family, £5 to the poor and £5 to the pastor. Then he added a codicil: "instead of wine, gloves, tobacco and pipes, which are usually expended on such occasions [his funeral], I order £5 more to be added" to his £5

---

* The State documents are full of his name and doings; there should be a biography of him.

for the poor. Samuel Penhallow's estate was inventoried at £1904 1s. 4d. so the proportion for the poor was hardly excessive.[45]

The family tradition is that there was an eldest son, Samuel, who went to England, married there and remained there —if so, he was disinherited; that there was a daughter Phoebe who married four times and had a numerous progeny. What we know for certain is that son John, born in 1693, succeeded to something of his father's place. He carried on the family trading connections under the name of John Penhallow and Company.[46] In 1711 his father had made him clerk of the Superior Court. In 1719 he was engaged in making a new settlement to the east, sixty miles east of Piscataqua. This brought on further fighting with the Indians, and we find young Captain John Penhallow serving against them and carrying the war eastward.

John's second son married a daughter of Hunking Wentworth—Mark Hunking had served on the council with Samuel Penhallow—and had eleven children. A younger son of this marriage married Harriet Pearce and had a family of six. After many years as a shipmaster, Hunking Penhallow entered business at Portsmouth. For his last twelve years he was member of either council or senate of New Hampshire, and was one of the Committee of Safety during the Revolutionary War. His youngest son, Benjamin, followed family tradition and became a judge of the Court of Sessions. In the fifth generation Captain Pearce W. Penhallow followed his father to sea and commanded a ship in trade with the Southern States, about 1850. While another member of the family, about the same time, joined the gold-rush to California, starting a San Francisco line.

Thus they spread. All these names—Penhallow, Hunking, Pearce—are Cornish. We may observe in this group the apparent eugenic fact that the expansive circumstances of life in the New World in general favored a much larger increase of stock than in the Old.

NOTES

1. cf. R. Hakluyt, *Principal Navigations* (MacLehose ed.), VIII, 315–17.
2. Alexander Brown, *The Genesis of the United States*, I, 209ff.
3. *Ibid.*, II, 540ff.
4. *Virginia Magazine of History and Biography*, vol. 1, 195.
5. *Ibid.*, vol. 4, 302.
6. *Ibid.*, vol. 2, 363.
7. *Ibid.*, vol. 2, 183.
8. *Ibid.*, vol. 25, 118; vol. 27, 149; *William and Mary Quarterly*, series 1, vol. 22, 78.
9. *Va. Mag.*, vol. 26, 356.
10. *Ibid.*, vol. 25, 119.
11. S. M. Ames and F. S. Philbrick, *County Court Records of Accomack—Northampton, Virginia, 1632–1640*, 127.
12. *Va. Mag.*, vol. 3, 285.
13. cf. *The Trelawny Papers*, ed. J. P. Baxter, for the following account, from which quotations come.
14. C. H. Pope, *The Pioneers of Maine and New Hampshire*, 61, 93, 105, 114, 115.
15. *Va. Mag.*, vol. 97, 347.
16. *Ibid.*, vol. 88, 386.
17. *Sprague's Journal of Maine History*, vol. 13, 229.
18. *Ibid.*, vol. 7, 154–55.
19. A. V. Chadbourne, *Maine Place-Names*, 82.
20. For the following account cf. Baxter, *op. cit.*, and C. E. Banks, "The Bonython Family of Maine," *Va. Mag.*, vol. 38, 51ff.
21. For the following account, see R. P. Stearns, *The Strenuous Puritan: Hugh Peter, 1598–1660*.
22. *Ibid.*, 96, 97, 98.
23. *Ibid.*, 139.
24. *Ibid.*, 153, 162.

25. *Dictionary of National Biography*, under Thomas Peter.
26. D. N. B., under Hugh Peter.
27. J. Savage, *A Genealogical Dictionary of the First Settlers of New England*, IV, 328.
28. *State Papers of New Hampshire*, vol. 23, 235; *Records of the Colony of Rhode Island*, III, 256.
29. cf. the Boston and Montreal telephone directories.
30. *Va. Mag.*, vol. 2, 154.
31. *Winthrop Papers* (Massachusetts Historical Soc.), III, 200.
32. Savage, IV, 322.
33. *Winthrop Papers*, V, 205, 280, 288.
34. *Va. Mag.*, vol. 46, 173; Savage, IV, 322.
35. *Va. Mag.*, vol. 38, 441; vol. 41, 273; vol. 43, 274; Savage, III, 388.
36. Savage, III, 579.
37. C. H. Pope, *The Pioneers of Massachusetts*, 119, 461.
38. *Ibid.*, 118.
39. See D. N. B., under Charles Morton.
40. cf. *Dictionary of American Biography*, under Morton.
41. cf. Pearce W. Penhallow, *Memoir of the Penhallow Family*.
42. D. A. B., under Samuel Penhallow.
43. *Documents and Records Relating to Towns in New Hampshire*, ed. N. Boulton, IX, 43.
44. Pearce W. Penhallow, *op. cit.*
45. J. N. McClintock, *History of New Hampshire*, II, 283.
46. Pearce W. Penhallow, "Penhallow Papers—Indian Affairs," *New England Historical and Genealogical Register*, vol. 32, 21ff.

4 *NEW JERSEY AND NEW YORK*

The Quakers sprang up in England out of the turmoil of the Civil War, and with their conspicuously inconvenient ways were being persecuted before ever the Commonwealth came to an end and the king was restored. But the Restoration of King and Church, with a Tory view of society, redoubled the persecution. Thousands of Quakers were fined or imprisoned, and after a decade or more they began to turn their eyes, like the Pilgrims before them, to the New World for a refuge.

They found no comfort in Massachusetts, and not much in New England in general; for where orthodox Congregationalism was dominant it persecuted Quakers too. So they looked to the unoccupied lands of the great Delaware Valley, which offered promising prospects for settlement, with a fine river for a main artery of communication. They settled first on the east bank of the river, which had good loamy soil, mainly shore-side plain rising to undulating hills, with easy communications with the lower Hudson across the narrow neck between the rivers, as one went further up the Delaware. This was the land that became West New Jersey, the first province of Quaker settlement before they shortly turned their attention to the west bank—what became the great province of

Pennsylvania. "If all had succeeded, the Quakers would have controlled a domain extending from New York to Maryland and westward to the Ohio."[1]

Actually William Penn made his first acquaintance with the problems of American colonization and his first entry upon that scene through his concern with the affairs of West New Jersey. He became involved in these through becoming one of the trustees to straighten out the tangled affairs of the Cornish Quaker, Edward Billing, the promoter of Quaker settlement in West Jersey.* Billing must have been a curious and interesting man, if only we could elicit his submerged and somewhat elusive personality. Pepys, who knew him, regarded him as a "cunning fellow," and one of Oliver Cromwell's former guard reported him to Charles II's Secretary of State as "a close, subtle, witty [i.e. clever] man . . . no man more busy stirring up and down, inquiring after news than he . . . He does not want a friend at Court amongst the rest."[2] We may conclude that Billing had a scheming head—in both senses of the term—a restless temperament, a somewhat febrile nature, poor health and circumstances and, what was even more discouraging, no luck. If he had had Penn's resources along with his stable temperament, Edward Billing might have emerged as one of the leading colonial founders. As it is, even the credit that properly belongs to him as the framer of the West Jersey Concessions and Agreements—regarded somewhat enthusiastically as a model charter of colonial liberties—has been annexed to the more fortunate Penn. We have authority for thinking that "to him that hath shall be given, and from him that hath not shall be taken away even that which he hath." Edward Billing's is a sad, a cautionary, tale.

He evidently belonged to the family of Billing of Hengar in the parish of St. Tudy—small gentry—for he used their coat of arms of three stags' heads on his seal, and even when operating as an unsuccessful brewer at Westminster is yet described as "gentleman." His daughters, Loveday and Grace,

---

* Billing is the regular form of the name; there is no point in retaining the rebarbative form Byllynge.

were called after Loveday and Grace Billing of Hengar, the former of whom as Loveday Hambly after her marriage became celebrated as a pillar of Quakerism in Cornwall. The name Philadelphia was a favorite one in three generations of this family. Loveday Hambly had been converted by George Fox on his tour of Cornwall in 1656. In the very next year we find Fox interesting himself in Billing, then a cornet of horse in Monk's army in Scotland, at loggerheads with his wife. They had separated, but the power of the Lord by George Fox's ministrations had brought them together again. This miracle fixed Billing in the faith for good. The faith brought him many tribulations. Pepys was a witness of Billing's illtreatment by his own comrades at Whitehall, "where in the Palace I saw Monk's soldiers abuse Billing and all the Quakers that were at a meeting-place there, and indeed the soldiers did use them very roughly and were to blame."[3] This was before the royalist Restoration, while the Saints still held the reins.

It must be admitted that Billing was one to ask for trouble. A couple of days later he was standing at the door of the Parliament house in Westminster, and when the Parliamentarian leader, Sir Arthur Haselrigg, came out very angry at the turn of events Billing seized him by the arm and cried, "Thou man, will thy beast carry thee no longer? Thou must fall!" The absurdities of their behavior did not improve matters for the Quakers. When Billing was called into court from jail, he clothed himself literally in sackcloth and ashes, tying the ashes in a "pretty big heap" under his hat; so that when his hat was forcibly removed—for Quakers would not doff their hat in a court of law—the ashes fell all about him and at the same moment he unloosed his sackcloth garment so that it fell down. Everybody was taken aback, even "the bench being struck and the people confounded."[4] It is hardly surprising that, neglecting his business for these delights, and spending his time in and out of jail, Billing eventually went bankrupt.

However, he had a ready pen and employed it to express

the sufferings of his people, of which he had full share. (Penn, on the other hand, was a favorite at Court and suffered little.) Billing wrote tracts advocating religious toleration, at least for Christians.[5] With his experiences Billing naturally urged that magistrates be permitted no coercive powers in religious matters; that in a trial the accused might take exception to judge, juryman, or witness; that every person be free to plead his own case in court; that debtors be obliged to pay as far as their estates allowed and then be set at liberty. We observe, as usual with people's statements of "principle," to what an extent they are simply generalizations of their own personal grievances.

More important than principles, what to do about Billing's bankruptcy?

By 1673 he was heavily in debt. Apparently Billing, too, had a friend at Court, for the West Country Lord Berkeley of Stratton offered to sell him his interest in one half of undivided New Jersey, if Billing could raise £1000 for the purchase. Here was something for Billing's working head to get down to: many Quakers were anxious to find a refuge in the New World, as the Pilgrim Fathers before them, and Billing was a promoter. This was seven years before Penn's grant of Pennsylvania but, unlike Penn, Billing had no resources. The idea was to raise the money for the purchase, and so recoup himself on the sale of sections, the "proprieties," of the country —West Jersey, some 4,600 square miles of land.

To effect the purchase Billing associated himself with another Quaker, John Fenwick—the whole project was to be within the Society of Friends. In 1674 Berkeley made over his interest in West Jersey to Fenwick in trust for Billing—a common form of transaction. The next thing that happened was that the two Friends quarrelled. Fenwick seems to have behaved badly: he got the title-deeds into his possession by a subterfuge, and refused to deliver them back to Billing unless the latter made over to him a tenth of the whole grant. Billing was in no condition to hold out, and thereupon Fenwick jumped the gun. He disposed of some 150,000 acres of land to about 50 purchasers. In 1675 Fenwick himself went out, with about 150 settlers, and founded Salem on the Delaware. Most of his settlers were small tradesmen from London and the neighborhood. Among them we meet only one Cornish name, Roger Pidrick (a form of Petherick or Pedrick), who subsequently moved: "John Fenwick would not let us set out our land, except those that were concerned would set their hands to such papers as he drew up, which would have been to ensnare us and all that come after us."[6] Even the Saints had their share of guile.

Meanwhile, Billing's affairs had gone from bad to worse—an open scandal to the Society. To remedy it three Friends, with Penn in the lead, became trustees for Billing's interest in New Jersey. They decided to form a joint-stock company of one hundred shares, worth £350 each. Thus, what Billing had purchased for £1000 should be worth £35,000. Not bad business!—Billing's creditors would be paid off, some of them with shares, and there might still remain over a patrimony for Billing.

In better spirits Billing proceeded to indite the famous Concessions and Agreements for his colony, about which historians have waxed so eloquent—and then attributed them to Penn! Actually in the original manuscript of them we find Billing's signature, large as life, at the head of the subscribers—a firm, educated, somewhat elaborate signature. William Penn comes second in the second column, straightforward and clear, except for a large pompous flourish.[7] The *Dictionary of American Biography*, thirty years ago, opined that "historians are in general agreement that this great charter of liberties came largely from the hand of William Penn. It was the first fruit of his hard schooling in English politics, and his first gift to American government."[8] It can now be seen that this is rather humbug. An historian of New Jersey observes, "the absolutely liberal and democratic character of the Concessions and Agreements has often been justly praised by historians. The sincerity of the proprietors, who reserved practically no peculiar power to themselves, is demonstrated beyond all doubt."[9] As to that, we shall see what happened in the upshot. Even an eminent historian, C. M. Andrews, describes poor Billing's Concessions, thinking them to be Penn's, as "the broadest, sanest, and most equitable charter drafted for any body of colonists up to this time."[10]

We see in them, without exaggeration, nothing but what might be expected of a Quaker reacting to the experiences of his time. "The guarantees of individual liberty were the crowning glory of the West Jersey Concessions. Asserting that none had the power to rule men's consciences in religious matters, no person under any pretence whatever could be called into question because of his opinion, faith, or worship of God."[11] What else was to be expected considering Billing's background? Though it was a pointer to the future, and was to be ratified in the easier circumstances of the New World—was indeed a necessary condition there with all the different sects and peoples coming in—it said nothing to the problem of order in older societies, where there had to be some limits placed in more restricted and intensive environments. The absurdities of the early Quakers were hardly more absurd than other people's absurdities, but they did have an erosive effect upon respect for law and order.

The Concessions merely repeated the secular principle of trial by jury. Billing added that if a convicted person proved, upon the testimony of three compurgators, that he was unable to pay his fine he should be discharged. We can see that this reflects Billing's own bias as a debtor, but was it fair to a creditor? Would it not undermine the security of credit transactions, if applied? I do not suppose that it was applied, or was generally applicable. Of course, the colonists always were sympathetic to the debtor, rather recalcitrant about the payment of debts—it was an element in the motivation of the Revolution; nor did it cease to be a problem with the attainment of independence. As to government the General

Assembly was to have wide powers to enact all laws for the province, provided that they were in conformity with the Concessions and the fundamental laws of England. The assembly was to be democratically chosen from the male freeholders of the province—a hundred members, one from each projected tenth or division. We shall see how Billing came up against his own doctrinaire provision when he got the governorship—and put the settlers up in arms against his rights. However, in politics there is nothing easier to eat than words: it is the politician's diet.

More important than all this were the actual provisions for settlement. Billing's trustees adopted the usual headrights system that had provided the best inducement to settle in the colonies: each settler would receive a lot of seventy acres, with an additional seventy for each able manservant and fifty for a less able, male or female. Upon the expiry of each indentured servant's term of service he would receive fifty acres. We regularly find that, in the freer circumstances of illimitable land in the New World, the running away of indentured servants is a familiar social feature. What is really important in America—far more important than any doctrine—is the *fact* that, with land illimitable, it was impossible to reconstruct the hierarchical structure of the historic societies of the Old World. To offset the disadvantages of this it was possible only to exploit Negro slavery as an alternative; and it was exploited to the hilt.

Equipped with these good intentions, the trustees planned an exodus of Quakers to West Jersey far larger than the Plymouth Pilgrims who have been made so much of in history. In 1677 the *Kent* arrived in the Delaware with 230 settlers to found Burlington. These came mainly from Yorkshire, and the exodus was so large as to alarm the authorities there. During the next few years additional ships brought further contingents, until by 1682 close on 2,000 folk, mostly Quakers, had come to the east bank of the Delaware. The colony on the east bank was thus rooted, and the Quakers were able to turn their attention to the west bank, where Penn's concession was on a much larger scale than Billing's, and was to have a resounding future.

The success of these arrangements, the sale of most of the tenths into which the province had been divided, got Billing out of debt and still left him by far the largest proprietor. In 1680 the Duke of York, who had overriding rights in all this area, acknowledged that the right of government went with the soil and that government was vested solely in the chief proprietor, Billing. This eventuality had not been provided for in the democratically minded Concessions. Never mind: Billing now saw a future for himself and announced, to the surprise of all, that he would go out as governor. He later defended himself on the reasonable score that it was impossible to divide the right of government into a hundred tenths: it must reside in a single person or corporation. This set off the usual quarrel between the settlers on the spot and the proprietor at home which became endemic in the proprietary colonies. Not even the arrival of an angel from heaven, in the shape of William Penn in his own Pennsylvania, could stop the bickering.

At first Billing was optimistic. We see how elated he was—and also what an excitable type—from a public letter he circulated at the end of 1681, when he was clear. His continual cry during his troubles had been that "the Lord God of the whole earth and all the treasures therein (according to the integrity of my heart) would, in his infinite mercy and for his blessed Truth's sake, raise me above the reproach and contempt of mine enemies and fully deliver me out of that pit which the righteous God well knew was not of mine own digging, although I was fallen therein."[12] We diagnose a touch of persecution-mania in him. He thanked God for finding a way to vindicate his integrity, so that "at least such of my friends who had known and tried me at heart . . . might see and feel that I was yet an honest man in my mind." There is much more of the same sort about his often watering his couch with tears and audibly crying to God. No recognition that he had got out of his troubles simply through the shares to West Jersey having been taken up satisfactorily.

In his enthusiasm Billing now offered to give, free, a hundred acres each to a hundred familes of Quaker poor. Then, resuming his promoter's note, "And yet I may tell you, and 'tis true, that land in West Jersey is sold at a far greater rate than it was four or five years since: it being now considerably peopled, a free and well-settled country, and many good Friends and large Meetings there are. . . ." We know that this offer was made known to the Quakers in Cornwall, for a record remains in the Monthly Records for Falmouth: "1682. A paper from Edward Billing was read in the meeting offering 10,000 acres of land in New Jersey to one hundred poor families of Friends."[13] Apparently Billing intended to circulate the offer in other counties where the Society was represented.

Meanwhile, in 1680 Billing had sent out Samuel Jennings as his deputy governor. Jennings saw very well which way his bread was buttered and went over to the side of the settlers. He proceeded to ratify the laws drawn up by the assembly without any reference to Billing—after all, the famous Concessions had said nothing about a governor. The assembly went forward to lay out the lands, taking no notice of their creator—at least they would not have been there if Billing had not conceived the idea of the colony and promoted it. Billing sent out Thomas Mathews, as his attorney, to locate and apportion his family lands—still almost a third of the whole. Mathews reported to the apostle, George Fox himself, the unjust proceedings in the assembly at which Penn was present, having crossed the Delaware and reached Burlington "in such a night of rain that I have never seen the like." In the assembly, Penn and Fenwick knew "very well how to tune their instrument to suit the hearers . . . Never man was more minced and run down than E[dward] B[illing], not being there to speak for himself, and old dirt thrown upon him by W[illiam] P[enn] in the face of the assembly."[14]

The assembly voted Jennings as governor, and he accepted.

But this put them plainly in the wrong. The assembly climbed down and delegated Jennings and another, Budd—a West Countryman, from Somerset—to go to England and settle the matter. In 1684 the arbitrators to whom the dispute had been referred pronounced that the right of government had been vested, by the grant of 1680, in Billing, and even the deputies admitted that his was the legal right. But they remained on in London to pursue their campaign, and issued a discreditable tract arguing that Billing had disposed of all his shares. This was untrue, and they were forced to admit it. The scandal to the Society was highly displeasing to George Fox, who gave Billing his support throughout.

Confirmed in his rights, in 1685 Billing appointed Skene as his deputy governor, a Scottish resident in West Jersey who had remained loyal to him throughout the controversy and had been removed by the assembly from his place in council for his loyalty. Billing owned twenty-two out of the hundred shares; his son-in-law Bartlett—a West Country name—owned another six.[15] Five of these were in lieu of money Billing had owing to him; in addition Bartlett had acquired Billing's daughter Grace as wife. (It reminds one of the terms upon which Milton acquired Mary Powell to wife: Squire Powell owed Milton's father money.)

By now Billing was a sick man; he died, apparently of consumption, in 1687. Unlike Penn he had no son to succeed him and carry on the struggle. His daughter Loveday died next year, and Bartlett in 1691. The remaining daughter decided to dispose of the family interests in West Jersey. Jennings remained to carry on the argument. "The controversy between the successors of Billing and the proprietors here," he wrote, "was never yet determined: which hath occasioned jars and misunderstandings, to be kept on foot betwixt them and us."[16] It would seem that colonists everywhere much enjoyed these disputes: they became an endemic element in the colonial scene.

Edward Billing had no luck; for all that he had given the

colony of West Jersey its initial impulse, and himself was an
essential link in the chain, he has been forgotten. The simple
truth is that he didn't have the money that Penn had behind
him. It is characteristic that where Penn's name has been
given the widest reverberation in the name of a proud, imperial state, Billing's, in Billingsport, once a little shad-fishing
village down river from Camden, should have been forgotten,
obliterated even in the maps and guides to the state he
launched.

The first settlers of West Jersey were mainly from the
London area, Yorkshire and Dublin. Edward Billing's contact
with Cornwall was marginal: he lived most of his life in
Westminster. Only a very few recognizably Cornish folk
trickled into New Jersey. Roger Pedrick, or Pedderick, came
to Salem in 1676.[17] Ten years later he got a grant for 140
acres to be called Pedderick's Neck at the mouth of Ould-
man's Creek.[18] The Pedricks flourished in New Jersey in the
eighteenth century; a settlement was named for them—
Pedrickstown. In 1683 Ralph Trenoweth was assigned a lot of
100 acres on the south side of Crosswicks Creek, in Burlington County. He was evidently one of those who took advantage of Billing's offer to poor Quakers in Cornwall, to judge
from his assignment of 100 acres. Subsequently we find
Trenoweth chopping and changing his holdings, until he ends
up better off with 200 acres out of Budd's original 300
acres.[19]

George Rescarrick came over before 1700.[20] This is evidently the well-known old name of Roscarrock (meaning the
rocky promontory), from the barton on the east side of Padstow haven, where the family had lived since medieval times.
Roscarrock was a small gentleman of impoverished means. In
1700 he got a grant of 300 acres between Cranberry Brook
and Millstone River on the Great Post Road halfway between
Burlington and Perth Amboy, the port and capital of East
Jersey on the eastern shore.[21] This was land from a

large tract purchased from the Indians, and the grant was made to encourage Roscarrock to settle there and "keep a good house of entertainment for strangers and travellers on the said great Post Road." This road ran across the northern neck of West Jersey at its narrowest to Perth Amboy, opposite Staten Island at the mouth of the Hudson. Roscarrock settled his family there—we hope he kept a good house of entertainment. We find him a reliable citizen, called in to witness people's wills and make inventories of their few possessions. In 1709 the council wrote to him to go forthwith and summon an Indian chief, Weequohela, to the governor's presence.[22] Evidently Roscarrock lived out on the edge of Indian country—not a pleasant assignment, for ultimately Weequohela was executed for killing his relatives. In 1714 Roscarrock himself was dead: not old, for both his children were minors. The Book Debts were £101 3s. 5d.; among his possessions were a silver tankard, a dozen spoons and a cup—pathetic insignia of gentility—and seven slaves.[23]

The Roscarrocks built up a holding there in Middlesex County. We learn from *The American Weekly Mercury* in 1725 that three indentured servants had run away from the son, another George. "William Hide, of a middle stature, lightish coloured hair and curls very much, of a fair complexion, an Englishman born." John Miller was "of a small stature, black complexion, having his hair cut off and wears a cap under his hat, having a suit of dark grey homespun clothes made plain and but little worn. He wears over them an old drugget coat, fashionably made, of a light colour, good shoes and stockings, and has with him a pair of cinnamon-coloured drugget breeches and wears an old beaver hat." Thomas Sowthrop was "a thick well-set fellow, with very short reddish hair, a Yorkshire man and talks broad," a carpenter by trade. "Whoever can secure the said servants so as their master may have them again shall have £10 for all, and in proportion for one or two of them."[24]

In 1729 George Roscarrock, Jr., was dead, also quite

young, for his mother was left executor with William Hartshorne—of that Quaker family to be Loyalist during the Revolution.²⁵ Roscarrock had moved to Perth Amboy, where the sale of the estate was to take place.²⁶ At Cranberry there was a house and farm of 400 acres, whereof 200 acres were cleared and within fence. On Millstone River was a small house with orchard, and half of a tract of 300 acres, of which 50 acres had been cleared. There was one half of a lot of 80 acres with half of a sawmill thereon, with another third of a sawmill. Evidently the Roscarrocks had done a good deal of clearing; when death took him, the son was extending his interests to East Jersey, for he had a proprietary right for 250 acres there and a lot in the little capital, Perth Amboy. Next year the family home, the inn, was to be let: "the house has three rooms on a floor, a barn, stable, other outhouses, a large orchard, 60–70 acres of land cleared and within fence and 200 or 300 acres of woodland." From these notices we can imagine the circumstances of life there on the edge of Indian country. It does not seem that the Roscarrocks made much of a success after all; the father and son died young, and the name died out.

We find only a clutch of indubitably Cornish names in early New Jersey. In 1693 Nicholas Tregidgo is an indentured servant at Burlington, who has several times run away from his master and put him to great charge in sending after him.²⁷ In the same year there was a good deal of controversy among the Friends at Salem, which led many to separate from the Society. Proposals to bring them together again were signed by John Penrose.²⁸ When we look into the telephone directory for Princeton alone today, we find no less than seven Penrose entries; Trenton yields another seven, Camden two. So there must be more. The most remarkable example of the proliferation of old stock in favorable circumstances is that of the Pedricks: there are no less than fifteen families of them listed in Camden, others in Trenton and Newark.

Before the end of the century we find a Penquite as an

active citizen in Burlington County, and shortly after a Trelease family in Hanover Township, Morris County—today there are two Trelease families in Newark.[29] By about 1700 we find a Chenoweth family established in Burlington.[30] Today Newark has five Chenoweth families, and three Trevaskiss (there is no point in doubling the s, as if it has anything to do with "kiss": it has not, and it should be dropped). Among Cornish names represented in New Jersey today we find the following: Tredinnick, two families in Newark, one in Camden; Trevena, three in Jersey City, two in Newark; Trevenen, two in Newark, one in Jersey City; Trevarthen, three in Princeton, one in Trenton. We find also more than one family of the name of Pendarvis, Carew, Chellew, Trembath, Tregurtha—a rare catch—Trewin, Vivian, Edgcumbe; besides Trethewey, Trewhella, Trengove, Trenhaile, Roskelly, Penberthy, Pascoe. And these are only a small sample.

We shall see that numbers of Cornish miners coming into the country in the later nineteenth century went to work first in the iron-mines of New Jersey, particularly around Mount Hope, or in the coal-mines of Pennsylvania, before moving out west to the better prospects of Michigan, and later Nevada, Dakota, Colorado, Montana.

Naturally, since the beginnings of New York were dominantly Dutch, we find few Cornish names in early days. But the moment the English take over New Netherland the Cornish begin to trickle in along with them. In October 1664, since "there is no public notary in this place that understands the English tongue," Thomas Carveth was appointed, the first of his kind.[31] In the same year Nicholas Pengelly became one of the first settlers on Staten Island.[32] The name does not seem to have continued there, though today we find Penhallow, Penrose, Tremaine, Trethewey, Trevena. In the mid-eighteenth century a John Tremaine appeared as the first musical director in the city, who later held the stage as an actor for some years. He combined these activities with his profession of cabinet-making. In the 1750's a harpsichord of his making was played at the John Street theatre. In 1751 an advertisement appeared that he was declining the stage; next year a benefit performance was given for him, himself playing the part of Richard III.[33]

We come up against the problem of the New York Tremaines, to which a couple of Victorian antiquaries devoted a portentous book of two volumes, each of a thousand pages, *The History of the Treman, Tremaine, Truman Family*;[34] it reminds one of nothing so much as Macaulay's hilarious account of Professor Nares's life of Burghley. The book is confused by the assumption that Trúman and Tremáine are the same name, and this is what comes from confusing the accent. I repeat that with most Cornish names the accent properly falls on the second syllable: Tremáine, Penróse, Trevéthan, Trebílcock. Truman is a perfectly good old English name, and even West Country; but it is not Cornish. Hence it is probably mistaken of these enthusiastic genealogists to derive the Tremaines of New York from Joseph Truman of Nottingham, who arrived in Connecticut in 1666. They begin their book with an account of the ancient Cornish family of Tremayne, who were much to the fore in the Elizabethan Age. It is quite likely that some of the Americans of this name descend from this medieval stock. But the name in its various forms—Tremain, Tremaine, Tremayne—is fairly common in Cornwall. And there are now so many of them in America that it is clear that they descend from a variety of bearers of the name arriving at different times.

In the earlier eighteenth century there was a clutch of Tremains in western Massachusetts, located at Westfield.[35] John Tremain had moved there from Pittsfield; he had brothers, and cousins, and they were a prolific stock. Of their sons almost a dozen served as soldiers in the Revolutionary War. Afterwards they got grants of land in upper New York State, in the tremendous push to open up the hinterland after the war—of which the Wadsworth achievement in the Genesee Valley offers a classic example. John Tremain himself moved before the war to Hillsdale, Columbia County, New York. A cousin, Philip Tremain, had served in a Massachusetts regiment in the Indian troubles in Maine in 1724. Each of them had a mass of sons. The pattern they follow is westward, from the rocky hard-faced land of western Massachusetts along the valleys to the better soils of the Finger Lakes region of upper New York —of which they made such excellent farmland, the slopes flourishing with vineyards and peach orchards. Of John Tremain's sons Philip settled beside Cayuga Lake; Julius moved to Otsego County, Daniel to Chenango County, Gains and Abner also came into New York State.

Let us take the example of the youngest boy, Abner Tremain, who made a name for himself in the Revolutionary War. He enlisted at sixteen and served throughout the war, just over five years. "He was one of the picked company selected by Washington himself to accompany General Anthony Wayne in his hazardous and successful attack on Stony Point."[36] A brave young fellow, he was chosen for several special tasks, and at the end of the war was given a large grant of six hundred acres in what became Trumansburg. Who would have guessed that it was originally called Tremain's Village, "but in making out his commission as postmaster the name of the place was misspelled Trumansburg, and so it has remained." In 1792 young Tremain took possession with his family, together with his brother Philip and his son Benjamin. They started clearing the land, building a grist mill, their log cabin and eventually a substantial frame-house.

Abner Tremain was the progenitor of a family that prospered in Ithaca and became influential in state politics. Three of his grandsons, Leonard, Lafayette and Elias Tremain, moved to Ithaca and rose with the prosperous development of the town.[37] The brothers began with a hardware store, but they had initiative and branched out into gas- and waterworks, then banking. In the next generation the Tremains again demonstrated their fighting spirit in the Civil War, three young cousins being killed, and one showing gallantry all through the war, to emerge as a general. He was in all the principal engagements before Richmond and in the battles of Pope's campaign, ending with Second Bull Run, where he was taken prisoner. He was exchanged, however, to serve at Fredericksburg and Chancellorsville, and win the Congressional Medal of Honor for conspicuous gallantry. Promoted brigadier-general, he fought at Chattanooga, and in all the engagements of the Petersburg campaign. He returned from the war to a distinguished career at the New York bar, writing many papers and addresses, publishing some books and founding the *New York Law Journal*.

We cannot follow the ramifications of this particular branch further, under its various spellings. Some members of it, under the form Treman, remained at Ithaca, prominent in business, banking and Democratic politics. Lyman Tremain was eminent in his day as lawyer, scholarly book-collector, orator. Henry Barnes Tremaine won himself a place in the *Dictionary of American Biography* as a manufacturer of mechanical musical instruments, developing the pianola, etc. We must retrace our steps to the origins of this clan, and then, coming closer to Cornwall, to fresh immigrants of the name coming over.

A son of Julius Tremain, Roswell Tremaine, as he is spelt, provides an example of how this prolific clan spread westward from New York.[38] Born on the Hudson in 1780, he was four times married, having a considerable family by each of three wives. He moved into Ohio about 1815, some of his sons into Indiana, a brother into Illinois, another into Pennsylvania. So there are Tremaines all over the place. One of those Revolutionary War soldiers, Solomon Tremaine, moved from Massachusetts to take up land in New York State after the war and founded the village of Tremaine's Corners in Jefferson County. One prosperous Tremaine family was lost to New York as the result of the Revolution. A Jonathan Tremaine, born at Portsea in 1742, became a New York merchant. But at the evacuation by the British at the peace, he was one of the numerous Loyalists who left for Halifax, Nova Scotia.[39] There he resumed business, did well and left a large family. So there should be Tremaines in the Maritime Provinces of Canada.

Enough of these Tremaines! It is amusing to think that the name should have secured a place in a Louis Auchincloss novel as exemplifying all that is genteel in an old New York family.

More to our purpose is to observe the widespread representation of Cornish folk in upper New York State today. There are several Tremain, Tremaine and Tremayne families in Buffalo, Syracuse and Rochester. In Buffalo alone there are no less than nine Pascoe families, and eight Pasco; seven Edgecombe, five Coad, five Vivian, four Tredinnick, four Pellow, three Hocking, three Curnew (for Curnow); two each of Trenberth, Trevillian, Treen, Clemo, Carew, Pengelly, Carlyon, Minear, Hambly, Hender, U'Ren (for Uren). It is pleasant to find, among rarer names, three Penvose, two Penhallurick, a Mellow, Penhollow, Penwarden, Pelmear (for Polmear). We find also represented Trerice, Penhall, Nancekivell, Chenoweth, Petherick, Jagoe. Altogether Buffalo must have a large Cornish representation. In Syracuse we find an immense number of Coons, some of whom are indubitably Cornish; ten Pearce families, seven Couch, two Rowse (a dozen Rouse), besides Edgecomb, Vivian, Trevethick, Treloar, Trembath, Penrose. In Rochester there are seven Penrose families—it has become, with Pascoe, one of the most common of Cornish names in America; four Trescott (for Truscott), two Trezise, a Trembeth, a Trerice, a Penhollow, along with numerous Rowe, Rouse, Pollock, Pollard and such names among which Cornish folk are to be found.

Perhaps we may give a direct example of a nineteenth-century immigrant coming into this area and making a success of things. A young Cornish carpenter, William Pidrick, landed at New York in 1849.[40] He was going to join a friend at Milwaukee when an accident interrupted his journey along the Erie Canal, and he walked into Rochester. Funds were low, he found work, and "when again in funds he had lost the desire to proceed and Rochester had gained a permanent and a useful citizen."-He built up a large business as builder and contractor; his biographer says that "the finest structures in Rochester erected prior to 1882 are monuments to the skill, energy and business ability of William Pidrick."

Pidrick married Jane Hosken; their son, William H. Pidrick, became an expert worker in wood under his father and added to this a second trade as cloth-cutter. This dual equipment enabled him to make a fortune as a manufacturer of coffins. The Victorian biographer waxes eloquent upon the subject of the trade. "Probably no business in the United States has undergone a greater transformation in the last century than that of caring for the dead. In no branch of that business, a sacred one from its very nature, has the change been more complete than in the manufacture and distribution of caskets." (In England we use the good old word "coffin.") "The business transacted at the Rochester plant is simply enormous, caskets going to every part of the United States, to Cuba, South America, Australia, Canada, and European countries. These are not caskets of an inferior character but include caskets of the finest woods, upholstering and decoration. The greatest and most honored of the nation's dead of recent years sleep in caskets prepared under Mr. Pidrick's supervision, including President Grant, President Garfield, James Gordon Bennett, and thousands of others, great in their day and generation." From which we may perceive that the Forest Lawn of our time, caricatured in Evelyn Waugh's *The Loved One*, has nothing on the Victorian humbug shrouding the subject.

At about the same time, the 1870's and 1880's Cornish

folk were being employed in the iron-mines of the Lake Champlain region. In a gorge near the headwaters of the Little Ausable River was the Arnold Mine, celebrated in its day. Captain Richard Kitto was its overseer, who showed a party of newspaper-men over the mine.[41] Kitto had been fifteen years altogether in the Company's service, ten years in working the Cliff copper-mine in Lake Superior country, and five here, "as thoroughbred a gentleman as ever clasped your hand, and as efficient and practical a miner as ever followed the track of a vein of iron or copper ore through the underground depths of the earth . . . Captain Kitto has had the assistance of no mining engineer since he has been here; and yet so well has his judgment guided him, by the aid of outside indications and his previous thorough knowledge of his business, that it would be hard to point out a single mistake which he has made here."

Captain Kitto was evidently well pleased with himself—a recognizable Cornish type. It appears that he had installed one of the famous Cornish beam engines to pump water out of the mine. The newspapermen were surprised by the absence of an air-chamber, which they had thought indispensable. "But do you not lose a great amount of force by dispensing with it?" they inquired—by "the expansion force of the air which is compressed into the chamber, and which keeps up a constant pressure on the surface of the water." "That," replied the doughty Captain, "is a popular fallacy of mere theorists. You get just the amount of force back which you lay out, not a bit more, but, if anything a little less on account of friction. When you have done all, you must lift the water, and your compressed air does not help you one bit, unless it is desirable to get a constant stream."

I am incompetent to pronounce on the technical point, but I recognize the type. It is likely that a number of the miners were Cousin Jacks—they are described as "nearly all of them Englishmen, and are distinguished for their sober and industrious habits. They are far above the average of their class with respect to intelligence . . . An excellent cornet band has been organised, and their music would reflect upon musicians of much higher pretensions." That, too, is a recognizable touch: everywhere the Cornish miners had their brass bands.

The Cornish Arms Hotel, down on West 23rd Street in New York, has a nostalgic interest for us. It is close to the waterside, the quays where the immigrant boats came in. The Cornish folk, those who could afford it, put up at the Cornish Arms (then run by the Blakes) before they mostly went on into the interior to their destinations or looking for work. If only we had some memoir of that hotel, some reminiscences of the life that passed through it, with its mingled gaiety and sadness, its chance encounters, its happy reunions and partings for ever! . . .

When I visited it a few years ago in search of its memories, I found that it was too late, they had all been dissipated. The name "Cornish Arms" remained, but no one even knew what it meant. The place was run by Italians: where the Cornish had once thronged and passed on, the Italians had taken possession. We shall learn a little more of its story later.*

In its heyday it used to print a *Cornish Arms Hotel Bulletin*, published by Sid Blake, giving news of the whereabouts of Cornish folk in the United States, linking up friends and relatives, keeping them in touch with each other.[42] It was full of anecdotes and stories with the characteristic turns of humor—hardly definable even by Bergson—often turning on the ignorance or obtuseness of another, and with the traditional cracks of one place against another at home, Camborne against Redruth, Falmouth against Penryn, in West Cornwall jokes against St. Ives as in Mid-Cornwall against Mevagissey —everybody's butt. Two St. Ives men met at Calumet, in the Upper Peninsula. "Well, Bill, I'm glad to see 'ee. 'Aven't seen 'ee for 'ears." Bill: "I seed 'ee awver t' 'Ancock last week." "Why ded'n 'ee spaake?" Bill: "Well, thee's went roun' th' corner 'for I seed 'ee."

Or there were two Cousin Jacks from Holmbush working

---

* See below pp. 422–23.

at Albany Mine. The superintendent came to measure the work done in the past month—how far they had "drifted" (shifted rock). "Iss, two lengths of this chargin' stick, two pick and pick 'andles, two dag (axe) and dag 'andles an' two big nubs—tha's the exact measurement." Sometimes they are stories from home. "Jan Penberthy drawve to station last evenin' to mit 'is son comin' 'ome from 'Merica. Jan said it must a bin a excursion train, 'cos three people got out all to wance." Or there is the macabre story of the man condemned to death at Bodmin Assizes, who, when asked if he had any particular wish at the end, said: "Ess, you, I'm ticklish roun' the neck; put the roape doun' roun' me waist." Rather Elizabethan, in its way.

Some of these early Cornish folk found no better welcome in the New World than in the Old, life as hard and as bitter. Here is a paragraph from the *West Briton*, October 8, 1819. "Mr. Hoskin, a wheelwright who resided in Luxulyan [near St. Austell], sometime since took himself, wife and several children to America, thinking to better his condition. He found that country so overstocked with people of all trades from Europe that he was unable to obtain employment. Finding his family reduced to a state of wretchedness, he put a period to his existence, in a fit of desperation, leaving his wife and children in the greatest distress."

This bleak paragraph may stand for the Hardy-like tragedies that often enough underlie the impersonal statistics.

The 1840's were a period of cruel hardship at home, with bad harvests all over the country: my grandmother used to speak of them as "the hungry forties." Hundreds, nay thousands, were forced to leave home for a living, and, fortunately, the copper-mines of Lake Superior, the lead-mines of Wisconsin, the iron of New York, the slate and shale of Pennsylvania, all offered their opportunities. We read the other end of the story in the *West Briton*, one of the oldest of provincial newspapers still flourishing. July 2, 1841: "The ships *Adelaide* and *Cornwall*, which sailed from Falmouth in April last with a large number of emigrants chiefly from this county, reached New York in safety about a month ago." Evidently a ten-week passage such as that described by Dickens, with horrifying veracity, on his first visit—and hardly differing essentially from the voyages of a century and a half before. However, "all the passengers landed in good health and spirits to pursue their several destinations in the interior of the country. In passing the quarantine station the superintendent expressed his highest satisfaction at the good order and cleanliness of the vessels and the healthy and respectable appearance of those on board."

Three years later, April 5, 1844: "our Camelford correspondent informs us that the rage for emigration continues, some scores of men, women and children having passed through that town from the north of the county with wagon loads of luggage on their way to Malpas to emigrate in the *Clio* for Quebec." An appropriate name for the ship, since Clio is the Muse of History. "Great numbers are preparing to start from Padstow for the same destination." A notice a few years later, April 7, 1848, advertises a first-class, one thousand ton American packet ship sailing from Falmouth for New York. "Persons about to emigrate to Mineral Point or the neighbourhood of Wisconsin or Lake Superior will find this a favourable opportunity as vessels sail so infrequently from this part of the kingdom for New York."

Though New York was only a port of entry for the vast bulk of Cornish immigrants moving inland, a considerable Cornish sediment remains behind. Of the Tremaine clan so prominent in this chapter there are ten entries, beside two Tremain, one Tremayne. There are eleven Pascoe entries, five Pendarvis, four Hocking, four Penrose, four Trebilcock (including the distinguished painter); three Treleaven, plus one Treleven; three Ugelow, three Tredennick, three Tregenza; two Treloar, two Polgreen, two Nancarrow, two Treherne, two Trezise. There is one Rowse, amid a score of Rouse and Rous. Among other names represented are Retallack, Tregellas, Trelawny, Trembath, Treseder, Trevillion, Trewhella, Trewin, Pengelly. There are two Clemo entries, besides Clemo Milk Products, and a variant of the name in Clyma. Among rarer names it is pleasant to note a well-known Oriental rug and carpet shop—Ernest Treganowan, Inc.; Penglase and Pengloan are also rarities. Among recent immigrants we find a Trevorrow—a St. Ives name: a Methodist minister who, after various pastorates in California, where he had been educated, ended up in New York.[43]

In Brooklyn it is striking to come upon a large Pendarvis clan, no less than fourteen families; eight Pascoe, and an interesting spread of not so common names: Tregillies (for Tregellas), Menhinick, Nankervis, Polglase, Penberthy, Pengilly, Penketh, Coon, Curnow, Treherne, Trevaskis, Trevethan.

And we must remember at every stage that these names, specific and recognizable, are only a small minority of those of Cornish descent.

NOTES

1. J. E. Pomfret, "The Proprietors of the Province of West New Jersey, 1674–1702," *Pennsylvania Magazine*, vol. 75, 117.
2. L. V. Holdsworth, "The Problems of Edward Byllynge: His Connection with Cornwall," in H. H. Brinton, *Children of Light*, 87–88.
3. *Diary and Correspondence of Samuel Pepys*, ed. Lord Braybrooke, vol. 1, 19, 20.
4. J. L. Nickalls, "The Problem of Edward Byllynge: His Writings ... and Influence on the First Constitution of West Jersey," Brinton, *op. cit.*, 112.
5. cf. J. E. Pomfret, *The Province of West New Jersey, 1609–1702*, 94ff.
6. *Ibid.*, 78–79.

7. They are reproduced in J. P. Boyd, *Fundamental Laws and Constitutions of New Jersey, 1664–1964*, 100ff.
8. *D. A. B.*, under William Penn.
9. Pomfret, 95.
10. *D.A.B.*, under William Penn.
11. Pomfret, 97.
12. J. E. Pomfret, "Edward Byllynge's Proposed Gift of Land to Indigent Friends, 1681," *Pa. Mag.*, vol. 61, 88ff.
13. L. V. Holdsworth, *loc. cit.*, 107.
14. Pomfret, *op. cit.*, 137.
15. J. E. Pomfret, *Pa. Mag.*, vol. 75, 140.
16. Pomfret, *op. cit.*, 145.
17. *Ibid.*, 75.
18. *Cal. N.J. Records*, vol. 1, 571.
19. *Ibid.*, 364, 400, 423, 425, 489.
20. *Ibid.*, 143.
21. *Minutes of the Board of Proprietors of the Eastern Division of New Jersey*, vol. 1, 9, 236.
22. *Docs. of the Col. Hist. of N. J.*, XIII, 331.
23. *Ibid.*, XXIII, 381.
24. *Ibid.*, Part I, *Newspaper Extracts*, 90–91.
25. *Ibid.*, XXIII: Cal. of Wills, 381.
26. *Ibid.*, *Newspaper Extracts*, 235, 275.
27. H. C. Reed and G. J. Miller, *The Burlington Court Book, 1680–1709*, 152.
28. J. Clement, *First Emigrant Settlers of Newton, N. J.*, 217.
29. *Docs. of the Col. Hist. of N.J.*, Cal. of Wills, X, 431; XII, 45, 296; XIII, 164, 432.
30. J. E. Stillwell, *Historical and Genealogical Miscellany of New York and New Jersey*, II, 49.
31. *New York State Library Bulletin. Colonial Entries*, V, 1, 125.
32. O. E. Monnette, *First Settlers . . . of Piscataway and Woodbridge, N. J.*, vol. 1, 123.

33. J. G. Wilson, *The Memorial History of the City of New York,* IV, 166; *New York Historical Soc.,* 1938, 119.

34. E. M. Treman and M. E. Poole, *The Hist. of the Treman, Tremaine, Truman Family in America.*

35. *Ibid.,* I, 36ff.

36. *Ibid.,* I, 44ff.

37. *Ibid.,* I, 98ff.

38. *Ibid.,* I, 81.

39. L. Sabine, *Loyalists of the American Revolution,* II, 362.

40. C. E. Fitch, *Encyclopedia of Biog. of N.Y.,* 56ff.

41. *New York State Historical Associations,* X, 193ff.

42. I am indebted for these extracts from this rare publication to a typescript, made by Mrs. Helen Paul, at the Marquette County Historical Society Library, Michigan.

43. *Who's Who in New York,* 1918.

5 PENNSYLVANIA

Of all the old colonies along the Atlantic Coast it would seem that the Cornish contribution to the splendid province of Pennsylvania was the most varied and interesting, perhaps the most influential. There was not only the Quaker element, distinguished in itself, but the non-Quaker Cornish, who became far more numerous. The Cornish element not only began in the first decade, the 1680's, within a few years of William Penn's original grant, but continued to be recruited by individuals and small groups all through the eighteenth century. Then, in the nineteenth, it grew to sizable proportions with the incoming of hundreds of miners to work in slate-quarries, iron- and coal-mines, such as those around Pottsville. From this last the Cornish were apt to move to the Middle West; they did not take permanently to coal-mining: that was a province of the Welsh. Among the earliest recruits, however, were four families that have played a leading part in the life of province and state, two of them right up to today, or yesterday: Growdens, Foxes, Rawles and Penroses.

We have seen that William Penn first became interested in American settlement through his concern with the affairs of New Jersey. In 1681 he got a grant from the Crown of an immense tract of land west of the Delaware, in discharge of a large debt owed to his father, Admiral Sir William Penn. In honor of the unromantic Admiral this province in the New World was named, romantically, Pennsylvania. In the autumn of 1682 William Penn came to take possession, landing at Newcastle on the Delaware—that beautiful old town gathered around its green, standing unchanged since the eighteenth century. From the first the colony was intended, in part, as a refuge for the persecuted Quakers. In its constitution and nature the province exemplified a wide measure of toleration, in contrast to Massachusetts.

Among the largest purchasers from Penn were Lawrence Growden, a rich pewterer of St. Merryn, and his brother Joseph. Together they bought ten thousand acres; only the twenty-five largest purchasers bought on this scale, the average freeholder contenting himself with a farm of three hundred acres. Clearly the Growdens believed in Penn's scheme to invest so much, and the younger generation was evidently opting for the New World. Lawrence Growden sailed in his own ship from Fowey, bringing a company of forty-five with him—family, servants, dependents—and after a nineteen weeks' winter crossing arrived safely in January 1684.[1] His home was the substantial barton of Trevose in St. Merryn, and this name he gave to his large estate on the Neshaminy Creek. Trevose has come through the changes and vicissitudes consequent upon the Revolution, is now a suburb of giant Philadelphia with a railroad station of the name.

Lawrence Growden returned to Cornwall to die about 1708–9.[2] Most of the property he had to dispose of was in Pennsylvania; his son Joseph was to succeed to all of it, except three thousand acres to his grandson Lawrence, who, after his father's death, was to have the whole. This was to constitute something like an entailed estate, after the model of the English gentry; he named a number of Padstow and St. Merryn neighbors as trustees for the grandson, with power to depute two or more friends in Pennsylvania to act. The grandson was also to have the moiety or half of Trevose barton in Cornwall. William Hooper, his grandson-in-law, was to have the barton of Treveglos, paying Thomas Leverton, a trustee, one hogshead of good cider, "if any be made of the orchard in the said barton." Bequests of money and property at St. Austell to the Hoopers attested the pewterer's wealth. A modest bequest of £5 was to be distributed to poor Friends at two quarterly meetings, with £5 for rebuilding the walls of Tregangeeves burying-place—the tall and grisly walls, enclosing that haunted place with its will-o'-the-wisp which are just now, while I write this, being swept away for road-widening. The will was proved in 1716 by the grandson who was then of age. The male members of the family being now in Pennsylvania, it came to an end, in the male line, in Cornwall.

The province had the usual teething troubles incident to such ventures, and shortly settled into the pattern of a struggle on the part of the settlers against the interests of the Penns as proprietors. In 1689 we find Joseph Growden printing a large number of copies of Penn's original *Frame of Government*, against the latter's wishes—understandably, since Penn had committed himself to some very democratic sentiments: "Any government is free to the people under it (whatever be the frame) where the laws rule, and the people are a party to those laws."[3] He was now being taken at his word, and his words used against his proprietary rights. Two years later Penn was appealing to Growden among others of his "loving friends" not to quarrel over the government of the colony.[4] Growden, however, became a member of the popular party against the deputy governor Penn sent over during his long absence.

Penn had spent only some twenty months in the colony during 1682–84; he did not return till fifteen years later and then only for another spell of some months in 1699–1701. The original constitution Penn drew up had proved unworkable: he was a doctrinaire optimist rather than a practical statesman, unlike John Winthrop and the hard-faced men who made New England. In 1700 Growden was chairman of a grand committee with Penn, the council and assembly, to draft a new charter. Penn could not even get his legislation through the assembly to introduce marriage among the Negro slaves now held in large numbers by the settlers, or for the protection of the Indians.[5] He saw no evil in owning slaves himself, though ready to free them in his will. Frustrated on every side he made haste home in 1701; we find him writing next year, "Pray quiet Edward Farmer, Joseph Growden [and others of the settlers' party] till my son come."[6] His son William Penn, Jr., did no better with the contending factions in the colony, and added to his father's griefs by his dissolute life.

Power inevitably came into the hands of the people on the spot. Growden was a leading settler in Bucks County, constantly on the commissions of the peace there and from 1695 elected to represent it on the provincial council.[7] For many years he was a member of the General Assembly, fairly constantly its Speaker, in the end Chief Justice of the Supreme Court of the province. He was a leading figure in its public life, active in all its concerns; he added to his interest by acquiring a further tract of ten thousand acres.[8] At his death in 1730 he must have been the largest landowner apart from the Penn family.

Joseph Growden, Jr., was the first to practice inoculation against small-pox in the province from 1731, "the first person of note who then devoted himself as a forlorn hope for the purpose of example."[9] Whether on account of this exhibition of public spirit or no, he died quite young in 1738—not until he had achieved the office of Attorney General, however. With the third generation and Lawrence Growden, Jr., (1694–1770) we reach the apogee of the family fortunes. From 1734 he was one of the eight members of the assembly for Bucks County, later a member of the council.[10] A silversmith's book of this time reveals, in his purchases, something of the finery with which he set up house: a dozen knives and forks with ivory handles, pairs of gold and silver shoe-buckles, a gold girdle-buckle, knee buckles, and an arched moon clock and case. He not only owned a four-wheeled coach—one of eight in the place by 1760—but had been married in church "by a priest." Fie on him!—no good Quaker.

He and Jeremiah Langhorne set on foot the famous Durham ironworks of which they were the principal proprietors.[11] Part of the Langhorne estate came to Growden, who had other business enterprises and extended his holdings in land. With him the male line failed: he had two daughters, coheiresses, Elizabeth Nicholson and Grace, who in 1753 married the brilliant young lawyer, Joseph Galloway. This match gave Galloway a promising start at twenty-three: by twenty-six he was the second judge of the Supreme Court.[12] From this basis he launched himself into provincial, and ultimately imperial, politics. This is not the place to deal with the tragic career of this leading Loyalist. A lawyer and a conservative, a rich man, he naturally feared the revolutionary consequences of the colonies' break with Britain. A patriotic American, he worked to the last to bring about an accommodation between the mother country and the colonies; a lawyer, he believed that their respective rights should be laid down by a written constitution for the whole Empire; a conceited man, with more than average public spirit, he proposed to write it himself. But the revolutionary tide of events swept him to one side; drummed out of public life by mob-spirit and himself distrusting the populace, he opted for the Crown as a Loyalist. Thereupon all three of the family estates were confiscated —Trevose, Durham and Vandergrift—and even long after the Revolutionary War was over, in 1793 his petition to return to Pennsylvania was summarily rejected. He died after twenty-five years of exile in England, having devoted much of them to the service of his fellow Americans there and to literature.[13]

Thus the great Growden inheritance in Pennsylvania came to an end.* Grace Growden was herself a woman of strong personality, who wrote verse and kept a diary. She was an

---

* No member of the Growden family has a biography in D.A.B.; it would be useful to include them in an expanded edition of this standard work in the future.

unhappy woman, ill-attuned to marriage with Galloway: she disliked his politician's egoism and had a mind of her own. Naturally the events of the Revolution—of which she gives a vivid, tell-tale picture—increased her alarm and despondency. From her diary we can observe the Loyalist or neutralist attitude of the upper class in Philadelphia as against the aggressiveness of the Whigs, the confiscations put through by the vindictive revolutionaries.[14]

The Rawles also suffered severely for their Loyalism in the end, but managed to come through to continue making a distinguished contribution to public life. They were a family of small gentry from the parish of St. Juliot high up on the tremendous cliffs of the north coast of Cornwall not far from Boscastle—that parish so beloved of Thomas Hardy and celebrated in his poems. A younger son of the family, Francis Rawle, moved to Plymouth where he engaged in trade, and was one of a considerable number of Cornish folk of good substance who were struck by George Fox's gospel of the inner light. He was several times fined and imprisoned for the pleasure of his peculiar convictions, without doing him any good. With a group of Friends he determined to take advantage of Penn's opening and to emigrate among the first. Rawle combined with James Fox—not a relative of the founder of the sect, George Fox, but one of a St. Germans family—to purchase a large tract of five thousand acres in what is now Montgomery County.[15] Others with them were Richard Gove and John Shilson. Rawle left Plymouth with his son Francis in April 1686, in the ship *Desire*, and landed in June with six servants. With his friends they settled in the Schuylkill Valley and set up the Plymouth Meeting House; subsequently they moved into trade in Philadelphia, where the senior Rawle died in 1697.[16]

In 1689 Francis Rawle, Jr., married a well-off wife, and thereafter prospered in trade and public life. In the same year he became a judge of the county court, in 1691 an alderman of Philadelphia, and deputy registrar of wills.[17] He was a member of the assembly from 1704 to 1709, and again from 1719 to 1727. In spite of his father-in-law having been Penn's intimate friend and adviser, Rawle became a leader of the popular anti-proprietary party, along with the Growdens and other settlers. He was active on most of the important committees of the house, but refused to accept appointment as a member of the provincial council in 1724. He died in 1727.

Rawle's chief interest was in economic matters: he is said to have been the first person in the colonies to write on them —a change from theology—and in this sensible interest he was followed by Franklin, who took up Rawle's ideas on a paper currency. The colony suffered distress and trade-depression owing to the scarcity of currency; Rawle was right to advocate a moderate dose of inflation to cure it—a Keynesian before his time. In 1721 he offered to the General Assembly *Some Remedies Proposed for the Restoring the Sunk Credit of the Province of Pennsylvania*. He followed this in 1725 with his *Ways and Means for the Inhabitants of Delaware to Become Rich*. The ways and means he suggested were no less Keynesian: bounties on exports, discouraging tariffs on imports; prohibition of foreign liquors and luxuries to protect the local production of beer and cider; the import of molasses from the West Indies to be free, to encourage the local manufacture of rum. It all seems very sensible. In 1723 he had the pleasure of signing the bills of assembly for the issue of paper-money he had advocated. Meanwhile, we find Friend Gove wrestling with Governor Keith—of delightful Graeme Park, that unchanged small Queen Anne mansion in the country not far from Philadelphia—over his misrepresentations of the Quaker position, signing "Our Ancient Testimony" as to Jesus Christ, the Scriptures, etc. with other protesters.[18] He did not prosper.

Since Francis Rawle had six sons, as well as four daughters, the family increased and ramified. It is not my purpose to write its history—that has fortunately been done; but perhaps it may be proper to notice a few members of this family without parallel in the length of its service to province and state.[19] A third Francis Rawle, great-grandson of the original settler, was born in 1729 and as a cultivated young gentleman made the Grand Tour of Europe.[20] He died quite young, from a shooting accident, in 1761, and his widow married Samuel Shoemaker, who during the Revolution was a leading Loyalist. Most of the upper class were, more or less, loyal to the Crown—at least their sympathies were not revolutionary. When Shoemaker's estate was confiscated, his wife's Rawle property was confiscated along with his. Laurel Hill, the pleasant Georgian house in Fairmount Park, looking out over the Schuylkill from the back, which had been bought by Francis Rawle in 1760, was taken over as a summer residence by General Reed, one of the most active persecutors of Philadelphia Loyalists. After the Revolution it was forcibly "sold" to Parr, a leading investor in confiscated properties. Later, young William Rawle was able to buy it back, and the family returned for another generation to the house, familiar in Rawle diaries and letters as their country home on the Schuylkill.

During the Revolution the family was broken up for a time and young William went to England to study law at the Middle Temple.[21] After the fuss was over he decided to return to Philadelphia, though he regarded it as "in some degree humiliating." Benjamin Franklin, whose own son had been a Loyalist, was accommodating and kind; young Rawle was granted a passport in 1782 and admitted to the bar in 1783. The present law-firm of Rawle and Henderson goes back to that date and is thus the oldest in Philadelphia. Later Rawle was invited by Franklin to join his Society for Political Inquiries. He became a member of the American Philosophical Society and served a term in the state legislature. President Washington made him United States attorney for Pennsylvania. This was the prelude to a distinguished and varied public career. A successful lawyer, he wrote an influential *View of the Constitution of the United States*, which attracted all the more attention coming from a former Loyalist; an abolitionist, he argued against the constitutionality of slavery. All his life he maintained the family connection with the Society of Friends, and himself exemplified their high standards in his life of public service.*

His grandson, William Henry Rawle (1823–89), carried on the family tradition, at the bar, in religion, and in public service.[22] Though a Quaker, he enlisted to fight against slavery, serving as a private in the artillery in the Civil War. He also continued the family tradition not only in practice as a lawyer, but as a jurist writing on legal subjects. In the next generation his nephew, William Brooke Rawle (1843–1915) got leave from the University of Pennsylvania in time to serve at Gettysburg and received his B.A. while on active service. He served through the Wilderness campaign in 1864 and at Appomattox in 1865. In later years he became a student of the war and wrote several studies of the Gettysburg campaign based on his own experiences. In the tradition of his family he was immensely public-spirited: an active member of the Pennsylvania Historical Society his great-grandfather had founded and of other societies which the family had advanced and supported. His mother was the only daughter of William Rawle, Jr., thus reinforcing the strain. In the next generation a later Francis Rawle (1846–1930) was a member of the Philadelphia bar for nearly sixty years. As with his predecessors he combined practice with writing: he wrote a biography of Edward Livingstone, edited a standard law dictionary, and wrote numerous legal and historical articles. When he died only a generation ago, the *Dictionary of American Biography* was able to pay this tribute: "from the arrival of the first Francis in Philadelphia to the death of the last, nearly a quarter millennium had elapsed with no generation failing to include a Rawle among those prominent in the civic life of Philadelphia. It is a record equalled by few American families."[23]

---

* There is enough material to warrant a biography of him.

Yet, even a generation later the family still remembers its Cornish origins, remote as they are.

We learn more about that original group of Cornish Quakers that came over in the *Desire* in 1686, in connection with James Fox.[24] Francis Rawle and his son came with six servants, James Fox with his family and eight servants, John Shilson with his wife and four servants, Nicholas Pearce with two servants. Most of the names are unknown to us, but the bulk of the group would be from Cornwall or Plymouth. Their intention was to set up a woollen manufacture, but this did not take effect, and Fox removed with Rawle to Philadelphia. However, the Plymouth Meeting continues to this day—it was at first established in Fox's house in Plymouth Township—to testify to their intent.

James Fox was the son of Francis Fox of St. Germans—this is the family from which the distinguished Quaker family in Cornwall today is descended—and his wife Dorothy Kekewich of Catchfrench, where the shell of the old Elizabethan house remains, a melancholy reminder, behind the modern house. James Fox married Elizabeth Rickard, of a Cornish family engaged in making woollens at Plymouth. After moving into Philadelphia Fox became a member of the assembly in 1688, and again from 1693 to 1699. Penn's first charter to the city of Philadelphia, in 1691, which appointed Francis Rawle, Jr., one of six aldermen, made James Fox one of twelve councillors.[25] In 1693, when the government was in confusion upon Penn's withdrawal, Fox was on the committee of the assembly to draw the tax bill.[26] In 1699 he died. John, Richard and Justinian Fox had arrived with him as servants, though they were probably members of the family since they witnessed family marriages. Justinian Fox left seven children, of whom Joseph played an important part in the life of the province.*

---

* There is no notice of this interesting man in D.A.B.

Joseph was apprenticed to a prosperous carpenter, who left him half his property, a good bit of real estate. He became a prominent property-holder in Philadelphia, brought into association with Franklin, Galloway and other leading figures. In 1745 he was made city commissioner, in 1748 city assessor, and in 1750 one of the two burgesses for Philadelphia in the assembly; he was an early promoter of the famous Philadelphia Hospital. In 1763 he was Master of the Carpenters' Company, presiding in the historic hall that still remains; for many years he was the barrack-master of the city, and trustee of Province Island, the quarantine quarters.

In 1764–65 he was Speaker of the assembly at the height of the Stamp Act agitation; he was one of the signers of the Non-Importation Agreement, and was chairman of the assembly that declared against Parliament's right to tax the colonies. After the Stamp Act was repealed Fox came round, like a good many people, to sympathize with the home government —for this he was ousted from the Speaker's chair. The revolutionary minority was determined to push things to a break. Fox was really a moderate, though he was forced to take a modest part in war-preparations, until his barracks were taken over by the revolutionaries. In 1777 he took the oath of allegiance to the state, renouncing allegiance to the Crown. A sociable, agreeable man, he was a member of the fascinating old club, the State in Schuylkill, that still keeps its marble busts of George I and George II looking down upon its festive assemblies. Fox died before the end of the war, in 1779; his son George at one time owned the bulk of the Franklin Papers. He had numerous descendants in the professions, especially of law and medicine. Foxes of old family in Pennsylvania are thus apt to have some Cornish tincture in them.

In 1692 there arrived the founder of a family which was to make as important a contribution as any, in the fulness of time, to the power and prosperity of Pennsylvania; for it was they who founded the great Cornwall Ironworks, and named it in honor of the county of their origin.[27] This was Peter Grubb, who settled at what became known as Grubb's Landing on the Delaware, near Wilmington, and here his son Peter was born. The Grubbs lighted upon the rich iron deposits near Lebanon, and with the native Cornish instinct for mining began to exploit them. The second Peter Grubb became a successful iron-master, who erected the first bloomery about 1735, not far from where the famous ironworks subsequently grew up. In 1742 he built the first furnace here, the Cornwall furnace, adjacent to land where Samuel Grubb was also at work. An early account tells us, "Cornwall, or Grubb's, Ironworks in Lancaster County. The mine is rich and abundant, forty feet deep, commencing two feet under the earth's surface. The ore is somewhat mixed with sulphur and copper. Peter Grubb was its discoverer." He died in 1745, when his estate came to his sons, Curtis and the third Peter Grubb. Both these became colonels in the Revolutionary War. Curtis's son, a fourth Peter, sold a part interest to the Colemans, and together they engaged not only in mining the ore but in manufacturing the iron. Their descendants "are still identified with the manufacture of iron, and the Cornwall ore-hills are still relied upon to furnish large quantities of iron ore for furnaces in Eastern Pennsylvania. Prior to the development of the Lake Superior iron ore region the Cornwall mines were annually the most productive group of all the iron ore mines in this country, and this distinction they held for several years after Lake Superior ores came into general use."

Here was a field to which Cornish miners came in the nineteenth century, in smaller numbers before the decline of mining at home precipitated the flood. Then, a witness writes, "if you want to see our Cornish miners you must go to Pennsylvania, to Lake Superior, to Nevada; you'll find very few of them in Cornwall."[28] We shall observe later on that it was fairly usual for some Cornish miners to have a spell at mining or quarrying in the East, before they passed on to the Middle West or Far West. They raised iron, copper and zinc in New

Jersey, emery in Massachusetts, iron and nickel, with some coal-mining and slate-quarrying, in Pennsylvania. Their skill at tunnelling rock had many uses: "most of the men who between the 1850's and 1870's drove the Hoosac railroad tunnel through the Berkshires were Cornish."

A number of Cornish folk came over with these families, as we have seen, but we have lost track of their names. Occasionally a recognizable one pops up: in 1689 John Penquite's father is so poor that the son is unlikely to pay the debt he owes to John Nicholls.[29] We have observed too that the early settlement of Pennsylvania is to some extent connected with that of New Jersey. Charles Read, a Cornish tailor, emigrated to Burlington County, New Jersey, but soon moved to Philadelphia.[30] His son Charles Read (1686-1737) became mayor of the city, and the family married well into its Quaker oligarchy. Another pioneer settler of Burlington was Henry Grubb, of Stokeclimsland. He had only daughters, but other Grubbs may have come along with him; for later we find them active not only in Pennsylvania iron-furnaces in the eighteenth century but in professional circles in the nineteenth.

About 1700 there arrived someone who was to be the ancestor of a foremost Pennsylvanian family, which made the most varied and significant contributions of any to American life, both inside and outside the state. This was Bartholomew Penrose of Bristol—though, like all Penroses, he was of Cornish origin. He and his brother Thomas were shipwrights and substantial people; for Thomas owned a dock at Bedminster, and a manor in the parish of Compton Martin with a number of small properties round about.[31] Batholomew purchased a property in Philadelphia at what is now Market Street and Delaware Avenue. In 1703 he followed the admirable pattern we have observed by marrying a daughter of one of the large landowners of the province. In 1707 Penrose established his famous shipyard on the Delaware, which lasted for nearly a century and a half.[32] With the Penns as partners he launched its first ship, the *Diligence* of 150 tons. Bartholomew died in 1711 and was succeeded by Thomas Penrose, to whom Bartholomew left a legacy and who probably came over later. For the whole family group was connected with the shipyard, while other members engaged in trade. Thomas Penrose was succeeded in the shipyard by his son James; while there were two more Thomases in this and the next generation who were shipbuilders. Joshua Humphreys, one of the designers of the United States Navy's first vessels, was an apprentice in the yard. We find Ann Penrose listed as shipwright, evidently during a widowhood, followed by the third Thomas (1734–1815), who was called into consultation on the design of the United States Navy's first frigates. Last of this remarkable dynasty to build ships was Charles Penrose, head of the Philadelphia Navy Yard, who died in 1845 and this was the end of the family's ship-building activities.

We find notice of other members of the family. Another Bartholomew Penrose (1708–58) was a merchant, and assessor of taxes for the city in 1759. His daughter Polly married General Anthony Wayne of the Revolutionary Army. We hear a good deal of Colonel Joseph Penrose in Grace Growden Galloway's Diary. Southeastern Pennsylvania was very much divided over the Revolution; to the struggle between Whigs and Tories was added that between Quakers and Presbyterians, carrying the war into every household in this region. It was "torn by an internal dissension which almost reached the proportions of a civil war . . . only a bare majority throughout the Colonies favoured separation from the mother country."[33] In April 1778 Colonel Penrose's patrol was surprised by the Bucks County Volunteer Company, and shortly after his whole detachment was captured. Colonel Penrose thereupon resigned his command of the 10th Pennsylvania Regiment.

The real efflorescence of the family that Bartholomew Penrose founded came in the nineteenth century with two Biddle marriages. Clement Biddle Penrose was one of the three commissioners appointed for the immense territory ceded to the United States by the Louisiana Purchase. His son, Charles Bingham Penrose (1798-1857) married another Biddle. A lawyer, he collaborated with William Rawle and another in three volumes of Reports of Cases in the Supreme Court of Pennsylvania, and became prominent in state politics.[34] He served in the Senate as a Whig for some years, and was Speaker for a term. When the Whigs came to power in Washington he was solicitor of the United States Treasury, 1841-45. From this he returned to state politics as state senator till his death. He had six children, of whom one, an eminent physician, produced a family of seven sons: four of these were men of mark and achieved fame.

The most famous of these was Boies Penrose (1860-1921).* He followed in the family tradition of law-practice at first in the family firm and then state politics. He gradually built up a position as leader of the Republican Party organization in the state and became the undisputed boss of Pennsylvania politics. Elected United States Senator in 1897 he remained so for the rest of his life, ultimately becoming head of the Republican Party in the Senate—an opponent of Woodrow Wilson, and Wilsonian idealism, one of those who bequeathed Harding as President to the nation. A cynical aristocrat, who had no use for democratic cant, he was a man of immense power and influence, who dedicated his life to politics in the lower sense of the term.

His brothers, Spencer and Richard A. F. Penrose, made immense fortunes in Western mining—perhaps it would not be fanciful to see an atavistic element in this, the Cornish nose for minerals, the genius for mining.[35] Richard Penrose (1863-1931) was a gifted geologist, who made extensive surveys of mineral deposits for the states of Texas and Arkansas in 1888-92—in those days the whole vast country lay open to be rifled, much of it virgin territory. In his middle

---

* cf. D.A.B. There is no adequate biography of this important politician.

years he was professor of geology at Chicago, until the growth of his mining interests along with his brother's called him to exploit the gold, silver and copper of Colorado, Arizona, and Utah. He became one of the founders of the Commonwealth Mining and Milling Company at Pearce, Arizona—called after the Cornishman who discovered the silver there. (The profits flowed in to the Penroses.) In 1903 he joined his brother in founding the Utah Copper Company, which in its time was the largest copper producer in North America.

The career of his brother Spencer Penrose (1865–1939) was virtually coterminous with the history of modern Colorado. As a young man, spurning the safe allurements of banking, he went west to Colorado Springs, hit the gold boom in Cripple Creek and shortly became a millionaire. Gold, however, proved only the foundation; a bigger fortune was made from copper. Turning his attention to milling and smelting ores, he also joined with his father and brothers to organize the Utah Copper Company. When he eventually sold out he became a multi-millionaire. He proceeded to extend his interests into real estate, agriculture, banking, investing in tourism, building hotels and a road to the top of Pike's Peak, pioneering the sugar-beet industry of western Kansas. Dividing most of his estate between wife and step-daughter he was still able to leave a residue of over $11,000,000 to his El Pomar Foundation. He had a creative life, which he much enjoyed, like his famous brother Boies.

A fourth brother, Charles Bingham Penrose (1862–1925), was a distinguished surgeon, professor of gynaecology at the University of Pennsylvania. Among his public services he founded the Pennsylvania Board of Health, and was president of the Philadelphia Zoo, which he made outstanding. Though others of the family carried the name beyond the confines of Pennsylvania to Missouri and elsewhere, he was the only one of the brothers to have a son. This is the present head of the family, another Boies, scholar and historical geographer, president of the Historical Society of Pennsylvania. It is pleasant to record that this distinguished society, founded by a Rawle, should today be presided over by a Penrose.

This eminent family was Quaker neither in its origin nor its subsequent affiliations; but other Penroses came in who were Quakers. In 1717 Robert Penrose arrived from Ireland: he was from a Yorkshire branch of the clan which had settled in Ireland, probably with the Cromwellians.[36] His son was a tanner, who settled on a tract of two hundred acres in Richland. They were a numerous stock, who continued Quakers into the nineteenth century. So the name begins to be fairly frequent in the province. When Graeme Park fell from its high estate—it has now been restored as a museum—the "longhouse" which had been servants' quarters and guest-wing was pulled down by Samuel Penrose, a neighboring Quaker farmer, who used the materials to build his house nearby in 1810.[37] In Whitpain Township in Montgomery County Benjamin Penrose owned the Waggon Inn from 1779–83; while there was a Penrose's tavern in Roaring Creek.[38] In 1848 a Samuel Penrose, son of William Penrose of Horsham, was killed while logging.[39]

Among other Cornish names Nathaniel Edgcumbe was in Philadelphia by 1719: not a Quaker, for his family appears now and again in the records of Christ Church.[40] Thomas Polgreen died there in 1730. In 1733 Thomas and Mary Williams arrived from Bristol with four young sons.[41] They were Cornish Quakers. Williams was from my native town of St. Austell, where his father was the miller at Trevarrick, a substantial yeoman. Thomas Williams had married Mary Reed of Menheniot up at Tregangeeves—Loveday Hambly's old home and a spiritual center for the Cornish Friends. Young Samuel, the fourth son, remembered being carried in a pannier on the back of a mule, with the buildings of Bristol being pointed out to him on the way to the ship. Samuel Williams was the founder of a business in Philadelphia which has continued up to our time—one of the Association of Centenary

E

Firms in the United States. Samuel's son Thomas died in 1846, worth a good deal of money and real estate; his will was witnessed by four Williamses—the family was very prolific. He had been a member of the city's Common Council, and taken much interest in its development, particularly in the Waterworks at Fairmount Park, of which we still see the fine classic buildings on the Schuylkill river-front. The business continued in the family for yet a century, and in the family name: "the corporation's ownership and management has been continued to date by direct heirs," with only one recruit from outside.[42] Other direct descendants of Thomas and Mary Williams have carried their family bible—with its memories of Tregangeeves and Menheniot and St. Austell—as far as Cincinnati, Ohio.

In 1749 Richard Kimber and his wife sailed from Bristol, and settled at West Bradford in Chester County.[43] Already there were Cornish settlers among the very first in this county, for we find Peter Tremaine there as early as 1687.[44] The Kimbers were Quakers and the tradition of their family is that it originated in Zennor—hence an earlier coat of arms with the Mermaid of Zennor for crest, who still appears on a carved bench-end in the church there, and with a comb featuring upon it. This is a rebus on the name—though the meaning of it has nothing to do with a comb: it means a confluence of two streams, as in Quimper in Brittany. A later coat of arms sports three Cornish choughs. Richard Kimber was a younger son, brother of a well-known Dissenting divine; he farmed a mere sixty-seven acres, and died not many years after his arrival. He set a pattern of emigrating in the stock; in several generations Kimbers emigrated to America and to Australia.

His son moved about between Chester County, a farm at Radnor—he married a Welsh wife—and a house in Philadelphia. He was buried at Kimberton. A descendant became an approved minister in the Society of Friends, and for thirty years conducted the Kimberton Boarding School for Girls, with success or without mishap; he took a public-spirited part in local life and, an earnest opponent of slavery, was given to sheltering runaway slaves in his house. The clan achieved no prominence—unlike the Penroses, Growdens and Rawles, they gravitated around the modest reaches of middle and lower-middle class life, as farmers, glass-blowers, booksellers, printers, steamboat-captains, coal-merchants, railroadmen, occasionally blossoming into a Quaker or Methodist minister. In this century a young Kimber was a Stanford University student who volunteered for the American Field Service, and had the honor of carrying the first flag authorized by the United States Government to France in May 1917.[45] He was subsequently killed flying over the German lines in September 1918. He was not a descendant of the Quaker Richard Kimber, but of another line.

They all apparently go back to Cornwall. Again one observes the interesting eugenic fact: there is only a handful of Kimbers in Cornwall; there are hundreds of them in the United States, across the country to California, and in Australia.

There must have been a great many Cornish folk of whom we have lost track. In mid-eighteenth century we find a James Treviller, yeoman, in Chester County—probably a mis-spelling of Trevillian.[46] From 1743 a prominent Philadelphia shipmaster was Captain John Bolitho. He was one of the subscribers to the second edition of Fisher's Chart of Delaware Bay and River, with its creeks, shoals, and guide to navigation. Unfortunately he had no male descendants of his name, but various Philadelphia families, Dalletts and Suttons among others, descend from his daughters.[47]

Before the Revolution John Nancarrow, a Quaker from Penzance, came over; in September 1779 he married Susanna Jones, daughter of the provincial treasurer of Pennsylvania.[48] Grace Growden Galloway was a close friend of the bride—if that is not an unsuitable word for a Quaker; though Mrs. Galloway did not grace the meeting with her presence, she signed the marriage-certificate. Mrs. Nancarrow frequently appears in her Diary, and shortly the Nancarrows appear among the leading folk in Pittsburgh. John Nancarrow engages in the brewing business, getting his equipment from Philadelphia, to set up an establishment at Petersburg on the Kentucky. Next he appears in 1792 as one of the superintendents laying out the Philadelphia-Lancaster turnpike. Later on in that decade, in Tarlton Bates's *Journal of a Voyage down the Ohio*, at a house-warming in Cincinnati we find Miss Nancarrow dancing minuets. The Nancarrows are over the Alleghenies: thus these families begin to fan out and spread westward.

It so happens that there has survived, out of the flotsam and jetsam of time, a scrap of autobiography of a young Cornish trader who came to Philadelphia just at the end of the American Revolution.[49] This was Paul Burrell of Illogan, a devout Methodist of the second generation, who made a trading voyage to America, with Thomas Stephens and his wife, in 1783. Burrell brought over with him a stock-in-trade worth some £400. Landing in New York they found life too expensive and the prospect of setting up a business unfavorable. So they determined to move to Philadelphia. The weather was bad, and the passage by sea took seven days. Burrell was much impressed by the journey up the Delaware to the city, with houses, farms and plantations on either side: "it did Give A butifull Aspick." Arrived at Philadelphia, "we met with our friends that went by land, and Mr. John Nancarrow that went from Market-jew [i.e. Marazion] about ten years before . . . And he got me lodgings and board to an old gentleman Quaker where I was greatly cared for. And then it was the first thing to look out for a shop and to get our goods on shore, and to see what business was to be done. And Mr. Thomas Stephens and myself took a shop in Second Street . . . and this we continued on for about three months and sold out most of our goods." Business was so successful that the partners joined with two others to buy a vessel with a consignment of goods for England. "And then we moved shops to Market Street, and there did very well by buying and selling. And we went through many hot days—hard to keep up our spirits, and got over it better than all our fears."

Burrell records that at that time, just on the close of the war, the Methodists were at a low ebb—only one meeting house, "and Mr. Asbury the only preacher that was there (and some others come before I left) and most of the society was the negroes." Burrell much enjoyed the horrid delights of their sharing experiences, "so simple, so free, and so artless . . . that if I was to tarry here these people would be my people." But the Quakers, who were much more prominent, with four meeting houses and a numerous attendance, were no less spiritually satisfying. At the large meeting house in Second Street, the Friends were as lively "as to a Methodist love-feast, and full of love, and full of heaven, and full of God." Burrell testifies to the prosperity of the city, "eatables in great abundance." Business increased at the shop in Market Street, where they continued till December, 1783. They had a good prospect of getting orders for goods from England. "So we made up our minds to take orders and get ready for England, and left our business to a friend to settle in our absence. And we got a passage for Williams of Redruth and myself on board an Irish vessel bound to Belfast . . . with a view to go out again in the spring following." They freighted the ship in part with flax-seed and tobacco, with every expectation of returning to Philadelphia. "For, if I thought I should not see it again I should not be so hasty of coming home, for I was delighted with the country and could turn my hand several ways to make a very genteel living."

There is first-hand evidence of the motives that led a good tradesman to seek his living in the new country, and the satisfaction such people found in settling there. Paul Burrell did not return, however: on getting back he married a wife and that settled his fate. He spent the rest of his life in Cornwall and, rather surprisingly, prospered. Those were the days of the Industrial Revolution and trade and business were on the upgrade.

After the Revolutionary War, in 1793, there arrived in Philadelphia a Cornishman who made a signal contribution to the new nation: this was Josiah Fox, the shipbuilder, who along with Humphreys designed the first frigates for the United States Navy.* Joshua Humphreys learned his shipbuilding in James Penrose's yard; Josiah Fox learned his in the royal dockyard at Devonport, then known as Plymouth Dock. Fox was born at Falmouth in 1763, a member of that Quaker family to have a distinguished record in Victorian science and literature. After completing his apprenticeship young Fox made a number of voyages aboard the *Crown*, owned by the family company—which still operates its business from the quayside at Falmouth. This gave him opportunities of visiting the principal shipbuilding yards in England, Cadiz, the celebrated Arsenal at Venice; he even went so far afield—or, rather, at sea—as Archangel. In 1791 he was employed in the royal dockyard at Deptford. A recent student of the subject concludes, that "Fox was, in fact, the only formally trained shipwright concerned with the design of early American ships."

Late in 1793 he arrived in Philadelphia, then the capital of the new nation, to visit friends and relatives. Fox was recommended to General Knox by a kinsman, Andrew Ellicott, who was also descended from the Cornish Foxes, the branch already settled there. The General was anxious not to lose Fox's expertise to the nation, and discussed the proposed navy with him, the design and construction of the ships. Fox was given a clerkship in the War Department eighteen days after Hum-

---

* M. T. Westlake, "Josiah Fox, Gentleman, Quaker, Shipbuilder," *Pa. Mag.*, vol. 88, 316ff. Quotations are from this admirably documented study of Fox. There is no biography of this important figure in *D.A.B.*; it is to be hoped that there will now be technical studies of his work, as well as a full biography of him.

phreys. Both were equally involved in preparing the designs for the new 44-gun frigates; but Mr. Chapelle tells us in *The History of the American Sailing Navy* that "Fox was far better trained than Humphreys in all respects, and was a far superior draftsman."[50] This was hard for the local man to take, and the two men—in spite of being Friends—were on unfriendly terms for the rest of their lives. Fox was given the job of designing the largest of the frigates to be handed over to the Dey of Algiers, upon peace being made with the Barbary States in 1795. In 1797 he was in consequence discountenanced by the Society of Friends, "on account of his deviation from our discipline by going in marriage with a woman not in membership with us and in accepting employment under government in which he hath assisted in building vessels intended for the purpose of war contrary to our peaceable principles." One hardly knows which was worse—marriage with a non-Quaker or war. However, in 1807 Mrs. Josiah Fox became a Quaker, was accepted and all was well.

Not long after his discountenancing he had been transferred to Norfolk to establish the Navy Yard there, where he proceeded to construct the famous frigate *Chesapeake*. Of this charge he wrote, "that during the whole of the period he was employed in building and equipping that frigate, he had the *sole charge* of conducting the business as no naval officer was appointed to that yard, which has been the only instance of the kind in the Navy Department." When the government called on the principal ports to furnish new frigates to face hostilities with France in 1798, both Philadelphia and Charleston commissioned Fox to design theirs. "It was the famous frigate *Philadelphia* that was burned by Stephen Decatur at Tripoli in 1804." Jefferson's administration brought about a reduction in the size of the Navy, nevertheless he reappointed Fox, though an active Federalist. In the next five years he was responsible for designing "the greater part of the numerous gunboats," as well as the sloops *Hornet*, *Wasp* and *Ferret*. However his dabbling in politics and his habit of buying

Negro slaves to free them did not endear him to the authorities and in 1809 his appointment was revoked. He thereupon removed to the headwaters of the Ohio "with plans to build boats for trade with the West Indies"; but the War of 1812 put an end to that scheme. In 1833 Fox inherited a sizable estate and retired to the life of a gentleman farmer. He himself had never ceased to be a Quaker, and in Ohio was a leading figure, where he took the part of the Quietist preacher, Elias Hicks, in the separation that took place from less liberal Quaker orthodoxy. He died in 1847, a venerable old gentleman in his eighties, after a life full of constructive achievement and varied activity.

It seems that his part in the construction and design of the original United States Navy has been totally underestimated in favor of the local man. It is certain that it was consistently depreciated by the Humphreys—and Joshua had a son to carry on the work, in an advantageous position as chief naval constructor from 1826 to 1846. However, this historic injustice is now being put right. It is clear that Fox, no less than Humphreys, was a key-figure "in the designing and construction of the first ships built for the United States Navy: the 44-gun frigates *United States, Constitution* and *President*, and the 36-gun frigates *Constellation, Chesapeake* and *Congress*." The numerous papers left by Josiah Fox, at length studied, "indicate that his contributions were of major importance and had a marked influence on American naval design." And, no doubt, there are Fox descendants in Ohio and elsewhere.

Now that we are over the divide of the Revolution and into the nineteenth century we can pursue only one or two of the individual immigrants who are coming in direct from Cornwall, as samples out of the mass-immigration of scores of thousands characteristic of this period.

Richard Esterbrook (1813–95), who patented the celebrated Esterbrook steel pen, made a fortune from it in Pennsylvania.[51] (The regular form of the name in Cornwall is

Easterbrook.) His family came from the tin-mining district of East Cornwall, near Liskeard, and had made money out of tin. They were comfortably off, but the enterprising young Richard emigrated to Canada and, with an uncle, began the manufacture of steel pens. They were unsuccessful, and moved to Philadelphia, where their efforts again failed. Young Esterbrook would not give up, however, and in 1858 persuaded his father to come over and invest his small fortune in the enterprise. He himself collected a band of skilled workers in Birmingham and brought them over. In a few years he was able to buy the old water-pumping plant of the city of Camden and build his factory on the site. Esterbrook kept the establishment as a family affair, his son proving a very able sales manager who secured a wide distribution for the pens. With the spread of elementary education and literacy, and the increase of population, they were on a moving escalator, on to a good thing. The business expanded so rapidly that they got into financial difficulties after the panic of 1873. "Esterbrook, however, had already gained the reputation of a man who always kept his promises, and his largest creditor, who supplied the steel, volunteered to continue to furnish on credit the much-needed raw material as long as necessary." The business came through its troubles and by 1930 was "the largest and most modern establishment in the United States for the manufacture of steel pens."

Richard Esterbrook continued president of the company to the day of his death. The family had been Quakers for several generations, and Richard himself served as a minister of the Society. No doubt this was a factor in his success. But the exodus of so many Quakers to Pennsylvania left the Society of Friends much depleted in Cornwall, where in the beginning it had been strong.

In the 1850's James Gribbel—the regular form of the name at home is Gribble—came with his wife from St. Austell, where the family had been for generations, to New Jersey.[52] Their son, John Gribbel (1858–1936), made a fortune in business, becoming the proprietor of a large concern which became the American Meter Company—another moving escalator.[53] He himself moved with it to Pennsylvania, where—unlike so many English businessmen—he became both distinguished philanthropist and book collector, president of the Historical Society of Pennsylvania, yet another Cornishman to become so. This St. Austell family flourishes in Pennsylvania, but keeps up its contacts with Cornwall in its present head.

Into the Wyoming Valley, with its variegated mining population, there came a number of Cornish miners where we can follow their careers if we wish.

The largest single element in the nineteenth-century immigration was that of the miners, but it is not likely to have been a majority of the whole. We may take, for example, a group of better-to-do farming folk, who came to take up land around Beach Lake, and of whom we have—somewhat exceptionally—records.[54] This land was opened up by the completion of the Delaware-Hudson Canal in 1830, of which word was sent home. The typical promotion poster said that this "has opened a wide and promising field of enterprise. The subscriber offers for sale valuable lots. Also a number of farms and 10,000 acres of unimproved land. The titles are indisputable." A group of related families got the word—no such chances offered in Cornwall: they came to Beach Lake pioneering, cleared the land and made a good thing of it.

They were already farmers, with large Victorian families to provide for. Of those who came to found this new settlement in the 1840's there were thirteen Tamblyns, twelve Penwardens, ten Olivers, fourteen Olvers (the more Cornish form of the name), seventeen Bullocks. We can see the background of the hungry forties in a flash, from the letter written by the Venners to their daughter, who married George Spettigue, from Bude, April 4, 1842.

Richard and Mary are thinken if the can get money
sufficient to take them there in the same vessel that you
sailed in shee is going to sail May 12 an land to Quebec
because the price is so high to New York it will be a
great tryel but there is no living here . . . There are
thousands going to America. Your Uncle Richard and
Aunt Nancy Allin . . . he hath given notice to his Lord to
take the place (i.e., has given up the lease of his farm).

From this we see that members of the family were already here. The *Springflower* had brought the Olver family from Plymouth in 1829—so like the *Mayflower* two centuries before—first to Montreal, where they did not feel at home and came on to Wayne County. William had owned some land in St. Pinnock parish, near Liskeard, which he sold to come over, with wife and six children. He had been a curate, but "settled at Beech Pond, he became trustee of the newly organised Methodist society and so continued many years. He was also justice of the peace and was to the last deferentially called 'Dominie' and 'Squire Olver.' " Two more brothers, Richard and Thomas, and a sister Grace also came to Wayne, but it was a fourth brother, John, who lived to become the venerable patriarch of Beech Pond. When John and Sara Olver left their farm of Caduscot, near Liskeard, they brought eleven children, by sailing ship to New York. Thence to Kingston on the Hudson, and then by canal barge for a hundred miles to their destination.

There came also on the *Springflower* a young St. Pinnock neighbor, Jonathan Tamblyn, whose brother Thomas's farm included Bury Down where—they all knew—the beacon had been lighted at the approach of the Spanish Armada. Jonathan married his companion on the voyage over, Mary Olver, and had a large family. The first generation, naturally enough, almost always made a Cornish marriage, and often too the second generation. Two years later the Tamblyn brothers came to Wayne, Henry, Jeremiah, William and a sister Anne; in 1849 young David. Jonathan had acquired by 1835 two hundred acres at Bethany, by Chestnut Lake, cleared them and sold them to an incoming Cornishman, Ambrose Davey, who parted with half to John Stevens; he in turn sold the holding to more Olvers, Edmund, Richard, Moses, Joseph. We see how prolific these families were. In 1834 Grace Olver's husband, Samuel Doney, acquired one hundred acres, which he sold later to William Treverton from St. Minver, with whose descendants the lot remained: the Orville Treverton place. Jonathan Tamblyn moved away to New York State, but came back about 1842.

There had been living in Bethany William Bryant, a relative of William Olver's wife: it may have been he who set all this activity going—and one knows the way in which these people sent home the money to help the others out. They certainly needed to come: long afterwards Jeremiah remembered the forties: "Wan year there was nothin' to ate but taties and banes." Nor had these simple folk any illusions about the society they left: one of the Tamblyns was heard to sum up Queen Victoria, "She be good for naught but to ate the good things and to brade children." They carried earlier, and deeper, memories with them. The miners had always believed that there were little people who made the noises in the mines, the knackers, "no bigger either of them than a sixpenny doll." They remembered all about wishing wells—St. Keyne's, famed in the Middle Ages for its healing power, was not far from John Olver's Caduscot. Even in the New World, James would take alarm at a mirror being broken or believe that salt pork tied round the neck was a cure for whooping cough. And was not Cornwall "cigged on to a furrin' country," held by ferry chains at the River Tamar?

In 1830 George Spettigue had come, progenitor of a large family, and with him his brother Edmund and his brother-in-law, John Brownscombe. Spettigue's land is still in possession of the family. Brownscombe sold some of his to a Hicks, some more to an Orchard, whose daughter used to go back to it for the summer up to the age of ninety-five, not so long ago. The early 1830's brought these families to the Beach Lake neighborhood, with others, Daveys, Sprys, Marshalls, Hams. "In the early thirties the incursion into north Berlin, now Oregon, brought to the Torrey area James Oliver, Peter Davey and others. About 1842 these came: the Slumans and the Woodleys, who after a stay in Quebec came by way of Lake Champlain. William Budd came here; later moved to the Beech Pond area. Brice Davey came a little later. The emigration from Cornwall tapered off near the fifties with the coming of James Orchard, Jennie Hicks, John Robbins, the Bullocks, Richard Brock, the Neales, and others."

Altogether, as these authors say, it made "a little Cornwall."

Thus it is that all over Pennsylvania today one finds Cornish names. In Bethlehem alone seven Trembath families appear in the telephone directory—almost half the number of those that appear for the whole county of Cornwall; and there are no less than five Pascoe families. It is perhaps not surprising that in Philadelphia there should be twenty Penrose families—two-thirds the number listed in Cornwall—besides the corporations, clubs, stores, to which the famous family has given its name, or, rather, from which the name has been taken. In the city there are three Pascoe families, three Penberth, three Tregear, three Trenwith, two Trevaskis, two Treherne, two Trescott, two Hender. There are seven Coon entries, at least one of whom, with Wesley for first name, would be Cornish; over forty Rouse, of whom some would belong, as we say in Cornwall, certainly the two Rowse families. Among the specific names well represented it is pleasant to see that there is a Nancarrow, along with Lanyon, Hocking, Annear, Pengelly, Penglase, Pendarvis, Tregea, Tregembo, Treglown, Tremayne, Trembeth, Trethaway (for Trethewey), Trengove, Trevathan and Trevethen. This is only a small proportion, for how many of the Cornish are lost among such common names as Rowe, Mitchell, Hancock,

Dunn, Harris, Rogers, Roberts? Altogether, in that great city there must be some thousands of them.

At Harrisburg we find a whole clan of Menears, no less than eleven families, seven Chenoweth, two Nancarrow, two Trevenen, two Chellew, along with Trethaway, Coon, Combe, Penrose, Rouse, Gear, and so on.

We can only dip here and there into this vast inexhaustible reservoir. It must be clear by now that we can only give samples; nevertheless, however incomplete, our picture can be taken as representative.

NOTES

1. I am indebted to Mrs. Balderston for this information.
2. *Pennsylvania Magazine of History and Biography*, vol. 28, 466.
3. D. A. B., under William Penn.
4. *Pa. Mag.*, vol. 34, 144, 153.
5. D. N. B., under William Penn.
6. *Pa. Mag.*, vol. 36, 305.
7. *Ibid.*, vol. 3, 211; vol. 26, 195.
8. *Ibid.*, vol. 55, 32.
9. *Ibid.*, vol. 27, 265; vol. 75, 403.
10. *Ibid.*, vol. 7, 74; vol. 29, 122; vol. 55, 32.
11. *Ibid.*, vol. 7, 74, 81.
12. *Ibid.*, vol. 26, 163.
13. D. A. B., under Joseph Galloway.
14. *Pa. Mag.*, vol. 55, 32; vol. 58, 152ff.
15. *Ibid.*, vol. 3, 119–20.
16. W. J. Buck, *Hist. of Montgomery County, Pa.*, 81.
17. D. A. B., under Francis Rawle.
18. *Pa. Mag.*, vol. 26, 351.
19. cf. E. J. Rawle, *Records of the Rawle Family*.

20. *Pa. Mag.*, vol. 35, 385ff.
21. D. A. B., under William Rawle.
22. D. A. B., under William Henry Rawle.
23. D. A. B., under Francis Rawle.
24. A. H. Cresson, "Biographical Sketch of Joseph Fox, Esq., of Philadelphia," *Pa. Mag.*, vol. 32, 175ff.
25. *Ibid.*, vol. 18, 504.
26. *Ibid.*, vol. 8, 43.
27. J. M. Swank, *Progressive Pennsylvania*, 216–19.
28. cf. R. T. Berthoff, *British Immigrants in Industrial America, 1790–1850*, 58, 60.
29. *Ibid.*, vol. 40, 376.
30. I am indebted for this information to Mr. James F. Dallett.
31. *Pa. Mag.*, vol. 25, 285.
32. *Ibid.*, vol. 63, 104ff.
33. C. H. Smith, "Horsham Men in the Revolution," *Bulletin of Historical Society of Montgomery Co., Pa.*, vol. 1, 158ff.; vol. 2, 280.
34. D. A. B., under Charles Bingham Penrose.
35. cf. D. A. B. for their careers.
36. C. V. Roberts, *Early Friends Families of Upper Bucks*, 396.
37. *Bull. of Hist. Soc. of Montgomery Co., Pa.*, vol. 4, 266.
38. *Ibid.*, vol. 6, 140; vol. 14, 194.
39. *Ibid.*, vol. 13, 257.
40. *Pa. Mag.*, vol. 33, 72; vol. 3, 105.
41. H. W. Lloyd, *Lloyd Manuscripts*, 328ff.
42. i.e. to 1915, from the Association's leaflet, 1916.
43. S. A. Kimber, *The Descendants of Richard Kimber*, 31ff.
44. *Record of the Courts of Chester Co., Pa.*, 94, 310.
45. Kimber, 28–29.
46. *Pa. Mag.*, vol. 32, 244.
47. Ex inf. James F. Dallett.
48. *Pa. Mag.*, vol. 58, 179; vol. 56, 43; vol. 42, 237; vol. 58, 179.

49. *Cornwall to America in 1783*, ed. K. M. Burall. The usual Cornish form of the name is Burrell, which I adopt. I have modernized the text in quotation, except for one phrase—the spelling is very odd.
50. H. I. Chapelle, *The History of the American Sailing Navy*, 122.
51. D. A. B., under Richard Esterbrook, from which quotations are taken.
52. Ex inf. James F. Dallett.
53. cf. *Who Was Who in America, 1897–1942*, under John Gribbel.
54. I. N. Baldwin and K. E. Baldwin, *Your Heritage in Beach Lake: The Story of Beach Lake*, from which quotations are taken.

6   THE OLD SOUTH

We must not expect anything like so large a Cornish element in the South as in the Middle colonies and New England. For one thing, the South had its own slaves, and for another, geographical and climatic conditions made it less attractive to Cornish folk, adverse to their settling. Nevertheless, individuals and families trickled in. By the end of the seventeenth century there was a little group of Cornish kin settled at Lynnhaven and on the lower James River in Virginia. These were Bolithos, Cocks, Trevethans. As early as 1636 a Richard Cock, gentleman, had patented three thousand acres of land in Henrico, near John Pearce and Thomas Harris: these names are very common in Cornwall.[1] By the end of the century two Cock cousins, Captain Thomas and Captain Christopher Cock, had arrived, apparently from Helston. Thomas patented land in 1687 and died young in 1697, leaving two daughters.[2] He left mourning rings to his cousins, John and Mary Bolitho; to cousin Christopher he left "my black horse with bridle and saddle, and my rapier, belt and one broad piece of gold and 10,000 lb of tobacco for his services in collecting my debt." To his daughters all his plate, jewelry, gold rings, a gold chain and five or six broad pieces of gold—he was evidently a gentleman. When Christopher Cock died in 1716, also quite young, he left John Bolitho a bible, his books on practical divinity, with his seal, ring and other trinkets. He too had only daughters: he left the tuition of two of them to his uncle and aunt Bolitho, and of the third to his uncle William Cock—the eldest to have all his plate, his physic books to them in common.

John Bolitho had settled in Princess Anne County, where he was a vestryman of Lynnhaven parish in his last years. Upon his death in the 1730's his heir-at-law was Thomas Bolitho at home in Cornwall.[3] William Trevethan, esquire, had come over as surveyor of the enumerated commodities in the Elizabeth River—those, like tobacco, rum, rice, of which the entry was controlled under the Navigation Acts—and took the oath as such in 1697.[4] Sampson Trevethan lived in lower Norfolk County, but returned to Penzance in 1715. He left his estate to his wife, afterwards to go to the two daughters, Mary and Anne, whom he had left in Virginia: they were to have all his lands in Lynnhaven, besides £200 each from the rest of his estate. By 1678 we hear of Anthony Trevillian, a merchant of Whitechapel, and Samuel Trevillian of Virginia, planter, engaged in shipping tobacco.[5] This was the pattern: perhaps they were brothers—at any rate it was more reliable to do business in this way with one's kith and kin. In 1734 Thomas Trevillian was licensed "to keep a ordinary" (tavern) in Hanover County. In the eighteenth century references to this name are already frequent in Virginia.

A John Triplett of Cornwall had married a Joan Yeo of Devon; the Yeo family was prominent in early Virginia, and the Tripletts became numerous there.[6] In 1666 Francis Triplett patented 1050 acres in old Rappahannock County; by his will in 1700 he devised to children and grand-children the plantation of 200 acres on which he had lived, with the 1050 acres and other tracts besides. His family spread into Prince William County, other branches to Westmorland, King George and Loudoun counties. In Truro parish, Fairfax County, William Triplett was a friend of Washington; it was he who did the reconstruction of the old house at Mount Vernon into the present fine mansion. A son Francis served as a captain in the Revolutionary War, and by his will in 1794 was able to leave 37,000 acres in Kentucky to his children. Simon was a friend of Washington and fitted out a company at his own expense to serve under the great man. John was present at the siege of Yorktown with four of his sons. Altogether some dozen Tripletts received bounty lands for service in the Revolution. Robert Triplett, of the sixth generation, moved into Kentucky, opening the first coal-mines and building the first railroad there in 1834; he also built a woollen mill and a cotton factory. In the depression of the early 1840's he was ruined by a partner, but recovered, made a second fortune and left his children well off. He fought a duel with the Honorable Philip Thompson; Triplett shot Thompson and thus cured him of his lameness in walking. They made friends later; Thompson said that Triplett was "a good surgeon but severe in remedy." In the next generation, George Triplett from Kentucky was a member of the Confederate Congress.

The Virginia Footes descend from Richard Foote, born at Cardinham in 1632.[7] He married the daughter of a London grocer, who traded with Virginia, and his subsequent father-in-law gave Foote power of attorney to manage his business there. About 1689 Foote, with his brother-in-law and two others purchased an immense tract of thirty thousand acres in the present Prince William County. The son, another Richard Foote, was the first to come and settle there, dying in 1729. He had numerous descendants, many of whom moved into Kentucky, Alabama, Mississippi, Illinois.

One who achieved distinction was Henry Stuart Foote (1804–80), United States Senator, and governor of Mississippi.[8] Born in Virginia, educated at what is now Washington and Lee University, he moved to Mississippi, where he became a successful criminal lawyer. After a term in the state legislature he was elected to the United States Senate along with Jefferson Davis. Davis was of Welsh descent; he and Foote could not abide each other and came to blows in their boarding-house. Foote ardently supported the compromise measures of 1850—over California, admitted as a free state, and the southwestern territories won as the result of the war forced upon Mexico in 1846. Jefferson Davis was all in favor of slavery and of the right of the slave-states to secede from the Union. Foote was not; in spite of that he defeated Davis in the election for the governorship of Mississippi. Foote was a good stump orator. But his administration was marked by the increasing bitterness of the struggle between the supporters of the Union and the secessionists, with the latter constantly growing in strength. Five days before his term expired Foote threw up his governorship in disgust and departed to California, where he spent the next four years. Jefferson Davis, in line with the tide of opinion in the South, had won. When the war broke out and the Southern States set up their Congress, Foote entered the lower house with the idea of supporting a moderate course, a compromise peace. He attacked Jefferson Davis's uncompromising stand on secession and, when Lincoln's peace-proposals were not accepted, Foote threw up his membership, was imprisoned briefly by the Confederates, and moved over to the Union. Here he found that his ideas of compromise were no more acceptable to Lincoln than to Davis. Both sides were determined to fight to a finish, and the sensible man in the middle departed for Europe for the duration of the war. Foote always believed that the Civil War could have been avoided. The results were grievous, to the United States and most of all to the South itself.

Yet again, for the third time—as with the Revolutionary War and the War of 1812—the historic English elements had the folly to fight each other, leaving other elements to pour in and rip ahead. The demographic effects, little appreciated as they are, were not least among the important consequences of the Civil War.

Foote was not only an able speaker, a charming conversationalist, but a good writer. His first book, *Texas and the Texans*, evinced his sympathetic interest in the independence of the country. His account of the Civil War, *The War of the Rebellion*, expresses his independence of mind. He was out of step with both dominant points of view; that does not mean that he was wrong, indeed the country would have avoided a great tragedy if only his moderate line could have prevailed. But sense is sometimes irrelevant to human action: men are determined to have their heads. Those who are determined to keep theirs are swept to one side, out of the mainstream of human action and historic folly. And so it was with Henry Stuart Foote: he left much less of an imprint in history than he promised. He presents the case—not infrequent with Celts —of an essential moderation in thought and action expressed with immoderation, and ordinary humans are apt to mistake the manner for the matter. Foote was a better man than Jefferson Davis, but Davis has his place in history—because he fell in line with men's emotions. Foote was out of line. Though independent of both sides, there was no ataraxy about him: he remained engaged.

He was a little man, with a large head, a bantam cock forever getting into quarrels and fighting duels. He knew quite well that he ought not to have done so; his engaging *Casket of Reminiscences* admits as much—one of its qualities is its complete honesty, totally without humbug; indeed Foote was as much anti-humbug as he was anti-drink. His book is also generous in spirit, generous towards everyone except Jefferson Davis; it is most convincing in its depiction of the greatness of Lincoln. Talented and temperamental, individualistic to a fault, incapable of co-operating with anyone for long, generous, public-spirited, ultimately frustrating himself, in Foote I diagnose the Cornish temperament as much as the southern, atavistic and even recessive.*

"One and All" is the Cornish motto: there never was a greater joke—unless its interpretation is given a subtler twist.

---

* There is no biography of this fascinating figure: there should be one. It is much to be regretted that his private papers are apparently lost: they should have been extremely interesting.

For the Cornish, co-operation takes place at a subliminal, intuitional level, rather than on the conscious plane upon which politics operate.

It is interesting to see how successful eugenically the Trevillians have been in Virginia: today there are nineteen families of them in Richmond alone, when there are only two listed in all Cornwall. Two more families of them appear in Norfolk, Virginia, where there are also no less than five Trevathan and five Chenoweth entries; a score of Nance—some of whom qualify—nine Pender, along with Trebilcock, Pascoe, Vivian, Tremaine, Trewhitt, Trescott, Uglow. Richmond has fifteen Rouse families—and some Virginia Rouses claim a Cornish ancestry—along with four Pascoe families, four Coon, three Pender, three Chenoweth, a Treglown, Retallick, Penhallow, Rosevear, Hocking, and eight Oates entries, some of whom may be Cornish. Washington, D.C. has eight Pender entries, six Vivian, five Toy (with two Toye), five Pascoe, four Penrose, two Pendarvis; a Nankivell, Tremaine, Treleaven, Trethaway, Trewhella, Trewhitt, Trezise, Pengelly, Ugelow. Among rarer names we find Penkert, Tremearne, and a Wesley H. Trewolla—no doubt about him! Cornish folk do not seem to have penetrated in any number beyond the Blue Ridge Mountains into the great Shenandoah Valley. We do, however, find several Trevillian families, as we should expect; and among others Tremaine, Nankivell, Chubb, Pendrey, Edgcumbe. The Edgecomb Steel Company is located here and elsewhere in Virginia.

We discover an amusing variation on the theme of temperament with the career of Colonel John Coode in Maryland.[9] Colonel Coode was actually a cleric in holy orders, who seems to have been turned out of his living at Penryn—we do not know for what, though he was not unfrocked. He usually appears in the books as a rascally adventurer, a flagitious and debauched priest, a blasphemer, though the more serious crimes are not imputed to him; we shall see whether these charges are altogether fair—he certainly was troublesome.

He emerged from obscurity, says the *Dictionary of American Biography* sagely, when in 1676 he took his seat in the Maryland assembly for St. Mary's County where he lived. He had married a daughter of Thomas Gerrard, a member of council under Governor Fendall.[10] Perhaps this qualified him and gave him ideas; for the House of Commons at home Anglican orders were a disqualification, the provincial assemblies were anxious to ape their great model at Westminister, and this tincture of holy orders—the "infectious hand of a bishop"—dogged the Colonel's attempt at a political career all his days. Coode ganged up with Fendall in 1681 to make trouble: Fendall hoped to revenge himself upon the establishment—the Baltimore family held the proprietary government—by raising a revolt of the disaffected with aid from Virginia. Virginia resented the grant of the territory to the Baltimores, out of land she claimed as her own, and treated Maryland with constant hostility.

This first attempt to make a mark back-fired and Coode lost his seat in the assembly. He was acquitted of the charge of mutiny and sedition, but was reproved for his "love to amaze the ignorant and make sport with his wit"—a recognizable trait. Not that his addresses can have been any more edifying than his sermons had been: it was charged that when sitting as a justice of the peace he had behaved so debauchedly and profanely that the court had to bind him over to keep the peace. Perhaps he was just tight, but he was put out of the commission—and reacted with flaming speeches against the authorities. The Baltimores were Catholics, and there was a small minority of Catholic gentry among the population. Under the benign rule of the Baltimores no one was molested for religion, and a number of Quakers took refuge in Maryland from the persecution they met with in New England and Virginia.[11] There was some trouble with the Indians, though far less dangerous than usual; it was an easy step for Colonel

Coode to win popularity and get his revenge by taking an aggressively Protestant line and directing the colonists' fears of the Indians against the Catholics as well.

The Revolution of 1688 gave the fire-eating Colonel his chance. An unfortunate accident delayed the recognition of the new monarchs, William and Mary, by the Maryland proprietary government. Coode hastened to form a Protestant Association after the English model, put himself at the head of it, and marched on St. Mary's—the tiny capital with hardly more than a score of houses. He put forth a proclamation, with the usual charges about the Catholics combining with the Indians to massacre the Protestants. It is the first document to be printed in Maryland.[12] Coode's force nearly fell to pieces and went home again on the road to St. Mary's; however, the governor and council ran away to the shelter of a fort on the Patuxent, whither the gallant Colonel pursued them and they soon surrendered. The Colonel now took the title of general and a fine time was had by all, commissioning officers, confining opponents whether Catholic or Protestant, helping themselves to cattle and horses. Nobody seems to have suffered much—it was all *opéra bouffe* rather than serious politics. However, General Coode summoned a sort of assembly and represented to King William that the Lord Proprietor had forfeited his rights and that they had acted only in the interest of the Crown and the Protestant religion. Addresses were organized from the counties petitioning the king to take the government into his hands. The episode was really a colonial caricature of what had taken place in England; what was serious behind it was that the Protestants outnumbered the Catholics by fifteen to one, and the proprietary government had been left behind by time.

Thereupon Coode sailed for England, evidently hoping to be made governor, or at least a councillor. There was nothing doing, however; the very fly William appointed the respectable Sir Lionel Copley as the first royal governor. Though Copley recommended him, Coode was not even made a councillor: he came back to Maryland with empty hands. Nevertheless this not altogether respectable instrument had been the means of an historic change in Maryland, from private palatinate to crown colony. It is as well that the validity of the sacrament does not depend on the character of the minister.

The conflict between the Reverend Colonel's sacred and profane functions gave trouble again when he took his seat as a member of the assembly in 1696.[13] The governor of the time sent a message that the Colonel was incapable of being a burgess of the House, since he was in holy orders. The House replied that he had been a member almost twenty years, that he had held commissions from king and proprietor for exercising both judicial and ministerial functions, that they conceived themselves the proper judges of their own members and they resolved that the Colonel was legally qualified to sit. Messages flew back and forth—dispute was at any rate something to occupy the empty colonial days, with so little else to do. It was agreed that a committee of the House should investigate the matter; it reported of course that the Colonel *was* qualified to sit. At this governor and council brought up their guns, appealing "to the whole House whether in his life and conversation he does not appear so heinously flagitious and wicked scarce to be paralleled in the province, whereof the House must needs be conscious . . . Divers of the members have at some time or other in his debaucheries heard him publicly blaspheme. It is left to the consideration of the House whether he has not at this present cost the country more tobacco than perhaps he is worth or will ever do them good."

This consideration gave them pause: tobacco was the colony's chief currency; money talks, and this was talking. One of the council deposed that the Colonel had been ordained by the bishop of Exeter, and that he had not been degraded or unfrocked—an ironic turn, for if the Colonel had only been unfrocked there would have been no trouble. At this the Colonel offered to depose that he was not a priest. (Perhaps the simple explanation is that he held only deacon's orders, but no one has put this point forward.) The House at this gave way and resolved at length that he was not qualified and put him out of his elected seat. Drink apparently was the Colonel's trouble, and when he was drunk there was nothing he would not say. Governor Nicholson had more interesting vices, but at least he kept them private; and when the Colonel was drunk and disorderly in public during divine service the governor caned him with his own hand.[14] Enraged beyond endurance the Colonel gathered a few of his old following, hatched a plot against the governor, was indicted by a grand jury, and fled across water to Virginia, always ready to receive the disaffected from Maryland. Here Governor Sir Edmund Andros protected him and refused to yield him up: Coode now made a fine bone of contention between the two governors. Not until 1701, reduced in circumstances and therefore in spirit, did the Colonel petition for pardon —which was granted on the score of his services at the Revolution a dozen years before!

In 1708 the Colonel was back in the assembly as burgess for St. Mary's and, large as life, put himself forward in its business, the assembly sending him with their formal messages to governor and council.[15] This was too much; it asked for trouble, and shortly the Colonel was challenged again on the ground of his sacred calling. Once more he braved it out: it seems that he was still representing St. Mary's County when death called him in 1709. Shortly after, his son William Coode, late sheriff of St. Mary's, was summoned before the House for his misdemeanor over the election returns: evidently he had used his position as sheriff to return his father. The son refused to appear. It was not until a year later that he was brought before the House and ordered to pay a fine of 700 lb. of tobacco to the sheriff of St. Mary's, 300 lb. to the clerk of the House. Pleading poverty and begging pardon, he was let off. After all, all this was between gentlemen, and hadn't the Colonel saved the province from the papists at the Glorious Revolution?

The Coodes continued, though in a more modest way; the Colonel had left three sons, three daughters and four plantations, probably small affairs. John Coode, Jr., was licensed to practice law by the governor and council; Captain Coode served as a member of the House in 1714.[16] A generation later, in 1749, a William Gerrard Coode makes a transitory appearance—evidently named for the Colonel's father-in-law, who had been a member of council, by which fact the Colonel's grand ideas probably came. His temperament and means had not been such as to support them, yet he had played his part.

It would be interesting to know in what condition the Coodes continue today. There are few evidences of Cornish names in Maryland in colonial days. There is a John Treleague, an indentured servant, in 1649-50; John Tregear appears as a planter.[17] A Jacob Tregaskis served as armorer in the Revolutionary War, a Thomas Rowse was a lieutenant in the 5th Maryland Regiment, an Edward Chenoweth enlisted in 1776.

Captain Humphrey Pellew was a Penryn merchant largely interested in American trade; he purchased in Maryland a large tobacco plantation of two thousand acres, on which Annapolis is now built. Three of Pellew's grandsons served against the Revolution and the estate was confiscated. One of these grandsons became the famous Admiral, Viscount Exmouth, who as a young officer nearly captured Benedict Arnold in a chase on Lake Champlain—his stock and buckle left behind in the scramble ashore were handed down in the Pellew family.[18] Exmouth's descendant, who became the sixth Viscount, came to settle in America in 1873, on marrying his deceased wife's sister—then (absurdly) illegal in England.[19] Son of an Anglican dean, this Pellew was given to good works: he organized the Bureau of Charities in New York with Theodore Roosevelt's father, then moved to Washington to work among the Negroes and help to build Washington Cathedral. He organized numerous night refuges, coffee houses, circulating libraries, improved tenement dwellings, societies for improving the condition of the poor and for sanitary reform. All this we owe to the deceased wife's sister.

Today what is surprising from our particular point of view in the population of Baltimore is the immense proliferation of the Chenoweth clan: there are no less than sixty families of them listed, and six under the meaningless form of Chenworth. There are four Trevillian, four Trezise, four Pender, three Tregellas, two Pendarvis, a Pascoe, Treganowan, Trevail, Trewin, Penrose, Penvose, Behenna, Gear, Jago, Uglow, Trehearn, Treewolla (sic). There are twenty-five Rouse, one Rowse; many Courtney, Pomeroy, Nance, Pollard, Kendall, Rowe, Thomas, Couch, Oates, among whom there must be many Cornish. Finally there are two Coad families, the more plebeian spelling of the ancient Coode name.

Moving into North Carolina we find hardly more Cornish folk than in Maryland, and a great many fewer than in Virginia. From 1695 there is a Penrice family—a name that is very rare at home—that builds up a substantial position in Perquimons and Chowan precincts.[20] We can follow them in the records serving in the militia and at length in the Revolutionary War—one on either side: Francis Penrice with the patriots, Thomas in the 1st North Carolina Regiment with Sir Henry Clinton. In the earlier eighteenth century John Tremain is a justice of the peace for Onslow, Jonathan petitions for land; Trevillians, Trewins and Trewhitts serve in the militia; Rouses are taking up land in Craven and New Hanover; William Trevathan and John Trevaile are named.[21] There is an excruciating confusion of names, making it very hard for the researcher. Treweek becomes Truheek, Tremaine becomes Truman, and so on. One does not know whether the Nances and Hickses are of Cornish descent, though the names are common enough in Cornwall, and many American Hickses of later descent are definitely Cornish.

We reach firm land with a nineteenth-century immigrant who made a significant contribution to the industrial development of the state. This was Egbert Barry Cornwall Hambley, whom we see a dark handsome bearded type, with intelligent eyes.[22] His father, James Hambley, was a mining engineer who had travelled about the world, to Brazil and Argentina, and helped to develop the mines of the Transvaal. Young Egbert Barry Cornwall—his names must surely represent his mother's tastes rather than his father's—was sent to the Royal School of Mines at Kensington. He was sent out early as assistant to the superintendent of the Gold Hill Mines in North Carolina, and, after some further experience in South India and on the Gold Coast, he settled in the state. He organized several London companies to develop mines, and installed a pumping plant—no doubt with the famous Cornish beam engine—on the Yadkin River to supply them with water. He became manager, director, president of cotton mills, gas and electric light companies, local banks; he developed the Rowan Granite Quarry and Yadkin River water-power. On his place at Rockwell in Rowan County he built up a Jersey herd of cattle; he had considerable interests in California. His biographer tells us that he was "a man of very captivating, persuasive and winning manners, and a very fine conversationalist." With all these charms he married into a gubernatorial family, had several children and lived happy ever after. Nevertheless, he imparted to his sympathetic interviewer, he had had many obstacles to overcome in his early life; he was a strong believer in the (now antiquated) gospel of work.

Naturally, we find Cornish names sparsely represented in North Carolina today. In Raleigh, the capital, Tremain, Trethewey, Trevathan, Pascoe, Tippett, and an immense clan of Pearces, some of whom may qualify. In Charlotte one comes across several Penders, a Pendarvis, and—a nice catch —a Menhinick.

At Charleston in South Carolina we come upon the early and interesting Pendarvis clan, which might have cut a more important figure than it did—the opportunity was there. Joseph Pendarvis was one of the original settlers of the town, on the tongue of land between the Ashley and the Cooper rivers, where they unite to form that harbor, in time to become historic. Pendarvis arrived in the first fleet in 1671, and was allotted a good lot and 250 acres on the east bank of the Ashley River.[23] In 1694 he died, leaving a long will from which we may read the comfortable, gentlemanly circumstances the family was in. To his son John, he left a house and tract of land, one-third of his cattle and goats, "the old silver tankard," a silver-headed cane, a cedar chest, a mare, a Negro named Caesar, two Negro women and a girl Friday. To his daughter Mary a house and lot, one-half of his cleared plantations from the bridge to the marsh, one-half of his household stuff, one-half of his flock of twenty sheep, one-third of his cattle and goats, an old mare Strawberry, a silver tankard, a Negro Mingo and woman Peg. To his daughter Ann, a brick house and a lot and a half, one-half the household stuff, one-half of the twenty sheep, one-third of the cattle, a young mare, a silver tumbler, a silver dram cup, two coconuts tipped with silver, a Negro man with two women. He directed his friends to look after his daughters and "see that no wrong be done them."

In 1719 John Pendarvis left land along the Cooper River to his younger sons, Benjamin and John, which Joseph, the eldest son, acquired from them.[24] But in 1735 Joseph left land opposite Belmont to trustees for his children by a Negro woman, Parthena. This land was acquired by one of the trustees, and Belmont itself, with an estate of 175 acres on Charleston Neck, was made over to Charles Pinckney, who made it his country-seat. So where the Pendarvises might have ruled, the Pinckneys reigned in their stead: two of the latter married prominent women, became major-generals on the Revolutionary side and both of them aspired to the Presidency.[25] The Pendarvis luck was out: Josiah's son Richard was well-known as "Tory Dick" for his Loyalist activities during the war. South Carolina was deeply divided: a large number of militia officers and magistrates accepted royal commissions, and in consequence their property was confiscated after the war, Richard Pendarvis's estate among others.[26]

The family lost its chance to establish a leading position, though in the 1750's Josiah was appointed as a person of credit to arbitrate on disputed wills, and in the 1760's James contributed £20 to building the Willtown Congregational Church.[27] A hundred years later we find a William Pendarvis a private in the Confederate army.[28] However, in the Charleston telephone directory today there are no less than nine Pendarvis entries, with two more in Summerville. Others of the family moved into Georgia and northwestward into Illinois, and increased mightily: they are a numerous stock, besides all the others of that name coming in.

Among other names we descry the rare and fascinating name of Tregeagle (or Tregagle)—Jan Tregagle is the leading spirit in Cornish folk-lore, the unjust steward who foreclosed on mortgages, dispossessed people of their inheritance, persecuted the innocent, made himself rich by wicked deeds, sold his soul to the Devil, and is heard crying and howling around exposed and windy places like Roche Rock, pursued by the Devil and his hounds, condemned forever to dip out Dozmary Pool with a hollow limpet shell and make ropes out of sand from Kynance Cove. In historic fact John Tregeagle was steward to the Puritan Lord Robartes during the detested Commonwealth.[29] It is a very rare name—and here is a Mr. Nathaniel Tregeagle, evidently another lawyer, turning up in South Carolina in 1757 to settle a suit.[30]

In 1737 a William Trewin was a justice of the peace for Berkeley County.[31] The Trewins multiplied in the South. From 1760 to 1776 John Carne was a leading cabinet-maker; a John Vivian was to the fore in the parish of St. David. There are plenty of Trawicks, and this is probably a form of Treweek. Meanwhile, the early days of the Carolinas are not without their pathetic evidences in the records at home. In the autumn of 1699 a ship from Carolina was lost with all hands on the hazardous coast of North Cornwall—evidently near Padstow, for there some of her papers were recovered.[32]

Marching into Georgia, we do not find that the Cornish made any discernible contribution to its early populating by convicts and charity children. But there were a few individuals and families that moved in. As early as 1736 a Mr. John Penrose—evidently a middling kind of gentleman—was with General Oglethorpe, the founder of the colony, at Frederica.[33] He got a grant of pine land, but complained that unless he could get a stock of cattle and turn his farm into a cowpen it would not be worth planting, the land being very poor. Penrose set up a public house instead, which the malcontents—a familiar feature in early days—made their rendezvous. Penrose was not with them, but at his door they harangued for a new set of men in power. Next year, 1742, he opened his mouth wide for five hundred acres of land in Hutchinson's Island; his petition was rejected on the score that he was never industrious in cultivating land. We hear of him reaching a private understanding with one Adams to buy cattle, kill and salt them, and hold out for higher prices; while Mrs. Penrose made a compact with her fellow-chandler to double the prices of candles and butter. John Penrose owned a boat, for we find the colony's agent hiring it to take him to Darien. Penroses continued in Georgia—as they do to this day. William Trewin was a merchant in Augusta who got a lot in the fourth row from the river in 1759.[34] In 1764 he was made a justice of the peace for the parish of St. Paul. Next year he and his three partners, Indian traders, got a large grant of fourteen hundred acres on the Satilla at Pike's Bluff. That year, too, he was a commissioner for building the fort and barracks at Augusta. In 1768 he died at sea in passage from Savannah to Charleston.[35] The family went on: we find a David Trewin petitioning for redress for robbery and damage to crops by Creek Indians, and granted one hundred acres in Christ Church parish.[36] We can hardly blame Americans

The Old South 133

for sometimes spelling the name Truan, for the English make the same mistake in its pronunciation.

When we move on to Atlanta today, we find a good spread of Cornish names: a Travillion and a Trevillion; five families of the Menhenett clan, under various spellings; several each of the following, Pascoe, Gear, Furse, Chenoweth, Carne, Pender, Tregellas, Hunkin, Goldsworthy. Among others we have Pendarvis, Trevena, Treglown, Trehern, Uren, Roseveare, Kellow, Hocking, Yelland, Minear, and—more rarely—Dungy and Chegwidden. There is the usual spread of names that must include more Cornish—large numbers of Mitchell, Rowe, Rouse, Triplett. These must be mainly nineteenth-century recruits, coming in to the mining areas of Georgia and Alabama.

Moving to the iron and steel district of Birmingham, Alabama, we find a considerable contingent, as we might expect. A dozen Trawick and half a dozen Traweek families: those would be old stock. There is a remarkable clutch of Trevarthens, no less than nine families; five Angwin entries (with an Angwen Mortuary Center). There are three Jagoe, and among rarer names, Penhale, Penhallegon, Polglaze and Hender. There is an enormous number of unspecific names among which there will be many Cornish—such common names with us as Hancock, Rowe, Mitchell, Cox, Dunn, Williams, Perry, Richards.

Tennessee seems to provide few, to judge from Knoxville: three Trevena, two Trovillion (*sic*), a Trethewey, Trebella (for Trewhella?), Trewhitt, Pasco and—more rarely—a Higman. However, just before the Civil War copper-mining started up in the Copper Basin of Polk County, and this drew a considerable number of Cornish miners.[37] F. L. Olmsted gives us a characteristic glimpse of them in his *Journey in the Back Country* of 1860. He tells us that there were several hundred of them and "more are constantly coming. They are engaged in Cornwall, and have their expenses out paid, and

F

forty dollars a month wages. Two, whom I found at work together [the regular custom in Cornwall] one hundred and fifty feet from the surface, told me that they had been here about six weeks and were well pleased."[38] Their wages worked out at over twice what they would have got at home. "Some of the miners, including some of the Cornish men, had been getting ready a pole and hoist a flag upon, on the fourth of July. I heard a report the day before I reached the mines that the Englishmen were going to hoist the English flag and hurrah for the Queen on the fourth of July. The country people were much excited by this report, and on the third I met a great many of them armed with rifles, coming in 'to see about it.' I could not persuade them that the Englishmen were intending in good faith to celebrate the day, so strong was their belief in the continued hostility of the English people to independence." We know what popular cant that was—and soon North and South were fighting each other. However, the interesting thing is that Olmsted should have been able to distinguish so clearly between the Cornish and the English. For all the Cornish tendency to move west to Lake Superior, and further west to California, there should be some of their descendants left in Polk County, as of the Welsh in Scott County.

And so to Louisiana where the Nicholls family has played a distinguished part in the state, particularly in the person of General Francis Nicholls, its governor and Chief Justice, an heroic fighting type.[39] He was the descendant of Edward Church Nicholls, a Cornish Catholic, who was educated for the priesthood at St. Omer's. The family tradition is that, stopping in Paris one time, he decided that the Church was not his vocation. For this he was said to have been disinherited, emigrated to Maryland as a teacher, studied law and married a Crauford. He returned to England to arrange his affairs and, after the Louisiana Purchase, he settled at New Orleans, where his fluency in French helped. He built up a lucrative practice, but, haughty and reserved in manner, he incurred the resentment of the Creoles and got no further than a county judgeship. He had three sons. The oldest died in camp at Washington in the War of 1812; the youngest had an adventurous life, among other things serving under Captain Perry in the action on Lake Erie. The second son, Thomas, became a judge of the Court of Errors and Appeals—all three of his sons and two of his grandsons were judges. In 1815 he moved to Donaldsonville, which became the home of this eminent legal family.

Its fame was made by Thomas's youngest son, Francis (1834–1912). "More by accident than because of military taste, he entered the United States Military Academy at West Point." He served in Florida in the Seminole campaign, then was stationed at the lonely outpost of Fort Yuma in California, where he resigned from the service—it was so unhealthy there that he overheard the army doctor predict his death if he stayed. He returned home to study law, marry, and start a promising practice. This was interrupted by the outbreak of the Civil War, and though—like Henry Stuart Foote—he opposed secession, he followed his state when he had to choose. He and his brother raised their own regiment from Ascension and Assumption parishes, but Francis Nicholls was immediately promoted lieutenant-colonel and proceeded to achieve one of the most gallant careers of the war. He was in the first battle of Manasses and served throughout the first year in northern Virginia. Next year, in Stonewall Jackson's famous campaign up the Shenandoah Valley, Nicholls fought at Front Royal and Winchester, where he lost an arm and was taken prisoner. Exchanged that autumn, he was promoted brigadier-general and commanded the 2nd Louisiana Brigade at Chancellorsville, where his horse was shot from under him and his foot was torn off by a shell. He was rewarded with the offer of a major-generalship, but was too conscientious to accept, since he could no longer serve actively in the field.

After the war he resumed his law-practice, until he was

called, reluctantly, into political action. The period of carpet-bag Reconstruction was to be seen perhaps at its worst and most corrupt in Louisiana.[40] At the Democratic convention of 1876 there was nominated "all that is left of General Nicholls." One-armed and one-legged he stumped the state, and—after a prolonged struggle, punctuated by violence, for possession—he was installed as the first governor of the state to be regularly elected since the war. His own party turned out no better than the Republicans, and when a group of city politicians got control and brought the term of this honorable man to an end, he refused to stand again and went into semi-retirement. He was called out of it eight years later to fight another campaign—against the Louisiana lottery company seeking to shackle itself on a debt-ridden state. After the bitterest of campaigns he was elected governor once more, and during his term of office succeeded in bringing the lottery to an end. His third period of service covered practically the rest of his life—twelve years as Chief Justice of the state. As such, through his voluminous and clear reports, he built up the structure of its constitutional law. Public service was thrust upon this man rather than sought by him; as upright as he was intrepid, as modest as he was gallant and courageous, he made a noble figure in the history of his state. It is a matter of reproach that he should not yet have had a biography devoted to him, where many lesser men have.

Representatives of this family continue in New Orleans today, along with several Treleavens, Tredinnicks, Treloars, Carveths, Penroses, Pendarvises, and Pentecosts, who may or may not be Cornish by descent.

A more immediate, if less distinguished, contribution was made to the public life of Florida by Samuel Pasco (1834–1917), United States Senator for that state, who was born in London of Cornish parents.[41] In 1842 they emigrated to Prince Edward Island, and then settled in New England, so that young Samuel was enabled to go to Harvard. Given charge of a school in Florida he became an ardent southerner, and enlisted as a private at the outbreak of the Civil War. He was wounded at the battle of Missionary Ridge, taken prisoner and spent a year and a half in hospital and internment camp. The rest of his long life he spent as a devoted and adroit southern politician.

Removed from office by the carpet-bag régime in 1868, he returned to law-practice until the end of Reconstruction—which he helped to bring about in Florida as Nicholls did in Louisiana. Pasco was much more of a professional politician, going up the regular ladder of state conventions, party committees, membership of state legislature until he finally became United States Senator from 1887 to 1899. Earlier he played a useful moderating role in the compromise that achieved home-rule for Florida after Reconstruction. In the United States Senate his role was of a routine character, and he confined himself mainly to matters affecting his own state. He lost the nomination for a third term in 1899, but was consoled with an appointment to the Panama Canal Commission, which carried him on to retirement in 1904. He had sons, one of whom was killed in the Philippines in the Spanish-American War, another served as a doctor in the Medical Corps in the First World War.[42]

A useful rather than an exciting career—it may be seen that Cornish folk, though far fewer in number there, have made their contribution even to the South.

NOTES

1. *Va. Mag.*, vol. 3, 285.
2. *Ibid.*, vol. 5, 182ff.
3. *Ibid.*, vol. 30, 39.
4. *Ibid.*, vol. 25, 380; vol. 28, 174.
5. *William and Mary Quarterly*, series 1, vol. 26, 33; vol. 21, 57.

6. *Ibid.*, vol. 21, 34ff., 115ff.
7. *Va. Mag.*, vol. 7, 73ff.
8. cf. *D. A. B.*, under Henry Stuart Foote.
9. cf. *D. A. B.* under John Coode. The article is mistaken in thinking that he was a renegade Catholic priest.
10. N. D. Mereness, *Maryland as a Proprietary Province*, 38.
11. W. H. Browne, *Maryland, the History of a Palatinate*, 92.
12. *Ibid.*, 57.
13. cf. *Archives of Maryland*, XIX, 435ff., 469, 497ff.
14. Browne, *op. cit.*, 188ff.
15. *Archives of Maryland*, XXVII, 186, 270, 333, 410, 455, 520.
16. *Ibid.*, XXV, 236; XXIX, 414; XLVI, 265.
17. *Ibid.*, IV, 541, 552; XVIII, 52, 170, 298, 364.
18. Sabine, *Loyalists*, II, 157–58; G. C. Boase and W. P. Courtney, *Bibliotheca Cornubiensis*, 11, 442.
19. *Who's Who in America*, 1914–16, 1829–30.
20. *The Colonial Records of N. Carolina*, ed. W. L. Saunders, vol. 1, 415, 449; vol. 15, 400; vol. 16, 1139, 1140; vol. 22, 253, 257, 356.
21. *Ibid.*, vol. 2, 89; vol. 4, 346, 1240, 1246; vol. 4, 275, 349, 589, 710, 853; vol. 22, 324, 417; vol. 25, 186.
22. *Biographical Hist. of North Carolina*, ed. S. A. Ashe, 11, 133ff.
23. *Records of the Court of Chancery of S. G., 1671–1779*, ed. A. K. Gregorie and J. N. Frierson, 60; *South Carolina Hist. Mag.*, vol. 10, 14.
24. *S.C. Hist. Mag.*, vol. 19, 33–35.
25. H. K. Leiding, *Charleston Historic and Romantic*, 107.
26. *S.C. Hist Mag.*, vol. 20, 35; vol. 34, 63.
27. *Ibid.*, vol. 62, 47.
28. *Ibid.*, vol. 59, 88.
29. cf. my "Jan Tregagle: In Legend and History," *History Today*, 1965.
30. *Records of . . . Chancery*, 489.
31. *S.C. Hist. Mag.*, vol. 11, 188; vol. 19, 108, 137.

32. *Records in British P. R. O. relating to S.C.*, 106.
33. *The Colonial Records of Georgia*, ed. A. D. Candler, XXI, 149, 468; IV, Supplement, 34; V, 664; XXII, pt. II, 445, 447; XXIII, 294.
34. *Ibid.*, VIII, 197; IX, 179; XVIII, 641.
35. *S.C. Hist. Mag.*, vol. 16, 37.
36. *The Colonial Records*, ed. cit., IX, 61; XIII, 491.
37. J. B. Campbell, in *East Tennessee Historical Soc.*, vol. 20, 94.
38. F. L. Olmsted, *The Slave States* (Capricorn Books), 214–15.
39. cf. *D. A. B.*, under Francis R. T. Nicholls; Anon, "The Nicholls Family in Louisiana," *La. Hist. Quarterly*, vol. 6, 5ff.
40. For the squalid, complex story cf. E. Lonn, *Reconstruction in Louisiana after 1868*.
41. cf. *D. A. B.*, under Samuel Pasco.
42. W. T. Cash, *The Story of Florida*, III, 204–5.

7 STEPPING WESTWARD

The movement westward over the Alleghenies down the Ohio River into the promising timbered lands of the vast Ohio territory had begun before the Revolution—indeed the desire of the government in London to keep its word to the Indians and give them some measure of protection was one of the contributory factors to it. But no power on earth could have stopped this human movement, this inevitable push over the mountains through the gaps and down the rivers; the successful outcome of the Revolution removed the last barriers and released the flood.

We can watch the process individually, turn a spy-glass on it briefly, in the story of one such Cornish family. John Chenoweth, a blacksmith, came to Baltimore before 1730.[1] One part of the family moved to Frederick County, Virginia, and each branch had numerous children in each generation—under various illiterate spellings, Chennerworth, Chenworth and Chinworth. By the time of the Revolution a number of them served as soldiers—Jonathan, John, William, Thomas, and Richard a captain, who commanded a company in Kentucky. He had brought his family with George Rogers Clark across the Alleghenies to float down the Monongahela and Ohio rivers; they alternately drifted and propelled themselves by poles, men and boys in the bow of the craft, women and children in the stern.[2] They built themselves a blockhouse with stockade in December 1778 on Corn Island at Ohio Falls, and experienced the severity of the winter in which one could walk across the falls, the spring frozen. In 1780 Louisville was founded in honor of the great American ally, Louis XVI; Richard Chenoweth is regarded as its principal founder. In 1782 he contracted to build a fort at Beargrass Creek; he both lost on it and suffered a repulse at the hands of Indians at Blue Licks. But he got a large tract of land, some fifteen miles east of Louisville, now known as Chenoweth's Run.

In 1788 Tom Chenoweth, a boy of fourteen, was captured by Indians, and brought up as a son of the chief. Exchanged some six years later, he did not welcome giving up his freedom for civilization, even pioneer civilization: he was clad in warpaint and feathers and was said to walk like an Indian, a young brave. Next summer there was an Indian attack on Chenoweth's settlement, which has got into the history books as Chenoweth's Massacre. Mrs. Chenoweth was scalped but recovered—the spring-house to which she was dragged for this customary operation still stands; a boy was wounded, but the father was not killed, as generally reported, merely grazed by a tomahawk. He was ultimately killed, in more regular fashion for a pioneer, by a falling log while clearing land.

By 1796 the settlers in Jefferson County were numerous. Captain Richard had been sheriff there, but there were other Chenoweths too. In 1792, for example, William Chenoweth had seven Indian blankets stolen from his wagon at Owen's tavern near Lexington.[3] John Chenoweth and his wife moved from Winchester, Virginia, to Jefferson County, but they ultimately went on to Indiana and died at Columbus, where "their graves are lost."[4] In 1814 Jacob Chenoweth was appointed surveyor of the road from Berry's Lick to Greenville.[5] The Chenoweths marched on and on, proliferating as they went. Up to the last generation they remained a leading family in Louisville, where their name is commemorated by a plaza in the city and a John A. Chenoweth Elementary School, as by Chenoweth Flats out in the country. (The

F*

Chynoweth family there will be more recent.) In Indiana today there are three families of them in South Bend; in Columbus, Ohio, there are no less than eleven, at Dayton fifteen, two of them with the more exact spelling Chynoweth —evidently more recent recruits. Nor have they failed to increase elsewhere, notably in California and as far afield as Honolulu as well as in the Old South. During the Civil War, we learn, "there were a number of colonels by the name of Chenoweth—if we read the name aright"![6] In West Virginia Lemuel Chenoweth was active as a bridge-builder in the mid-nineteenth century.[7]

In Louisville today there is a sprinkling of Cornish: no less than eight Ennis families, a dozen Oates (of whom some will belong), six Berryman, five Tippett and five Kellow (a less frequent name), three Ede, two Trevarthen (both doctors), one Trevathan (an attorney), two Wherry, two Treece. Among other names represented are Tamblyn, Tonkin, Toy, Trefry, Treharn, Opie,. Vivian, Jagoe, Hambly, Goldsworthy, Coon. Many more, however, will be found among such names as Triplett, Pollard, Merrifield, Nicholls, Edwards, Harris, Rowe, Rouse.

Edward Church Nicholls's third son, David, who fought under Perry on Lake Erie, moved into Kentucky and had many adventures there.[8] He had a dispute with a friend as to who was the better dancer. Nicholls said, "I am going to spoil your dancing." The friend's fire missed; Nicholls aimed at his leg, carried the friend to the doctor's house, rang the bell and departed. The friend never told how he had been wounded, but he did not dance so well after. It sounds very like Old Kentucky.

A more useful recruit to the state was a direct immigrant, Robert Peter (1805–94), of the well-known Launceston family, who was brought over as a child to Pittsburgh.[9] Employed in a drugstore, he developed a passion for chemistry—perhaps inspired by the brilliant career of Sir Humphry Davy; he educated himself, lecturing on chemistry to the Western University of Pennsylvania. In 1832 he moved into Kentucky, studying medicine and publishing articles as he went on chemistry and medicine. For nearly twenty years he was professor of chemistry and pharmacy at Transylvania University, researching and publishing on urinary calculi. He inspired the Kentucky geological survey, the first large state undertaking of its kind, and was the first to perceive that the productivity of Kentucky blue grass was due to its high phosphorus content. He served as chemist for the surveys of Arkansas and Indiana, during the Civil War as surgeon in the medical hospitals of Lexington and then returned to professoring. His son spent over forty years as chemist in the Kentucky Agricultural Experiment Station. "Father and son together gave nearly a hundred years of service in chemistry to Kentucky." They evidently were good servants of the state.

Neither Kentucky nor Indiana has been much of a stamping-ground for Cornish folk. I think we are in a position now to say that most of the names that appear are those of old Cornish stock in the country. Indianapolis, for example, has five Tremain families, besides Tremaine and Tremayne, and five Trefry, evidently from New England. But in addition we find three Minniear (for Minear), three Edgecombe, two Nankivell, two Tremear (a sugar company in this name), besides Trethewey, Trewartha, Pengilly, Vivian, Dungey, Ivy, Oates, Pasco and seven Penrose (one a Wesley C., to make doubly sure). We find also a rarity, the Reverend Alfred Edyvean (little Eddy) and two Killigrews, so rare as to be improbable—in Cornwall this famous name has long died out. In South Bend, Indiana, it is interesting to find a whole clutch of Tretheweys, six entries, several recent Warricks, along with Penrose, Pascoe, Trezise, Chenoweth. A strong thrust of these last leaves five families of them in Des Moines, Iowa—though this may be a case of old Cornish-American stock meeting new recruits. Here there are seven Trevillyan entries, seven Minear, five Pender, two Glanville, along with

Trevethan, Pendarvis, Penberthy, Petherick, Curnow, Grenfell. This gives us a nice mixture of old and new Cornish.

Perhaps Ohio gives us the best example of this process—the old stock from across the Alleghenies moving upwards to meet the much larger stream of Cornish immigrants coming into the area of the Great Lakes, with the rich mines in Michigan and Wisconsin, in the nineteenth century. We see the older stock, with its numerous clans of Chenoweth, Tremain and Penrose, in Columbus and Dayton. It was a New York Tremain who settled on Lake Erie in 1823: Calvin Tremain was appointed postmaster and so the place became Tremainsville—an example of a frequent process.[10] Now it is a suburb of Toledo, giving its name to Tremainsville Gardens and other amenities.

Cleveland, with its immense industrial development, swarms with new Cornish. It has a clan of Tresises, ten entries, ten Santo, eight Pascoe, seven Ede, seven Chenoweth, seven Gear, four Penberthy, four Rodda, four Hocking, four Hunkin, four Tregenna (a rare name), three Tamblyn, two Penharth, two Retallick, two Pethick, two Treharne, two Jago, two Trembath, besides Carew, Chegwidden, Curnow, Pendry, Penhollow, Wedlake, Angove, Kitto, Uren, Pendarvis, Menhenett, Trevillian, Trevorrow, Trevarthen, Trevathan, Tregear, Treen, Tregoning, Hambly. There is a clan of twenty-two Pender, a smaller one of seven Treece, perhaps mainly Cornish, besides all those disguised under English names like Mitchell and Harris. There are probably not less than two or three thousand people of Cornish descent in Cleveland today.

In Akron there is a wide spread of old and (mainly) new Cornish: a dozen Chenoweth, and a fair number of the usual names in Tre- and Pen-. Perhaps I may draw attention only to the rarer names. There is one great rarity—the medieval name of Tripcony; I thought that this had become extinct long ago—the place it comes from is pronounced Trekenning. There are two Angwin entries, two Carlyon, three Behanna (a form of Behenna?), three Uren, two Gear, along with Pellow, Warrick, Gundry, Lanyon. There are twelve Couch, of whom some will be Cornish, and five Hocking.

We see how little is understood about Cornish names from what a useful immigrant into Ohio, William G. Pengelly, thought that his meant, "the name indicating that the family is descended from Druid chieftains"![11] This man came over from Plymouth at seventeen, and was employed in a bank for over thirty years. In the later nineteenth century "practically all bankers were in a measure judges of handwriting," and Pengelly made himself "one of the best handwriting experts in America." As such he was employed as an expert in legal cases relating to forgery, for the state departments of Ohio and Michigan, for the United States Post Office as well as the British intelligence service and other governments. He often appeared in the courts, was well versed in the history of handwriting, and compiled a work on *Foiling the Forger*, besides various papers. It was an idiosyncratic contribution to make—one sees him beaming out from his portrait like a private detective, very Cornish, with bright eyes and frog-face, marked creases from the nose to the corners of the mouth.

Stepping westward to the Mississippi, in St. Louis there is quite a Penberthy clan, twelve entries, nine Tremain altogether, eight Vivian, eight Penrose, six Trebilcock, six Hambley, besides a representative spread of Pen- and Tre- names, including the rare Tregerthen, Treloggen and Trenwith. Kansas City, Missouri, has a much larger representation: sixteen Chenoweth with one Chenowth, nine Tremaine, eight Vivian, eight Tonkin, eight Tamblyn, seven Pender, six Penrose, four Hocking, four Penfold, three Pellow, three Pascoe. Among the more usual names there stand out these rarer ones: Penprase, Penquite, Polkinghorn, Chellew, Santo and Pellmounter—that name which has taken the odd form of Palamountain in New York and California.

St. Louis was the scene of the labors of one of the greatest of American botanists, William Trelease, in honor of whom Mount Trelease at the head of Clear Creek, Colorado, is named.¹² He was for many years, 1889–1912, director of the Botanical Garden at St. Louis, virtually its creator, and also professor of botany at Washington University, St. Louis, from which he moved to become professor at the University of Illinois. Born in New York State in 1857, he was trained at Cornell as most of the members of his staff at Shaw's Garden, St. Louis, had been. In turn he trained up a school of distinguished pupils, among them a leading Danish botanist, Christian Bay, foremost collector of Western Americana, who paid a tribute to his master as "the perfect botanist." I do not know if Trelease kept contact with Cornish gardens—he did with those in Europe, particularly at Copenhagen. He published numerous papers, making original contributions to botany and entomology, along with standard works on *The Agave in the West Indies, The American Oaks, Plant Materials of Decorative Gardening,* and *Winter Botany*. Many plants are named after this famous botanist and he received a number of international honors. He died, after an immensely long life full of achievement, in 1945.*

His son, Sam F. Trelease, carried on his father's work, becoming an eminent plant physiologist. Born in St. Louis, he had a long and varied academic career, making a number of contributions to his subject and ending up as professor of botany at Columbia University.

About 1850 there came to Ohio a Menhinnick from the fine old Tudor farmhouse of Pengenna in St. Kew: he was married and the couple came to Ohio where they had relatives. They moved west to Lawrence, Kansas, a new community on Mount Oread, that hillock that rises so surprisingly out of the illimitable plain. During the Civil War, on August 21, 1863, the town was raided by a guerrilla band under the

---

* There is no notice of him in D. A. B. This should be remedied in an expanded edition, which is greatly needed; he is worthy of a separate biography by a qualified botanist.

murderous Quantrill—Quantrill's raid—most of the town was burned and a hundred and fifty people butchered. Menhinnick had hidden when a band came to the house, its leader sent the little son back into the house to get matches. Mrs. Menhinnick came to the front porch, where she was made to turn out her pockets and petticoats for money. "Where's your husband?" She didn't know. "You must know . . . Anything else you've got?" She fetched out her little box decorated with shells, such as the Cornish folk made—we had one in early days in our home. Of no value, she said she would like to keep it: "I brought it over with me from England." "Where do you come from in England?" "Cornwall." "Well, I'm Cornish too." He gave orders that that house was not to be burned.

One of the Menhinnick daughters became an early professor at the University of Kansas, and had a good deal of success as such. Of the granddaughters, one of them wrote a book, *The Wind and the Rock*, which has this story, badly handled and missing the whole point of it. The other granddaughter went west to Salem, Oregon, marrying into a leading family from pioneering days.[13] So the Salem Browns are descended from the Menhinnicks. That name, rare now in Cornwall, is not uncommon in America under its various forms, particularly Menhenett.

We have now reached the Mississippi, and even in the lesser story of the incoming of Cornish folk we can see how it conforms to, and illuminates, the larger rhythms of the peopling of the continent. The end of the War of 1812 released a further surge westward of the American people: the days of the Indians east of the Mississippi were numbered. "The postwar Indian policy had only one objective: to bring the tribes so completely under American control that they could be pushed from their ancestral lands."[14] The first period of settlement of the Great Lakes plains, from 1815 to 1830, was mainly a movement out of the Old South across the Ohio into southern Indiana and Illinois, to reach the Mississippi at St.

Louis with Missouri beyond. This movement, then, was dominantly southern: we have an historic illustration of it in the trek of Abraham Lincoln's family from Virginia through Kentucky to fetch up in Illinois. We have a no less authentic illustration, though of no historic moment, that led the Chenoweths westward, so that today we find four families of them in Carbondale, in southern Illinois—along with two Trovillion (probably old Cornish stock also from Virginia), two Tregoning, a Carlyon, Pearce, Varcoe, who would be new recruits.

The opening of the Erie Canal, from the Hudson to Lake Erie, in 1825 offered a far easier and more direct route westward into the great, rich, teeming plains for the impoverished farmers of New England and immigrants alike. People swarmed along it into Michigan, northern Indiana and Illinois, Wisconsin and beyond. These two streams met, to fill the plains east of the Mississippi with people. The great river itself formed a third route, if a subsidiary one. By 1830 the lead-mines of the Galena area, at the junction of the Fever River with the Mississippi, in northwestern Illinois and southwestern Wisconsin, inspired a mining rush thither; many miners went up the Mississippi route, the lead came down. This stream also met with the larger stream coming across the Great Lakes to the copper-mines of Lake Superior. Both these streams carried large numbers of Cornish miners with them: the first mass-movement, amounting to many thousands, direct from Cornwall to the United States.

Before portraying it, a subject in itself, perhaps we may round up various individual or group contributions, and then tackle the miners *en masse*.

A very characteristic contribution was that of Cornish Methodism. At home, simple folk—especially the miners, farmers and fishermen—took to Methodism from the first. It offered an outlet for their emotionalism, and answered their emotional demands, in a way that the quieter and more sedate services of the Church of England could not. One institution that Methodism carried with it everywhere was that of itinerant local preachers—preaching laymen. Here is one such old body at work in northern Michigan, Samuel Rowe. "He had the most tenacious and retentive memory of any man I ever knew . . . He sometimes used to say, if the Bible were lost, he could replace by his memory the four Evangelists, the Acts of the Apostles, the Epistle to the Romans, and the greater part of the Epistle to the Hebrews."[15] John Glanville spent a year on the Sangamon in Illinois, and then travelled about in Mexico. He held a number of responsible appointments and was presiding elder in Illinois 1843–45. He was "a man of superior preaching ability and Christian character, a companionable, intellectual, able minister of the Gospel, distinguished for his originality."[16]

Pachuca, the great silver-mining center fifty miles northeast of Mexico City, had—and still has—a considerable community of Cornish miners. A Methodist class had been formed among them as early as the 1850's.[17] By the 1870's there were two or three local preachers and several Mexicans had joined; they had weekly services in their hall on the public square. Christopher Ludlow had come from home to install a Cornish pumping engine, and he was a good preacher. Bishop Butler put him in charge of the three missions, Pachuca, Real del Monte, Omitlan—some five thousand inhabitants at nine thousand feet. He was assisted by a Paull and a Treloar as preachers; they had a chapel to hold a hundred and fifty, Cornish and Mexicans, a Sunday school and a boys' school. Extraordinary to think of those familiar efforts in so remote and exotic an environment!

Richard F. Trevellick (1830–95) was one of the most important labor leaders in nineteenth-century America.* He was born on St. Mary's in the Scilly Islands, and to the end of his days remembered the cottage smothered in rambler roses, the

---

* There is a notice of him in D. A. B., but he merits a short biography.

wallflowers and gilliflowers in front, the little orchard at the back, the farm noises, the cows, the cuckoos in spring, the seagulls forever crying. Trevellick's father had lived at Silver Lake, New York, in the early 1800's; he talked of American freedom, but lost all his savings in a financial panic. He buried two brothers there, but went back to Scilly where he had a family.

Young Richard turned after his mother in independent spirit and initiative. He learned his trade as a ship's carpenter at Mumford's, and at twenty-one left for Southampton, where he helped to build a large vessel, the *Parana*, for the South American trade. Dick was a handsome fellow, tall and dark, with fine eyes, a lot of hair brushed across a wide forehead, well-shaped nose and ears. All the girls fell for him and several tried to catch him. When at length he fell for a girl of his own choice at home, his mother wouldn't have her inside the house. He left home telling his mother that he would never see her face again; nor did he. She repented, but too late for Dick. He went as a ship's carpenter on a boat for Calcutta, and on the voyage had a curious telepathic experience: his girl appeared to him at the same moment as she was received as a daughter by his mother at home. Next year, 1852, he went on to Australia in the gold-rush; going on to Auckland, New Zealand, he put himself forward in the agitation for the eight-hour day. Back in the Australian gold-fields, he had various hardships and adventures, in one of which he was had up before a judge for resisting an officer. The judge turned out to have been a playmate of Dick's mother, a man named Rose Price. Price had been in love with his step-sister, was refused a license to marry, and emigrated to Australia, where he became a judge.

In 1855, sailing to San Francisco, Dick was wrecked on the coast of Peru, lost everything and joined the Peruvian navy. The local war with Chili ending, he was paid off. A vessel from Scilly, William Lakey captain, calling in at Callao took Dick on to Panama. In the employ of the Pacific Mail Steamship Company he helped to construct the wharves at Aspinwall (Colón) for the rapidly increasing traffic to California on account of the gold-rush. He worked his passage to New Orleans, where he was elected president of the ship carpenters' union and led a successful fight for a nine-hour day. His brother Sam and a fellow-Cornishman, Obadiah Hicks, were working in New York when Dick joined them.[18] In Brooklyn—the Brooklyn of Walt Whitman (who should have met Dick)—he worked as a foreman and was active in his union. He moved up to Franklin where, sick, he married one of his landlady's daughters. On a steamer on the Mississippi he refused a Confederate offer to take the command of a gunboat; his wife, who was a southerner, came north with a British passport. They made their home in Detroit, lived there the rest of their days and there their family of five children were born and brought up. So there should still be descendants of his about.

The rest of Trevellick's life is part of the history of the American labor movement. In 1864 he became the first president of the Detroit Trades' Assembly, and after that worked no more with the tools of his trade. Next year he was made president of the International Union of Ship Carpenters and Caulkers. Trevellick led the first torchlight procession in Chicago to demand the eight-hour day—his good looks were too much for one woman in the crowd: "Oh, I do dearly love that man!" In 1867 he was a delegate to the congress of the National Labor Union, and there he bravely advocated the admission of Negroes: without unity the unions would be "killed off." Trevellick, always an idealist, insisted that Negro membership would be an asset, and all along "had stood his ground nobly when a member of a trades union."[19] The question was shelved. That year Karl Marx's First International was formed and met at Lausanne; Trevellick was named as delegate, but the funds could not be raised to send him.

He became the most popular and respected of all labor

speakers of his time. Eugene Debs, the Socialist leader, said of him later, "from his thirty fifth to his fifty fifth year he talked to more working people than any man on the American continent." Immediately after the Civil War he toured the South with Sylvis, the leader of the Iron Moulders' Union, but the South was too stricken to respond. In 1867–68 on his strenuous speaking tours he made some three hundred speeches and started nearly fifty trade unions. In 1870 he made efforts to organize the anthracite miners of the East; in that year he toured sixteen states and formed nearly two hundred local, and three state, unions. He was a persuasive orator, of an old-fashioned idealist type, who for over twenty years carried on his campaign, mostly single-handed, for the rights of labor. And mostly, we may add, in vain: he was a pioneer before his time. In 1868 Trevellick went to Washington to carry out, at his own expense, a four-month lobby for a national eight-hour day law. In the circumstances of the time it was out of the question, and the effort crippled him financially. Nevertheless he returned in 1870 to lobby the Capital for legislation. Though he failed, Congress made a gesture in his direction, passing a law to put letter-carriers on an eight-hour day. It gave official currency to the idea, and Trevellick must be regarded as the pioneer of the eight-hour day in the United States.

In 1870 he became president of the National Labor Union; as such he had to accept the majority vote for the exclusion of Chinese labor, though he always stood out for welcoming the Negro into the unions. The economic crisis of 1873 strengthened the employers' hands and unionism declined, but "the collapse of organization after organization never undermined his belief in the general principle of organized labor struggle."[20] He favored the idea of an independent political party for labor—again before his time—as he advocated the Rochdale principle of Co-operation and votes for women. His ideas mostly came from Britain, his experience from all round the English-speaking world.

However, America was still dominantly a rural and farming country. In the mid-seventies the prairies were alive with discontent, grain prices going down, prices of what the farmer bought going up—"Raise less corn and more hell" was to be the incisive advice of a female Populist in a later decade. Trevellick devoted his energies to helping to organize the Greenback Party, which grew rapidly in 1874-76, establishing Greenback clubs throughout the Middle West. Their aim was to get the government to continue the issue of greenbacks, the unbacked paper currency of the Civil War; this meant a sensible dose of inflation, almost certainly what the economy needed, as against the dominant vested interests, the banking and business of the East. Trevellick was in the thick of all this hopeless, high-minded activity, presiding as chairman at two of the party's national conventions. He found, however, that they were dominated by farmers and agrarian politicians, with little interest in the rights of labor. The return of prosperity in the later seventies ended the Greenback party; the experience left Trevellick with an abiding interest in currency questions —that last infirmity of noble minds.

In the 1880's he devoted himself largely to spreading the ideas of Co-operation, particularly among the farmers. It must be supposed that what Co-operation there was must have owed something to him; he certainly received a special tribute from Co-operators—tributes were what he mostly received. The *New York Sun* said that he "has done more than any others to organize the working men of the West, especially the agricultural laborers who have been forgotten or ignored by others." What did it all add up to? He took his ideas and energies with him into the Knights of Labor, for whom he campaigned arduously. At length he suffered a stroke, and died two years later in 1895.

In the last year of his life he wrote a treatise on money; though he got up the subject and consulted the standard authorities, the book remained unpublished. He was, of course, a forerunner of the idea of a controlled economy against the contraction of credit and deflation. He was a kind of J. A. Hobson, who also was before his time and on the right lines, as Keynes later acknowledged in his book that inaugurated a new era. Trevellick argued that it was for Congress to decide upon and control the amount and flow of credit, not the banks, and should issue a full supply at 3 per cent per annum. He advocated a graduated income tax, government ownership of railroads, prohibition of the sale of liquor, industrial arbitration in place of strikes, the eight-hour day for labor, no child labor under fourteen, free schools, all paper money to be government money.

His ideas seem common sense now, and most of them have been put into effect, though he has received little credit for them or for his life of struggle on behalf of others. He was a singularly noble, unselfish fellow. With his talents (and looks) he could have made a fortune. A couple of Michigan politicians offered him $300 a lecture for ten lectures. Poor Mrs. Trevellick (not unlike Dame Alice, the down-to-earth wife of highminded Sir Thomas More) thought that $3000 would be a nice thing to educate the children with. Her husband thought it would be a disgrace and refused, as he refused tempting offers for his oratory from both the big parties. He did canvass Pennsylvania for Grant on the tariff issue, but that was because he believed in protection for infant industries. Evidently he believed in his ideas. As Yearley says, "his scanty recompense would have disgusted even an itinerant Methodist preacher"—which, in a way, he was. He received many tributes of esteem: "in a venal age he has escaped corruption; in the turmoil of party strife he has maintained a character above reproach. A frivolous sentiment never escaped his lips."[21] Perhaps that was the trouble: there is not much evidence of a sense of humor in such a career of altruistic devotion, when America was the country of rugged individualism, in the age of the robber barons.

We can continue to follow the westward migration into the lands across the Mississippi representatively in the Cornish folk: wherever we step westward we come upon them. If it is Oklahoma we find old southern names: in Oklahoma City six Chenoweth families, five Pendarvis; to them we must add three Tremain or Tremaine, three Trezise, three Pender, a Tredenick, Trevathan, Penrose and—more rarely—a Chegwin.

Since we cannot follow the process in detail, let us look at Iowa, organized as a territory in 1838, as an example. Ira H. Tremaine (1822–1902)—Ira was rather a favorite name with Victorian Cornishmen—moved from New York to Wisconsin, where his son Orlando was born.[22] Orlando became a doctor; the father represented his county in the representative assembly of the new state. In a Civil War time diary of 1862 we find a William Minear, brother to the diarist's sister-in-law. In the next generation the Reverend George Lafayette Minear ended up as Wesleyan superintendent of his district.[23]

Members of the Treloar clan moved on to Iowa and prospered farming.[24] Joseph Treloar, born at Wendron in 1827, worked his way to the States on a freight boat in 1848. He settled at first in Wisconsin, mining, carpentering, farming; here in 1855 he married Susan Crase of Camborne. His brother Temby was already in the new country opening up in Iowa and persuaded his brother to come out: prospects were good. James's first trip took six weeks: he had three teams of horses, one yoke of oxen, three cows, a colt and several sheep for Temby. Nearing Temby's place, they got lost in a swamp; in old Swede who lived in a haystack helped them to find the vay. James Treloar signed up for 240 acres to begin with; whenever he wanted more land, he borrowed the money from Uncle Sy Crase back in Wisconsin. In 1886 James sent the money for his nephew to bring his family out. The two families lived at first together in a small house, 14 feet by 26 feet—twenty-four of them: when the men moved out first to their work, then the children were fed; they must have slept in relays. Yet the two families lived in the closest harmony all their days. They were all converted by a Baptist revival in the vicinity—all except old James, who wouldn't give in. The rest besought and plagued him, at length besieged him, until he owned that he might as well surrender. One son became a minister. James had had a successful life; when he retired he owned 640 acres, and moved into the city, Des Moines. One finds members of this immediate family, in considerable number, in Iowa and Kansas, back in Wisconsin and on in California.

We notice a number of instances of Cornish folk moving on from Wisconsin or Michigan to farm in Iowa. It is probable that a close study would reveal a respectable contingent in that state. James Henry Trewin (1858–1927) moved on from Illinois to live with his brother on an Iowa farm.[25] He taught country school for six years, then read and practiced law. He served a number of terms in the state assembly, and on retiring set up a law partnership, in which his son joined, as Trewin, Simmons and Trewin. He continued to make useful contributions to the public life of the state as president of its board of education 1909–14, and chairman of the commission which produced the code of state laws in 1924. We learn that, a man of ability and force, he left his impress upon the state.

Emlin G. Penrose (1844–1930) was born in Ohio and moved with his parents to Iowa in 1860.[26] He first taught school then made money in the hardware business. Public service followed, on the school board and as mayor of Tama City; finally as state senator for several terms. Senator Penrose accompanied a delegation of Musquakie Indians to complain to the governor about a road across their reservation. Their chief said: "These are my chiefs and my councillors. The earth was made for us when they came here to this country . . . You came from across the ocean, and when you first came over here you leased lands from our chiefs. That is why we

call ourselves the friends of the white man."[27] And the result
... ! This speech was made hundreds of times as the irresistible tide rolled west. We may take it as an epigraph for the whole movement.

In our pilgrimage westward let us narrow down to an instance in our own time, a career of signal public service of which I have personal knowledge.* Carleton College, Minnesota, is one of the foremost liberal arts colleges in the Middle West; it has a greater importance as a pioneer in this field where so many have followed since. For Carleton College got going early and was thus able to set a model. Its achievement was the life's work of Donald J. Cowling, president of the college for nearly half a century, from 1909 to 1945. He was born at Trevalga, on the north coast of Cornwall, in 1880 and taken to America as a child of two. His father was a Methodist minister, who died young, and the boy was educated at the care of the church. He did well at Yale, and went forth to teach philosophy. At the age of twenty-eight he was made president of Carleton, then the youngest college president in the country; he lived to be about the oldest. The years between were filled with fruitful, creative achievement. An "unusual looking" young man of very dark complexion and glittering eyes under already heavy eyebrows, he had "a boldness of purpose which seemed unbounded . . . He envisaged a college in the Middle West equal in standards and equipment with the best in the country."[28] His life's work was to achieve it, virtually singlehanded; for this was accomplished by his own initiative, before the regardless expansion of higher education made things too easy and lowered standards throughout. With his firm Methodist upbringing, a man of principles as well as of persuasive charm, Cowling believed in education as a buttress for democracy without its becoming wholly pro-

---

* I am indebted for my introduction to Carleton College and to Dr. Cowling to my old friend, Mr. Louis J. Hill of Minneapolis-St. Paul. It is a pity that Dr. Cowling did not write an autobiography.

vided by the state and dictated by the state. An independent-minded Cornishman, he believed in independence in education. It is a rare type today.

His influence radiated far beyond his own college, in the educational field in general, in religion and philanthropy, in citizenship. He served as president of the Association of American Colleges, president of the American Council on Education, chairman of the Founders Committee of the famous Mayo Clinic. He received many awards and citations, one of them "in recognition of the great debt America owes its adopted citizens." It may be appreciated how well such a career of service rewarded the adoption. He was before the time of generous educational pension schemes: when I saw him in retirement, he was still working for his living in an office at the age of eighty-seven.

In Cowling's home-state of Minnesota, where the Scandinavian element is strong—St. Olaf's College is the rival to Carleton at Northfield—the Cornish element is nevertheless noticeable. It is recent and mainly owing, no doubt, to the iron-mines. In Minneapolis there are no less than eight Pascoe families, five Pellow, five Pengelly, three Polkinghorne, three Vivian, three Trethewey. In the fairly wide spread of names represented we find some less common names, Angove, Annear, Bosanko, Polgreen, Kitto, Carlyon, Pendroy (for Pendray), Trezona, Nankivell, Curnow, besides more familiar ones. There is an unusual deformation of the name Trelawny —Treglawny, which should be rectified.

When we sweep south again into Nebraska we find a still stronger contingent in Omaha. Perhaps the influence is to be seen in the name, Cornish Heights, for a section of the town. There are eight families of the name of Cornish, fourteen Couch (some of whom will belong), thirteen Rouse, nine Courtney, eight Toy, five Nance, four Trebilcock, three Pasco, three Jolley, three Tremaine, three Carew, three Chenoweth, three Coad: with a wide spread of familiar names by now, from which I select a few of the rarer, Penhollow, Penquite, Hender, Jago, Santo, Granville, Bunney, Bunt, Trevarrow.

We are now in a position to tackle the first mass-immigration of Cornish folk, to meet the first wave of miners coming into the Great Lakes country in the 1840's.

NOTES

1. *Tyler's Quarterly Hist. and Geneal. Mag.*, 186ff.
2. J. S. Johnston, *Memorial History of Louisville*, I, 40ff.
3. C. R. Staples, *History of Pioneer Lexington, 1779–1806*, 76.
4. *Kentucky Hist. Soc. Reg.*, vol. 45, 169. This journal, to be used properly, needs a better general index.
5. *Ibid.*, vol. 42, 193.
6. *Ibid.*, vol. 47, 198.
7. D. B. Steinman and S. R. Watson, *Bridges and their Builders*, 121.
8. Anon. "The Nicholls Family in Louisiana," *La. Hist. Quarterly*, vol. 6, 5ff.
9. *D. A. B.*, under Robert Peter.
10. N. O. Winter, *Hist. of N. W. Ohio*, I, 340.
11. C. B. Galbreath, *Hist. of Ohio*, III, 118.
12. *Missouri Hist. Rev.*, vol. 28, 62.
13. Mrs. Keith Powell, to whom I am indebted for the above information.
14. R. A. Billington, *Westward Expansion*, 291.
15. W. C. Barclay, *Hist. of Methodist Missions*, Part I, vol. 2, 436.
16. J. Lenton, *Hist. of Methodism in Illinois*, 182.
17. Barclay, *op. cit.*, vol. 3.
18. Obadiah Hicks, who became a Labor journalist, wrote, anonymously, a *Life of Richard F. Trevellick, the Labor Orator*, or the

Harbinger of the Eight Hour System, Joliet, Illinois, 1896, from which these personal details come.

19. P. S. Foner, *Hist. of the Labor Movement in U.S.*, I, 396ff.
20. D. A. B., under Richard F. Trevellick.
21. Hicks, 84.
22. *Annals of Iowa*, 3rd Series, V, 637; VI, 159.
23. *Ibid.*, XV, 156, 457.
24. *Treloar Genealogy*, (privately printed), 88ff.
25. *Annals of Iowa*, XVI, 237.
26. *Ibid.*, XVIII, 79.
27. *Ibid.*, III, 130.
28. L. Headley in *The Voice of the Carleton Alumni*, vol. 10, no. 3, 3ff.

8 THE FIRST WAVE OF MINERS: MICHIGAN

*A*t home in Cornwall, in the middle of the nineteenth century, mining—particularly that of copper—was in full blast. The dozen square miles or so around Camborne and Redruth were at that time the most heavily, and the most deeply, mined area in the world. It had its outlier in the mining parish of St. Just at the Land's End, where the mines went out under the sea. So they did in the St. Austell area, the second to come into full production, in Mid-Cornwall—where my father's folk were miners. This area was shortly surpassed in production by East Cornwall, centering upon the immensely rich copper-mines of South Caradon—with its outlier across the Tamar in Devon Consols—that high, bare, windswept country which is the background from which starts Newton Thomas's admirable novel about the Cornish miners in the Upper Peninsula of Michigan, *The Long Winter Ends*, a book full of compassion and understanding of their hard lot and brief vivacious lives.[1]

In the 1850's Cornwall's copper production reached its peak, with 209,000 tons in 1856.[2] But already its dominant position as producer was receding. From 1800 to the 1830's it had produced two-thirds of the world's copper; in the 1850's it was down to one-quarter. Even so its value was twice that of the tin mined in Cornwall, and three out of four miners were mining copper. But the outside world was fast catching up; even in the 1830's Chile was producing one-fifth of the world's copper, and the long years Richard Trevithick—Cornwall's greatest inventor—spent in Peru and Chile gave a marked impulse to production in South America. (He had gone out to install Cornish pumping-engines in the mines of Cerro de Pasco).[3]

Along with the tremendous expansion of mining in the little county there was a no less remarkable development of the Cornish steam pumping-engine—indeed, it was only this that made the former possible, with the greater depths worked and the volume of water to be pumped out. It was a Scotsman, James Watt, who made the fundamental improvements in the West Country Newcomen engine that turned it into a true steam-engine, in which steam became the actual driving force. Subsequent Cornish engineers, notably Trevithick and Woolf, made further improvements applying high-pressure steam and expansive working. Thus evolved the classic Cornish beam-engine which held supreme place throughout the world for the remainder of the era of steam.

Within Cornwall the second quarter of the century, 1825–50, witnessed an intensely competitive period in raising the duty of the engines, i.e. their performance in raising water for coal consumed. By 1838 there had been a four-fold increase of duty in a generation.[4] The ablest engineers—Trevithick, Woolf, Grose, Sims, Hocking, Loam, Taylor—gave their minds to raising the duty of their engines; there was great excitement over the climbing duty-figures—until 100 million lb. duty was reached—and intense competition among the engineers over the engines they submitted to tests, as other people raced horses. By 1850 the duty-race was over and the Cornish beam-engine had reached its peak of perfection. "Nowhere in the world," we are told, "has pumping been carried out on a scale even remotely comparable to that in Cornwall in the last century, and by 1850 Cornishmen had more experience of deep mining, and with it deep pumping, than the rest of the world together."⁵ This preponderance continued till 1865—the sudden collapse of copper-mining; by then, at the peak, there were 650 Cornish beam-engines at work in the county, with another 60 in West Devon.

This led in turn to the development and achievement of the Cornish foundries. We learn that "by 1830 the work produced by the three leading Cornish foundries was the equal of any in the kingdom and within another decade they had gone on to excel them. For twenty years more they held their pre-eminent position, achieving a world-wide reputation for the building of engines for mine-use."⁶ "The greatest and most long-lived of all the Cornish foundries was Harvey and Company, of Hayle," established by John Harvey (1720-1803), who began as a humble blacksmith, and is still venerated in the historic firm as the "little Captain." This firm, in 1844, built the world's largest steam-engine for the drainage of the Haarlem Meer, now preserved in Holland as a national monument. "As the world's largest steam-engine it fittingly commemorates not only the Hollander's successful battles against the North Sea, but also the international standing of Cornish engineering in the great days of steam."⁷

Harvey's built engines for Mexico, South Africa, South Australia. Quite early on, a Camborne mining engineer, John Rule, installed machinery at Real del Monte in Mexico—and the miners and engineers followed the engines.⁸ Perran Foundry—established by the Quaker Foxes of Falmouth⁹—built engines for Spain, Mexico, South America and Australia. The smaller St. Austell foundry also built engines for Australia. The Holman foundry at Camborne specialized in boiler-making before they concentrated on the rock-drills and air-compressors for which they are now known all over the world.

The Cornish pumping-engine, though the most famous, was not the only steam-engine to be developed in Cornwall. There were whim-engines, to draw the ore in buckets, and ultimately man-engines in deep mines to lower and raise the men and obviate climbing hundreds of feet of ladders. (There is an old mining maxim, "Cornishmen do not like to hang to a rope.") There was a gradual introduction of steam-stamps to crush the ore. "Californian stamps," developed on the goldfields, were merely a development of the normal type in use at home, but the former had round heads and rotated slightly.[10] The Californian type gradually replaced the original Cornish. But stamps are stamps the world over—I remember the curious clacking noise they made in the distance from the village of my childhood.

When the total depression of Cornish mining came in the late nineteenth century, these engines were sold off in hundreds, sometimes for other purposes at home, or for mines abroad. Then, as before, the mining engineers and enginemen went with their engines. For decades they had had a reputation for speed and dispatch in erecting them—and again I recall from childhood the pride the engine-men had in their engines, the care they took of them, the polished brass, sometimes a vase of flowers for decoration. (Was not an engine a feminine creature?)

"The emigration of Cornishmen to foreign mining fields was partially responsible for the world-wide foreign trade of the Cornish foundries."[11] The Hornblowers were from Staffordshire originally, but they came down to Cornwall to install Newcomen engines before the mid-eighteenth century; there they remained for several generations and proliferated. Jonathan Hornblower had thirteen children who were all given names beginning with J—the father was a Baptist; one of these, Josiah, took the first Newcomen engine to America in 1753.[12]

Later on, the Harveys built two regular Cornish beam-engines in 1835 for an unsuccessful gold-mining venture in Virginia. About 1849 a Cornish pumping-engine was installed at the copper-mine at Perkiomen. "The engine was one that had been used in Cornwall, but still perfect in all its parts. The success attending it has caused several to be constructed there; and Messrs. J. T. Sutton and Company of Pennsylvania are building one ... to be used near the one alluded to; and I. P. Morris and Company are building two of the same size for supplying the city of Buffalo with water."[13] In 1872 the largest engine in the United States—with 110 inch diameter—was started at the Lehigh Zinc Company's mine in Pennsylvania. Though built by a Philadelphia foundry, it was designed by the Cornish engineer, John West, who had emigrated some years earlier, and was erected by "Simeon Noell [Noall], who has had twenty-one years experience in this kind of work in Cornwall." It was, moreover, worked by two emigrant Cornish engine-men. "West ... had earlier erected a 50" Bull engine at these same mines." By the 1860's the Vivians had moved their engineering works bodily from Camborne to Pittsburgh and were supplying the mines of Lake Superior.[14]

With the lasting depression from the late 1860's the engine-reservoir of Cornwall was dissipated over the face of the earth. A considerable number yet remained to serve the contracting tin-mines; a few were transferred to serve the needs of the newly developing china-clay works. But mostly they were scattered to the coal-mines of South Wales and Yorkshire, the lead-mines of Derbyshire, the water-works of London. Abroad they went chiefly to Spain, some to France, more to Australia and as far afield as New Zealand. "There, transplanted fragments of the contemporary Cornish scene, they must have gladdened as well as saddened the hearts of the many Cornish miners who went with them or who came across them in their wanderings."[15] At home, "the most striking surface remains of former mining activity ... are the derelict engine-houses scattered throughout the county, and their numbers, even today, serve as a reminder of the once pre-eminent position of the county as the world-centre of metalliferous mining."

The late 1860's saw the catastrophic collapse of copper-

G

mining in Cornwall; and by 1880 hardly forty thousand tons of copper were raised, a mere quarter of the output of a few years before.[16] In the two years, 1865-67, some six hundred men emigrated from the three districts of St. Austell, Helston and St. Just; on average they left behind them a family of wife and three children, to whom their remittances could be but irregular at first. Public relief had to step in: in St. Austell and Redruth it increased by 50 per cent in those years, in Helston and Penzance-St. Just by 100 per cent. But by 1869 Camborne men in California and Nevada were faithfully sending home some £15,000 to £18,000 a year—the combined monthly wage of a score of mines then working. Soon, there were as many Cornishmen at work in Johannesburg and Butte as in Redruth and St. Just. While, by the late 1870's "there were more Cornishmen working at Calumet and Hecla mines in Michigan than there were at any other copper mine in the world."

Jutting out into Lake Superior from the Upper Peninsula of Michigan is the Keweenaw Peninsula, with the Ontonagon River as its base on the west, the deep indentation of L'Anse Bay on the east. Half way up it is cut in two by Portage Lake, with its outlet on either side—that on the west deepened by ship canal—into Lake Superior, with its communications with the outside world through the Sault Sainte Marie channel. The inlet from Portage Lake runs between the twin towns of Houghton and Hancock (which is dominated by famous Quincy Mine, "Old Reliable," now dead) like a river: in early days crossed by canoe and ferry, then by a bridge, today by a big suspension bridge. Here is the base, running up to Copper Harbor at its tip, of what was the richest copper country in its time. Further south, where the peninsula broadens out between Lake Superior and Lake Michigan, are the great iron-ranges, Menominee and Gogebic, also among the richest in the world, the United States' chief source of iron ore up until quite recently. This is the country to which the Cornish miners came in their thousands; many thousands of their descendants are all through it today, and wider afield in Michigan, particularly in its metropolis, Detroit.

The Keweenaw Peninsula is singularly beautiful—not unlike another Cornwall, far away from home; and the Cornish became attached to it, regarded it as a second home. As one stands in the derelict mining waste of Quincy, on the high ground above Hancock looking out over Portage Lake, it might be the mining landscape of Camborne and Redruth: the old people must have felt it not unfamiliar. The chief contrast is that this is forest country, and now that the mines have mostly closed down, the forest is recovering its hold: in the fall the vegetation is all colors, ruby and wine-colored, cherry, peach, strawberry, purple-grape of sumach, many varieties of green. Then, in the ferocious winters, it is all white. The miners were warm enough underground.

Today, as one stands in one of their cemeteries—the little country graveyard at Eagle Harbor—one remembers them. Trampling down the dry autumn bracken—maples in flame, wind in the pines above, and over all the noise of Lake Superior washing in on the reef—one reads the names on the headstones. Half of them are Cornish: Job, Rosewarne, Opie, Martin, Bawden, Kellow, Cocking, Richards, Saunders, Barrett, Rule, Sampson, Williams, Paull, Nicholls, Uren, Trethewey. One is struck by the youth at which they died: young couples in their twenties, many children—such were the hardships of those early years, the fierce winters. Then, too, there was the toll of the mines. "Sacred to the memory of William Roberts, who came to his death while performing his daily labor in the Amalgamated Mine, May 18, 1864. Aged 28 years." Or there are two Berryman brothers, Thomas and John, aged twenty-seven and twenty-nine, "both killed in Central Mine, April 29, 1872. They fought the fight." The headstone has the chain symbol of the Oddfellows upon it. Then there is one tough old Cornishwoman who lived through almost the whole story: Harriet Uren, born in 1808, died in 1909.

Douglass Houghton, the state geologist who first surveyed

this fascinating country—himself drowned off Eagle River in 1845—observed the close similarity between the copper deposits of Cornwall and Michigan, the main difference being that in Michigan there were solid blocks and bunches of native copper, immensely rich, but difficult to prise out. It was here that the tried skills and tools, the methods and techniques, that the Cornish brought in were invaluable. "If there is a difficult shaft to be sunk or a tunnel to be driven in hard or dangerous ground," a state official reported, "as a general thing it is Cornish miners who are the men to do it."* A Michigan Commissioner of Mineral Statistics concluded that in the days before mining became an engineering science the traditional Cornish methods were best, and long experience gave them great success. "Yet they also perfected new mining machinery and techniques, and in the 1880's their sons were among the first graduates from the new Michigan College of Mines"—now the Technological University at Houghton.

They brought not only their skills, but their individual contracting system of work, by which a couple or more miners would contract to shift so much material on a percentage basis. This was customary at home: it put a premium on the best workers, and it appealed to the gambling instinct, though the game had its downs as well as ups, and the men were sometimes hard put to it to subsist. Above all, it appealed to Cornish individualism and meant that they had little interest in strikes or collective action. The strikers on the Marquette iron-range in 1874 were Scandinavians: the Cornish would not join them. The big copper strike of 1914 was of unskilled miners—Finns, Slavs, Italians; the Cornish were skilled workers, foremen, bosses, mining captains, to whom the unskilled objected.[17] It was natural that they should move up the ladder, since they had the skill: "as foremen, mining captains and inspectors, though seldom as owners, they long

---

* R. T. Berthoff, *British Immigrants in Industrial America*, 60. This excellent book is the only one on the subject to deal with the Cornish separately among other immigrants from the British Isles.

dominated the pits."[18] After a strike of 1895, when conditions of skilled miners became unsatisfactory, the skilled Cornish moved off to the Rand in South Africa, and the Italians and Slavs poured in.

Notice that the Cornish did not make the fortunes—they were "seldom owners": the mining fortunes were made notably by New England promoters and investors, particularly in Boston. No doubt they contributed to the *rentier* affluence of the Miss Olivia Chancellors of *The Bostonians*.

In 1842 by a treaty with the United States the Indians ceded their land—or they were jockeyed out of it in the usual manner: the land lay open to exploitation.[19] By 1844 there were two companies operating, with a little stamp-mill at Eagle River; already some twenty Cornishmen were on the spot. Next year 25,000 lb. of copper were produced. In 1847 Horace Greeley—"Go West, young man!"—visited the peninsula and publicized it in his letters to the *New York Tribune*. A rush to upper Michigan followed in the late forties and fifties—something comparable to that to California. Except that there was no Bret Harte or Mark Twain to write it up. Longfellow's interest—like Parkman's with the *Oregon Trail*—was with the Indians, and the country in fact provided the background, the legends and the folklore of *Hiawatha*.

In the 1850's the rush was on, with the usual accompaniments to life in a pioneer community of men in virgin forest: the clatter of hammers and axes, the shouts of teamsters and stevedores, blasting in the echoing hills. Boarding houses sprang up, beds unmade, men sleeping in them in three shifts around the clock; saloons with their drinking and fist-fights, the hard life of miners away from their women. "The pioneers were a wild and hardy lot, but honest and neighborly."[20] Manners improved when the women came over, and settled family life began.

By now the Irish were coming in, and there were some famous fracases between the Cornish and them. At Front Run, some twenty miles up from the mouth of the Ontonagon

River, Henry Hocking had his saloon bar; Patrick Dolan came in and put up his on Hocking's claim. Hocking bided his time, until Dolan went down to the mouth, then took his axe and knocked the Irishman's shanty down. Dolan came back one January night in 1854 with his friends, built a fire and proceeded to re-erect the cabin. Hocking went out to face them and forbade them to build on his land. Dolan braved him with "If you think this land is yours, why don't you take the legal course?" There was no legal course. Hocking pulled a pistol from under his red flannel and shot him dead; he then faced the others: "I have but one life and I will sell it dearly."[21]

One April Sunday morning in 1857, at Rockland, Richard Kestle was in a fight with two Irishmen, when a fellow Cousin Jack told him not to strike as there were only two of them! One of the Irishmen drew a long knife. Another came up with an axe and felled a Cornish fellow called Terrell, practically severing his back. Terrell was taken into Thomas's bar-room —a Cornish saloon—where he bled to death. At that the Cornish went wild: several score of them gathered and surrounded Ryan's grocery. They smashed the windows and set fire to the building; Ryan leaped from the roof and disappeared into the wilderness—forever. The Cornish thereupon drove the Irish out of Rockland. At Portage Lake four hundred Irish swore revenge and set out for Rockland, where the outnumbered population took refuge on the steamer *Illinois*. But the Irish never turned up; something had distracted their attention: they fell to drinking on the way.

After these exploits of *l'homme moyen sensuel*, let us turn to more solid achievements.

From producing a mere 25,000 lb. of copper in 1845, Michigan produced 14 million in 1865; and in 1895, half a century from the beginning, 130 million.[22] The peak was reached in 1909—the year of old Harriet Uren's demise— with nearly 230 million.[23] The catastrophic decline came twenty years later with the great depression of 1929. Today, except for the most famous mine of all, the Calumet and Hecla combine, the place is even more derelict than the area around Camborne and Redruth: a shadow of what it once was, the forest closing in, mining villages empty, the miners' houses falling down, a few old people creeping about them; the haunts of the former folk given over to ghosts and memories.

From the beginning the mines depended on Cornishmen for their mine captains, bosses, shift-managers, foremen, as well as in earlier days for the miners. Let us take a few examples out of a great many. Captain John Hoar, born in Cornwall in 1817, after a few years in Ireland and Germany engaged himself in 1846 to open a mine on Keweenaw.[24] When he landed at Copper Harbor in July—that beautiful bay sheltered behind its reef—there were only three families on the whole point. (At Copper Harbor today the manager of the country store is a Cousin Jack, whose father arrived by ship from New Jersey into Eagle Harbor, where all the people came out to the ship for provisions.) John Hoar in his day found no accommodation, and returned to the boat to sleep. Thence he made his way further down the peninsula to open up the Boston Mine. Not satisfied with prospects he took two years off, coal-mining in Pennsylvania. He returned to be put in charge of pumps and underground work at North-West Mine, then became captain of the Cape Mining Company. In 1859 he retired from mining to open a business in Houghton and contracted to build the first tramway, from Isle Royale Mine to the stamp-mill on Portage Lake. His brother Richard emigrated to Canada in 1854, then came over to form a partnership with John. Richard purchased the steamship, *Ivanhoe*, and organized the Overland Transportation Company, a winter line, employing over a hundred teams, travelling three stages a day each way, the freight largely copper for export. This younger brother served in most of the community's public offices and as a member of the Michigan legislature; he ended up Vice President of the Mineral Range Railroad, and with a family of six.

Let us look at the Edwards family. Richard Edwards was born in 1809, and emigrated to Brooklyn in 1849.[25] In 1850 he came on to take charge of the Eagle River Mines; in 1853 he took over the Albion Mines at Houghton. Next year he built a sawmill and, considerably invested in mineral lands and stock in Calumet, was able to retire. In association with his second son he held some twenty thousand acres in the peninsula. We are told that, "having acquired considerable wealth, he died lamented by the whole community."[26] We shall hear of him again later.[27] His eldest son, Joe, began as a miner and in 1860 went as agent to the North Carolina Consol Mines. On the outbreak of the Civil War he went to California, mining in Grass Valley before crossing the high Sierra to Virginia City, Nevada. He came back to Lake Superior to the family sawmill, running a steamer, and went off mining for a couple of years in South Dakota before settling down in Houghton to various public offices. James, another son, was educated at Ann Arbor; a civil engineer he was chiefly instrumental in building the bridge across the inlet between Houghton and Hancock, and was the largest stockholder in it. A third son was president of the Bridge Company, had a half share in the sawmill and in the good steamer, *Ivanhoe*. He was president of the Wolverine and other mines in the Black Hills of Dakota and, comfortably invested in copper, was able to sustain the burdens of office as supervisor and chairman of the board of Houghton County for several years. Captain Buzza, after mining in Ireland, came to the mines of New Jersey and Pennsylvania, but removed to Lake Superior as agent for Ridge Mine and various others.[28] He had good literary and statistical attainments, was a regular correspondent of the London *Mining Journal*, and ended as treasurer of Ontonagon County. Captain Richard Uren was secretary and treasurer of Lake Superior Native Copper Works.[29] He emigrated at sixteen, became a mining captain, and entered into a partnership with Dunstan and Blight to exploit a safety fuse he invented at Eagle River. In 1868 he went to California to establish a safety fuse factory. He returned in 1872 to lease the Pewabic and Franklin mines, and then became agent for the Madison Mine. Three years later he had a spell of gold-mining in the Black Hills of Dakota, but came back to Lake Superior. Captain Josiah Hall, of Pewabic Mine, was the inventor of the dumping skip which came into general use: he first introduced it at North American Mine.

The Honorable William Harris was one of the pioneers of 1846.[30] He first investigated the Canadian shore of the lake and then opened up the Bruce Mine. From 1850 to 1864 he was a mining captain of the Minnesota Mining Company, and from 1864 to 1872 its agent, then the most prosperous in the region. It was while he was captain that his men discovered, in 1857, the immense five hundred ton mass of native copper, that took twenty months to cut up, starting with forty men. It was said to be the largest mass ever taken out in the history of copper-mining: it would have loaded two good trains of trucks. Harris took charge of the Allouez Mine for three years. In 1860 he had already started a business as a side-line, and now branched out into several stores, a dock and warehouse. He occupied various offices, and served from 1871–75 in the Michigan legislature. An Illogan man, married in Cornwall, if he had remained there would he have ended up as an Hon?

The same holds good for the Honorable Thomas B. Dunstan in the second generation. Born at Camborne in 1850, he was the only son of a mining captain and given a good education at the University of Michigan.[31] Becoming a lawyer, he was elected a judge of probate; thence he became a Republican state legislator, next state senator and ended as lieutenant-governor of Michigan. Possessed of large mining and banking interests, when he died in 1902 "it was a day of deep mourning in the city of Hancock." One sees him in his Victorian frock-coat, a fine-looking fellow with full beard and serious stare. Another probate judge was William Lean, who was brought up as a miner and became a captain before leaving home in 1855. After mining five years in Ontonagon he was elected probate judge for the county. He had eighteen children—the eldest son killed in a mine at Ontonagon, the eldest daughter drowned, falling from a steamer into the Mississippi near St. Louis. But how prolific these families were!

From 1846 the Cliff Mine was the first to give a good yield.[32] Then it was surpassed by Central Mine, which produced richly for the next forty years, until it closed in 1898. From 1860 Quincy became profitable, and remained so up to the depression of the 1930's. Captain John Cliff, who emigrated in 1854 and spent the summer of 1858 surveying the Apostle Islands, joined the Quincy Company next year, and after many years' experience ended as captain, and the company's leading man. Captain William Stephens was a captain of Quincy for four years; he then went to become head of the Hecla branch while William Daniell was captain of the Calumet branch of the combine. This great concern produced over 100 million lb. of copper by 1906, exceeded only by Anaconda, which had taken first place before the end of the nineteenth century.

The most remarkable story of achievement comes here, and is that of Captain John Daniell of Laurium.[33] He was born in 1839, and at twenty-four went to California for a couple of years. Coming to the Upper Peninsula, he became captain of Osceola Mine and later general manager for the syndicate. He advised the purchase of the Boston and Montana group of mines at Butte, Montana, which became a good producer and he was mainly responsible for the construction of the copper smelting works at Dollar Bay. He was already a very experienced man, and a sharply observant mind, when he noticed that the regular dip of the Calumet Lode at an angle of 37½ degrees indicated that ore should be found outside the property's western boundary. But the Calumet people would not listen or extend their boundary.

After several years of planning and calculation, he got his own directors, of Osceola, to buy the land. Sinking the shaft would be a very expensive operation: he calculated that it would need a vertical shaft of 2260 feet to intersect the dipping Calumet Lode. The money was raised, but at the end of three years the lode was still not reached. Doubts began to circulate about the project and about its projector's judgment and even sanity. Daniell had to go to Boston to raise more money to complete the shaft. Fortunately the syndicate backed their man, for, shortly after—after three and a half years' work—the shaft cut the lode only ten feet lower than Daniell had calculated. The Tamarack Mine soon became a rich producer; it was ultimately, in 1917, bought by Calumet and Hecla, by which time it had produced nearly 400 million lb. of copper and a record of large dividends—a pretty price to pay for not listening to Daniell's advice. But the strain of it all had been too much for his mind: "his genius was not properly appreciated until a short time before his death, which was brought about by a disease of the brain by his incessant mental labors . . . He was regarded as half cracked by the majority of people, but lived to see the verification of his every prediction and the opening of one of the great mines of the world along his plans." Starting with nothing, he ended with a considerable fortune, and a mental breakdown. He had married a Cornish girl at Copper Falls, daughter of Captain William Edwards, and had eight children.

After Daniell's breakdown Tamarack Mine was captained by William Parnall, who had left Cornwall after some poaching escapade. He spent two years mining in the South, then came to the Upper Peninsula, where he won renown as a wrestler, especially after knocking out some notorious local bully. Captain John Chynoweth persuaded the rising young fellow to study, which he did lying in his bunk with his candle stuck in his miner's helmet. From being captain at the smaller Franklin Mine, he became assistant superintendent at Tamarack in 1890, and died its captain in 1903. Two of his sons were in the first class graduated at the Michigan College of Mines.

I have cited only a handful out of the scores—or possibly hundreds—of mining captains who made and worked the copper-mines of Michigan, and said little of the thousands of miners who dug the rock, sank the shafts and extracted the ore. They came to this new country to make their living, from the poverty of the old. "Who can say what England owes to these men? They produced riches and scarcely enjoy common necessaries themselves."[34] A leading mining authority tells us of the third generation: "the day of the old Cornishman has gone; his place has been taken by sons that are native Americans; and these, although better educated, lack the distinctive character of their fathers . . . Nevertheless, when technically educated men, Americans—whatever their fathers were—had the management of the mines, in 1904, I found the underground work still in charge of a Cornishman in every mine that I visited."[35]

It is time to turn to the iron-mines, where the Cornish contribution was second only to that in copper.

By the dramatic deflection of the needle of Burt's magnetic compass in 1845—he was assistant surveyor to Douglass Houghton—the immense iron-ranges of the Upper Peninsula were discovered. These were located in three districts: the Gogebic range at the southwestern end of the Keweenaw Peninsula; the Marquette and Menominee ranges to the east and southeast. In each of these the Cornish are still strongly represented today: in the first at Ironwood; in the second, at Ishpeming and Negaunee, which were dominantly Cornish mining townships, and now to a lesser extent in the local capital of Marquette; in the third, at Iron Mountain. But they are also scattered, in varying degrees, all through Michigan, with a notable concentration in Detroit.

The pioneer Jackson Mining Company was formed in 1845. "Today a pyramid of rock and ore marks the site of the first iron mine in Michigan."³⁶ Others shortly followed: a second company started operations at Ishpeming.³⁷ A plank road was built over the steep gradients from Ishpeming to Marquette, where soon an iron-loading dock was built out into the lake. The Menominee range was discovered in the 1860's and developed in the 1870's, with the advantage of railways. With the iron-boom of the 1880's the Gogebic range came into production, at the southwestern base of the peninsula, where the Ironwood mines were located. In 1869 production had been a quarter of a million tons, by 1909 it was 13 million tons—first in the nation until latterly surpassed by Minnesota.

Plenty of work for the Cornish pouring in, in greatly increased numbers from the later 1860's. In Menominee County, at the southeastern end of the peninsula, Iron Mountain grew from a mining camp of 150 people to a town of 8000, incorporated as a municipality in 1887.³⁸ William Bice was one of the first settlers, who did a lot of prospecting and made some rich discoveries of lodes: he became captain of Ludington Mine.³⁹ William Bray was captain of the Hewett Mine: he had emigrated at twelve to Vermont, then went to the Carolinas for a few years. He moved back and forth between South Carolina, Michigan, Illinois, Missouri, Duluth, Ontonagon—wherever prospects beckoned—until he settled at Iron Mountain. The Hewett Mine, which he opened up, was one of his finds. The celebrated Chapin Mine was opened in 1878 and Thomas Rundle became its captain. He had begun mining at nine and left home in 1856; he was ten years in Ontonagon, twelve years in Marquette County, in charge of various mines, before coming to Iron Mountain. Among its earliest citizens we find Vivian Chellew, a Hosking, Rule, Robbins, Hambly, Alderman Hancock, and William Andrew was clothier and furnisher. At the beginning the gospel was preached by a Cornish miner in the dining room of Hambly's boarding house: he was shortly after killed for his pains in the first accident in Chapin Mine. At Quinnesec the Vivian Mine was at first put in charge of a Curnow from Milwaukee, but it turned out an irregular producer. William Pengilly came from the Cornish community in Milwaukee to become treasurer of Menominee County.[40] Of the captains in the iron-mines, Peter Pascoe was captain of the Republic Iron Mining Company.[41] William Trestrail became inspector of mines for Dickinson County.[42] His father was a stonemason of Redruth who went mining in Cuba, returned to Cornwall, then emigrated to the peninsula, where he helped to build the first highway from Hancock to Keweenaw Point. He spent a couple of years in California, then came back to work in Hecla Mine, transferred to Chapin Mine, and died at forty-six. Young William had been in California with his father, where his uncle was farming. The boy returned to work in Hecla and at Iron Mountain, then set off gold-mining in Dakota and Colorado. He returned to Chapin Mine, until he was appointed a mine-inspector—he had certainly garnered a wide experience.

Captain Thomas Stevens of Ironwood, on the other coast from Iron Mountain, was captain of the Pabst Mine.[43] He was born at Leedstown in 1850, where his father worked in the mines at famous Godolphin—the wife's father was killed in a mine in Cuba. (The Pascoe-Grenfell firm was heavily invested in Cuban mining.) Of five children three came to America, one went to South Africa. Young Tom worked at a mine from eight and a half, and at nineteen went to work at Abercarn in Monmouthshire—the most dangerous mine in Wales from ever-present fire-damp. Tom realized the danger in which he worked and, after a few months, emigrated. Three years later the entire working force was killed in one of the worst explosions in mining history—282 miners, including two of Tom's uncles and two cousins. He went to Scranton, Pennsylvania, then back to Cleator Moor for eleven years. He returned to the United States to work in Alabama and Massachusetts, until 1888 when he came to Iron Mountain. He worked thirteen years as miner, shift boss, timber foreman—the usual steps up the ladder—until he was made a captain in 1902.

From these outlines we can see the regular patterns of their lives. So far we have concentrated on mining, but the Cornish played their part in many other activities in the community they helped so largely to form. I like to think of Stephen Cocking, keeper of the Main Light at Eagle Harbor for years, and Peter Treleaven, one of those for whom Stephen kept the light: for Peter sailed the Great Lakes as marine engineer for thirty-five years.[44] Stephen Cocking, the light-house man, had served throughout the Civil War—he enlisted as brigade bugler in the 23rd Michigan Volunteers. There is the characteristic Cornish interest in brass bands, which they took with them wherever they went. Keeper of the light station at Copper Harbor was William Tresize; he had come with his parents to Pennsylvania, thence to Wisconsin and Keweenaw. He worked in the mines till 1862, when he enlisted in the 27th Michigan Volunteers and was wounded before Petersburg. On receiving his discharge he went to Colorado for a year, thence to New Mexico, Arizona and California, before returning to Keweenaw to keep the light at Copper Harbor.

Later on, we shall observe a regular rhythm in the excellent dairy-farming country of Wisconsin, of lead-miners moving off to California for a spell of gold-mining, and coming back to invest the proceeds in a farm. The rocky Upper Peninsula offered no such extended opportunities. But we find Thomas Trevethan a large farmer near Chassell.[45] His father was a mining captain who left Perran with wife and four children in 1841—among the earliest to come. They sailed to Quebec and had a six weeks' journey up the St. Lawrence and the Great Lakes to Chicago; thence 160 miles by team to Galena on the Fever River to work in the lead-mines. The father came to the Copper Country when it was a pathless wilderness, surveying for mines for the Gratiot Company till 1850. He spent most of his life thus before retiring to his former home at Shullsburg. Of his six children by a Padstow girl, three went to California, two others to Iowa and Minnesota. Young Thomas began work at the Cliff Mine at twelve, then kept the store at Eagle Harbor. He built the first stamp-mill that shipped stamp-copper out of Portage Lake—it used at first to be loaded on flat boats and taken out to deep water. By 1877 he was able to purchase four hundred acres of good land at Chassell, half of it in cultivation. A large farmer, he was able to fill public office as alderman at Houghton; as several of these Cornish fellows mention about themselves, he formed one of the new middle-westerners who gave solid support to Abraham Lincoln's brand of Republicanism.

Other Cornish folk had other jobs. Take the little township of Red Jacket, at first "a mere hamlet in the woods." Richard Burge kept the Commercial Hotel, which in time came to accommodate, if somewhat tightly, thirty-five guests. The Holmans had the grocery store. George Jacka had prospered as a timber contractor for Calumet and Hecla, and ended with a fine farm of 380 acres, 100 acres of it under cultivation. A kinsman manufactured harness—he had served his apprenticeship in Cornwall. William Tonkin, from St. Agnes, was elected village marshal and deputy sheriff to keep order in the nursery.

From these simple bases they spread out in the next generation. The father of Edward Rawlings Penberthy came to Montreal in 1840, where he died, leaving a widow with six children.[46] They came on to Cliff Mine, where the sons worked; son Edward taught school, however, learned accountancy and became a merchant. His son, Grover Cleveland Penberthy—one sees that the father was, *par exception*, a Democrat—became the leading surgeon in Houghton, with a long and distinguished career. A family of Pascoes made their impression on the life of Detroit. William Pascoe was a successful portrait painter there, though he travelled a good deal, dividing his time between the United States and Europe.[47] His brother, Edward, was a leading real-estate merchant of the city and headed a firm, with his sons, that took a large part in the development of Detroit eastwards. Of his twelve children, Richard achieved fame with the immensely popular (and immensely sentimental) Edwardian ditties he wrote for the famous tenor, John McCormick. In the rapid development of Detroit perhaps it is the less surprising that the leading architect, who built many of its large buildings, and some of those at Ann Arbor, was H. M. Maxwell Grylls.* Born in 1865, of an old Cornish family which had come down in the world, he emigrated in 1881. The firm he founded was named Smith, Hinchman and Grylls. Grylls had won the public competition for the County Hall; the firm put up the Penobscot Building, then the highest in the city. Perhaps its best claim to fame is that an architect of genius, Yamasaki, worked with them as a young man.

Nor is it surprising that today Detroit has such a large Cornish population, while other Michigan cities—such as Lansing and Grand Rapids—have considerable elements. In addition to the drift into the cities of the older country folk, there has been the continuing immigration into the automobile capital of America. Detroit's Cornish population is so large that it is possible to give only the merest sample of it. To take the Pascoe families listed in the telephone directory: North Detroit has fifteen, and one Pasco; East Detroit has eleven, and three Pasco; West has six. The Cornish are thickest in North Detroit, where there are fifteen Goldsworthy families, twelve Nancarrow, eight Polkinghorne (some without an e), ten Uren (and one in the silly form of U'Ren), eight Trerice, eight Tonkin, six Chenoweth, who would be earlier over here, and six Chynoweth, more recent, six Rosevear, four Angove (and one under the meaningless form, Angrove), no less than fifteen Vivian, seven Tippett (and two Tippitt), nine Opie, four Trevillian, five Trevarrow, with one

---

* C. M. and M. A. Burton, ed., *Hist. of Wayne County and the City of Detroit*, V, 576. It should be possible to learn more of this man: he would be worth an article.

Trevorrow. Out of these hundreds, let us pick out a few of the rarer names represented: Penhalligon, Reseigh, Rodda, Trewern, Whear (for Wheare), Faull, Pedrick (for Petherick), Edyvean, Dungey, Chellew, Carnwath, Pedlar, Bosanko, Colenso (seven families), Pendray, Kellow, Chenhalls. It is much the same story with West Detroit, where we find nine Angove, five Chynoweth (and one Chenoweth), four Penhale, three Nankervis, eight Santo, seven Jose, ten Rickard; among rarer names, Gummoe, Reseigh, Ivey, Rodda, Carne, Spargo, Pellow, Polglase, Trevail, Treweek, Grenfell. In East Detroit the Cornish are less numerous, but we find five Curnow families, five Chynoweth, five Ede, four Trudgeon; and among rarer names, a Lanyon, Chegwidden, Tamblin, Pellow, Jose, Esterbrooks (for Easterbrook), Grenville, Penprase.

There is no point in going into any further detail: the point is made.

In an area where the Cornish population is so large it is impossible, within the confines of this book, to analyze it in detail. But one general point of importance we may make: in an area like this English names that are commonest among Cornish people belong, it is fairly safe to assume, to people of Cornish descent. Such names as Santo and Jose, in this area, will denote Cornish folk, not people of Spanish descent as in California and the Southwest. It is pleasant to notice that many of the names of the earlier mine captains are represented and have increased: Chynoweth, Bawden, Hoar, Vivian, Trevorrow, Uren, Edwards, Dunstan, Goldsworthy, Gribble. At Houghton and Hancock there are no less than eight Dunstan families, four Edwards, three Uren, two Chynoweth, two Pascoe, one Bice; while at Calumet there are four Chynoweth, three Gribble, one Hoar, one Bawden, one Trevethan. At Marquette we find two Uren, one Buzzo, one Rickard (and one Rickerd); at Iron Mountain no less than ten Uren, two Trestrail and one Pascoe; at Ishpeming six

The First Wave of Miners: Michigan 183

Pascoe; at Negaunee no less than ten Pascoe, and one Blight; at Ironwood four Gribble, one Pascoe. These families will not all descend from the earlier mine captains; on the other hand, these are by no means the only captains' names represented.

Apart from these two general considerations we must confine ourselves to individual points that strike our attention.

Let us consider the Copper Country first. At Houghton and Hancock we find three Masters families—and Job and Jane Masters were among the very first to arrive in 1843-44. Among the rarer names are six Moyle entries, of that interesting old family much to the fore in Utah; four Combellack and five Verran—an infrequent West and East Cornish name respectively; four Nettel (or Nettle). There are four Vial families—its historic form was Vyell: there is a fine painted slate-tomb of this family of gentry in the church of St. Breock. There is only one Vial (with another Vials) listed in all Cornwall today. We find three Carne entries, one Chegwidden, five Congdon, one Eva, one Pethick, one Pelmear (for Polmear), one Jose, and one Colestock (a rarity: perhaps for Calestick). Among the more numerous names are Opie (seven), Coon and Hocking (six each), Spear (five), Harry, Cornish, Trevethan, Trudgeon (four each), Hosking and Snell (three each). There is the usual spread of Tre-, Pol-, Pen- names, and it is good to think that a Berryman family has survived. At Calumet the most striking thing is to find eight families of an exceedingly rare name, Rosemergy: there is only one, in the form Rosemurgey, listed for all Cornwall. There are four Vivian entries, three Yeo, three Sincock, three Lobb. Among rarer names these: Penhallegon, Hendra, Penpraze, Polglase, Ivey, Trezona, Verran, Wearne, Roskilly and one Roskelly.

Turning to the Iron Country, south of the Copper, let us notice again only what is striking. At Marquette there are four Britton families, one with a bulldozing firm. In Cornwall this name means that these people originally were Bretons, who had come across from Brittany. Most numerous of the specific names are Libby and Sleeman (five each), Carlyon, Chubb,

Menhennick, Kimber, (four each), Luke, Lutey, Goldsworthy, Pellow, Trevillion (three each), Hawke, Inch, Lowry, Penglase, Pelmear, Yelland. The great bulk of Cornish people will be found here, as elsewhere, with common English names.

At Ishpeming we find a tribe of Argalls—no less than fifteen families. This is a rare Truro name—the obstreperous Sir Samuel Argall of early Jamestown was a Cornishman. Hardly less interesting is that there are six of the uncommon West Cornish name, Boase. There are three entries under the rare name, Dowrick—which means "watery place": hardly more in Cornwall. We find four Cowling and four Grenfell, three Carlyon, three Polkinghorne, three Pellow, two Rule, two Nankervis, two Kitto, one Rodda, one Rashleigh. No less than seven Snell, six Pascoe, four Grenfell—still most of the Cornish will have such names as Jacobs, Perry, Pope, Prisk, Pryor, Rowe, and Simons.

The same holds good for Negaunee, as indeed everywhere. Rarer names that strike one here are Borlace (no less than six), Veale and Stanaway (five each), Cory (four), Verran, Vercoe, Yelland and Annear (two each), Blewett, Blight, Viant. There are no less than six Trewhella, and ten Pascoe—but we appreciate now that this is one of the commonest of Cornish names in America. Iron Mountain has eleven Hosking, ten Uren, five Grenfels, five Rouse, three Sandercock. Among rarer names, two Colenso, one Dawe, one Rodda, two Tregillis, which probably represents the proper pronunciation of Tregellas, the usual spelling. Ironwood on the western side has a considerable Cornish population, second to the Finns; when one comes across a name like Hjalmer Hill, one sees that there has been some intermarraige.

Let us return to the more endearing early days.

The early folk brought everything with them, their customs and folk-lore, their dialect and mining terms along with the techniques, their religion. At Calumet the Methodist Church was first organized in 1867; among its trustees were William Hambly, S. B. Harris, J. Vivian, Thomas Buzza, James Pascoe, Joshua James, Richard Noell (for Noall), John Allen—all Cornishmen.[48] At Central, south of Copper Falls, the first Methodist Church was built in 1868; it had a membership of sixty then, under the care of the Reverend R. Nichols.[49] At Republic or Iron City, the first Methodist society had Alfred James for preacher—plenty of Cornish folk in that mining community to hear him. The community at Allouez—where Ned Rescorla was the first captain of the mine—had their Methodist Church, as most of them came to have. Among the pioneer preachers was Solomon Minear, who took charge of the Detroit Methodist circuit, which embraced all that was then settled of Michigan.

Their vivacious and revivalistic religion was not incompatible with other entertainments, though it provided plenty of enjoyments of its own. There is an authentic story of a miner, at the end of his week's work (and perhaps at the end of his tether), going into Hancock to shack up with a well-known woman of the town. Meeting with a fellow-miner, his mate asked him what he was up to; and, being told, noticed that he was equipped with a Bible under his arm. What was that for? "Well, you see, if she be as good as they say, I may stop awver Sunday."

Chapel provided plenty of fun, as at home, with their choirs and their tea-treats for the children. Christmas day was always taken off from work in the mine, as in Cornwall. Then there were the clubs. Cornishmen were members of the Sons of St. George, in the Upper Peninsula, or else Oddfellows—and at odds with the Molly Maguires. Much more rarely were they Masons, though the first lodge at Eagle River was founded by two Retallacks and a Ham; it had a Vivian and a Harris among its first wardens. Further afield there were the Cornish societies in New York, Chicago, Detroit, Boston, earlier this century, that held their reunions, playing the old children's games, "Kissing Ring, French Tig and Jolly Miller," and in the winter banqueted on "kiddley broth, marinated pilchards, fermades [furmity], limpets, turmut [turnip], taatie [potato], lickey [leek], gurty-mait, hogs pudding, stanning pie, saffron cake, figgy hobbin, junket and cream."[50] This list of favorite Cornish dishes inexplicably omits pasties and several others—squab pie, for example. Even today, at deserted Central Mine in the peninsula—the success of which was first due to Captain Dunstan—the old people return every year for a Sunday reunion in July—sometimes "more than a hundred of the old faithful. Religious services, picnics, renewing old friendships are the fare. It is like the huge, boisterous family Sunday picnics of a few generations ago."[51]

In the mines Cornish terminology prevailed. The superintendent, in American usage, was always the "captain," and the term "royalty" was used for mineral leases even in the United States. A surface boss was a "grass captain"; a bucket was a "kibble," the mouth of the shaft a "collar." A "whim" was a capstan for pulling up ore; a mine that was "hungry" was poor in ore; a "sump" was a depression where ore collected; a "braave keenly lode" was a promising lode; "gob" or "deads" meant waste rock; "gad" was a steel wedge; "jig," a vibrating machine for crushing ore; "tut-work" was contract work. And so on: many of these terms and more I have heard in the Cornwall of my childhood.

It was the distinctive Cornish dialect that most struck Americans, for, of course, these simple folk were illiterate—hardly any of the first two generations would have been to school.[52] Their speech betrayed a wonderful mix-up of personal pronouns after prepositions—such as one can still hear in out-of-the-way places in Cornwall: "Us don't belong to she," for example. Or a mother instructing a child to put the dinner on: "Your fayther is comin': tell she to 'eave 'ee on." Somehow the nominative "she" is more emphatic to a Cornish ear: I feel it in my bones myself. Correct speech is less forceful.

It is the forceful individuality of the Cornish temperament, even in the third and fourth generation, that so strikes a practiced observer in the Upper Peninsula. Robert Traver, in his novel *Laughing Whitefish*, is familiar with the local names and the characteristic temperament. "I stood watching these men, fascinated by their swift pulsing talk and animal vitality. Cornishmen might also be Englishmen, I reflected [in fact they are not: British, but not English], but there was a distinctly different quality in their lack of restraint, in the way they seemed compelled to act everything out . . . Even the idlest bit of conversation was apt to bring on a full-dress drama: eager noddings of the head, shruggings of the shoulders, thumbs suddenly hooked this way or that . . . sudden digs in the listener's ribs."

The Cornish are as expressive as other Celts, to whom and with whom they belong.

From outside evidence—"Robert Traver" is the pen name of Judge Voelcker—let us narrow our focus down to the internal, to family records, the autobiographical. That will tell us something more subtle about the process of assimilation, about becoming good Americans while retaining an individual temperament, distinctive traditions and memories—an enrichment, not an impoverishment, of the contribution we have to make.

Donald S. Rickard, of Exeter School in New Hampshire, has been able to reconstruct a delightful portrait of his grandfather from the old mining captain's letter-books.[53] "When my brother Eric and I were little boys and our schoolmates boasted of being German or Irish or Yankee, we felt we had to be something too. We dared timidly to echo, at recess time one day, my father's assertion that we Rickards were *Cornish*. This statement was met by some derision and some curiosity which we were unable to satisfy, for we had no idea of what Cornish was . . . Gradually we learned more about this tribe, *our* tribe, but never were able to find anyone very interested or willing to be aware of its importance."

This would seem to indicate that there is a real need for this book: it should help people to be more aware of the Cornish in their midst.

It was not until 1950 that Mr. Rickard explored his grandfather's letter-books; he followed it up by going back to Cornwall, in the third generation, where he found his people awaiting him, his family not forgotten. His grandfather, R. H. Rickard, was the son of a mining captain, who had been put in charge of the first ship-load of miners to the Australian goldfields. There were twelve children and times were bad, so in 1847 young Rickard left home and worked in various mines—a lead-mine in New York, at Perkiomen in Pennsylvania—before coming to Keweenaw in 1850.

Young Rickard was rowed ashore at Eagle River "to join the life of a typical frontier community." He mined first at the Albion, where Captain Richard Edwards was his boss; but, the son of a mining captain, Rickard was not content to be a miner. Very early he purchased a preemption on a stretch of land ultimately taken over by the Copper Range Company; he became a mining agent and prospector, investing for himself. In 1858 he took the decisive step of opening an office in New York, going back every summer to Keweenaw to keep in touch with the mines whose affairs he dealt in. "He had a finger in every mining pie, serving as treasurer, president or transfer agent of several mines at a time, selling the stock of these, buying stock in others, advising investors, receiving daily confidential reports from agents and professional friends . . . Passing through New York every month were Cornish miners looking for work and bringing news of the Old Country." By 1864 he was able to make his first trip back home— he had already been able to put his relations there on to a good thing or two in the way of mining investments.

It was at this time that he missed the chance of becoming one of the richest men in mining and a dominating figure in the peninsula—through over-caution. A young civil engineer brought to Captain Dick Edwards a specimen of ore so rich that Edwards was willing to go all out on it, writing to Rickard that he would put up $30,000 himself if Rickard would invest a similar amount. Rickard knew that Captain Edwards drank a good deal and was liable to be unduly sanguine during his sprees. Rickard made the great refusal; Edwards had to turn the chance down. The young discoverer of the lode turned to Boston for capital. The lode turned out to be the famous Calumet Lode. It was not merely that Edwards and Rickard missed becoming millionaires but that Boston capital gained control of the peninsula and, with it, at that time the control of the copper market. The Cornishmen on the spot, who were doing the work, were resentful. But they had had their chance, and were not big enough to take it—they afterwards invested in a small way in the concern, and did moderately well out of it. That was all. There is something symbolic about that story.

In 1855 Rickard had married one of the two daughters of a Newquay man who had come to New York to seek his fortune, after the failure of his pilchard fishery at home. (The catastrophic decline of the pilchard fishery, on which Cornwall had so long relied, was another factor in her distress in the later nineteenth century.) The other daughter lived to be ninety-three, keeping alive the traditions of the old home. "She corresponded steadily with her brothers and sisters and cousins who had remained in Cornwall and she kept Cornwall always present to the minds of her children, feeding them saffron buns and clotted cream and telling them tales of the family horses, of the great hauls of pilchards and of St. Columb's beautiful old church-tower . . . She was a delight to us in her old age with her look of an aged Cornish pixie and her homely Cornish accent . . . In those last years she was as it were still picnicking at Bedruthan Steps, plying an oar with an old ferryman across the Gannel, racing on little bare feet from the headland to the port to set out in her father's boat to meet a school of pilchards."

One observes the intense family spirit that impelled these people to help each other across the Atlantic. When his father died, Rickard paid for the schooling of his brother John as a civil engineer at Devonport dockyard. John came to America, where he built the docks for the New York, Oswego and Midland Railway at Oswego, New York; after a promising start he died early of consumption. Another brother went to Australia, where, having too large a family too young, he made no success: his elder brother found a job for him in California, at the mercury mine at New Almadén, where there were plenty of Cousin Jacks. Another brother remained in Australia, "caring for nothing but drinking and fighting." That enters into the picture, too.

Rickard kept loyally in touch not only with his family but with old friends at home. A boyhood friend, John Pascoe, made a success of things in San Francisco, while Rickard's favorite cousin settled in British Columbia. His eldest son, a civil engineer, disappointed his father by opting for railroads in New York, instead of the mines in Keweenaw. In the year before he died Rickard and his wife paid a last visit to Cornwall, renewing cousinships and old acquaintance. Even today, Donald Rickard adjures his children in turn—the fourth generation—to visit Keweenaw, that other Cornwall, where his father was born: "the place belongs in a sense to you, through R. H. R. . . . Have a look at it, if only from the Windsor-Winnipeg plane at 23,000 feet. When Houghton and Hancock lie tiny far below your feet, its thumblike shape is perfectly revealed and you will think of that greater peninsula of the Land's End whose needy sons sought a home and fortune there. Or else . . . have a go at Cornwall itself. Your cousin Dorothy Chown, the liveliest and friendliest of relatives, still lives there in Madron near Penzance." He bids them listen to the sound of church-bells coming over the moor—that characteristic English sound, fainter now, like everything that made the old country what it was—as his grandmother thought she heard the bells of St. Columb Minor ringing to evensong when she lay dying in Connecticut.

•

The First Wave of Miners: Michigan 191

In the year in which the United States came into the Second World War, 1941, Newton G. Thomas published *The Long Winter Ends*, which is not only the best novel about the Cornish in America, but one of the most authentic expressions of the Cornish in literature.[54] If it had not been for the turmoils of the year of Pearl Harbor the book would have had a better chance of being remembered. Indeed it should not be forgotten: it deserves to be reprinted. The theme is that of the inner difficulty of adapting from the intensely felt experience of the little world of Cornwall to the extensive experience of the enormous world of America. It presents in microcosm, and at its most poignant in the first generation of illiterate newcomers, the theme of this book.

It begins with the familiar experience of a mine closing down in East Cornwall—Newton Thomas's father was a miner who had had to leave home. The captain bids the men who are going abroad farewell: "I know w'ere you are goin'. I 'ave been there. The country is different, mining is different, the way the people live is different; but the facts of life, the foundation facts, are the same." The culture of these simple folk is based on their Methodist chapel. It adds to the authenticity of Thomas's book that he understands this from the inside and with sympathy. He gets the dialect absolutely right, too, as only a Cornishman can, and knows from intimate observation such telltale details as the forward stoop of the miner's walk. At the good-bye service in chapel a woman touches Jim, who is leaving home, on the arm and says, "My boay Jan be awver there, somew'ere. If you see un, tell un Mother would like to 'ear from un." Many a time that heartbreaking question must have been put in the early days; but, of course, these fellows in the first generation often could neither read nor write.

That is only a part of Jim's problem coming to the New World. He has left behind him a newly-married wife. The mining he can stand up to: it was in his blood. "For generations his ancestors had picked and pried, mauled and shovelled, blasted their way by candlelight in the Cornish pits. The miners accepted their assignments as soldiers go into battle ... none refused his turn when asked to go. The captain did not need to give instructions, and he knew it. He did not urge them to work. That was what they were there for. He knew that no Cornishman worked for a boss. It was their binding code not to move a tool in the presence of one." Other observers of the Michigan scene have commented on their independence of spirit, the absence of complaints at their lot, no shirking of work—so unlike the rotting English of today.

Jim and his comrade are torn between the opportunities offered by the New World and the pull of home. As one says of their fellows to the other: "They've been transplanted, but 'aven't took root. So far, they awnly 'ave a job. That bayn't enough to give a man a feelin' for a place." The experience of rooting took time, and something more than time: constantly in their new life there were reminders that "their grief over the old home was not wholly assuaged." All this is very sensitively realized and depicted—as also that it was the chapel-services that most completely recapitulated their former lives. With the first line of the hymn "every Cornish *émigré* present was seeing the walls of his little home chapel. Wives sat beside most of them, and children around them. People long unthought of and all but forgotten appeared in the mist."

The miners had their pride in their skill, in that first generation, to sustain them. Actually, at home, they would not move into the clay-pits, for there was no skill in it: they would rather go abroad.

> But Cornishmen are like the turf:
> Cornishmen roam all the earth.

The poignancy lies in the fact that this people, driven over the face of the earth, are exceptionally rooted in their home and are drawn back to it again and again wherever they may be. "Try as he might, he could not banish a yearning, an affection for England, for Cornwall, for the roads and lanes and fields of one parish." His head was with the New World and what it offered, but his heart was with the Old.

On the other hand, in his own land he had been not much better than a pauper; here something better offered. Jim decides to take the first step, with great effort to learn to read and write—now he will be able to write to his wife, left alone at home as so many were. However, at school, "the schoolmaster doesn't know much about Cornwall. Few folks do. The Cousin Jacks themselves don't know much of anything about it." They had never been taught; they were totally uneducated.

Here, then, was the choice. He could feel "an inner response to the appeal of America that he had never felt when England was mentioned." Cornwall had the pull of the past, America was the future. I think that this was true for these Cornish folk: this was the inner argument of their lives. "There is a saying in the Bible, 'With a great sum obtained I this citizenship,'" said Jim to his mate, who replied: "But this one can be 'ad for the askin', an' I fancy 'e's the best the world 'ave t'offer."

There was no more than the truth.

The time came when Jim was able to bring his wife and child over, and build a home around them—in the Upper Peninsula where, someone says, the flavor of Cornwall will remain a long while after the Cornishman has ceased to be.

NOTES

1. For this section I am chiefly indebted to two excellent books: John Rowe, *Cornwall in the Age of the Industrial Revolution*, and D. B. Barton, *The Cornish Beam Engine*.

2. Rowe, 305, 128, 145.

3. Trevithick left England with three other Cornish mining men in 1814; his second stay in South America lasted eleven years, 1816–

27. L. T. C. Rolt, *The Cornish Giant, the Story of Richard Trevithick*, 125ff.
4. Rowe, 126.
5. Barton, 253.
6. *Ibid.*, 148–49.
7. *Ibid.*, 87.
8. Rowe, 130.
9. cf. Caroline Fox's Diary, *Memorials*, ed. Horace Pym, for delightful descriptions of visits to it to watch a casting operation, etc.
10. Barton, 224.
11. *Ibid.*, 149.
12. E. Vale, *The Harveys of Hayle*, 51.
13. Barton, 259.
14. Rowe, 311.
15. Barton, 65, 169.
16. Rowe, 321ff.
17. R. T. Berthoff, *British Immigrants in Industrial America*, 94.
18. *Ibid.*, 61.
19. L. A. Chase, "Early Days of Michigan Mining," *Mich. Hist. Mag.*, vol. 29, 22ff.
20. J. B. Martin, *Call It North Country: The Story of Upper Michigan*, 70ff.
21. J. K. Jamison, "The Copper Rush of the '50's," *Mich. Hist. Mag.*, vol. 19, 383ff.
22. T. A. Rickard, *A History of American Mining*, 231.
23. A. L. Sawyer, *A History of the Northern Peninsula of Michigan*, 276ff.
24. *Hist. of the Upper Peninsula of Michigan* (1883), 281.
25. *Ibid.*, 279.
26. A. P. Swineford, *History and Review of the Copper, Iron, Silver, Slate . . . of the South Shore of Lake Superior*, 42.
27. See below pp. 188–89.
28. *Hist. of the Upper Peninsula*, 539.
29. *Ibid.*, 286.

30. *Ibid.*, 314.
31. Sawyer, 831–33.
32. L. A. Chase, "Michigan Copper Mines," *Mich. Hist. Mag.*, vol. 29, 479ff.
33. Sawyer, 1058; Rickard, 241–42.
34. J. Fisher, "Michigan's Cornish People," *Mich. Hist. Mag.*, vol. 29, 377ff.
35. Rickard, 248.
36. F. C. Bald, *Michigan in Four Centuries*, 240.
37. Sawyer, 281.
38. *Hist. of the Upper Peninsula*, 539ff.
39. *Ibid.*, 498ff.
40. Sawyer, 819–20.
41. *Ibid.*, 1149.
42. *Ibid.*, 818.
43. *Ibid.*, 1181.
44. *Hist. of the Upper Peninsula*, 337ff.; G. N. Fuller, *Historic Michigan*, III, 689.
45. Sawyer, 1295.
46. C. M. and M. A. Burton, ed., *Hist. of Wayne County and the City of Detroit*, V, 552.
47. *Ibid.*, V, 69.
48. *Hist. of the Upper Peninsula*, 301.
49. *Ibid.*, 343ff., 457ff.
50. Berthoff, 175.
51. From an illustrated Supplement, *The Milwaukee Journal*, October 2, 1966.
52. J. H. Forster, "Life in the Copper Mines of Lake Superior," *Historical Collections of the Pioneer Society of the State of Michigan*, XI, 175ff.
53. *Blessed Shall Be Thy Basket And Thy Store*, printed by the Phillips Exeter Academy Print Shop, Exeter, N.H., 1960.
54. Published by the Macmillan Company.

9 WISCONSIN AND ILLINOIS: THE LEAD REGION

*I*n the southwest corner of Wisconsin and the northwest coign of Illinois, bordering on the Mississippi, is the Lead Region that made history in the mid-nineteenth century. Actually it attracted attention before the Copper Country of Michigan; the movement thither set in in the early 1830's and ceased with the gold-rush to California. So the flood was brief in duration, from 1830 to 1850; but it left its mark on the land and a larger settled population—the fertile soils made good farming land—than the Upper Peninsula. Thus its story, which has many points in common with that, also offers some contrasts.

The entrance to this region, and its supply-center, was the town of Galena, which grew up a few miles from where debouches into the Mississippi the Fever River, which in those days was still navigable a short distance beyond the town.[1] Perched in a striking situation upon steep bluffs, Galena— quiet enough today, rather a shadow of itself, haunted by the ghost of President Grant—presented a busy spectacle in its heyday. One observer saw a dozen or so full-sized river steamers tied up at its wharves loading ore, and unloading bacon and supplies from St. Louis. Grant's later Secretary of State described it in the 1820's: "The mud in the streets was knee-deep, the log and frame buildings were all huddled together, the river full of steamboats discharging freight, busy men running to and fro, and the draymen yelling."[2] By the time Herman Melville spent a summer here with his uncle in 1840, and it was visited by one of the Orléans princes, the Prince de Joinville, the same year—for its fame had spread far and wide—the town was much improved; many of the porticoed houses of a century ago remain today.

It had long been known that there was lead for the taking in this region—the Indians themselves scratched the surface and smelted the lead after a fashion—but after the repression of the Winnebagos in 1828 the white man began to take it. T. A. Rickard invites our attention to the performance of Henry Dodge in 1827-28: "with fifty men well armed, he squatted on the lead-bearing land of the Winnebago Indians in the Wisconsin valley and started to produce the metal forthwith."[3] The Indians' protests went unheeded: "the hills are covered, more are coming and pushing us off our lands to make the lead. We want our Father to stop this before blood may be shed." This refers not to their Father in Heaven, but to the President of the United States. Of course, nothing was done, except that Dodge built a fort and raised several hundred rifles among the miners. They for their part had the usual frontier scare about Indians and were willing to a man to serve in the scuffles, dignified by the name of the Black Hawk War, that ensued. Rickard sums it up as an operation which, though it "looms large in the story of frontier days, was merely the dying protest of a brave savage when subjected to unendurable mistreatment." It is better remembered today on account of young Abraham Lincoln's having shouldered a gun in it, though he said that they did more blackberrying than fighting. Dodge was their general; after enforcing a "treaty" upon the Indians he acquired a thousand acres of their land, waxed wealthy, shipping his lead in his own steamers down the Mississippi. He emerged as governor of the Territory of Wisconsin, and in the fulness of time United

H

States Senator. Dodgeville was suitably named for him: a monument to his prowess.

The way lay open to progress, and a rush to the Lead Region followed. At first the Americans, then the Cornish. Mr. Copeland tells us that "some of those who came in the 1830's say that there was no real mining done by the Americans, before the Cornish came. As soon as the rock became hard, the Americans deserted the mines for the surface diggings, seeking only the 'float mineral.' The Cornish introduced into the district the safety fuse for blasting; before they came there was little blasting done; the Americans were surface miners, and consequently had little use for it."[4]

This country they came to became known as the Blue Mounds country, from the blueish haze the low mounded hills took on in the distance; with its ravines and slopes where the lead outcrops were apt to appear it is an attractive landscape, if not as spectacularly beautiful as Keweenaw. Soon the hills were covered with miners scrabbling away at the surface, and digging deeper: one of the settlements which became dominantly Cornish was at first known as Hardscrabble, subsequently changed to Hazel Green; another was New Diggings. The men went out at first "prospecting," in the regular fashion to which they were accustomed at home: two by two with pick and shovel, later came the tunnelling into the hillsides, the sinking of shafts, the blasting and pumping. One can still see the slopes pock-marked with small pits that came to nothing; the whole country now is honeycombed with levels and adits and tunnels invisible. For it turned out very rich in lead. After the first period of discovery and exploitation, 1830–50, there was a pause, when more than half of the miners caught the gold-fever and rushed off to California in the fifties. Very many of them came back with their earnings, for the Cornish took to the Blue Mounds country, as they did to Michigan. They were natural stayers, for all their restless excitability where mining prospects were concerned; it seems paradoxical but they had a great liking to be rooted. Many of the men came back from the goldfields of the West to put their gains into buying farms. By 1860 practically half the farmers of Hazel Green were Cornish, about eighty in all, the wealthiest of them John Edwards, "whose rating was $34,100 real estate and $12,350 of personalty."[5] At Platteville perhaps a quarter of the farmers were Cornish, some thirty. Today there are several hundred farmers of Cornish descent in this region. Others of them re-opened old workings or opened up new ones with improved apparatus, and gave the Lead Region a new lease of life, with excellent figures of production, in the 1860's and 1870's.

We may take an example of this renewal of activity from Hazel Green.[6] At Richard Eustice's Diggings the shafts were 90 feet deep, the length of the drift (i.e. tunnel) 150 feet, the ore sheet 1 foot thick. From June 1872 to June 1875 it produced 40,000 lb. At Bininger range, then worked by Stephens, Nankivell and Rowe, four men were employed, with a horse pump in the second opening; the year's production might be 30,000 lb. Tregenza and Son began work in the fall of 1874, at a flat sheet about 5 inches thick, the top lead, the lower zinc; their production 20 tons of zinc, 20,000 lb. of lead. Rowe and Vivian were at work in the southern pit at the end of the village, which was abandoned in 1854. When they opened it up again in November 1873, the mine produced 24,000 lb.; the shaft was 106 feet deep, the drifts were 190 feet long. We see that the Cornish came back and persevered after others had dropped out. Something of their excitable enthusiasm emerges from the report of Richard Eustice and his company working a new locality and finding "one of the handsomest displays of ore ever seen on the grounds"; the sides at the bottom of the shaft "presented an unbroken mass of cubic crystals ... and of very perfect shape, affording very handsome cabinet specimens. There were not less than 10,000 lb. of lead ore in sight, in a place about 10 feet long." I do not altogether believe them, but I respect their spirit.

Similarly at Linden, near Mineral Point—at both these

places the Cornish element was the largest in the population.[7] Poad, Barrett and Tredinnick Brothers resumed working an old mine in 1869; they had been at it four years and sunk ten shafts—it looks as if they were going to fail. To the west of their ground were Kisselbury Brothers, Hammerson and Trewartha; to the east, Poad Brothers, Tredinnick, Vial and Geach. Treglown and Sons and Captain Wicks were working a range discovered forty years before, which had worked continuously since, and was then (early 1870's) producing 5000 lb. lead a year, 100 tons of blende. The Linden Mining Company's mine was first opened in 1833 and worked until 1853, producing perhaps 40 million lb. in twenty years; work was resumed in the 1870's cleaning out old shafts, installing an engine of 30 horse power, a lift pump and so on. It was producing ore worth $500 a day. Richards and Faull Brothers had made a good strike in May 1875. So too had R. S. and W. J. Jacobs in March 1875. They had struck four east-west sheets at 20 feet below surface; the ore in large isolated masses, one of 1527 lb. sent to the Centennial Exhibition. Production in 1875 was 70,000 lb. of lead, in 1876, 40,000 lb. "The mine has not been worked much during this summer, as the owners are engaged in farming."

At Dodgeville—also a largely Cornish settlement—Diggs's Mine had been discovered in 1836 and worked till 1850, when it was discontinued until 1870.[8] It was then revived by Joseph Pearce; its deepest shaft, 80 feet, was "drained by horse pump. During the last two years it produced 200,000 lb.; prior to that it only paid expenses." At Mineral Point the mining ground on the ridge was owned by several parties. It was "found impossible to obtain information of the amounts of ore obtained on this ridge," but it was "safe to estimate $600 a year for each man," and this was thought probably much beneath the actual amount. The names of the concerns are given: Mitchell and Pollard, Prisk and Paynter, Prisk and Coad, Samuel and William Richards, Jacka and Waggoner, Pascoe and Collins, Hendy, Davey, Lovey and Company.

We see that all this was on a small scale compared with the big undertakings developed in Michigan. These were nearly all small independent producers—no vast world-famous combines like Calumet and Hecla. And this had its social consequences. When the mines gave out, or even before, these men were able to make the transition to farming, which in earlier days they had despised. Mr. Copeland, himself half-Cornish, knew some of these old folk; one of them said to him, "I'd rather work for 50 cents a day in the mine than work for a dollar a day on the old farm."[9] John Treloar described to him the simple conditions that prevailed in these mines. They were not deep; a couple of men working at a windlass with ropes would bring the stuff up. A horse or a couple of shaft-horses worked the pump. The ores were blasted and hoisted to the surface, where they were "jigged" by hand; ox-teams took the ore to the boats at Galena, or to the railroad which eventually reached Mineral Point, and for long stayed there. When the prospectors got to the end of their venture they would move on and stake out another claim. They worked for their own independent subsistence and for something over; Treloar once had five hundred dollars in gold hidden under a stone—the Cornish wouldn't trust the United States paper currency. Though some became comfortably off, no one made any big fortunes—except, of course, the Artful Dodger.

We must turn back to the beginnings, the first diggings.

The first Cornishman to arrive as early as 1827, was a very experienced hand: Francis Clyma, of the parish of Perranzabuloe.[10] (This appears in the books as "Paranzatatoe!" etc.—it is simply the medieval Perran-*in-sabulo*, i.e. Perran in the sand, from the dunes on the coast.) Most of the folk coming to this region came from the Camborne area, or to a lesser extent from the coast of North Cornwall, from Perran —the patron saint of miners—to St. Issey. Clyma had emigrated to mine in Maryland in 1819 and had been sent by his company to prospect for copper in the Blue Ridge Mountains of Virginia. Failing in this, he moved into Kentucky to engage in salt-making. Thence he crossed the Mississippi to mine in Missouri, and so up the river to Galena where he struck lead. He arrived in the excitement of the affair with the Winnebagos, and moved his family into Ferguson's Fort. His wife was a St. Ewe girl, who had emigrated in 1821, and was the first Cornishwoman in the Lead Region. Clyma served as a lieutenant against Black Hawk. When the Indians were broken, he was able to settle on his farm, clearing it and mining, until he was able to retire—having spent two years in California, and made two trips back to Cornwall—to Apple River.

The first person to come direct from Cornwall was Edward James of Camborne—a forceful, intelligent, restless character—who came by way of Quebec, Cincinnati and St. Louis in 1830. He came to mine at Mineral Point, enlisted with the rest of the lads in the Black Hawk War, and was with Dodge at Bad Axe and other skirmishes. After the war he mined with Dodge at Dodgeville, and when the latter became the first governor of the territory he appointed James his secretary and gave him a commission as marshal of it. In 1841 he gave up and went to Missouri, where he disappeared and, with him, his story: it would be interesting to have it. In the same year as James came Edward Rowe, and next year James's brother.

In 1832 arrived Francis Vivian, who became a leading figure in the life of Iowa County.[11] A Camborne man, born in 1801, he came to New York, thence via the Hudson and the Erie Canal to Buffalo; then by boat to Ashtabula, Ohio, by stage to Millville and down La Belle River to Cairo; and so from St. Louis to Galena, much pleased with the amateur boatmen. He got by ox-team to Mineral Point on a Saturday evening, and on Sunday morning enlisted against Black Hawk, though he spent his time on garrison duty at Mineral Point. After a year's mining, he set up a store, which he combined with mining and smelting; during twenty-five years at Mineral Point he prospered. Having acquired a farm of 280 acres, he was elected treasurer of Iowa County for eight successive terms on the Republican ticket, sixteen years in all: "a greater length of time than any man in the North West in the same office." He married first a Camborne girl, by whom he had three children, then a Penzance woman, by whom he had five, one of them named Abraham Lincoln Vivian—which speaks for itself. In the same party came Matthew Edwards and his wife; the same year the brothers Terrell from Camborne—Stephen served in the Black Hawk affair, and died shortly after. Thus the flood of Cornish began.

We know so many of their names, since nearly all the fellows served in the little war and received their pay. A few settlers were killed, but after a couple of engagements the Indians were crushed. Black Hawk surrendered and moved off to Iowa, where he died and was buried on the banks of the Mississippi. Settlers poured in. Take the case of the "Stephens Colony" in 1842—fifty-two persons, almost all of the same family or closely related, came from "Peyrdinzabuloe" to Platteville, north of Galena.[12] Here they all settled together until the California fever swept many of the menfolk away in the 1850's. Some of them returned to purchase good farms with their winnings, others remained in the West. "All the Stephens brothers were married in the same parish church in England and now all the sisters and sisters-in-law are buried side by side in the cemetery at Platteville."

An interesting feature of the migration to this region is the number of families that came together. To Mineral Point there came no less than six Lanyon families, from the Truro district.[13] William Lanyon, senior, a blacksmith, came in 1840. "When he began life he had nothing"—"now he has a prosperous business and fourteen children," and was, moreover, city alderman and assessor. Simon Lanyon had come in 1838, and prepared a place for his wife: "the first house in Linden was built for her, and it was built of white walnut, lined with white pine"—there they had nine children. Lanyon's uncle, Henry Lanyon, had "piloted the British fleet up the Potomac River to take Washington in 1812; he was afterwards captain of a man-of-war and was known as 'Captain Cork,' on account of his having a cork leg." The Lanyon couple remembered the day on which they were converted together—it was just as well—March 29, 1843.

William Rablin arrived at Mineral Point on Saturday evening, June 27, 1835: "the next day, Sunday, the first day spent in the new home there were seven fights; it was a new experience to them and it did not create a very favourable impression."[14] At first he built a sod house into the side of the hill at Linden, which he shared with his brother until his wife came out to join him. "On Sunday when there was preaching at some cabin they were obliged to cross a swampy place: he would take his wife in his arms and carry her from one bog to another." To Mineral Point there came no less than five families of the name of Toy; to Linden six Rule families, two Sampson, two Viall; to Dodgeville two Prideaux, two Hocking. Numerous Rogers families came to the region. William Rogers married Mary Polkinghorne in Illogan church on July 26, 1839 and "at once left the church for their new American home." I find this somehow touching —one has known instances in one's own lifetime.

Charles Bilkey came to Mineral Point in 1837. Shortly after there came a band of Indians led by old Whirly Thunder. The Chief made overtures of friendship to the whites, who responded with plenty of fire-water and a grand orgy began. There were the bucks and squaws, "big Injun" and lesser, all half naked and wholly helpless—a disgusting spectacle, Bilkey considered. He mined at Wiota for three years, then went into partnership with Henry Eva as drovers and butchers. They went to Illinois and even into Missouri in quest of cattle, often being away a month. He ended as "the veteran butcher of Dodgeville." John Bilkey came to Mineral Point with a largish party in 1834: five Lanes, Kendalls, a William Fine, Stephens, Nicholls, Crowgey. They came with teams from Detroit, the isolated settlers not yet having built up the waste places left by the Indian war, and via Chicago then a village, the country a howling wilderness.

An institution full of character and long remembered was Abner Nicholls's tavern—he was known to everybody, in the Cornish manner, as Uncle Ab.[15] This was the social center of Mineral Point, in the later 1830's generally known as Shake Rag. It was then a village of log huts and shanties along the ravine—seven dry goods stores, four public houses, four grocery and liquor stores, two smithies, a couple of hundred or more houses, a population of twelve to fifteen hundred of whom four hundred were miners. At that time the jail was of unhewn logs barely tall enough for a man to stand upright in, and the wolves howled round the town at night.

Stage-coaches with six horses each ran between Galena and Mineral Point—Bob Nancollas among the old drivers. At Mineral Point the stage stopped at Ab Nicholls's hotel, where there was "always room for one more," and Mrs. Nicholls was an excellent hostess.[16] Uncle Ab's establishment consisted of three or four log cabins put together, a large bar with a faro bank in one corner, in another roulette, a third was given to cards. Here the miners gathered to drink and gamble, frolic and make music from Saturday night to Monday morning. It is the world of Mark Twain—if only the Cornish had produced a Mark Twain to describe it! One man would be playing a fiddle, while a couple of men danced together in the middle of the room. Hundreds of dollars lay about on the tables, among the crowd the principal men of the territory. When the landlord showed his guest to his bedroom, two men were playing cards there with a third drunk on the floor. They all slept together in bed in their clothes, the guest with bowie knife in belt and pistol in hand, lying awake, for he had $100 on him.

G. W. Featherstonhaugh in his *A Canoe Voyage up the Minnay Sotor* has a snooty description of Mineral Point as it was in 1837. The people were very hospitable, but their free

H*

and easy ways were not welcome to a Featherstonhaugh. In particular, at Uncle Ab's there was a man who took the fire from Mr. Featherstonhaugh and stood there in front of it in his nether garments and nothing else. We hear of no complaints from the Prince de Joinville who stopped overnight with his suite at Uncle Ab's in 1840. Uncle Ab, who had come over with the earliest, was good-natured but a terror when aroused. Once he had a fight on the street with Burris the grocer, who was aiming his pistol shots at Uncle Ab; the latter replied with a volley of stones so much more effectively aimed that Burris was put to flight before anybody could intervene. Sunday amusements were varied with gambling and racing, on foot as well as horse-racing. Sometimes there was a more sinister turn. Phil Cox was an old Cornish miner who lived all alone and hoarded his money. He lived in a well-settled part of town, and rumors of his hoard went round. An intruder broke in and struck the old man from behind with an axe; the body fell forward into the fire and was partly burned. The murderer was never discovered.[17]

A Cornishman called Shaddick, who was nevertheless known as "the Scotch giant," was employed for a time at the Helena Shot Tower, making shot. Seven feet four inches in height, 370 lb. in weight, he had travelled with a circus in England. He was a teamster for several years between Mineral Point and Galena. Stories of his feats of strength were long told. At last he went back to the arena, and was a regular feature in one of the earliest circuses to travel the Northwest. While on exhibition at Laporte, Indiana, he died, and was brought back to Cottage Inn to be buried. It must have taken a team to bring him.[18]

The place was full of vendettas in earlier years and it was border—or frontier—justice that was administered, the usual punishment whipping. A couple of men hired four yoke of cattle at Galena to team mineral from Mineral Point, but they sold them to Francis Vivian and Thomas Jenkins.[19] There was a general hunt for the thieves and a thrashing administered. In 1837 a meeting was called at Uncle Ab's to organize borough government, Uncle Ab, Francis Vivian and O. P. Williams among the first trustees.[20] In 1844 the Miners' Guard was organized, in 1850 the first public school established—there had been a school of sorts since 1829. By 1848 Mineral Point was the most important town in Wisconsin and expected to be made the territorial capital.[21] It had a population of two thousand and was increasing; it was the center of transportation routes and had a dozen lead-furnaces working. Moreover, Governor Dodge lived only four miles out of town, where he operated his prosperous concerns. It was not chosen for capital, however; perhaps to console itself, it was incorporated as a city in 1857. The Methodist Church had been organized there as early as 1834—the first Protestant Church in Wisconsin—by William Kendall, William Phillips, Andrew Remfrey, and James Nancarrow. When cholera came to the town, the inhabitants were attended to by Dr. John H. Vivian, who lived there many years, influential in Iowa County and active on the State Board of Charities; we have a portrait of him: a charming old gentleman, with a kind expression.

The Cornish flocked to Dodgeville in the 1840's: we find a large number of their names among the store-owners: Penberthy, Thomas, Hocking, Prideaux. The town band—that typical institution—was formed during the excitement of the Lincoln-Douglas campaign; led by Thomas Bosanko, it included two Nankivells, a Rowe, a Glanville.[22] In the fall of 1863 the boys went on a visit to the Lake Superior mines. The Cornish manned the Primitive Methodist Church here—a break-away from Methodism proper; in Wisconsin in general the Cornish were divided half and half. The Dodgeville Rangers when organized became Company C of the 12th Wisconsin Volunteer Infantry. There was a grand demonstration at the fall of Vicksburg. The news was brought by parties from Mineral Point driving their horses hard and yelling at the top of their voices in the night. Ben Thomas and Sam Hoskins were first aroused; everybody got up and bon-

fires were lit in the street, fences and outhouses cast on. The
saloon was then thrown open. At 4 A.M. the stage arrived, and
a sick soldier on furlough stepped out surprised by the cele-
brations: "My God, how did you know that I was a-com-
ing?"

We see that the Cornish were already patriotic citizens.

The gold-rush to California produced a fever of excitement
in the Lead Region in the early 1850's—far more so than in
the Copper Country. In the Blue Mounds landscape the diggings and holdings were deserted, business was paralyzed,
stocks of merchandise went unsold. A veritable craze seized
the menfolk—the same kind of collective excitability that
manifested itself in religious revivals and mass-conversions.
(California was, however, a more rational excitement: there
was gold at the end of the rainbow.) At the height of the fever
some sixty teams and two hundred persons left Mineral Point
in one day—about two thousand miners and laborers left the
area, at least half of them Cornish, out to make their fortunes.[23] In 1852 teams advertised that they would take passengers across the long overland trail through to the western
slope for $125.[24] On April 12 and 13 fifty people gathered in
the village of Lancaster to depart, having sold or mortgaged
their farms. We are told that up to 1852 some seven hundred
left the Mineral Point neighborhood alone, apart from
Dodgeville, Mifflin and other townships.[25] Lists of the California emigrants have been preserved—one would guess a
good third of them to be Cornish. Again and again one notices in the lives of the pioneers that they spent the early
fifties in California and then a number of them returned. It is
a frequent pattern: we shall be able to notice only a few
instances and some odd adventures.

Mineral Point was early to the fore. In the winter of 1848-
49 three partners—a man with some capital, a carpenter and
a sailor—built a midget schooner for sea and sailed down the
Mississippi and out into the Gulf.[26] Off Cuba they were cap-

tured by a Spanish gunboat; at night, however, the gunboat's crew went ashore, the Cornish overcame the guard and escaped with their boat. Up the Nicaragua River they sold their boat for $1000 and so got their passage from Aspinwall to the Golden Gate.

From Jo Daviess County across the border in Illinois Henry Roberts took the Nicaragua route by the Vanderbilt Line. "Upon that trip he had the opportunity of becoming acquainted with the Vanderbilt disposition and the man who later gave utterance to the words, 'The public be damned.' The vessel carried a thousand passengers and, the ship's provisions giving out, they were upon the verge of starvation."[27] An indignation meeting was called and Roberts led a deputation to the captain, "whom they pressed at the point of the pistol to open the vaults of the steward." Conditions worsened in a crowded ship off the Pacific coast, and many men died from disease and starvation. This was familiar enough. From San Francisco he reached Hangtown, soon to be known as Placerville, in Eldorado County, where he mined three years. It was a profitable trip, and he returned by the same route: this enabled him to build a brick hotel at Scales Mound. In 1861 he made a second trip, placer-mining near Mount Shasta; it paid and he came back once more by the Isthmus.

James Bennett came with his wife to Dodgeville where he was mining till he left for California in 1854. He travelled via New York and the Isthmus, was gold-mining five years, and returned to buy a farm of 160 acres: "it was then as the hand of nature left it, not a tree cut nor a furrow turned."[28] In 1865 he went to Colorado, thence to Salt Lake City where he visited the Mormon Temple and saw Brigham Young and other notorieties. Onward to the gold hills of Montana (i.e. around Helena), and in the fall of 1866 he "left the headwaters of the Yellowstone on a Mackinaw boat and coursed down that and the Missouri River to Sioux City, a distance of 1400 miles." He must have had a good time—and was enabled to increase his farm to 280 acres, besides building a substantial house and barns. A Methodist and a Republican, he had seven children, the two eldest in Colorado.

Thomas Buckingham won his farm of 280 acres with a Mexican War warrant—he had come a miner in 1842, served in the war of 1846, bought his farm in 1848.[29] Good going! Sam Cornelius, a Redruth man, went to California via New York and Panama, and was there four years. His father returned from Brazil to die at home in Cornwall; next year the son brought his mother to Dodgeville, where a Cornish marriage gave him seven children. Joe Davies mined for a year there, then returned to marry a Camborne girl. He made three visits to California, the first by the Nicaragua route, when he stayed two years and nine months. From 1864–66 he was in Montana; in the fall he made one of a party of several hundred who floated from the headwaters of the Yellowstone "in the peculiar flatboats of that region." What fun it must have been! Returning to Dodgeville he was able to buy a farm of 178 acres, which he later turned over to his sons. In 1878 he went again to the Far West, visiting the Mormon capital— evidently already a tourist attraction—and Nevada. On his first trip to Montana his party spent eighteen nights exposed to the snows and blasts of the Rocky Mountains. His last trip enabled him to witness the "marvellous development of the Pacific slope" since his first trip twenty-eight years before.

We have an example of how they sometimes raised the money to go, in the case of John Penberthy, whose father had died in Canada, leaving a widow and seven children in Dodgeville.[30] The California fever caught him like everybody else. "Hearing glad tidings from his old friend James Roberts then in California, he wrote asking him to send a remittance that would enable him to join him." His generous friend promptly sent him the money—these simple people were very good to each other, trusting and confiding. Penberthy reached California and his friend in 1856 and mined for four years with success. He returned to go lumbering two years, spent part of 1864–65 in Montana, and came back to join with others in a general merchant's business. He made a Cornish marriage, was a Republican and ordained a Methodist local deacon. We see how this kind of thing helped to keep them on the rails and build a community.

We have space here for only a few examples of those who took the overland route. Here is young Richard Wearne of seventeen, who started with his friend William Jacka and a yoke of oxen for California in 1859.[31] When they got to Omaha Wearne had only three sovereigns left, and Jacka decided to go back. Wearne pressed on and somehow got across the plains, the desert and mountains to California, where he was three years mining and another four in British Columbia. He returned to Mineral Point, married a Cornish girl and went into business with his father. Thomas Jenkins, born at Kenwyn, came to Platteville—his father was in Brazil, 1837–42.[32] The son went to California by the overland route in 1861, and from there to Montana, lured by prospects of gold, from 1866–68. Then he returned to Platteville to settle, marry, become a member of the village board, and to represent the district in the state legislature from 1874.

These are a few examples out of many: they are enough to enable us to see the social and economic patterns that obtained, the *train de vie* of these simple folk.

In the 1860's there came the terrible experience of the Civil War to rack the nation and disturb the life of the Lead Region, now more populous and settled, no longer a remote frontier area, and fronting the great highway of the Mississippi, much contested lower down its course. In Wisconsin, we are told, "the southwestern part of the State had an excellent record in the war. Some of the counties furnished many more soldiers than required. One of the first companies formed in the State, upon the first call of President Lincoln, was formed in Mineral Point, where about a third of the population was Cornish. This was Company I, 2nd Regiment of Wisconsin Volunteer Infantry, and familiarly known as the

'Miners' Guard' ".[33] Their flag is still preserved. About a third of the company were Cornish, with a Cornishman for first lieutenant. "Shortly after this, another Company was organized in Mineral Point—Company E of the 11th Regiment, known as the 'Farmers' Guard.'" This had a score of Cornish, more than their proportion of farmers at the time. General Allen afterwards said, "Dr. J. H. Vivian was surgeon of one of our regiments . . . On the whole, the Cornish were as loyal as the Americans, and made good soldiers. The businessmen of the same nationality [a proper expression] were mostly patriotic and helped fill our ranks."

The Miners' Guard had a distinguished record all through.[34] They fought at Bull Run and Manasses, they were engaged with Stuart's cavalry at Thorburg. They were heavily engaged with Stonewall Jackson at the storming of Turner's Pass at South Mountain. They were in the bloody battles of Antietam and Fredericksburg, at Gettysburg itself with its fearful losses on both sides, and at the Battle of the Wilderness. In the end, terribly worn down—the 2nd Regiment of Wisconsin Volunteer Infantry was reduced to a hundred men and had lost all its field officers—they were withdrawn.

We have their names in the records.[35] From Mineral Point we have Pascoe, Prideaux, Tregeary, Tregea, Trevillian, Prisk, Crabb, Bennett, Thomas, Hosking, among others; from Linden, Goldsworthy, Jacobs, Treloar, Manuel, Penrose, Hocking, Arthur, Chynoweth, etc. Company E of the 30th Wisconsin Volunteer Infantry had many men from Mineral Point: James Trevillian, Matthew Trewhella, Josiah Tyack, Paul Prisk who came back there to die of disease in October 1863. Two Perrys were from Dodgeville; Enos Trahern from Oasis, who died of disease in 1864. We cannot go into all the names of the Cornish serving in Wisconsin regiments in the course of the war, merely note a few points that strike us. There were no less than ten Pascoe, since that is a very common name; three Pengilly, three Treloar, two Penrose, two Rowse, two Tregea, two Trevillian, two Nancarrow; names with which we are now familiar, Trewhella, Trewartha, Polkinghorne, Carlyon, or less so—Nancollas, Nanscawen, Treweek, Pengra. As usual, however, the majority are found to have names like Richards, Robins, Rogers, most of whom would belong.

Perhaps we may now look at a few of these Civil War soldiers individually. Thomas Goldsworthy was born at Mineral Point, but left an orphan. In October 1861 he enlisted in Company C of the 12th Wisconsin Volunteer Infantry, known as the "Dodgeville Guards." He served faithfully till July 21, 1864 when, in a charge upon the front at Atlanta, a rebel bullet shattered his right arm and he was taken prisoner. He was four months in the notorious prison-camp at Andersonville. After the war, sporting an empty sleeve, he was made postmaster at Linden.[36] Benjamin Prideaux, post-master at Mineral Point, and several times mayor, was a Civil War veteran.[37] Young Benjamin enlisted in Company C of the 31st Wisconsin Volunteer Infantry. He served in Sherman's Atlanta campaign, was at the battle of Averysville in North Carolina, at Bentonville and in the March to the Sea. He cast his first vote, for Abraham Lincoln, in the city of Atlanta.

Since there is a history of the 96th Regiment of the Illinois Volunteer Infantry, we know more about the individual fates of the Illinois Cornish.[38] One thing that emerges is the costly casualties they suffered at the battle of Chickamauga. Corporal David Isbell had his right elbow shattered as the regiment was falling back to re-form. Though ordered to the rear he went with his regiment on a third charge, and was last seen being carried back with a ball in his right breast. His body was never recovered. His brother Jason suffered a shoulder wound in that terrible engagement, and was wounded in the hand at Rocky Face Ridge. Though in every engagement, he came through and mustered out with the regiment. John Hocking enlisted from Vinegar Hill. He was badly wounded in the hip at Chickamauga, taken prisoner, then paroled. He was in the hospital two months, exchanged and at home three months; recovered, he returned to the regiment and finally mustered out with it. Edward Wearne was shot through the right thigh at Chickamauga, was months in the hospital, then transferred to the Veterans' Reserve. He ended happily farming in Dakota.

Cyrus Pomeroy enlisted as bass drummer in the regimental band. Wounded in the leg at Chickamauga, he was disabled by gangrene and discharged. Living on at Chicago, he kept his drum as a relic of the heroic days. Robert Pollard, a boy of eighteen, born in Cornwall, found the severities of the march from Kentucky to Danville too much for him. He died on the march, the first of the company to go, "mourned by his comrades." James Richards from Hazel Green enlisted as a schoolboy from Galena; he died at Nashville, Tennessee, May 9, 1865. There was a typhoid epidemic there, for Thomas Bray and Nicholas Tippett also died there that sad Maytime. Tippett's brother, William, fell sick of dysentery at New Orleans, but survived to farm at Galena.

At Lookout Mountain Sergeant John Vincent lost the sight of his right eye; but rejoined and survived the war to farm in Iowa County. Lieutenant Robert Pool, who had been wounded at Chickamauga, was disabled for six months by the fall of a tree at Lookout Mountain. He survived, to become sheriff of Jo Daviess County for two years, then went off to Oregon. Corporal William Richards, enlisted as a boy of nineteen, also suffered leg injuries by the crash of a tree at Lookout Mountain—it would seem that the regiment was caught by artillery fire among the trees. George Dimmick enlisted from Apple River. Wounded under the left eye at Chickamauga, he was taken prisoner, thence to Richmond where he lost his sight and fell ill of small-pox. He was moved round the prison-camps at Danville, Andersonville and Florence. It was testified of this boy—he was eighteen when he enlisted—that he was "always cheerful and ready to do anything in his power for his companions." He died at Wilmington, North

Carolina, just at the time of his release. William Perry was luckier: he enlisted at sixteen as fifer with the regimental band. Becoming orderly to General Steedman he had several narrow escapes, once at the battle of Chickamauga riding through the rebel lines. Though a mere lad he passed through the service without illness or absence from command, and mustered out with the regiment.

Of the officers of the 96th we have a notice of Major William Vincent.[39] Born in Cornwall in 1826, he embarked with his parents in 1837 from Falmouth for New York. They came by way of Buffalo and the Lakes to Cleveland, thence to Cincinnati and from Mark Twain's Cairo up the Mississippi to Galena. His father died in California in 1851, leaving twelve children. William married Eliza Bray, whose parents had come by the same route. In 1857 the young couple took their eighteen-months old baby with them to California by sea, landing at Placerville to mine at Weberville. They returned after six months via the Isthmus and New Orleans. In August 1862 Vincent enlisted in the 96th under the command of Captain George Hicks, who later settled in Jamaica. Vincent was with the regiment on duty at Kent, then at Louisville and Nashville. At Franklin, Tennessee, they had their first brush with the enemy; he was wounded at Chickamauga, where the 96th lost very heavily. After four months' leave Captain Vincent joined Sherman's army and served in the three months' campaign. Discharged in 1865, a Methodist and a Republican, he settled down as a prosperous farmer, with seven children.

Edward Kittoe, a Cornishman by birth, was General Grant's physician and personal friend. He became surgeon-general and medical director of the Army of the Tennessee, with the rank of lieutenant-colonel on Grant's staff. From Atlanta in 1864 General Sherman paid him a warm tribute on his direction of the medical department on that famous campaign: "I have never seen the wounded removed from the fields of battle, cared for, and afterward sent to proper hospitals in the rear, with more promptness, system, care and success, than during this whole campaign."[40] We have his medical reports as Chief Medical Inspector of the Army in the field. At the end of that arduous summer, we find General Wilson reporting from Alabama that "the old gentleman will not complain, or ask for anything, but he evidently looks with some trepidation upon the prospect of a campaign this winter and, I think, is getting rather too old for such work."[41] However, once the war was over, Dr. Kittoe went back to Galena, survived in private practice there for another twenty years, and died "in the old home on the hill in 1887."[42]

We are now in a position to scrutinize the settled Cornish population in the region as a whole.

With the gold-rush to California in the 1850's the main stream of the Cornish immigration was directed thither; that to Wisconsin and Illinois tapered off, though it did not wholly cease, particularly that to Illinois: as Chicago grew it became more of a magnet. Mr. Copeland, who knew the subject intimately, was able to estimate the Cornish population of the Lead Region by 1850 at about one-fifth, i.e. 7000.[43] By about 1900, when he made his investigation, "it is possible that the total number of pure-blooded Cornish in the Lead Region is about 10,000." We have seen how clannish they were—as they always are—and how they usually made Cornish marriages in the first and second generations. After that they began to widen their horizons as they began to spread out. More than half of the men who left this area for California came back to it—it evidently appealed to them. They took to farming and their descendants remained on the land. As the mining gave out, they moved further afield, to the West, or into the towns. A remnant remained, still recognizable, in the old haunts that had become their home.

The area in which the principal Cornish mining settlements were made in Wisconsin were: the southeastern part of Grant County, centering upon Platteville; the southwestern part of neighboring Lafayette County, around Benton and Shullsburg; almost all the southern half of Iowa County, including Mineral Point, Linden and Dodgeville. And, across the Illinois border, the northwestern part of Jo Daviess County, focusing upon Galena. All this territory was, of course, one area; the Cornish tended to settle thickest where the best mines were, outwards along the northern rim from Platteville to Mineral Point and Dodgeville, where they still are today. But they settled also in many smaller villages throughout: Hazel Green, Cornish Hollow, New Diggings, Gratiot's Grove, British Hollow, Coon Branch, Mifflin, formerly known as Black Jack. And in Illinois we find them strongly entrenched in Council Hill, Elizabeth, Apple River, Guilford, Scales Mound, and smaller places like Woodbine, Stockton, Thompson and Vinegar Hill (there is a Vinegar Hill in Cornwall). It is a pity that they were too late—or too illiterate—to impose some of the names of the places they had come from—Camborne and Redruth, Illogan, St. Agnes, St. Allen, Kenwyn, St. Day, Perranzabuloe. For, in fact, the population of the Lead Region came from quite a small section of West Cornwall.

They certainly had the demographic advantage of a high birthrate—and, respectable, hard-working, Methodist, they had a low rate of infant mortality. The vast majority of the Cornish children grew up in turn to contribute to the populating of America. The most frequent numbers of children in a family were eight, seven, or six, though nine was quite common.[44] The prize seems to be won by Thomas Paynter, who lived at Mineral Point and died, a venerable old patriarch, in 1901. He had twenty-one children, who scattered all over the United States. This notwithstanding, he prospered: kept a barber's shop, added a hotel, held office and was even able to contribute to charity. William Lanyon came next with fourteen children.

Many Hoskins families came to Dodgeville; James Hoskins, an attorney, had fourteen children; John Crase had a family of twelve there, so had John Uglow Baker. Nicholas Arthur, a professional assayer at Dodgeville, had a valuable mine and also ten children, who eventually scattered all over the United States. Stephen Tonkin, who came first to Copper Harbor in 1845, eventually settled at Linden, where he accumulated 525 acres and thirteen children. Seven years away in California enabled James Roberts to purchase a drug-store on his return to Dodgeville; he had eleven children, one of whom became a qualified pharmacist, an early graduate of the University of Wisconsin. Thus we go up in the world—and belonging to a large family was no particular disadvantage. Another family of eleven was Nicholas Tredinnick's; it is nice to think of the proliferation of so pleasant a name. He was a livery-man, whose grandfather mined in Pennsylvania and died young; Nicholas's father came to Mineral Point a drayman and got the government contract for carrying the mail to and from Linden. At Hazel Green, James Wills came in 1848, got 400 acres and begot thirteen children; James Harris got 400 acres and eleven children. At Platteville John Trenary, one of the founders of the Primitive Methodist Church, had ten offspring.

Nor were the Illinois Cornish behind-hand, if that is the word for it. At Guilford John Bastian had ten children; at Woodbine Edward Mitchell had ten.[45] John Jackson scored ten, but by several marriages, all Cornish.[46] He had a variegated life. Born at Pool near Camborne, a fortnight after his marriage there he embarked on the sailing vessel, *Siddons*, from Liverpool to New York. He spent two years in the iron-mines of New Jersey and three searching for gold in Virginia and as foreman in a Philadelphia mining concern. From 1852–60 he was at Hazel Green, combining a small farm with mining, in the traditional way miners had done at home for generations. The next three years he spent copper-mining in Michigan. In the fall of 1863 he started for Nevada, by way of New York and Aspinwall, crossing the Isthmus and arriving at San Francisco five weeks after. With his winnings he bought a farm of 240 acres back in Lafayette County, cleared the land and brought it to good cultivation. His wife and boys worked the farm while Jackson went back silver-mining in Nevada till 1876. Having been successful, he agreeably surprised the boys by sending them to the Centennial Exposition at Philadelphia.

We see that the menfolk had variegated lives, far more so than if they had lived at home in Cornwall. The women had a less changeable existence, once they had made the great change. Theirs were home entertainments.

First of these, in order of importance, was their Methodism: their Methodist chapels were the centers of their community life, as at home. Further, they provided not only the strongest integument binding the community together, but the most powerful continuity with their lives at home. Once the church was started—in America they called them churches, a nice differentiation: they were no longer inferior—and once inside it, they might have been at home. Many of the faces they saw around them they had known at home. The services, the Bible-readings, the hymns were the same. It was a great consolation, and it helped to keep them steady; it was an indispensable element in building a community, and it provided them with much fun. There was first of all the excitement and pride—and the social experience it gave them—in founding a church. Napoleon said of himself, "J'avais le goût de la fondation, et non de la propriété." Whether that was precisely true or no, there is no excitement like that of creating something, building something. These pioneering folk had that joy, and we can see from their reminiscences how proud they were of it. The rivalries, the competitive picnics, the ill-feelings between Methodist and Primitive Methodist—"Primitives" were wholly Cornish—gave no less enjoyment.

Judge Oscar Hallam's reminiscences take us straight into the heart of these endearing amenities.[47] Laxey Church was Primitive Methodist, a stone building set among trees, built before the Civil War. There was a cleavage between Laxey and Bloomfield, which was Methodist *pur sang*. All the Manx went to Laxey, named after the place in the Isle of Man; the Cornish divided according to taste, as in England according to class. To Laxey came Phil Allen from Point, "William Harris down-the-bottom" to distinguish him from "Chicken William" who bred Leghornes and "William Harris the blacksmith." Laxey churchyard was full of trees and the headstones of those who had built and maintained the little place.

There was begging for the annual picnic. A man recently arrived from Cornwall once contributed a whole dollar, and was loudly acclaimed for this act of generosity—or of greenhorn extravagance. Laxey picnic always outdid Bloomfield. The Linden Primitive Methodist choir led the singing, and dealt with the *h*'s in the uncompromising Cornish manner—omit them where they should be, and insert them where not:

> Then 'aste, oh 'aste to yonder bower,
> We'll 'ail the 'appy, 'appy *Hour*.

Sometimes Mineral Point Band honored the event, led by Sam Jenkins the hardware man, his son Jack as kettledrummer. But Dodgeville Tea Meeting was outstanding in the circuit. It required never less than eighty to a hundred chickens, four hundred pasties at twenty-five cents each, saffron cake and pies galore. All long over now. "Laxey and Bloomfield picnics are gone. Nick Jewell's grove is gone and its place is just another field. Nicholas Thomas's groves are all gone. No roundin' preacher is there to come, the choirs no longer 'practice for the picnic,' no more does Nicholas bring 'a barrel of water for the lemonade,' no more do the boys meet at Skillicorn's at 5 a.m. to make ice-cream. Who cares now whether it rains Thursday, who in Laxey cares whether Linden has a choir? Who in Bloomfield cares whether Point has a band? Bloomfield and Laxey church worship and their Sunday schools, as well as the social life centering about the annual Sunday school picnics and Tea Meetings have passed. Nothing remains but the burial grounds which recall the pioneers who once worshipped at the sites where they now lie buried. Their influence is a part of our heritage."

The Reverend John T. Mitchell was the first circuit minister from 1832, the circuit including Galena, Shullsburg, Platteville, Mineral Point.[48] The Reverend John Batten, who came over with his parents to Linden, was pastor of the Methodist Episcopal Church for twenty-six years.[49] At Platteville the Primitive Methodist Church was organized in 1847 by John Trenary, Mark Waters, Mrs. Verran and others; among its later pastors were a Hendra and a Hewitt.[50] At Hazel Green the Methodist Episcopal Church was organized in 1845; it came to have a congregation of two hundred. But in 1861 the Primitive Methodists withdrew from it, in high— or, more probably, low—dudgeon; they mustered sixty and built a new church—as a new colony of ants build a fresh ant-hill.[51] James Pryor came over in 1842 and kept a grocery shop; in 1851 he was admitted by the Methodist Episcopal Church, after their manner, "on trial."[52] He became an elder in 1855 and ultimately the Reverend James T. Pryor. In the second generation the son of James Gilbert and Julia Stratton, Albert Stratton Gilbert, became the pastor of Dodgeville. He had graduated from Lawrence University and proceeded to Columbia and Boston University; he served several pastorates in Massachusetts, New York and Milwaukee, but retired upon Dodgeville. Progress is registered.

Mr. Copeland observes that the Cornish, though quite uneducated, were sharp and shrewd. Some 75 per cent of the immigrants were illiterate; there had been no schooling for them in Cornwall in those days. And we may imagine that in the early days in the Lead Region schooling was rough and ready. Thomas Arthur, the "genial proprietor" of the leading general store in Dodgeville, taught school as a young man during the winter months—he evidently had something better to do in the summer. It is a Willa Cather world—if only there had been a Willa Cather to record the life of this pioneer generation of Cornish!

What struck people most, as in the Copper Country, was the strong and unmistakable Cornish dialect. In the summer of 1895, as a young man, Louis Copeland toured the Lead Region on a bicycle, collecting material. He was just in time to hear from the last members of the pioneer generation their habits of thought and speech from their own lips. He wrote down some of them, and again late in life this admirable, long-lived old gentleman recorded specimens of their speech on tape—for the authenticity of which I can vouch. The ignorance of the old people is rather touching. With no knowledge of geography they can hardly have known, some of them, where they were. One of them, asked how far Cornwall was from England, replied: "I cudn' tell 'ee 'zackly, but 'tedn' far apart." One old woman, noticing the Wisconsin moon for the first time, said to another, "Mary Ann, do 'ee come out 'ere. Do 'ee see that moon? I reelly believe 'tes the same old moon we d' 'ave in Cornwall." At a class-meeting an old miner was praying till he was out of breath: "I see 'n setten on a 'eavenly throne, surrounded with a passel ov angels." Coming to, he corrected himself: "I d'mean a multitude." We see that what instruction they did get was based on the Bible. This did not wholly obscure their common-sense judgment. Aunt Jane—old ladies were universally called "Aunt" in Cornwall —was not unduly impressed by a new preacher: "I d'feel fine and sorry for 'ee. 'Ee d' look wisht [miserable] sticked op there like nothin'." And then there is the rather macabre sense of humor we have observed before. Witness the following exchange:

> "'Ee warn't waitin' fur me when I come by. 'Ee was 'anged op be the neck in the staable."
> "Did 'ee cut'n down?"
> "Noa, I dedn' cut'n down. 'Ee warn't dead yet."

Uneducated as they were, and little chance as they had had, they made headway in the New World. We have noticed the numbers of them who, starting with nothing, by dint of hard work built up their own business, or bought and cleared land and ended with a good farm. Some few made more money, though not on a large scale. They fulfilled their obligations by holding local office, but they did not waste their time and talents—like the Irish—on the sterile business of professional politics: they had better things to do. And so they did not become important in the public eye, apt to be directed, or misdirected, on such things. Up to 1900, Mr. Copeland tells us, a dozen Cornishmen "have represented the Lead district in the Wisconsin Assembly": eight Republicans, three Democrats, one Liberal.[53]

To take one example only of these: the Honorable Joseph Bennett.[54] He was born at Camborne in 1822, a miner's son. He spent six years mining at Dodgeville from 1845, then went for a year to Lake Superior. In 1852 he bought a mining interest in Dodgeville, to which he added a smelter in 1858. A company was formed and heavy business done 1860-70, especially during the Civil War—with the demand for lead to settle an argument—when business averaged $100,000 a year. The firm owned considerable mining land, lead being sent mainly from Chicago east and south with the completion of the railroads. Beginning as chairman of the town board, Bennett held various local offices; a Methodist and Republican, he was elected a member of the Wisconsin legislature in 1876. Could he have achieved as much if he had remained behind at Camborne?

Even in our time the Lead Region has been represented in the legislature by an assemblyman of Cornish descent, Ben Tremain.

Judge Hallam who grew up among the Cornish of the district is an exact and reliable witness of their ways, character and speech. He gets the dialect perfectly, as few who are not Cornish can do. He notes that the Welsh spoke Welsh among themselves, and ordinary Dodgeville American to other people; so they did not stand out and were not remarked on. But the Cornish stuck to their dialect, by which they were immediately recognizable. Even Judge Hallam is defeated by the surnames, and does not get them all right.

> There were Treseder and Trezona the grocers, Trogilius [i.e. Tregilgas] the butcher, Treloar the stone-mason, Trelaway [?] down by the lime kiln, Tredinick the painter, Treweek the jeweller, Tregonning and Tremain farmers, and there were Trepenny [?], Trevelyan, Trevillian, Trevethan and Tremont, whose occupations I never knew. Then there was the Methodist local preacher, John Penberthy, the Penhallegons and the Pengelly brothers, who ran on opposing tickets for sheriff. One was elected: it helped the livery business. Then there was Penrose the butcher and Penhall whom I never knew. Then there were Polkinghorns and Kinghorns, not to speak of Edyveans and Eddashanks [!]. Some of the names have disappeared from the poll-list, I do not know why. We get to like names that signify origin. . . .

This passage has a double interest for us. It gives us a thumbnail sketch of the community; but it also draws our attention to the tendency to transmogrify and deform Cornish names in the United States, since nobody knows their meaning. Here we have Polkinghorne on the way to becoming Kinghorne; in some places it has become plain Polk.

As a boy Hallam loved to watch the blacksmith's shop, where the Welshman, Wynne, and the Cornishman, Wearne, would weld two hot rods into one. Then there was horse-shoeing: first paring the hoof, shaping, placing the shoe and nailing it on, then paring again all round the shoe—just as I used to watch the operation early this century outside the blacksmith's shop at Tregonissey. I don't know what the prices were there, but at Mineral Point it was fifty cents a shoe for new ones, thirty-five cents for setting old ones. The boy listened to the talk of the gaffers. Old Goorin (Goring?) cared nothing for London or Liverpool, but a lot for Falmouth and

Camborne. One day, sitting on a bag of beans, he was discussing some miscarriage of justice with the cobbler.

> Goorin: *There* we 'ad law an' justice. 'ere . . .
> Cobbler: Iss, fay. 'ere we 'ave no law, nor justice.
> Goorin: 'ere we 'ave plenty of law, but no justice.

From which we see that they were not incapable of a critical comment on their new surroundings.

Nor were they uncritical of their new country's heroes. Ste and Liza were dear friends from Redruth days. Ste had been to Pike's Peak mining in its best days, came back and bought a couple of blocks of land at Dodgeville. He didn't think much of Grant, however and considered the adulation of him nonsense. Ste had known the young Grant when he used to trek from Galena to Mineral Point buying hides for his father's tannery. He thought little of Grant as a general: "Anybody could 'a done so good as General Grant. I could 'a done so good." One recognizes the Cornish no-nonsense spirit, tinged with jealousy. The other side to this was pride in everything they possessed, "a bit boastful. They were proud of their house, proud of their barn, proud of their roothouse, proud of their well with the old chain pump and oaken bucket, proud of their three-year-old filly, proud of their old red and white cow, proud of their dog 'Lion.'" Asked about the grandeur of the Colorado mountain scenery, Ste replied, "No, there's no scenery like a good field of corn." They were hardworking and thrifty, provided for a family of seven boys and a girl, and left some to spare—they were willing to loan money to a neighbor. Though they never joined the church, they supported it and sent their children to Sunday school. They were good citizens, and "made substantial contributions to institutions which have made their adopted country great."

Old Gill had five girls, who could all sing and play the organ—he had spent $100 on their musical education. As possessive of them as his contemporary Mr. Barrett of Wimpole Street in far-away London was of his talented poet-daughter, old Gill would never tolerate any boy-friends near. Yet all the girls were attractive and married reasonably well —but they had to go away from home to do it. Bascoe— whose name must surely have been Pascoe—got up early and worked late, yet could never prosper: having acquired a farm before he acquired any capital, he could never better himself. He had fond recollections of home: he had seen Queen Victoria, approved of Peel for establishing the police-force, and taught his children nursery-rhymes about King Arthur and his noblemen. Yet he preferred America and would have stood for America against England.

Judge Hallam remembered from his childhood something of the impact of the Civil War upon the little community. There was Jack Pitts, at 6'4" the tallest man on Laxey picnic grounds, playing kissing games in the military dress coat and blue cap. There were bewhiskered Jim Bennett and Johnny his brother, returned veterans. Little Phil Lawrence often pointed to the place on his shoulder where lodged the bullet which he got as one of the Iron Brigade at the first Battle of Bull Run. Phil became postmaster as a reward. Eliza's brother Billy was of an age to be drafted, but he neither went nor hired a substitute. Soldiers came for him and bayoneted a pile of straw in the cellar; Eliza was harrowed by the thought that Billy might have been there. But he wasn't, and they didn't find him—sensible man.

We have had so much reason to regret the illiteracy of the early immigrants that it is useful to have, exceptionally, a fragment of autobiography by one who could write, if but simply.[55] Thomas Reed was twenty-seven when he brought his wife and two children to America in 1851. "We took a steamer at Falmouth for London, thence to New York by a big sailship named *London*. Came down the English Channel again from whence went up past the mouth of Falmouth harbor our dear Old Home, then for the Lezard Point and last of all the Land's End and watched it till we could see it no more and said 'Goodbye Old Home' if either of us would see it again . . . I am the only one that did. I have been back twice since. I was there in 1861 and 1892." He describes the route, familiar to thousands of incoming Cornish, up the Hudson, and along the Erie Canal to Buffalo, then by the Great Lakes to Chicago. "We are at Chicago now for Galena. There was no railroad. There were 2 teams there waiting for passengers we engaged one and went on. We were I believe four days coming to Warren. Slept there that night. In the morning got another team and put for Elizabeth . . . We got to Elizabeth by dark and continued on to Weston and came near being drowned crossing Apple River, arrived at Jenkins at 9 oclock. They were expecting us . . . We had a good time on meeting for we had not seen each other for many years."

Reed briefly describes the ups and downs of his life farming and mining. In 1871 his wife died leaving him with seven children; then a daughter died leaving him with two small children. "Four of the boys were working round. I made arrangements and went up on the Lakes in the Iron Mines with 2 of my boys. I was only there about 4 months and came home and soon found it necessary to try and get a good woman to Wife. I made it a matter of prayer and the 'good Lord' answered my prayer and I had a good woman and she was with me 11 years and 15 days and the children took her even as their own Mother and the good Lord saw it good and was pleased to take her from me and blessed be the name of the Lord and now I am a poor pilgrim on the earth awaiting the Lord's Righteous." Evidently a Methodist. It pleased the Lord to take away his second wife at a celebration in Elizabeth, when four drunks caused the horses to run away and overturn the buggy. Freed from the rigors of domestic life old Reed paid a last seven months' visit home. He came back to go to his son's in Montana, and visiting round at Sheridan and Butte. "Although it is so far west and north I can conscientiously say I spent the most favourable winter I ever spent." On that happier note let us take leave of him in 1899, in his seventy-sixth year.

From the uneducated to the more educated. We have something of the autobiography of an Illinois Cornishman of the third generation from the excellent printer, Hal W. Trovillion (i.e. for Trevillian), of Herrin, at the Sign of the Silver Horse. This is itself a reference to the ancient crest of the Trevelyans and the legend of the horse coming to land from the lost region of Lyonnesse. Mr. Trovillion recalls characteristics of his people that are very recognizable: "my grandmother smoked a clay-pipe; my mother 'dipped' snuff, using a brush made of hickory bark; and my father was a slave to the habit. He smoked; he chewed; and he virtually ate the stuff."[56] He died young. The son then quotes the Cornish miner-evangelist, Billy Bray's, pronouncement against the great American vice. "If God intended men or women to take snuff, their noses would have been turned upside down. And if the Lord intended men to smoke, He would certainly have made a little chimney at the back of their heads for the smoke to pass through. But as He has not, I don't think He intended men to smoke."

O sancta simplicitas!—the argument against smoking is a rational, not a teleological, one.

Trovillion was born and reared at Norris City, White County, and went to the university at Bloomington. With a widowed mother to support—that frequent theme—he left the university for the raw coal-mining town of Herrin, to edit and print a weekly newspaper. He consoled himself by putting out little books and brochures in admirable fount and format, and gradually built up a catalogue of *Books Beautiful*. He has authentic touches of speech from Cornish folk in Herrin still, and, achieving a modest success in life, did not fail to pay a visit to Cornwall, to the Lizard Point, to Tregarthen's hotel in the Scilly Isles, where Tennyson memorably stayed, to the Bishop's garden at Lis Escop on a June evening when the cathedral bells were ringing in Truro.

In Lancashire, it used to be said, it was three generations from clogs to clogs. In these regions it seems to be three gen-

Wisconsin and Illinois: The Lead Region 229

erations from miners to professors. It is pleasant to notice the exemplary transitions of such figures as Glen T. Trewartha, born at Hazel Green, to a professorship at the University of Wisconsin at Madison; of F. W. Tresize, born at Ironwood, to become dean of the Engineering School at the Chicago division of the University of Illinois. Other professors of Cornish name and origin are numerous: J. W. Spargo, born at St. Louis, professor at Northwestern, eminent in juridical folklore and bibliography; John D. Hicks, of Berkeley, historian of the Populist Revolt; F. J. Trelease, born at Buffalo, college dean and administrator; Allen W. Trelease, younger historian; P. J. Trevethan, born at Hancock, become a social welfare executive; or a William Ernest Hocking, born at Cleveland, for many years professor of philosophy at Harvard and prolific author on quasi-philosophical, quasi-theological subjects.

As one travels about the pleasant countryside of the Wisconsin-Illinois border one can see for oneself how the Cornish people have fanned out in the course of a century, and are now sprinkled all through it. At Beloit one day I noticed that there were no less than seven Goldsworthy, six Polglaze, five Rowe, four Oates families there, besides names like Tregoning, Tremaine, Trevethan, Trezona, Vivian, Wedlake, Cocking, Edgecomb, Welch, Berryman, Ivey. Starting down the street I came to Kitto the Printer and, walking in, was at once made welcome as a fellow-Cornishman. All Mr. Kitto's folk, for three generations, were Cornish on both sides—which illustrates our point that the early generations were apt to marry within their own people.[57] The Kittos came from Truro to Mineral Point. A great-grandfather, Christopher Hendra, turned from mining to butchering and made a good living. But he decided to study for the ministry, which he did by a correspondence course, including Greek and Latin. His first pastorate was at New Diggings: he would preach at one community on Sunday morning, another in the afternoon, a third at night. His daughter accompanied him to play the organ for the hymn-singing. "Often in the winter-time they would drive over snow as high as the fence-posts, always carrying the portable organ with them."

Passing once through the village of Hazel Green, I had to call on an old lady who kept in touch with Cornwall by reading my books. A similar experience happened to me at Normal, Illinois, where a Mrs. John Best came from my mother's village of St. Blazey Gate. She was the widow of a Methodist minister, who as a boy had worked in the mine at Wheal Eliza and then in the house at Menabilly—familiar to thousands of Daphne du Maurier's readers as "Manderley." Everywhere one goes in these parts there are associations and memories, some of them reaching far back. At Scales Mound in Illinois a great-aunt of a Cornish friend of mine lived to be a hundred and five. By birth she was a Treglown; on her hundredth birthday she received the customary congratulations from President Coolidge, while eleven children assembled in her honor. Her lifetime spanned the whole story in the Lead Region, much as Harriet Uren's had done a little earlier in the Copper Country.

At Mineral Point itself a memorable work of preservation has been accomplished in Shake-Rag Street by the devotion and skill, the scholarship and taste, of Robert Neal.[58] Many of the admirable old limestone houses of the first generation had been torn down, when he decided to save and restore what had been left, and fill them with the precious objects the old people brought over with them—pieces of good furniture, their Staffordshire china-figures, clocks, trinkets, their few books. The result is a charming, if fragmentary, late Georgian street, where one may fancy oneself in St. Day or Tuckingmill, Illogan or the outskirts of Camborne or Redruth. Within, amid recognizable surroundings, one may regale oneself upon Cornish pasty, veal and parsley pie, Beef Truro, saffron cake and buns, and even Cornish cream. The whole place is a work of re-creation, a labor of love for Cornwall.

Wisconsin and Illinois: The Lead Region 231

In the southeastern corner of Wisconsin, south of Milwaukee on Lake Michigan, there were several settlements that offered some contrast to those, at least in their original character. For these were settlements of independent farmers able to take up land on their own, not miners who were more numerous; in course of time, as the miners became able to move out and buy their own farms, the patterns merged into one. But from the beginning in the 1840's the East Wisconsin Cornish were real pioneers breaking in virgin prairie; their leaders were men of some substance, with their own capital, yeomen farmers, farriers and veterinarians and, since they were more literate, we know more about them. Their first points of entry were Racine and Kenosha, coming at first via Quebec and the Great Lakes; in the 1850's they came via New York, the Hudson and the Erie Canal across to Lake Michigan. The pivot of their settlements was Yorkville, which they created out of the prairie; but they spread out to adjacent places, Union Grove, Whitewater, Palmyra. As early as the 1850's they sent out one spur to Oregon territory, near Spokane in Washington, and subsequently to Iowa, around Lenox. Now their descendants, when they meet, come together from all four corners of the Union, though particularly from the sickle-shape which, we have noticed, contains most of the Cornish population.

The recognized leader in this group was John Foxwell of Mullion near the Lizard; when he came to die, in Yorkville, they put on his gravestone, "the Cornish Pioneer." His father, William Foxwell, was a fine type of fellow, a convert to Methodism who played flute and violin; he had won a medal, which has come down in the family, for the leading part he took in saving lives from the *Anson* frigate, when she ran in upon Loe Bar in 1807.[59] When the father died the hungry forties were in the offing, and in 1840 John Foxwell took ship at Falmouth, with a neighbor named Thomas, for the long haul to Wisconsin to spy out the prospects for his family, relations and friends. Favorably impressed with the prairie, good grazing ground with long grass and water for cattle, he bought government land at $1.25 an acre, built the first framehouse in the township and was soon staking out land for those who were to follow.[60]

On April 3, 1842 there set sail from Falmouth an emigrant vessel with nearly two hundred Cornish folk on board. This was the *Orient,* an old unseaworthy East Indiaman, with John Lutey for captain, a Cornishman who prayed long and loud on the way over that if the Lord would but save him this once more he would never take the old tub to sea again. Most of the emigrants were miners with their families—all were from West Cornwall—but a strong minority were farmers with a few craftsmen from the Lizard area, relatives and friends of the Foxwells. William was John Foxwell's brother; his brother-in-law, Thomas Moyle, kept a diary on board, which corroborates Dickens' horrid account of his crossing in *American Notes.*[61] At home Moyle had been a farrier and veterinarian; in all five generations of the family that he founded in Wisconsin there has always been a vet. To this, in the primitive conditions of those early days, he had often to add the avocation of country-doctor. One sees him called into practice on board. His portrait shows him a man much above average intelligence, bright and engaging; his wife has a Foxwell look, shrewd, reserved, forceful.

On his first day out Moyle recorded, "got sick when I looked at last of Lizard, and turned into bed." On recovering, he began to take an interest in the spiritual condition of the emigrants. Brother Gale, a local preacher, took a census and totted up "31 Methodists, 16 Associationists, 8 Bible Christians." Behavior, however, was not always according, in spite of prayer-meetings, bible readings and sermons. "Fraud discovered in water measure—pint and half for quart. Find every man's hand against neighbour and even friend if anything is to be got thereby. Every man serves his own end even when to the disadvantage of others." Moyle's simple skill in doctoring proved useful on board: "called by Captain to bleed one of the sailors. Captain gave me a rusty lance. Told him I could work best with one of my own tools. Bled him and he soon felt better. Gave him five pills." In spite of the trials of a six weeks' passage all the emigrants came through with a clean bill of health, except one Camborne woman who died. "At eventide sails were furled and ship hove to while funeral lasted. Captain read service. W. Gale acted as clerk. At five o'clock the body of her whose spirit had gone to glory was consigned to the great deep, wrapped in canvas with two bags of ballast. During the funeral some rogue entered the galley and stole some cake from the widower and hove the plate overboard."

In spite of the pains of uprooting Thomas Moyle never regretted his choice. As the ship neared New York he was "thinking of home, but not regretting." Next day, "thought much of Sunday School tea gathering. Would like to be with them. But satisfied with present prospects." Prospects, indeed, turned out to be good. John Foxwell was waiting for them: he had already staked out farms for them around Caledonia, near the Root River. His sister, Moyle's wife, immediately took to the new country and, with a woman's sensibility, recalled later its virgin state: "large prairies covered with long grasses and flowers. The first flower to bloom we called the prairie sweet william. Then came the wild rose. I can well remember how delighted I was with the first one I saw. No garden rose smelled sweeter. Large yellow lilies grew abundantly in some places, which made our young friend give the name 'Lily Grove' to his farm." This was John Foxwell's first place; having broken it in, he was able to sell it at a profit and moved on. By 1850 he was already prospering, as he could never have done at home. After a few years he came back to fix himself at Yorkville, where he built up a valuable holding, by 1860 worth not much less than $10,000. There was no difficulty in recognizing his leadership in the new community, "a power among his neighbours for good, one of the founders and a lifelong member of the church [Methodist] and society at Yorkville."[62] A local preacher and an Abraham Lincoln Republican, he was an out-and-out Abolitionist on the issue of slavery.

His sister Elizabeth was no less literate, and even more religious. She was the wife of Hannibal Shepherd; Hannibal was a frequent name in the ancient Vyvyan family that lorded it in the Lizard Peninsula—and there were Vyvyans, farming stock, who came to this community. The Shepherds had arrived in 1841: "I again resume my pen," she writes, "to record the goodness of God toward me in not only bringing me and family to the shore of America in safety, but this month was born in safety my third child."[63] However, "I sensibly feel and my husband also feels that we are as few sheep without a shepherd, having had no class meeting or prayer meeting, but we hope for better days." Next year their spiritual drought was alleviated: "1842—this year has brought some local preachers and class leaders from my native land. How rejoiced was I to see them."

In the end some hundreds of Cornish folk swelled the numbers of these agricultural communities, where their mark remains strong today. We cannot go into their individual stories, but merely notice what is significant in their motivation. Samuel James, another Foxwell brother-in-law, hesitated at first, but the increase of taxes in an already tax-ridden country in 1841 decided him, as it would anyone with any initiative today. In October 1841 he wrote to John: "I am at last determined by the Divine assistance to wind up my affairs here and set my face toward the land of promise . . . I should like if such might be obtainable to have a gently inclined surface with here and there a living spring. Let us hear from you immediately for what sum you can purchase and how we can remit you the purchase money."[64] In 1843 he found a gently inclined surface all right with no lack of water; but in 1850 he decided to move on to the less rigorous, more West Country, climate of the Oregon territory. Since Samuel James left a diary, his story is part of that of the Oregon Trail, while he

Wisconsin and Illinois: The Lead Region 235

and his progeny made their pioneering contribution to the state of Washington.[65]

Few enough of the Cornish in southeast Wisconsin today are recognizable by specific Cornish names as the Moyles, Goldsworthys, Bosustows, Roskilleys, Lorys and Vyvyans are. The Georges, for example, are a numerous clan allied with the Moyles and both of them sent contingents to the peopling of Iowa. The Georges came from Mullion, and go back to a child who was baptized in the house, presumably by the midwife, "because of danger of death," and more regularly at church four days later.[66] This was in 1814, the year of Napoleon's escape from Elba. This William George died a century later at Coon Rapids, Iowa, in December 1915, with the Germans well along on their first attempt to conquer Europe. The Goldsworthys, Martins, Shepherds, Robertses, Richardses, Prices, Dales, Luggs, Harrises, Iveys, and others pioneered in and around Yorkville. Thomas Dale looked after the large farm of 450 acres while his brother soldiered in the 2nd Wisconsin Cavalry in the Civil War. The Vyvyans helped to settle Raymond Township and Union Grove, where Henry in the second generation built up a large business as a cattle dealer. John Hodge captained the *Annie Wilson*, the first steamer that plied Lake Geneva and was afterwards engineer on *The Lady of the Lake*.[67] Henry Waters came via Pennsylvania and Illinois with twelve children to help to populate the prairie. Samuel Skewes, farmer, carpenter, builder, came from a very ancient stock that had provided a counsellor and confidant to Cardinal Wolsey back in Tudor days.

Most interesting of these tribes remained the Foxwells and the Moyles. Thomas Foxwell had gone back to Cornwall to bring out another group in 1849—his nephew Thomas James, John Hodge, James Skewes and Walter Humphry. Thomas Foxwell later married Humphry's daughter and the two families moved to Fayette County, Iowa, where their progeny is numerous. Since most of the Foxwell children were daughters, the name has often been continued in the female line, as in the case of the Albrights. Daughter Zephine married a Methodist missionary who worked for years in Chile, where a son was born, William Foxwell Albright, who became a leading authority on the Semitic languages and the archaeology of Palestine. An internationally known scholar—one sees into what fruitful paths the old family fixation on the Bible has led. One sees also the toughness of the stock in the survival of one of the daughters to almost her hundredth year, to take part in the centennial of the Iowa Foxwells, a large clan, in 1963.

These Moyles—there are other Moyle clans in the United States, the most important of them those of Utah—have been no less prolific and in the male line. The main stock has remained in the old location in southeast Wisconsin for five generations now. John Foxwell Moyle in the second generation carried on the family leadership in the community at Yorkville, for they had bookish and musical interests in addition to the usual Methodism of the group, and they had brought their books with them. In the third generation "Old Doc Moyle" carried on the family profession; even today Alton Moyle, the family historian, and his father "ride in the footprints of the emigrant Thomas along the same trails to the same farms. They own some of the medical books he brought from Cornwall, a contrivance for making pills for sick cattle, and the account book of the manor of Chiverton, the spaces in which he had utilized for his journal, so scarce was the supply of paper."[68] In one spur of this clan its biblical fixation degenerated into a somewhat *mouvementé* connection with Jehovah's Witnesses, a too close proximity that ended in the law-courts. More normal developments led this fruitful stock to branch out not only into Iowa, Minnesota and Dakota, but as far afield as Colorado, Texas and Louisiana. In them the biblical injunction, "Be ye fruitful and multiply," has been notably exemplified.

With the decline of mining and the rise of urban civilization—in this century America has ceased to be a dominantly

Wisconsin and Illinois: The Lead Region

rural country—Chicago has become the chief magnet of Cornish folk from all this area. They always have been an element in its population, from the time of Richard Trevellick. Today, its Cornish population must be considerable, larger than in any other American city, amounting perhaps to several thousand. There are literally hundreds of families with names in which Cornish people are most numerous, such as Pearce, Rowe, Hicks, Harris, Ivey, Dyer, Rogers, Richards, Tucker, Jacobs, Hancock. There are scores of families with such specific names as Pascoe, Vivian, Penrose, Rickard, Grose. Omitting to notice all the usual Tre-, Pol-, Pen-, names that have become so familiar to us, let us single out only those that are less so. We observe five Lanyon families, five Dungey with three Dungy, two Spargo, two Wedlake, two Behenna, Blamey, Trevan, Ede, Clymo, Sara, Chubb, Tremelling, Trewin, Tregay, Trevena, Tredrea, Tremethick, Pethick, Uglow, Cloke, Coad, Annear, Carew, Rosewarne, Penfound, Trevenen, Treweek, Treneer, Geach, Treharne, Nancarrow, Nankervis, Nancollas, and that very rare name, of old Cornish gentry, Anstiss.

Coming to occupations to which these folk have graduated we note with interest a Reverend Louise Nankivell, a Reverend John Tredrea, a Dr. Kenneth Penhale, a Dr. Benjamin Spargo, a Petherbridge who is a patent attorney. Among businesses we find the ubiquitous H. O. Trerice and Company, temperature instruments; Harry Pascoe Incorporated, erectors; a Rowse manufacturing company; a Rodda insurance firm; a Trescott watch-repairing firm; a Penberthy manufacturing company; a Treloar truck and car-rental concern; a Hunken Agency; and finally to put us to rest, a Lanyon Undertakers Incorporated, with two offices—perhaps according to destination.

NOTES

1. cf M. S. Carter, *New Diggings on the Fever, 1824–1860*; G. T. Trewartha, "The Earliest Map of Galena," *Wisconsin Magazine of History*, XXIII, 40.
2. E. L. Buchard, "Early Trails . . . in the Lead Mine and Black Hawk Country," *Journal Illinois State Historical Society*, XVII, 585.
3. T. A. Rickard, *A History of American Mining*, 168ff.
4. L. A. Copeland, "The Cornish in Southwest Wisconsin," *Collections State Historical Soc. of Wisconsin*, XIV, 319–20.
5. J. Schafer, *The Wisconsin Lead Region*, 145–46.
6. *History of Grant County*, (Chicago, 1881), 360ff.
7. *Ibid.*, 378ff.
8. *Ibid.*, 383ff.
9. Tape recording in 1952. By courtesy of Mr. Robert Neal.
10. Copeland, *loc. cit.*, 305ff.
11. *History of Iowa County*, (1881), 903–4.
12. *Hist. of Grant County*, 922ff.
13. *Hist. of Iowa County*, 865.
14. *Ibid.*, 871.
15. *Ibid.*, 661–62.
16. G. and R. M. Crawford, *Memoirs of Iowa County, Wisconsin*, I, 169.
17. *Coll. Hist. Soc. Wisconsin*, XV, 382–83.
18. *Ibid.*, XIII, 362.
19. *Hist. of Iowa County*, 674–75.
20. *Ibid.*, 664, 678ff.
21. *Coll. Hist. Soc. Wisconsin*, XV, 363; Schafer, 62.
22. *Hist. of Iowa County*, 754–55.
23. *Ibid.*, 676ff.
24. *Hist. of Grant County*, 647.
25. *Hist. of Iowa County*, 678–79.

26. *Ibid.*, 677–78.
27. *Portrait and Biographical Album of Jo Daviess and Carroll Counties, Illinois* (1889), 779–80.
28. *Hist. of Iowa County*, 881.
29. *Ibid.*, 883–86.
30. *Ibid.*, 895.
31. *Ibid.*, 879.
32. *Hist. of Grant County*, 909.
33. Copeland, *loc. cit.*, 332–33.
34. G. and R. M. Crawford, I, 75ff. For the military history of these regiments as a whole cf. Chap. VI.
35. *Roster of Wisconsin Volunteers*, vols. I and II, *passim*.
36. *Hist. of Iowa County*, 910.
37. *Ibid.*, 870.
38. C. A. Partridge, *Hist. of 96th Regt. Illinois Volunteer Infantry*, 882ff.
39. *Portrait and Biographical Album of Jo Daviess and Carroll Counties, Illinois*, 193–95.
40. *The War of the Rebellion: Official Records*, series 1, vol. 38, Part I, 84.
41. *Ibid.*, vol. 39, Part III, 444.
42. F. G. Bale, *Historic Galena*, 17.
43. Copeland, *loc. cit.*, 311ff.
44. *Hist. of Iowa County*, and *Hist. of Grant County*, *passim*.
45. *Hist. of Jo Daviess County, Illinois*, 706, 774.
46. *Portrait and Biographical Album of Jo Daviess and Carroll Counties, Illinois*, 195–96.
47. Judge Oscar Hallam, "Bloomfield and Number Five," unpublished typescript, State Historical Library, Madison.
48. *Coll. Hist. Soc. Wisconsin*, XXVIII, 74.
49. Crawford, I, 119.
50. *Hist. of Grant County*, 727.
51. *Ibid.*, 752.

52. *Hist. of Iowa County*, 896.
53. Copeland, *loc. cit.*, 331.
54. *Hist. of Iowa County*, 880–81.
55. I am indebted for this ms. to his granddaughter, Mrs. Margaret Hunt, of Phoenix, Ariz.
56. Hal W. Trovillion, *Sharing My Note Book*, 26.
57. I am indebted to Mr. Charles S. Kitto, of Beloit, Wis., for the above information.
58. cf. Robert M. Neal, "Pendarvis, Trelawny and Polperro, Shake-Rag's Cornish Houses," *Wisconsin Magazine of History*, XXIX, 391ff.
59. H. C. Duckett, *The Generations of the Children of William Foxwell and Ann Harris*, Burlington, Wis., 1941.
60. T. H. Foxwell, *The Family and Descendants of Thomas Harris and Frances Humphry Foxwell*, I, Elgin, Iowa, 1963.
61. Duckett, 14–17.
62. *Commemorative Biographical Record of Racine and Kenosha Counties, Wisconsin,* 102–3.
63. *Ibid.*, 18–22.
64. A. C. Todd, *The Cornish Miner in America*, 39.
65. See below, pp. 375–78.
66. A. I. Moyle, "The American Descendants of John Moyle, Farrier, of Constantine in Cornwall, England," *The Detroit Society for Genealogical Research Magazine*, Fall, 1962, 59.
67. *Racine and Kenosha Counties*, 408; Todd, 40.
68. Todd, 40.

10 CALIFORNIA: GOLD AND OTHERWISE

It is probable that there are more Cornish people in California than in any other state of the Union. After all, it is the most populous state and mining has been of crucial importance in its development. All the world has heard of the "Forty-Niners," of the original gold-rush to California that opened it up and inaugurated the subsequent gold-rushes to Australia, to Nevada and Colorado, South Africa, Alaska. All that became part of the folk-lore of the past century, especially among mining-folk in Cornwall, well aware of what was going on in mining areas in other parts of the world. In many miners' cottages at home the songs of the Forty-Niners were familiar:

> I'm off for California,
> Susanna, don't you cry:
> Oh, Susanna, don't you cry for me,
> I'm off to California
> With my wash-bowl on my knee.

We were aware of California away on the other side of the world—"Califo'nia," we called it—and not only of gold-mining there. The mining of gold was California's essential contribution to the modern world, and it had immense historical effects. For one thing, California gold was a considerable element in enabling the North to outlast and wear down the South in the Civil War, and we hardly need a Keynes to tell us how immeasurably the vast increase in the medium of currency contributed to the expansion of business enterprise throughout the civilized world in the second half of the century. But California was rich not only in gold; there was silver, and there were other minerals: the New Almadén Mines of the Coastal Range south of San Francisco Bay were the largest source of quicksilver in the world, after Old Almadén in Spain. Behind all this were the incomparable riches of the land itself, the fertility of the great valleys, once water was brought to them. In the early decades of this century California meant to the outside world golden fruit—orange-groves and citrus-orchards—black walnuts and prunes, ruby apples. Though mining came first and foremost to the Cornish, they made their contribution in other fields as well, as we shall see, and they have not ceased to emigrate to California. Then, in our time, came the developments of the petroleum industry, steel, aircraft, defense—nuclear and otherwise—with the enormous increase in population to damage the most beautiful climate in the world.

A hundred years ago it must have been, from all descriptions, not only an El Dorado but paradise.

The leading historian of American mining, himself a Cornishman, T. A. Rickard, tells us that "the discovery of gold in California by Marshall in 1848 was the most portentous event in the history of modern mining, because it gave an immediate stimulus to worldwide migration, it induced an enormous expansion of international trade, and it caused scientific industry to invade the waste spaces of the earth."[1] Further than this, since California was the first state to undertake the mining of precious metal on a large scale, it became "the school in which the builders of the mining West learned their lessons. During the great boom of the sixties California-trained miners migrated to all parts of the Far West, carrying with them the knowledge they had acquired in the Golden State."[2] California gold-mining proved, in fact, "the prelude ... to the intensive exploration of the entire Pacific slope; it presaged the feverish exploitation of the mineral resources that the ubiquitous prospector soon uncovered all over our western domain."[3] In some respects the story may be regarded as typical; we may see its characteristics repeated in other areas, where we need go into the less detail in consequence.

The phenomena of the gold-rush are familiar enough. Here they are locally: "the whole country from San Francisco to Los Angeles, and from the seashore to the base of the Sierra Nevada, resounds with the sordid cry of 'Gold, GOLD, G O L D!' while the field is left half planted, the house half built, and everything neglected but the manufacture of shovels and pickaxes."[4] It reminds one of the mania for gold-seeking that seized the Jamestown colony in 1608, at the very beginning of English colonization in America.[5] John Roberts wrote home to his brother in Camborne in 1851: "gold seems to be the object of all; talk with whomsoever I may on the motives which brought them to California, there is the same answer with one and all, that is to get a pile of gold, and return to their families and friends in better circumstances than they were in before they left their homes."[6] In Virginia the gold was fairy-gold, in California it was real and in large quantities; as the news spread there concentrated upon the new state a flood of would-be miners, an influx of all sorts and conditions from all parts of the United States and from the outside world. In the previous two years the discovery of large copper deposits in Australia had directed a stream of Cornish emigrants thither, until overtaken by that to California, when a number of the miners moved from Australia to California in turn. In April 1847 it was reported that over 700 people had left Camborne that month for Australia and America; two years later a Truro agent received over 600 applications for emigration passages in a fortnight. In 1849, while 3690 persons left Plymouth for Australia in three months, over 1000 left for Quebec in a single week, thence to find their way over the continent.[7]

The find had been made in the Sacramento Valley up country from San Francisco, which gave convenient entry to the alluvial gold-bearing area along the rivers running into the Sacramento, up which thousands of men came to innumerable diggings. The country was turned upside down. If there were some 5000 men at work there by early 1849, within a few years there were 100,000, an almost entirely male population. During the early years, 1851 to 1855, California produced nearly 45 per cent of the world's output; the yield of gold in the first decade, 1848 to 1858, was some $550,000,-000.[8]

Men poured in by various routes. The speediest was to go by steamship from New York to the Isthmus, whence one could cross by land to Panama, or else go mainly by water across Nicaragua to the Pacific Coast—both fever-stricken routes—and thence up the coast to San Francisco. We have already noticed Cornish miners from Wisconsin going down the Mississippi to follow these routes. The healthiest route was the longest, round Cape Horn. For people already in the Middle West there was the long overland route by ox-teams, exposed to Indians or, much worse, disease: dysentery, smallpox in the plains, mountain-fever in the Rockies. We have some direct information from a St. Agnes miner writing home to his wife from Weber Creek, September 25, 1850.[9] Not all the miners were illiterate, and Edward Dale has a long description of the overland journey. Beyond Laramie they were told that the ferries were so crowded that in a couple of days his party set to work and made a boat of their own, "ready to cross the swift and once dreaded Platte, which at this place is a quarter of a mile wide." They were so successful that they stopped a day or two ferrying other emigrants over, earning $100 the first day. But, crossing the Humboldt Sink Dale lost an ox which he would not have sold for $100—he describes the fearful losses on this dreary stretch. He himself had kept well, but many hundreds died on the way and since their arrival that season.

In the early stages of placer-mining, i.e. digging the stuff out from the sides or beds of streams and then washing the detritus for gold particles or dust, shovels and picks were about all they needed, with, of course, the wash-bowls on their knees. Anybody could be a prospector, and many lucky strikes of whole nuggets of gold were made in early days. Shortly, improved equipment was developed: long toms with long handles to maneuver the washing better, next cradles, then sluice-boxes to direct a continuous stream of water in the process. All this was just like alluvial streaming for minerals the world over—the Cornish had used these simple techniques in their tin-streaming for centuries, before following up the lodes into the hillside and taking to mining proper. This was what shortly happened in California.

John Roberts, who seems to have been a long-headed fellow, describes the techniques, the processes, and weighs up the prospects very intelligibly for us.[10] He had come on from Wisconsin to Sonora, and tells us that "the long tom is nothing but a washing strake such as we use in the lead mines of Wisconsin, with a sieve at the end of it, under which is fixed a box called the rifle box, set in a diagonal position . . . The place where I am working is on the side of a hill; we take away from one to two feet in depth of the surface of the ground (just like the farmers carry away a stope of Camborne town earth for dressing their land.)" At first he made little more than enough for his board, and provisions were extremely expensive. Then he and his partner bought two mules, two carts, the privilege of a stream of water to wash with and a long tom, for $700. In six weeks he had cleared $300 profit after all expenses, and the claim was as good as ever. He had never worked so hard in his life, but "I think this is the best country for making money under the sun, and, as far as I have seen and experienced, it is very healthy, we very seldom hear of anyone being sick." He was very appreciative of the "romantic appearance" of the country.

Roberts was intending to speculate by digging into the quartz veins next winter: "they are formed exactly like the copper lodes in Cornwall, only they lie very flat." It was a natural turn of thought for a miner used to working the copper veins in Cornwall, and, as we shall see, it corroborates what Professor Rodman Paul says on the matter.

Thus came about the development of quartz-mining in the richest area, up in Nevada County in the lovely foothills of the Sierra—its center the twin towns of Grass Valley and Nevada City. This gave the steady and continuous yield of gold for nearly the next century—the biggest and deepest of the mines, Empire Mine, ceased production only with America's entry into the war in 1941. This was real mining, the whole country there honey-combed with shafts and adits, tunnels and levels. This was where the know-how of the Cornish came in, and it was here that they chiefly congregated—as we saw in Wisconsin: where the prospects of mining were best. Grass Valley and Nevada City became dominantly Cornish towns. Here they stuck, and still to some extent stick today.

Professor Paul tells us that "Cornishmen are credited with suggesting the presence of the buried deposits and with making the first attempts to reach them. The Cornishmen, approaching the problem as veteran underground miners, sank short shafts into the hillsides until they struck 'pay dirt.' "[11] That is an American expression; the process of seeking it was a logical one to the Cornish, though they were often baffled by the unaccustomed and unexpected geological complexities of the area.[12] *Solvitur ambulando*: gradually difficulties were surmounted, experience accumulated of new conditions within a familiar framework, and they became at home in their new world—often at one remove, via Wisconsin, Illinois or Michigan. Here, too, we find Cornishmen in charge of the mines, as mining engineers, examiners of mines and prospectors; also in the more specialized operations, such as timbering the drifts and stopes, as foremen, in blasting and drilling, as well as in the ordinary avocations of mining.

California gold-mining made its own contributions to the science and to industry: the hydraulic process, for example, as well as the rotatory Californian stamps for crushing ore. In all this "Grass Valley, Nevada county, early became and has ever since remained not only the most important centre of auriferous vein mining in California, but one of the best known in the world. It was in Grass Valley that much of the trial and error experimental work was done during the 'fifties."[13] Hence the conclusion of the San Francisco press: "Nevada is the leading mining county of California. It has the largest mining population, the largest gold yield, the most thorough system of ditches, the most profitable quartz and hydraulic mines; and within its borders many of the most important mining inventions were made or first applied in this State." The chlorination process, by which a higher percentage of gold could be saved in milling, came into use there, though "more than a half-dozen years passed before it was employed to any significant extent outside the locality of its California origin: Grass Valley and Nevada City."[14]

Though Grass Valley had quite a cosmopolitan sprinkling, to serve various needs, the local newspaper declared that "our mining is for the most part carried on by Cornishmen."[15] They brought not only their experience and skill, their inherited aptitude, but their tenacious adherence to old and tried ways. They bitterly opposed the introduction of the new and more dangerous dynamite for blasting, in place of the old black powder to which they were accustomed. They objected to the single-handed drilling that went with the use of dynamite, instead of drilling in pairs that was their habit—safer and more companionable, if slower and more costly. These pressures came about when the old idyllic days of individual prospecting were over and mining became necessarily more capitalized, under the control of San Francisco and other capitalists. At Grass Valley the Cornishmen formed a miners' league, and the years 1869-72 saw two serious strikes and a good deal of turbulence, especially when the management tried to import "scab" labor, mainly Irish. Some of the Irish stayed, however: now they form a considerable element in the population and there have been a good many Cornish-Irish marriages. The good days were over before the Second World War: today there is no mining in Grass Valley or Nevada City. Though they are not deserted ghost-towns, like Jerome in Arizona, they are shadows of their former selves, the forest once more closing in around them: their appeal is the nostalgic one of the past, as with Mineral Point or Houghton and Hancock. Here, too, we shall observe Cornish folk setting out for fresh fields, though a faithful remnant remains.

Much that is sensational and vulgar has been written about early social conditions in this area; its authentic expression in literature still remains the early stories of Bret Harte, with which he won fame, brought together in volumes like *The Luck of Roaring Camp*. Mining camps are mining camps the world over, and we have already seen something of pioneering conditions in Wisconsin. In the gold-mining area red-shirted men, covered with the red dust that made its impression on young Harte—his stories slightly altered the names of settlements in the neighborhood, Red Dog, Red Hat, Rough and Ready, Dutch Flat—camped out at first in tents under the trees, and put together cabin or shack as winter came on. They partnered—one of the best of Harte's stories, "Tennessee's Partner," is on this theme; they took it in turns to do the cooking. At first it was a community almost entirely of men. In 1852 Nevada County had 12,500 white males to 900 females; there were some 3000 American Indians, and nearly 4000 Chinese.[16]

Soon came in the saloons and brothels, necessary adjuncts to such communities, though in their dancing some men had to take the part of women. Notorious ladies of pleasure appeared—the famous *cocotte*, Lola Montez, retired to Grass Valley, where one may still see her house behind its prim

California: Gold and Otherwise 249

fence with the red bougainvillea and blue morning glory. (When an editor of the *Grass Valley Telegraph* attacked her ballet, she horsewhipped him; he slunk out of town, and later committed suicide.) Along came the actors, the travelling companies arriving by stage-coach, and even opera. The National Hotel at Nevada City, at which so many of these characters alighted, has been admirably restored with its fine verandahs and iron balconies. Out in the hills there were not infrequent hold-ups—there *were* desperadoes about—though shootings were even more frequent in town. In the end, when the women came and family life was possible, the Cornish communities settled down to their familiar round of regular work, Methodist Church and Sunday school, brass-bands and processions, choirs and tea-meetings, clubs and fraternities, all the incidents of their vivacious and customary demotic life.

We may now proceed to illustrate these themes. First for a sample of the Cornish men who flocked from the Mississippi to California to mine for a few years and then returned with their winnings to purchase a farm—we have already observed something of this pattern in Wisconsin, let us look at folk from Jo Daviess County, Illinois.[17] William H. Blewett went mining in California from 1851 to 1857; from 1860 to 1871 he was engaged in freighting from Omaha to California, making twelve round trips across the plains, i.e. one a year. He settled down eventually as general superintendent of the Galena and Southern Wisconsin Railroad. Henry Vincent was less fortunate: he made the trip to California in 1851, but died "shortly after he reached the Golden Land." Seth Glanville spent eight years there, and as a result was able to purchase a farm of 248 acres in Illinois. Edwin Jewell spent three years in California, then a couple of years cattle-dealing in Australia, and settled back in Illinois on 370 acres. Josiah Kestle was four years in California, six years in the lead-mines of Galena, where he fell eighty-five feet and crippled himself.

Nevertheless, he acquired a farm of 403 acres and became a road commissioner and school inspector. Eight years in California enabled Edward Mitchell to buy a large grist mill at Apple River; three years there—and bachelor John Old purchased his farm of 156 acres at Woodbine; three years—and James Phillips returned to buy a farm of 340 acres at Scales Mound. At Council Hill Thomas Harris bought a farm of 125 acres after three years in California; after a similar period William Oatey got his 160 acres—and a widow to wife, whose son by her first husband, a Rodda, was subsequently killed at Chickamauga.

This is only a small, but representative, sample of the Illinois Cornish who went to California for a spell in the first phase, mostly the early 1850's—these are they who are meant by the "Forty-Niners"—and returned to farm in Jo Daviess County. We must not assume that it was solely their gold-mining gains that enabled them to buy land, but no doubt it would be the principal element in their total savings.

We have had reason to regret that so few of these folk could give an account of their travels and experiences, they were so illiterate. But we know something of the overland trip of William Jewell, one of five brothers from Wendron who became Forty-Niners. They were mining at Scales Mound when the California fever first caught two of them, James and Edwin, who journeyed overland in 1849. The three other brothers, William, Francis and Alfred, followed in 1850 and they were six months on the road. At Council Bluffs, Iowa, they joined a train of twenty-seven wagons. When they got across the Sierra Nevada their brothers met them at Placerville, and took them to Sacramento to buy more teams and provisions. At first in Greenwood Valley they had no luck, so the brothers moved southward to Mud Spring in Eldorado County, "where they built a log-cabin and wintered at a little post-office station, there being good dry diggings all about."[18] In the spring they moved up to Spanish Bar, on the Middle Fork of the American River, where they operated a quicksilver machine, making about $8 a day. Provisions from Sacramento were fearfully expensive—and this was where the far-sighted, the Huntingtons and Crockers and Stanfords, began to make their fortunes.

Next the brothers moved north to the Yuba River, where they were snowed in; hence "with their packs on their backs they started for New Diggings, pitching their tents on the snow or clearing it away when the ground was not too far under." Here they were in good mining country, but provisions were scarce and the brothers divided. William went freighting in 1851 and saved his wages. Thus he was able to join a partnership that staked a claim near Placerville from which each cleared $1500, Jewell keeping the accounts. "When the expenses were paid and the balance divided, each man took care of his own, having his secret depository under a tree or some other place unnoticed by the others. Mr. Jewell frequently carried with him $3000 and $4000 and, when he wanted to go anywhere, would bury it in an old mine until he came back." With some of the proceeds he bought cattle, went stock-raising and dairying, until 1854 when ague compelled him to leave the country.

He returned via the Nicaragua route, and went home to Cornwall to marry a wife, Eliza Roskrow, and bring her out with him to the farm he had bought at Council Hill. After four years they paid a four-month visit home, and returned to farm at Scales Mound. He was the first to introduce Leicesters into the county, his cattle being mostly Short-horns. He retired from active farming in 1872 and paid a third visit home in 1875, where he had mining interests and his wife some property. His wife's grandfather was governor of Pendennis Castle, at the entrance to Falmouth Harbor; his own maternal grandfather proprietor of the Half Way Hotel, between Falmouth and Helston, where the Royal Mail changed horses. William Jewell prospered and was an early investor in land in Nebraska, where he stocked a farm and settled a nephew upon it. The uncle had travelled all through Nebraska—there was hardly a house in sight from Omaha to Fort Laramie in 1850. The nephew, however, walked out on him, and Jewell sold out, transferring his land interests to Iowa, where they became quite considerable. A Methodist and Republican, he looked after them all from his residence in Warren, surrounded by evergreens and Victorian shrubbery.

It so happens that we have an intimate account of the overland crossing from one of the very first settlers in Napa County, before even the gold-rush began. William Alexander Trubody was a child of eight when his parents made the journey across the plains; he died in his ninety-fourth year in 1933. His parents had come from East Cornwall a hundred years before to Pennsylvania, thence to Lexington, Missouri, where they remained ten years and had two children. Crossing the plains and mountains they reached Sutter's Fort in October 1847, then went on to San Francisco where John Trubody worked at his trade of carpenter. On the discovery of gold at Sutter's mill, "he, as did almost every other white man in California, went to the mines."[19] Being successful, after six months he went back to the embryo San Francisco and built the first brick house erected there, as also the first marble front, with marble imported from New York. In 1850 he bought a ranch in Napa County, where he first raised stock and grain, and later planted fruit—we see the growing diversification of Californian farming in this. This remained the home of this Cornish family for over a century.

In his late eighties the son's memories of childhood were still vivid—perhaps we may reproduce them in his own veracious idiom.[20] A chance visitor's talk, in 1846—year of decision—"was so favorable to California that both Father & Mother concluded to get ready and in the spring start for California. with this in view he hired a helper & the two built a wagon & the local blacksmith did the iron work. this done he bought four yoke of oxen, sold his little home, procured provisions for the trip & about the first of may 1847 started for

California." The family were four in number, at Lexington they joined up with some friends and made for Independence, where they waited for the company to form, over thirty persons, to make a hundred strong.

At the Platte River they joined with a much larger train, mostly making for Oregon; now altogether a hundred wagons and four hundred people, they decided to divide in two, with one train a day ahead of the other. It must have looked like the descriptions we have of these armies on the march: "For miles, to the extent of vision, an animated mass of beings broke upon our view. Long trains of wagons with their white covers were moving slowly along, a multitude of horsemen were prancing on the road, companies of men were travelling on foot . . . the display of banners from many wagons and the multitude of armed men looked as if a mighty army was on its march."

Young William naturally remembered the Indians: after Fort Laramie they met a large war-band of Sioux in full fig going to fight the Pawnees. The emigrants got ready their guns, "but the Indians made signs that they were friendly & got out pipes took a whif or two & then passed to the whites to show that they were frienly." They travelled along the North Platte and then up the Sweetwater until they came to Independence Rock where already several hundred men following the Oregon Trail had scratched their names: "my Father put his name there along with the others & most of the company did the same." After Fort Hall the trains divided, by far the greater number taking the northern route to Oregon. The California contingent taking the left fork consisted of some twenty wagons and a hundred people. This was the year after the horrible fate of the Donner party, most of whom died in the mountains, while one or two survived by taking to cannibalism. Up in the mountains they camped one night at Donner camp, not far from the lake then known as Truckee Lake; already everything had been destroyed "that might be a discouragement to future travelers wagons ox yokes and anything & everything that would burn were given to the flames." The train managed the ticklish business of getting over the summit better than most, making up the road first, doubling the team to a wagon, the men pushing upwards and on the way down holding the wagons back with ropes.

On the Pacific slope, not far from where Nevada City came to be built, the Indians stole four head of cattle, "two of wich were my Fathers thus weakening his team of four yoke." Someone loaned Trubody a couple of cows to strengthen his team for the rest of the trip. And so they came to Sutter's Fort, where he sold his wagon and oxen and went to work helping to build Sutter's flourmill. From there the family moved to San Francisco, where the news of the gold-find "spread like wild fire & everybody that could went to the mines." It took the family some seven days to get up the river in the schooner *Susanita* to Sacramento.

Later in conversation William Trubody remembered that "Father didn't stay in the mines in the winter of '48-'49, because he was afraid of robbery—had $12,000 worth of gold with him. He got out a few logs for a cabin, but decided to go to Sutter's Fort . . . When we landed at Sutter's in '47, I remember them accusin' Keesburg, the Donner party man, of killin' people at Truckee Lake, and saltin' 'em down. We kids were so afraid of Keesburg that we always ran away when we saw him." Trubody took his family down the Sacramento again to San Francisco, where he bought a fifty-vara lot for $7500 on Washington Street and built himself a house. "Prices soon advanced rapidly & he sold forty feet for $40,000 built on the remainder several small houses." After that they never looked back: the development of San Francisco gave good opportunities to a carpenter and builder.

In 1849 Trubody's brother, Josiah, journeyed overland by the southern route through Santa Fé, coming out at San Diego. He came up to San Francisco in time for Christmas dinner with the family. John Trubody deserved to prosper, and did. In 1850 he bought himself a ranch in the Napa Valley, which became the family center though he himself lived mostly in San Francisco. The boys were sent East, via the Isthmus, to school in New York; they came back to farm the ranch their father had bought in Napa, that excellent wine-growing country not far from San Francisco. Here they took to fruit-farming, planting some forty acres of blackberry vines, raising five tons of fruit at their height, and "Trubody's blackberries have a state-wide reputation."[21] Each brother had a family of four children; the younger became superintendent of the county and lived to be the oldest of its pioneers. When an old man he could still sing the emigrants' variant of the Susanna song:

> I've just got in across the plains,
>   I'm poorer than a snail,
> My damned old mule a cripple,
>   I pulled him in by the tail.
> I fed him last at Chimney Rock,
>   That's where the grass gave out,
> But I'm proud to tell
>   We stood it well along the Truckee Route.

It is as well that we have this direct evidence from a Cornish boy, for literary folk have been apt to be ignorant about the Cornish. Here is Robert Louis Stevenson, himself an emigrant to California some thirty years later, writing in 1879 in *Across the Plains*.

> There were no emigrants direct from Europe—save one German family and a knot of Cornish miners who kept grimly by themselves, one reading the New Testament all day long through steel spectacles, the rest discussing privately the secrets of their old-world, mysterious race. Lady Hester Stanhope believed she could make something great of the Cornish; for my part, I can make nothing of them at all. A division of races, older and more original than Babel, keeps this close, esoteric family

apart from neighbouring Englishmen. Not even a Red Indian seems more foreign in my eyes. This is one of the lessons of travel—that some of the strangest races dwell next door to you at home.

Stevenson was young, and may be forgiven his ignorance, though it was strange in a Scot. All the same it was an opportunity missed. If only this reporter had taken the trouble to penetrate their "mystery," he might have had something to tell us—about the lives and thoughts of these men, their motives in leaving home, their background, their individual stories, the inner hopes and beliefs that sustained them in their arduous lives of toil—all that the historian longs to know. And just at the moment when he himself was writing:

> And all that I could think of in the darkness and the cold
> Was just that I was leaving home and my folks were
>   growing old.

It denotes a curious defect of sympathy, and, for the rest, corroborates one of the theses of this book.

Grass Valley was so named from the lush grass that grew there: some immigrants coming over the Truckee route lost their famished cattle and found these pioneers fattening themselves in the luxuriant grass. Then came in the gold-miners searching the ravines: in 1848 one of them broke off a piece of quartz to discover that it was gold-bearing.[22] Next year gold was found in the neighboring Deer Creek Dry Diggings, which became Nevada City. (It was called Nevada a decade before the state over the high Sierra; later it had to add "City" to avoid confusion with the state.) Quartz-gold was richer and offered continuous exploitation along the lodes, as opposed to the chance discoveries, the irregularity and petering out of placer-mining. Grass Valley and Nevada City were launched: they became the center of the richest and most continuous gold-mining in California, with mines all about the hillsides—North Star, Eureka, Idaho-Maryland, Empire—the ground beneath a honeycomb. Before the end, in the 1930's the area had the deepest mining in the world. The great Hearst fortune started here: George Hearst, father of the too celebrated William Randolph, was a working miner, who had the luck to purchase what became one of the richest mines for $450. Herbert Hoover, one of the most successful of mining engineers and least successful of Presidents, worked a student year here at Mayflower Mine.

It is said that General Frémont, who helped to open up this country, himself suggested the importation of Cornish miners to tackle the rock-mining.[23] The idea was obvious enough, and the Cornish were already flocking there, as we have seen, among the Forty-Niners. But their regular introduction into mining proper was a subsequent phase: they came in continuously after the original impulse of the gold-rush had ended in the mid-fifties, and thousands—miners as well as non-miners—had left with their takings, or without. Those who came in were professional miners; they largely built these solid communities with the familiar idiosyncratic features continuing right up to our own day.

The best-known of these to the outside world is the Grass Valley Cornish Choir. "Although the Cornish carols floated up from the mine-shafts for years, it wasn't until some time around 1890 that John Farrell organised the choir. It met at the Methodist Church and has never missed singing there during the Chistmas season."[24] Evidently it was formed out of groups of carollers from the mines; the carols they sang were traditional, "little of this music has ever been published and the Grass Valley Choir has used some frayed notebooks in which earlier carollers set down the music by hand." The choir was directed for nearly half a century by Harold George, whose father came from Cornwall nearly a century ago. Under him the Choir won nation-wide recognition with its broadcast from the two thousand foot level of the Idaho-Maryland Mine in 1940, repeated after the war, and with the record of their carols which has sold all over the West and penetrated to their original home in Cornwall.

It appears that the choir is now coming to an end—as everything interesting is. (There is this to be said for history, that the past is far more interesting than the future is likely to be.)

The miners brought not only their industry and expertise but their stories, their dialect and folk-lore, their superstitions about the "tommyknockers," with their tapping on the timbers to warn the men of an impending fall of rock or some other threat of danger. The "little men" also played pranks, such as hiding tools, jamming drills, blowing out candles or tampering with fuses. It reminds one of the "gremlins" with whom R. A. F. men were so familiar during the war. Such phenomena are to be expected from the imaginations of men in frequent contact with danger, but there may also be an element of extra-sensory perception in premonitions of danger. Cornish miners carried their ideas of tommyknockers everywhere underground; they sometimes fashioned effigies of the little men out of clay and set them up in the tunnels. Perhaps they were a protection.

The women contributed their cooking to the local lore, created the tradition as elsewhere—Wisconsin and Illinois, Michigan, Colorado. The Nevada City handbook tells us that Timothy Giles arrived in 1853, was successful and sent for his wife and daughters. They came, via Pennsylvania and Panama, in 1855. "Members of the Giles families have lived in Nevada City ever since those early mining days. Mrs. Giles was renowned for her Cornish cooking and her recipes have passed down through the family."[25] We are then given recipes for saffron bread (from 1805), "heavy cake," saffron cake and pasty, as still made, now by the fifth generation.

Let us look a little into these people as individuals—the essence of history being the particular, according to the philosophers—and build up our picture from that.

The brothers William and Philip Nicholls came from my native town of St. Austell in 1852, mined for a few years, then went to Forest City where they started a gold-buying business.[26] In 1861 the brothers opened their bank at Dutch Flat. William's son, John, followed via Panama in 1865, learned the gold-buying business and ultimately succeeded to it. After fifty-six years John retired in 1920—the firm had handled $750,000 worth of gold in the heyday of hydraulic mining. In those days false weights and scales took in many Chinese; with John Nicholls "his word was his bond," and the Chinese round about all did their business with "John Nicholo." He did well enough, but made no fortune. At eighty he still went down to the bank each morning, kept the old scales and other relics of the good days, when "the early Argonauts used to line at his counter and throw down their sacks of dust for safe keeping." He had three sons, a doctor, an electrician, a mining engineer in Canada.

I once met his cousin, Philip's son, then a centenarian: William Nicholls, Jr., living at Berkeley. Born in 1850, he sailed through the Golden Gate on Christmas Day 1866, on his way to the family at Dutch Flat.[27] He worked in the family bank till 1904, when he sold his interest to his cousin and retired to Berkeley; but he maintained the old family home in Placer County, and told me that he had twice been back to his native St. Austell. He had a brother, three sons and a daughter, grandchildren and great-grandchildren, mostly in California. Four generations of them assembled for his hundredth birthday; he died at the age of a hundred and one.

John Tamblyn came via Panama in 1864 to become a foreman in the Eclipse Mine in Owens Valley, thence to Sierra City to build a chlorination plant for reducing gold.[28] Buying himself a little ranch of thirty acres to raise fruit, in 1875 he was ordained a Methodist minister and became a circuit-rider through the mountainous counties of the state, "earning his way to Heaven in half-soled shoes." He had four children, one of whom had a rather un-Methodist career. Spending his early years mining, he set up a photography business and then opened the Broadway Theatre in Nevada City. He next joined with partners to purchase the Strand Theatre in Grass Valley. Nevertheless, he was a trustee of the school district, active in pushing forward education. His brother was the "Village Smithy" of Grass Valley. He had followed his trade in Idaho, where he added tool-sharpening and pipe-repairing in the mines. Returning to his own blacksmith's shop at Grass Valley, at regular intervals he went down into Central and Empire mines to shoe the mules, that were never brought up to the surface.

It is difficult to know what to think of Bennet Penhall, born at Hayle in 1853—he is so given to stretching the long bow: perhaps we may regard him as an interesting example of the bragging which is a not un-Cornish characteristic.[29] He gives us an improbable account of his ancestry, while his grandfather was killed at Waterloo—not in itself improbable. His father was an engineer, whose six sons were at one time in six different countries—also possible. His mining experiences as superintendent of Imperial then of North Banner Mine should be verifiable. He went off to South Africa to become manager of Lydenburg gold fields under Barney Barnato. The Boers, under Joubert's nephew, held him up and took $10,000 from his safe; they held him prisoner for a couple of months, when he made his escape—like young Winston Churchill, we may add. He joined the British forces under Kitchener but as a United States citizen declined a commission and refused pay for his services. He accepted only a couple of rifles presented to him by Lord Kitchener himself. For many years he was manager of Le Duc mining property at Grass Valley, a member of the town-planning commission and vestryman of Emmanuel Church. We see a very Cornish type in his photograph under his wide-brimmed hat, a fine pair of moustaches, good features, a direct look, well set up—he looks like Cecil Rhodes himself.

John Cornish came to Iowa, where he had eight children.[30] One son was yardmaster at Park Station, Chicago; in 1891 he came to a similar job at Barstow. With an ear injured in a mine blast, he gave himself up to organizing the Order of Railway Employees. Beginning with a few meeting in a conductor's bedroom in Sacramento in 1911, by 1924 they were twenty thousand in number, operating both accident and health insurance. This benefit-organization operated in all the Pacific states and Colorado, with Cornish as the head organizer for northern California. James Williams came via Panama in 1862 and worked in the old Eureka, New York Hill, North Star, Empire and other mines.[31] He married Mary Cheynouth and had four children. One of them learned assaying, and opened an assay office at Grass Valley. He became the owner of one thousand acres of mineral lands in the county, upon which were many gold-mining claims. He had "great faith in the future of Grass Valley, where he has invested his money." Alas, there was no future: gold-mining was on its way out. Another Williams of the second generation did better for himself by entering the motion-picture business, which was on the way up.[32] He operated the Crystal Theatre, then remodelled the Strand Theatre and made a success of it—those were the days!

John Bree made three trips to California: the first, across the plains by ox-team; the second, around Cape Horn.[33] He then went home to marry Mary Tredinnick, and came back across the plains. Buying a four hundred-acre stand of thick timber and brush near Grass Valley, he planted an orchard of Bartlett pears. Bree was one of six fellows who discovered a rich gold ledge, and unfortunately sold their claim—for it became the great Idaho-Maryland Mine. One of his sons became the first horticultural commissioner in the county, another a Standard Oil agent in Los Angeles—with that we are moving into the modern world.

Wisconsin had offered a greater variety of occupations than the Upper Peninsula of Michigan; now California extended a still greater spread and, with its immense future development, far wider choice with bigger opportunities. In gold-mining, however, we find the Cornish to the fore as superintendents and foremen, if not to the same extent as in the Copper Country. Frank Provis, after many years' experience, became superintendent of the gold-mill at North Star.[34] Samuel Blight, who came to Grass Valley at eighteen, after years at both quartz- and hydraulic-mining became captain of various mines in the district. Frank W. Hooper—the second generation usually takes a second name—was superintendent of the mill at Empire Mine; in the course of forty years' service he is said to have extracted $35,000,000 in gold from the rock.[35] In 1920 he bought a 975-acre farm in Mendocino County, which his two eldest sons farmed, and came to own a group of mines—an optimistic Oddfellow!

William Luke came in 1863 via Panama; when his family followed in 1870 they came by transcontinental train taking two weeks to cross.[36] A daughter married John James, born at Hayle in 1848, who came to Grass Valley about the same time as the Lukes. After fifteen years mining John James was able to buy 360 acres in French Ravine, three miles below Grass Valley. His son Frank was proud of having seen more service in France 1917–18 than any other Nevada County boy: he was in each American offensive from Montdidier to the Argonne. This introduces a theme: one notices again and again that the sons of Cornish immigrants were quick to join up and serve against Germany in the two wars she unleashed upon the world in the twentieth century.

When we look at the names of soldiers from Grass Valley serving in the First World War, nearly half of them are Cornish names—so many of those with which we are familiar, all the way from Angove and Arthur to Uren, Warne and Woolcock.[37] We find no less than seven of the Rowe name, seven Harris, five Richards, five Martin, four Nancervis, four Crase, four Hooper, four Thomas, four Williams; among rarer names we find Trescothick, Nettle, Kneebone, Gribble, Eva, Chellew, Henwood, Juliff, Stuckie, Rowett, Sleeman. The telephone directory for the twin towns today gives us a great many more.

We have illustrations of what Grass Valley looked like early on, in 1852, sparsely scattered log cabins among the pines, charmingly situated some twenty-four hundred feet high, half way between Sacramento and the high Sierra. In 1855 it was devastated by fire but, rebuilt, continued to grow until the First World War. In 1924 there were still twelve hundred men in the mines; today none. Up to 1918 Nevada County produced $265,000,000 worth of gold, of which Grass Valley contributed $120,000,000. By 1877 Eureka was worked out; in 1874 North Star closed down, to re-open in 1884; after 1895 it was exceptionally prosperous, finding veins at depth which produced $1,200,000 a year. In 1918 Empire and Pennsylvania were producing $1,500,000 from great depths. The gold is still there at depth, but, with managed currencies, the world has less need of it. But in the future? ...

We have seen the exceptional contribution of the Cornish to the industry in its heyday. The individuals I have cited are fair samples of the people who made headway in their new environment. Even so, they are only a small minority, while there are a hundred times as many of whom we have no notice.

Nevada County was not the only area where the Cornish went gold-mining, though they stuck fast where the gold was best and lasted longest. Plumas County, just north among foothills, had the largest British enterprise, the Eureka Mine, and it brought in Cornish miners. Many of them lived in the neighboring town of Johnsville, now being restored. It used to be said there that the saffron sent through the post to Cornish housewives would scent the little post-office. Thomas Treleaven, born in my favorite moorland parish of Luxulyan, came here from Lake Superior in 1866 to mine in Indian Valley and then the Cherokee district.[38] Two years later he brought his family over. In 1875 he re-located the New York quartz-mine, selling his interest in it three years later. He did better than he would have done in sparse and bare, but beautiful, Luxulyan.

Staging and freighting were of the first importance in those days, and demanded skill and experience in the primitive condition of the roads and considering the difficulties of the terrain. The stage-coach drivers have been celebrated in the stories of Bret Harte and Mark Twain and some of their names have been remembered. Not so the freighters, they remained anonymous—though a number of Cornishmen took to freighting. "The stage routes were often treacherous, crossing both arid wastes and rapid streams . . . It was no easy job to drive the large teams of mixed mustangs, hitched to heavily loaded stages, along the rough and stony roads and over the steep grades of the Sierra."[39] Still more so for the freighters, we may say.

An interesting resident of Sacramento County, for more than sixty years, was Stephen Uren, who patented a number of inventions.[40] The son of a blacksmith, he emigrated to Ontonagon and came to California in 1858, where he worked at his trade and mined as a side-line. He ultimately settled down in the blacksmiths' shops of the Southern Pacific, where the rolling mills were under his direction. He patented a device for forming car-links, and followed this with a process of making nuts at one a minute, instead of each half-hour. His most important patent was for a slot attachment on a bolt-heading machine, which simultaneously headed a bolt and slotted the key. He became president of the International Blacksmiths' Association.

At Stockton we find an interesting group of Tretheways.[41] Their parents had emigrated to Robert Owen's socialistic community of New Harmony in Indiana, which turned out to be anything but harmonious. Naturally this did not last long, and after two years of it the sensible Cornishman returned to his shipyard in London. In 1863 the father set out alone for

California: his first job was building a gold-crushing mill in Tuolumne County. In the fall of the same year son Edward followed his father, and together they went timbering in the mines of Contra Costa County. Two years later the son went home to marry a wife and bring her over. Eventually the parents concentrated their family in California: there were eleven children. Son Edward became the mill-wright at Stockton mills. Another son, William, served his apprenticeship in San Francisco, helped to build the Hope Iron Works and turned out the patterns for the California Street Cable Company. Moving to Stockton he formed a partnership to operate the Stockton Iron Works, which turned out everything from traction engines to decorative iron-work, William Tretheway in charge of the pattern department.

William Trenouth, a bricklayer, provides us with an example of someone who was able to ignore the stampede to the gold-diggings.[42] He went to San Francisco in 1850, but remained there working at his trade until he took to ranching in Santa Clara County, where he spent the rest of his life farming, fruit-growing and stock-raising. With three sons in partnership he bought 550 acres near San José Mission. Another son bought his own fruit-farm in Irvington. They made a marked success of their fruit drying. When David Hambly fetched his family overland in 1852 there were twenty teams in the train; arrived at Henpeck Flat the Hamblys opened a boarding house in a large canvas-tent—there were many hundreds of men to seven or eight women at the beginning. His son William became a young member of the Plumas Rangers operating against cattle-thieves, outlaws and Indians. This fellow provides us with an example of the unsuccessful. Uneducated, he learned printing, but his firm failed in the collapse of mining stocks in 1878. Put in charge of the reduction works of the South Almadén Mining Company, he suffered a series of set-backs and accidents. Unlucky, he consoled himself with spiritualism and became an organizer of the California State Spiritualist Association.

John Trythall emigrated to New Jersey at eighteen, and then worked his way across the continent, mining in Pennsylvania, Illinois, Iowa, Missouri, Michigan, Wyoming, Nevada, finally California.[43] But, "longing to see more of the world," he soon drifted to British Columbia and Alaska. He had spells of silver-mining in Napa County, coal-mining in Contra Costa County, and in Arizona, before he settled down as superintendent of the Pittsburg coal mines in Contra Costa. Moving to Alameda County he turned over to fruit-farming —almonds, berries, a vineyard: who wouldn't?

Henry Ivey, a popular livery man of Concord, Contra Costa County, carried the freight from Concord to Martinez and had the contract for carrying the mail from Martinez to Concord and Clayton.[44] He had sixteen fine livery horses and a German wife. At Angels Camp, near Sonora, where took place in 1889 one of the worst mining accidents of the period, we find several Cornish names among those killed.[45] This was the place where Mark Twain heard Ben Coon's version of the famous story of "The Jumping Frog of Calaveras County," though it was not original with Coon. Mark Twain simply wrote out what was an authentic story of the people and won fame with it. Now we have a place in the vicinity named for the two writers who brought California into the consciousness of the English-speaking world: Twain Harte.

A dozen miles or more from the lower end of San Francisco Bay, tucked in the Coastal Range and guarded by two peaks, were the quicksilver-mines of New Almadén. Up at an elevation of seventeen hundred feet, they came ultimately to form a constellation of mines and, owing to the irregular formation of the red cinnabar ore, to have an extremely intricate system of shafts and tunnels.[46] The development of gold-mining in California made the fortune of New Almadén, for during its heyday quicksilver formed the principal part of the amalgamation metal used in the reduction of gold. There were heavy exports to China, but the chief market for the mercury lay at hand on the Pacific slopes—when the fabulous Comstock Lode was opened up in Nevada it became an especially good customer.

The mine was known from Mexican times, but not until the Americans took over California could proper exploitation begin. By the Treaty of Guadalupe-Hidalgo America got California and the whole of the Southwest for $15,000,000—within seven years New Almadén had produced as much. It worked over a longer period, 1846 to 1945, and yielded a greater total value than any other metal-mine in California. During that period it produced over a million flasks of quicksilver or 76 million lb., one-third the entire United States production. For the first twelve years the mine was dogged by a complicated series of lawsuits regarding title and claims, but from 1863 the Quicksilver Mining Company was organized and took over.[47] From that time, especially during 1863–70, a start was made of importing Cornish miners to work the mine properly. By that time the labor-force consisted of 115 Mexicans and South Americans, 90 American-born of various sorts, 172 English-born of whom the major element was Cornish. The Mexicans lived in the old town below; English Camp was a pleasant new town of bungalows running up the steep hill—in old maps it is sometimes named Cornish Camp.

From 1870 to 1890 nearly all the improvements in quicksilver-mining and reduction were made at New Almadén. The mine grew deep, twenty-four hundred feet, some seven hundred feet below sea-level. There were marked variations in both demand and supply for quicksilver, so the mine had many ups and downs. After 1881 Captain James Harry was in control, and he located a large body of ore—the "Harry ore-body"—which gave prosperity for another five years. After that profits dropped. By 1912 the company was bankrupt; the First World War led to a revival, which continued till the depression in the 1930's, and it was worked again during the Second World War until the final closure in 1946.

Captain Harry had worked in the mines in Cornwall from

the time he was a boy of ten, for his father was killed in an accident in 1846.[48] In 1869 Harry came to California, mining first in Nevada County and moving to New Almadén in 1872. An experienced man, he was put in charge of responsible jobs as timberman, pumpman, shaft-boss, until he became captain in 1881. As such, in addition to his remarkable discovery of fresh ore, he introduced the Cornish skip for raising and lowering the men. He married Elizabeth Carlyon and had six children; he was class-leader, steward and trustee of the Methodist Church the Cornish built and attended.

Let us look into the lives of a few only of the Cornish folk in the area—first, the miners. We have noticed the two Berryman brothers killed in Central Mine in Michigan in 1867, who lie in the little cemetery at Eagle Harbor. Another Berryman moved from Marquette to Grass Valley, and thence to his fate at New Almadén, where he was killed.[49] His son was appointed plumber-foreman at the mine; later, taking *his* son into partnership, he set up on his own at charmingly named Los Gatos. (It means The Cats.) Arthur Berryman seems a more restless type. He came to Pennsylvania in 1854, mining coal for a bit; from 1855–57 he was gold-mining in California, in Amador County.[50] The next seven years he was in Chile, Bolivia and Peru. Then for twelve years he worked in the New Almadén and New Idria quicksilver-mines; in 1876 off to San Francisco and British Columbia, then back to quicksilver-mining at Guadalupe till 1882, when he took the Los Gatos Hotel on the old stage-road from San José to Santa Cruz. In 1887 he gave up and went into an insurance and real-estate partnership. At any rate, this Berryman survived.

Captain Richard B. Harper had a variegated career. Born at Redruth, his father had been a mining engineer in England, Scotland, Wales and Spain, where he died.[51] In 1863 Harper came by sailing-ship round Cape Horn to Valparaiso, thence by steamer to San Francisco. He mined in Grass Valley, thence over the mountains to Virginia City. For six or seven years he worked at New Almadén, then went off to varied experiences as foreman at Mariposa, Grass Valley and in

Nevada. Returning to San José, he was "the fortunate discoverer of the North Almadén quicksilver mines," and here he built his first quicksilver furnace. In 1872 a company was formed, with himself as manager; but the lease was not renewed, and Harper went off silver-mining in Mexico, thence to British Columbia to erect the first gold-smelter in Cariboo. He spent another six years in Mexico, purchasing a quicksilver-mine for an American company and interests of his own at Chihuahua, which he was forced to abandon owing to revolutionary disturbances. From 1907 he was a mine-examiner for seven years, acting on behalf of the American and British governments. For years he travelled with George Hearst, and retired near Almadén where he optimistically owned mining land. One sees the old gentleman, bright-eyed, with a bird-like inquiring look and clipped moustache, under his broad-brimmed California hat.

Quicksilver-mining at New Almadén evidently owed a good deal to these old fellows, Captain Harry and Captain Harper.

We have already observed a number of Cornishmen retiring from mining to move over to farming. It is pleasant to notice them taking a share in the most delightful of Californian occupations, fruit-raising. The Spaniards had introduced vines, olives, walnuts, along with the pepper trees, whose delicate waving tresses are a feature of old forgotten roads in California. But not until the railroads came in the last third of the nineteenth century could fruit- and citrus-growing become the great affair it now is.[52] The Cornish were not southern Europeans, so they did not go in for vines; they went in for the fruits with which they were familiar, apples, pears, plums, berries. Later, when horticulture and vegetable-growing reached the scale of an industry in such favorable areas as the Ventura Valley, Cornish people moved in along with the rest. Hence the rather surprising number of Cornish names in that neighborhood, along with all the Mexicans.

Going out into the country round about we may cite a few

instances of these varied occupations. Louis Chynoweth, from Wisconsin, had mine holdings, but sold them to purchase a fruit-farm on the road between San José and Monterey, where he planted, prunes, pears and peaches.[53] Another Chynoweth became an attorney in San José.[54] William R. Pender had been a seafaring man, who came to California in 1854 and went mining in Sierra County.[55] In 1861 he went home to marry Elizabeth Coon. He embarked in 1862 from Southampton for St. Thomas on the *Trent*, the famous ship from which the Confederate agents, Mason and Slidell, had been extracted on the way over. Pender and his wife were passengers on the return trip from St. Thomas to Aspinwall. He became a fruit-grower in the Hamilton district. John R. Brokenshire's father died early mining; the boy was reared by relations at St. Stephens near St. Austell, whence he emigrated to Ironwood and married a Cornish girl.[56] In 1894 he came to mine in Amador and Placer counties, and later became an engineer in the railroad shops of the Southern Pacific at San José. He had seven children: one a mining engineer at the Shasta coppermines; three sons served in France in the First World War.

After ten years in Wisconsin John Treglown came to mine in Tuolumne County, then followed the trail to Virginia City and back to New Almadén.[57] He bought various mining properties and had seven children, one of whom worked in Gover Mine—a Cornish name—in which his father had an interest. The son subsequently became superintendent of South Spring Hill, and lived at Alameda. He was often called in as an expert to report on mines. An historian of the state says that for half a century "the Treglown family have taken more than a usually active interest in the development of mining properties in Amador county." In Alameda County we note the place-name Trevarno, named after the Cornish home of George Bickford, associated with the Coast Manufacturing and Supply Company, which made the safety-fuses invented by his father, William Bickford.[58]

California: Gold and Otherwise

After all these activities round about in central California in the nineteenth century, and with the drift to the big cities characteristic of the twentieth, it is understandable that there should be a very large Cornish population in San Francisco today, with its attendant cities like Oakland, as also in Sacramento. Impossible as it is to analyze these populations in detail, let us ignore for the most part the numerous and familiar Tre-, Pol-, Pen- names and notice only what strikes us. In San Francisco we find represented such very rare names as Boscawen, St. Aubyn (the Cornish name, not the French St. Aubin), Minidew, Dowrick, Carkeek, Visick. Among fairly rare names we find Faull, Kneebone (2), Annear, Vosper, Wedlake, Chelew, Carew (no less than nine), Spry, Pellow, Knuckey, Pelmear, Pethick, Jope, Menhenitt, Spargo (no less than six), Wearne, Chegwidden, Treganowen (3). Among larger groups we find Chenoweth (10), Hambly (8), Coon (8), Oates (8), Rickard (7), Carlyon (7), Polkinghorn (4), Tregenza (4), Pengelly (4). There are three Clemo, with its variants, one Clymo, and one Clyma. There are hundreds of common names like Rowe and Richards, among whom thousands of Cornish are hidden. Oakland, too, has its rarer birds: Tregea (2), Penrice (2), Penpraze (3), Prout, Chellew, Trengove (2), with the meaningless variant, Trengrove. Among larger groupings are Chenoweth (9)—which is one of the commonest Cornish names in America, though not at all common in Cornwall, Penrose (8), Tippett (7), Pascoe (5), Pender (4), Tremaine (4), Nancarrow (3), Trevorrow (3), Trezona (3).

Sacramento, the capital of California, has a very large element, and this is not at all surprising when one considers its relation to the gold-mining areas. It is far too large to analyze here, one can only draw attention to a few details and some salient points. Among rarer names we find Trestrail (2), Trewhitt, Treffry (5), Wearn, Bawden (2), Blamey (3), Daw (2), Anstess, Gover, Hender, Henwood, Endean, Hendra, Isbell, Jope, Gribble (2), Keast, Vickery, Deeble, Bunney (2), Pengray (2—one with the Cornish first name of Jenifer), Geach (3), Penwell (3), Cloke (3). We find a very large number of names of which the holders will, in such an area, be dominantly Cornish. The majority of specific Cornish names we have no space to cite, nor can we go any further afield in this region. We can only conclude that there may be three or four thousand of Cornish name and descent in Sacramento and San Francisco each. This places them alongside of such cities as Chicago, Detroit, New York, Philadelphia, Denver, and the Los Angeles district as regions where the Cornish are thickest on the ground.

Southern California was, and is, a rather different world from central and northern California. Though there was some early gold-mining, finds were sporadic and did not amount to much. Its development did not come until later; in the last century its dominant occupations were pasturing and fruit-farming—the cattle on a thousand hills, orange-, citrus-, walnut-groves, the land of *dolce far niente*. The wonderful climate attracted easterners, and eastern invalids, in thousands. Then there were the urban developments in a hundred country towns, along the coast from Santa Barbara to San Diego, and along the inland valleys from Bakersfield to San Bernardino and beyond. Later came petroleum, industry and the population explosion of our time. Southern California has been a magnet for the whole nation, particularly from the Middle West. The population of southern California is now far larger than central and northern, the urban area of Los Angeles with its dependent towns comparable only with New York, Chicago and Philadelphia.

The consequence is, though it is somewhat surprising, that this area has about as large a Cornish element as the San Francisco-Sacramento area: one of the largest in the United States. One marked difference may be observed. In the central and northern area Cornish folk may be found sprinkled all through the country, in the rural counties in addition to the large urban concentrations. In southern California that is much less the case—naturally so, considering the different climatic conditions (northern California has a climate not unlike Cornwall, whereas the south is arid, semi-desert)—and the Cornish are to be found chiefly in the towns: largely in Los Angeles, markedly in Pasadena, surprisingly in southernmost San Diego.

First, for smaller, quiet places. The old Spanish capital, Monterey, half-way up the coast, has a sprinkling. Coming down the coast to Santa Maria, we find fewer, yet still a sprinkling. In the rich agricultural and fruit-growing area of Ventura, where there are so many Mexicans, we find a surprising number of Cornish, old and new. Among those of old descent probably are Chenoweth (5); among the new we notice Bice (4—we have earlier come across a mine captain of the name). Omitting the more familiar Tre-, Pol-, Pen- names, we may point out some rarieties: Polmanter (2—probably from Polmounter), Sleeman, Angwin (2), Gummo, Ede, Carlyon, Chegwidden, Edgecomb, Dungey, Ivey; besides such names as Curnow, Nancarrow, Goldsworthy, Berryman, Wherry, Rowse, by no means rare at home.

At Santa Barbara we find the rare names Pellamounter (2), Pellow, Penquite, along with more familiar Treloar (no less than 7), Trefry (2), Trenwith (2), Tremaine, Nancarrow, Higman, Ivey, Goldsworthy, Furse, Coon (2)—in addition to many names like Hancock (8), Rouse (4), among which Cornish may lurk. In this delightful ocean-resort there lived a prominent old lady, who was a sprig of the ancient family of Hoblyn of Nanswhyden—the fine Queen Anne house there, with its splendid library, was lost to us by fire in the eighteenth century.[59] This lady in marrying a Figg and adding her maiden name of Hoblyn, came near to perpetrating an atrocious pun to a Cornish ear—for "figgy-hobben" is one of the least digestible of our dishes. On marrying, Mrs. Figg went out to British Columbia, to a lonely life on Mayne Island with nothing but Indians around. After ten years of it she moved to Santa Barbara for her health, where she took a leading part in the local life. In 1921 she organized the Santa Barbara Society to preserve the customs, dancing and lore of Spanish California; she became president of several Californian women's societies. Caught in the earthquake of July 1925, the old lady died from the shock; not without leaving a son, however, engaged in real estate and horticulture to carry on the idiosyncratic name.

Going inland to Bakersfield, we come upon the tracks of Henry Hosking, who came via Quebec to Kansas, and then joined his brothers in California.[60] Henry worked on the land as ditch-tender for the Kern County Land Company, until he became foreman of their canals and water-courses; twenty years—and he was able to buy his own farm. Thomas J. Cornish came via Toronto—where he worked in a bakery under his uncle, a Tonkyn—then via Buffalo and Pennsylvania, to California where he patented an oil-burner for bake-ovens, but had no capital to exploit it.[61] However, he built up a large baking business in Bakersfield, with three modern ovens and many employees: the largest bakery in Kern County in its time.

These instances show us the increasing variety of employments opening up. In the early development of Los Angeles a Wisconsin Cornishman, John C. Goldsworthy, took some part —from 1870, when he became city surveyor.[62] As a boy he had come to California to the mines, where he was known as "the kid" on account of his youth; he wrote the illiterate miners' letters for them—that authentic theme of *The Long Winter Ends*. He attended the university at San José to become a civil engineer, and moved out to Virginia City as surveyor, where he made a topographical map of the region. When he came to Los Angeles, "the unprecedented growth of the city brought a great expansion in his professional work."

In the next phase of the city's development another Wisconsin Cornishman, William A. Polkinghorn took a notable part.[63] Born in Dodgeville in 1851, he was bent on seeking his fortune in Colorado. He mined for seven years at Leadville, then opened a mercantile business. Accumulating interests in the mines, and a considerable stockholder in the National Bank there, he used to winter in Los Angeles; and in 1900 he decided to transfer his interests there. Settling at Ocean Park, he built up a big estate, subdividing large tracts in the vicinity, at Venice and Santa Monica. A farsighted business man, he became a prominent citizen, but died early, leaving his widow to manage his interests and three sons who grew up to make their mark in business. Hence the Polkinghorn name is well known in Los Angeles today.

Thomas Pascoe made his living as a hotel-keeper providing for the increasing number of visitors.[64] He had had a good training as chief steward on board a man-of-war in the Royal Navy. At twenty-five he emigrated with his brother; they went to Montana as marshals in the penitentiary at Deer Lodge for a time. Thence to Colorado Springs in its happy beginnings, where he opened "Pascoe's Hotel." In 1883 he came to Los Angeles; when the transcontinental railroad reached the city a year or two later, it gave a great impetus to its growth. Pascoe managed the Clifton Hotel with success for a few years and then built the first modern family-hotel in the town to his own specifications, the Hotel Lincoln on Hill Street. Selling out to a company, he gave himself a year and a half of European travel. He was director of the Los Angeles Chamber of Commerce. At Colorado Springs he had made a Cornish marriage, to Jane Retallack; a son, Dr. E. R. Pascoe, became a medical officer of the Board of Health. Joseph Hill Pengilly, born in Minneapolis, was assistant power engineer in the Southern California Edison Company for five years, then a partner in Brown and Pengilly, electrical products, a manager of various electrical corporations, and finally a director of the California Manufacturers Association.[65] He served in France 1917–19, as company commander of the 56th Engineers; and in the Second World War as major of the Corps of Engineers.

The sons of two Grass Valley miners, Prisk and Hosking, made their impact on the newspapers of Pasadena and Long Beach. William Frederick Prisk was apprenticed printer on the *Grass Valley Tidings* and then served on the *Grass Valley Telegraph*. He moved to Fresno, Sacramento and San Francisco, whence he returned to Grass Valley, purchased the *Union*, revitalized it and made a success of it.[66] With his cousin, A. J. Hosking, he bought the Pasadena *Star*, and in 1910 the Long Beach *Press*, in which he was joined by Hosking's brother. William Henry Hosking had started in Grass Valley as newspaperboy and reporter, and ended as business manager on the family paper.[67] Meanwhile a brother, Charles H. Prisk, had made good in Pasadena, and in 1916 the Prisks effected a merger of the Pasadena *Star* and the Pasadena *News*. This was followed in 1924 by a merger of the Long Beach *Press* and the Long Beach *Telegram*, with new buildings and plant; in 1932 the *Press-Telegram* purchased the Long Beach *Morning Sun*. In the early 1930's these brisk Prisk newspapers had a combined circulation of 120,000. W. F. Prisk served a term as state senator, 1898–1902, and has his memorial in the William Frederick Prisk Elementary School at Long Beach. He and his brother did not forget the Grass Valley of their boyhood: together they owned over one hundred acres there, with a fine orchard of Bartlett pears managed by another Prisk.

So there should be Pascoes, Pearces, Pengillys, Polkinghornes, Prisks a plenty. As indeed there are. In the central Los Angeles district alone there is a drift of fifty-seven Pearces —the Cornish form of the name—though these can certainly not be all Cornish, and many may be older American stock drifted west. In the same area we find the following: Pascoe (19, with a Pascoe Steel Corporation, and a Pasco Construction Industries Corporation), Pengilly is represented along with Pengelly and Pengilley, Prisk (3, and one Priske), Penrose (11, with a Penrose Machine Company and a Penrose Coping Company), Polkinghorne and Polkenhorn. Among

California: Gold and Otherwise 277

other numerous groups we find Dungey (12), Chenoweth (8), Chubb (9), Hocking (10), Oates (12), Tremaine (17), Vivian (15), Trezise (5), Tretheway (10), Curnow (5), Penberthy (5), Minear (5). There is the usual wide spread of Tre-names, which we will forego.

In a cursory look at the southern Los Angeles area we find our expectations borne out: there is still a W. F. Prisk at Long Beach, and five Hoskings. But there is a tribe of no less than forty-four Hoskins in that form, with Hosken (2), Hoskin (8). Of the Pearce name there are over a hundred entries in that form alone; Pascoe (17), Polkinghorn (2, in that form, with a Polkinghorn Construction Company, and two Polkinghorne), Penrose (16, with a Penrose Match Company), Vivian (8), Pender (13), Varco (5, with one Varcoe). Among rarities, Vosper (2), Restorick (2). Pasadena has an unexpectedly large Cornish element: no less than nine of the uncommon Prisk name; Pascoe (17, with 4 Pasko), Warrick (8), Yelland (6), Chenoweth (11), Coad (6), Kitto (4), Penberthy (4), Pengilly (2), Minear (3, with one Manhire, which is the same name and should be pronounced the same way, Minéer), Higman (7), Edgecomb (4), Hocking (4). There is one Ede, and at last we find a Hobba, a rare bird; Menhinick, Nancarrow (3), Pendray (with 3 Pendry) are not uncommon.

But this is a mere dipping into the rag-bag, and I have omitted the most numerous class, Tre-names. It is impossible to analyze even the Cornish element in the pullulating population of the Los Angeles area short of a chapter to itself.

From San Diego we have a pleasant autobiography which gives us a picture of life there in the 1880's from Henry Bond Restarick, who became first bishop of Honolulu.[68] The name Restárick—in America pronounced improperly Réstrick—comes from Mid-Cornwall; at St. Columb is Restorick mill, at St. Dennis, Restowrick farm, and it means plashy ford. As a youth Restarick borrowed the money for a ticket to Toronto, where he worked on farms. He moved on to Omaha to the farm of a man who came over as a Mormon—on the ship the elders were proposing to the girls they fancied for their second or third wives. Studying at night Restarick passed his examination to become a school-teacher at Council Bluffs; in the summer months he earned money harvesting. His forebears had been followers of Wesley, but going to the Episcopal Church changed young Restarick's course. He went to Griswold College, was ordained, married and set off for California. The train took him along the Santa Fé Trail to San Bernardino and San Diego, where he was to serve his first pastorate.

San Diego was a dead town in the 1880's, with a population of two thousand. The stipend was exiguous, but there was plenty of food and hospitality, and marvellous camping in the back country up in the mountains by Palomar, (where now is the observatory with its giant telescope). The bears had been killed off, but there were still bear-traps in the gulches. One of the young men in this small pioneering parish was Manning, who became a celebrated bishop of the Episcopal Church in New York: Restarick started him in Greek and theology. Other acquaintances were George Scripps, who made money and founded Scripps College at Pomona, and a lawyer who married a survivor of the Donner party. In 1902 Restarick was elected first bishop of Honolulu and consecrated in the little church at San Diego.

Several members of his parish volunteered to work with him on his mission. The Church in Honolulu had been divided into two factions—the British supporting the demoted royal family, when the Americans had annexed the islands in the wake of the missionaries. The good bishop managed to patch things up and keep these Christians together. He took an innocent pride in being summoned to the White House by Theodore Roosevelt: "it seems wonderful to me that I, who landed on the American Continent in 1872, a youth of seven-

California: Gold and Otherwise 279

teen without a friend or acquaintance in this great country, should now be going to have a private interview with the President of the United States."

Perhaps it is as the result of the good bishop's activities that there is a Restarick family in Honolulu today, along with Penhallow (3), Pascoe (3—and the Pascoe Buildings), Chenoweth (2), Trefry (2), Trevenen (2), a Tresise pastor —no doubt Methodist—and a fair spread of Tre-, and Pen- names. San Bernardino has a small Cornish element, with a Kellow living up at Lake Arrowhead in the mountains. But San Diego has an unexpectedly large Cornish population. I can only illustrate it selectively. We find Chenoweth (14, in various forms new and old), Vivian (10), Pascoe (10, with 6 Pasco and a Pascoe Nursery), Minear (7, including a naval commander, with also Minear Scientific Instruments), Oates (7), Hocking (6), Pendarvis (5), Penberthy (4), Grenfell (5), Hambley (4). There is a large spread of Tre- names, along with some rarities: Santo, (3, probably not Spaniards for they have English first names), Penwarden, Penhaligon, Tregilgas, Tremear (a former group captain in the R. A. F., evidently a recent immigrant), Wherry (4, and one Wheary), Eade (2), Lanyon (2, one with the unmistakable first names, Ethel Carbis). There must be hundreds of Cornish folk among the hundred or more Hicks entries, and such names as Rouse (20), Hancock, Pollard, Pearce, Bartlett, Coon (16), Rowe.

I do not know how to account fully for this large Cornish population in remote San Diego on the Mexican border— perhaps health was a factor, the attraction of the climate and proximity to the sea. There is, first, the drift thither from all the dead mining areas of the Southwest. The city has enor- mously grown in the post-war period, is now a great naval base and defense-center. So among the many thousands of service-men there will be a good many of Cornish name, but old American descent, from other parts of the country—such as the Chenoweths, Trevillions and Trevillyans, Penroses and Trawicks, if that is an American form of Treweek. (There is a Treweek, who would be a recent comer.)

However we account for it, the fact is remarkable.

We may conclude with a couple of Cornishmen who made a significant contribution not only to California and mining but to the nation and beyond. T. A. Rickard probably had a greater knowledge of American mining in its heyday than anyone has had. With his scientific training and extensive practical knowledge of mines he combined a wide and exact scholarship with intense industry and a real capacity for writing. The result is that he wrote the standard history of American mining, a bigger book, *Man and Metals*—on the place of mining in the history of civilization—several other books of a technical character and some volumes of travel with an acutely observant eye, especially for minerals. He also wrote an informative autobiography, *Retrospect*, which is part of the history of mining round the world in his time. In addition to this he was able to boast that he had edited the three leading mining journals in the world: *The Engineering and Mining Journal* in New York, *The Mining and Scientific Press* in San Francisco, which he revitalized and virtually created anew, and *The Mining Magazine* in London, which he started. He was a vital and forceful personality, a tremendous worker, an eminent and upright man who was never afraid to state the truth in the treacherous world of mining promotion and journalism. He was a valuable public servant of whom Britain and America have both reason to be proud—and he has never received his due.

His cousin Edgar Rickard partnered him in his mining journals in San Francisco and in London, was for many years the trusted friend and business manager of Herbert Hoover and helped him to make his immense mining fortune. He then became Hoover's right-hand man in the Commission for Relief in Belgium and the Food Administration for Europe after the First World War. He came back to help Hoover in forming the American Child Health Association and in running for the Presidency.[69]

These two were grandsons of a Cornish mine manager, Captain James Rickard who "went to California in 1850 at the instance of the old London firm of John Taylor and Sons. He went thither to examine and appraise a group of gold-mines on the Mariposa estate, a Spanish grant then in the possession of General John C. Frémont. Captain Rickard was one of the first accredited mining engineers to go to California in those golden days; he crossed the Panama Isthmus and took with him a sectional ten-stamp mill, which was the first stamp-mill put to work in California—in June 1850, at Coulterville. . . . My father was the eldest of the five sons of this worthy man, and all of them followed the same profession. At one time our family had eight members in the American Institute of Mining Engineers: my father, two uncles, three cousins, my brother Forbes, and myself. Now the number is reduced to three. Most of us have taken to other occupations. This is in accord with the modern trend. The Cornishman, or 'Cousin Jack', has had his day; during the nineteenth century he was the acknowledged exponent of the mining art; today the American mining engineer is on top."[70]

There is in that one significant facet of the history of our time.

As a young man Rickard went out for his first practical experience of mining to Colorado, where we shall follow him later. He next spent a couple of years in California—where he had already spent Christmas with an uncle at Berkeley—as manager of the Union Mine in Calaveras County. "It was not much of a mine."[71] But Calaveras was "a picturesque region in the foothills of the Sierra Nevada; it abounded in quail, which I often shot before breakfast, twelve miles south was Angels Camp, where were the Utica and other rich mines." One day a drunk came into the office and pointed a six-shooter at Rickard's face, hoping to scare the tenderfoot. Fortunately, the young man never carried a revolver. "My bookkeeper, a Cornishman, John Roscrow, happened to be out of the office; if he had been present he would have pulled a gun, and there is no knowing what might have happened." Rickard made a very Cornish marriage, marrying his cousin, Marguerite Rickard. He first saw her as a boy of fourteen, when she was a pretty child in a perambulator, at their grandmother's house in Cornwall. Next, in 1898, when the girl was going out to her brother in Colorado, Rickard was asked to escort her, and—"I am escorting her still." They were married in the cathedral at Denver, and spent their honeymoon in California. Altogether, with all the families of all the uncles and their descendants, there is a numerous clan of Rickards along the Pacific coast, all the way from Los Angeles to San Francisco, and thence to British Columbia.

Rickard served his apprenticeship at mining journalism in New York. By 1906 he was able to buy the *Mining and Scientific Press* in San Francisco, made his cousin Edgar business manager and worked it up to a leading place in the profession. Rickard was an outspoken Cornishman without fear or favor, no smooth customer who dealt in humbug; moreover, he had high standards. He tells us that "at that time San Francisco was afflicted by two newspapers of the vilest type, the *Examiner*, owned by William R. Hearst, and the *Chronicle*, owned by Michael De Young."[72] Rickard did not hesitate to attack Hearst. "No university in America today is so potent an educational force for good as Mr. Hearst's papers are for evil. In four or five cities of this Republic he publishes a crop of journals, each of which preaches every day the gospel of hatred and undermines all the best instincts of popular government." In return, the Rickards were placed on Hearst's *Index expurgatorius*, no references to them being permitted in his papers. This did not prevent Rickard's cousin Tom from being mayor of Berkeley in the year of the earthquake, nor the *Mining and Scientific Press* from flourishing.

In 1909 Rickard started the *Mining Magazine* in London,

with Edgar again as business manager. Their plans were put out by the war. In their absence the San Francisco paper began to run down; in 1915 Rickard came back to restore it. His nephew Forbes was one of the first Americans to be killed in France. Edgar Rickard became absorbed in his work with and for Hoover. He had been brought to California as a child, and was educated at the University of California at Berkeley, which awarded him an honorary LL.D. at the end of his career. He worked from 1896 to 1905 as a mining engineer in America, Mexico and Australia, where the Rickards began their lifelong friendship with Hoover. Edgar became his administrative assistant in all his wartime and post-war organizations from 1914 to 1924. He received many international decorations and honors, and died in 1951.

T. A. Rickard succeeded in restoring the San Francisco *Mining and Scientific Press*, and sold it in 1922 for $250,000 to retire to British Columbia and write his books. Those are admirable books that he wrote, about the technical aspects of his profession, about his journeys of observation—across Colorado, to Yukon and Alaska—his larger histories of mining, all the way to his last book, *The Romance of Mining*. In addition he wrote a mass of excellent journalism, full of indispensable, scholarly information. His was a hard-working life, full of accomplishment. He died a couple of years after his cousin, full of years, if not of honors.

Why did he never receive his due? He was far more generous about other people than they were about him. He was not a "modest man"—that overworked *cliché*—for he was not one of those who have plenty to be modest about. He was an egoist, in the best sense—for his, unlike most people's, was an interesting ego. He was rather full of himself, but there was so much in him where so many are empty.

We are deeply indebted to him for his life and work. Let him stand as one type, and a very good type, of the Cornishman in America.

NOTES

1. T. A. Rickard, *A History of American Mining*, 20.
2. R. W. Paul, *California Gold*, viii.
3. Rickard, 82.
4. Paul, 19.
5. cf. my *The Elizabethans and America*, 192.
6. *The West Briton*, January 9, 1852.
7. D. B. Barton, *A History of Tin Mining and Smelting in Cornwall*, 86.
8. Rickard, 38.
9. *The West Briton*, August 29, 1851.
10. *Ibid.*, January 9, 1852.
11. Paul, 147.
12. I owe this information to Captain Dick Bennett of Grass Valley, formerly of the Empire Mine.
13. Paul, 257, 259–60.
14. *Ibid.*, 292.
15. *Ibid.*, 323, 327.
16. cf. *A Gentle Reminder*. (The Broadcaster Press, 1962).
17. *The History of Jo Daviess County, Illinois*, (Chicago, 1878), 627, 660ff., 698, 701, 774, 788.
18. *Portrait and Biographical Album of Jo Daviess and Carroll Counties, Illinois*, 302ff.
19. *Memorial and Biographical History of Northern California*, (1891), 373.
20. C. L. Camp, "William Alexander Trubody and the Overland Pioneers of 1847," *California Historical Soc. Quarterly*, XVI, 122ff.
21. *History of Napa and Lake Counties, California*, (1881), 570–71.
22. G. B. Glasscock, *A Golden Highway*, 123ff., 143ff.
23. E. E. Stevens, "The Cornish Miner," *Nevada County Historical Soc.*, vol. 18, no. 1.
24. "Cornish Carolers," *P.G. and E. Progress*, vol. XXXVIII, no. 12.

25. A Gentle Reminder.
26. W. B. Lardner and M. J. Brock, *History of Placer and Nevada Counties, California*, 943ff.
27. *The Colfax Weekly Record*, Dec. 14, 1951; *Oakland Tribune*, Nov. 5, 1950.
28. Lardner and Brock, 1101, 1164.
29. *Ibid.*, 519ff.
30. *Ibid.*, 754.
31. *Ibid.*, 1190.
32. *Ibid.*, 1157.
33. *Ibid.*, 1235.
34. *Ibid.*, 684, 1146, 1219.
35. Glasscock, 135.
36. Lardner and Brock, 1089.
37. *Ibid.*, 425ff.
38. *Hist. of Plumas, Lassen and Sierra Counties*, (San Francisco, 1882), 308.
39. Andrew Rolle, *California: A History*, 282–83.
40. G. W. Reed, ed., *Hist. of Sacramento County, California*, 993.
41. *An Illustrated History of San Joaquin County, California*, (Chicago, 1890), 516, 626.
42. J. M. Guinn, *Hist. of the State of California and Biographical Record of Coast Counties*, 752, 1201.
43. *Ibid.*, 677.
44. *Ibid.*, 667.
45. J. A. Smith, "Angels Mine Disaster," *Historical Bulletin, Calaveras County Historical Soc.*, vol. 1, no. 1.
46. H. W. Splitter, "Quicksilver at New Almadén," *Pacific Historical Review*, XXVI, 33ff.
47. K. M. Johnson, *The New Almadén Quicksilver Mine*, 93ff.
48. H. S. Foote, ed., *Santa Clara County, California*, 335.
49. E. T. Sawyer, *Hist. of Santa Clara County, California*, 1680.
50. Foote, 326.

51. Sawyer, 732.
52. Rolle, 350ff.
53. Foote, 344.
54. Sawyer, 337.
55. Foote, 460.
56. Sawyer, 1388.
57. J. M. Guinn, *Hist. of the State of California . . . Oakland and Environs*, II, 795–96.
58. I am indebted for this information to Mr. Harry M. Rowe, Jr., of Fullerton, California.
59. *Hist. of Santa Barbara County, California*, (Chicago, 1927), II, 371.
60. W. M. Morgan, *Hist. of Kern County, California*, 1201.
61. *Ibid.*, 948.
62. *An Illustrated History of Los Angeles County*, (Chicago, 1889), 744.
63. J. M. Guinn, *A Hist. of California . . . Los Angeles and its Environs*, III, 731–32.
64. *An Illustrated History of Los Angeles County*, 604.
65. *Eminent Californians* 1953, 175.
66. *California of the South: A History*, (Chicago, 1933), II, 71–78.
67. W. H. Case, *Hist. of Long Beach and Vicinity*, II, 532–33.
68. H. B. Restarick, *My Personal Recollections*, 1938.
69. cf. *The Memoirs of Herbert Hoover: Years of Adventure, 1874–1920*, 156–57, 196–97, 253, 273; *The Cabinet and the Presidency, 1920–1933*, 97, 191.
70. T. A. Rickard, *Retrospect*, 9.
71. *Ibid.*, 37–38.
72. *Ibid.*, 99, 108.

11 NEVADA, IDAHO, UTAH: MINERS AND MORMONS

Nevada was California's first colony. The fantastic riches of the Comstock Lode—just over the high Sierra on the eastern slope from Grass Valley and Nevada City—were exploited by Californian capital; "the twin Comstock towns of Virginia City and Gold Hill were operated as an industrial suburb of California, and more particularly of San Francisco."[1] It was understandable and natural enough: central California, with its rising city queening it on the Pacific, stood on the threshold of the new discoveries, and had now accumulated the experience and the capital to exploit them. In the new mining rushes that punctuated the later nineteenth century we shall see similar phenomena repeated that had characterized the original gold-rush of 1849, but in a reverse form—exploding outwards, east, north, southeast. Sometimes we observe the eastward movement of experienced miners, the "yonmen," meeting the westward drift of the inexperienced, the "tenderfeet" or "greenhorns."

The first discovery of gold in the Carson Valley was made by a small party of Mormons coming west from Salt Lake City in the spring of 1849. They were led by an elder, Thomas Orr; a young Mormon, William Prouse, took a milkpan to wash in a stream in the canyon and, himself a Cornishman, noticed that the specks among the gravel were gold. That creek became known later as Gold Creek and the canyon Gold Canyon. The best contemporary account of Comstock, that of Eliot Lord, tells us, while Prouse was still alive—at Kanosh City, Millard County—that he had noticed gold particles in that same creek bed the autumn before and had lingered there prospecting, promising his companions when they caught up with them to "show them a place, if they ever travelled that way again, where they could find gold."* It reminds one of Sir Walter Ralegh's promise, two and a half centuries before, to lead his men to "the treasure-house of the world"—in Guiana. Actually "the creek where Prouse prospected . . . was the door to one of the treasure-vaults of the world; but no-one surmised the connection."[2]

Orr's party were detained in the canyon for a few weeks by a fall of snow, but when it cleared they were anxious to follow the greater lure of California beckoning over the mountains. The news of their find spread, however, and soon there was a rush to the placer-diggings of the Carson Valley. A few Mormon farmers settled along the river-banks and did well enough, selling their farm-produce and cattle to the diggers, until Brigham Young ordered these stray members of his flock back to Utah. The early Mormons discouraged mining, and were wisely bent on building up a stable, agricultural community in their great valley before anything else. The placermen, with their cradles and sluice-boxes, worked their way slowly up the gulches, but it was not until a decade had elapsed that the great discovery of quartz-gold and silver was made at the apex of the two canyons, Gold Canyon and Six Mile Canyon, on the slopes of Mount Davidson. Here lay the fabulous Comstock Lode; here along a five-mile stretch grew up the twin towns of Virginia City and Gold Hill, with an exposed windy neck—the Divide—between them.

* E. Lord, *Comstock Mining and Miners*, 9. It is to be regretted that Prouse's diary and letters were not, apparently, collected nor has he been written up. This omission in Nevada history should be rectified.

Nevada, Idaho, Utah: Miners and Mormons

The miners were baffled by the presence of immense quantities of heavy blue quartz, until assays made at Grass Valley and Nevada City proved that it was rich in silver. Then, in the early spring of 1860, "there ensued an eager rush to the Washoe diggings, up the Sacramento river in crowded little steamboats, over the mountains on foot or on horse-back, through the snow, to the Comstock, as the lode was already being called in compliment to its supposed discoverer."[3] We have already come upon the tracks of Cornishmen taking part in that first phase of the "Virginia City excitement." "The mining of silver was unknown in the western States prior to the discovery of the Comstock Lode"; ultimately the mineral wealth of the Great Basin—Nevada, Idaho, Utah—proved far greater in silver. This meant acute technical difficulties to be surmounted, which are not part of my subject, and marked improvements in the mining art were made. An authority tells us that, for the Californians, the Comstock Lode "became an advanced school in which they discovered how to mine in depth and on a large scale, how to use powerful and intricate machinery and large numbers of employees, and how to cope with metals more complex than free gold."[4]

The same authority tells us that this meant bringing in experienced Cornish miners, along with others. The heyday of Virginia City coincided with the onset of the last and severest phase of the decline of mining in Cornwall. The miners poured in thousands out of the old county—the nursery of mining for all over the world—to help to make the fortunes of the new areas opening up in the Far West. Eliot Lord gives us contemporary figures of the working force in 1880—after the Big Bonanza, richest of lodes, was struck. The bulk of the miners were immigrants. There were 770 Americans, 816 Irish, 640 English, 191 Canadians.[5] The majority of those described as English would be Cornish; there would also be some Cornish folk, of the second generation, among the Americans and some among the Canadians. Professor Paul tells us that, in addition, "a discerning minority of the early

Nevada promoters hunted through the varied talents available in Nevada and California until they found veteran Welsh or Cornish smelting men."[6]

With the Big Bonanza in 1873 came what was the richest strike of silver in the century. This fabulous fortune came to two pairs of mines, coupled on either side of the Divide, and of these principally two. In some twenty years the Virginia and the California yielded $150,000,000 in metals, and paid out nearly $80,000,000 in dividends. Altogether "the total output of the Comstock mines was $350 million, of which 55 per cent was in silver and 45 per cent in gold."[7]

The effects of this brief, heady experience, this couple of intoxicating decades, were commensurate and important. "Technologically, by 1880 the new understanding of veins and of deep-mining on a large scale had already contributed to the revival of quartz mining in California and to a beginning of vein mining in Utah and Nevada outside Storey county. It was soon to inspire a boom in vein mines in Montana, Idaho and the South West."[8] T. A. Rickard has a more critical appraisal. He allows that it advanced the technical, particularly the mechanical, side of mining, and that the enormous output of the precious metals contributed vastly to American wealth and the expansion of business and enterprise. On the other hand, it led to an orgy of speculation, a feverish gamble in share-values: "the best mines were much over-valued, and many of those quoted at high figures were actually valueless. False reports were forwarded from Virginia City . . . The Comstock undoubtedly had a bad, and lasting, influence on the morale of mining."[9] Corruption of every kind, political, financial, judicial, thrived throughout the territory: Nevada got a bad name.

Rickard has a generous word of praise for the miners: "they met and overcame more obstacles and more difficult obstacles than any of the brothers of the pick and gad had ever faced before; and the hard-bought experience that they gained they carried with them all over the world, and most notably to the big mines of Montana, Colorado, and Dakota, as the history of those regions abundantly testifies."[10] The poor fellows worked under appalling conditions. For one thing, the heat was terrific: "rarely could one gang endure working more than every alternate hour; at worst, only fifteen minutes at a time . . . The temperature of the air increased about three degrees with every hundred feet of depth, and when the shafts finally got down to 3000 feet, late in the life of the Comstock, the miners encountered water at 170° Fahrenheit."[11] To all the other accidents to which mines are prone, there was here the constant danger of scalding water bursting out upon the men. Then they came up to the icy winds of Mount Davidson in winter, one knows with what results—no wonder that at home in Cornwall, where California meant a gay land of golden promise, Nevada had an ominous name: one remembers from childhood a miner returned home to cough his life out in his native village.

Lord gives us the figures of fatal accidents, with a peak of forty-nine in 1869, and still well over twenty in the later 1870's. He comments, "the most noticeable effect of the exceptionally high rate of mortality in the Comstock mines is the recklessness of temper and disposition towards fatalism which is thereby engendered among the miners."[12]

We have no such detailed information upon which to build up an intimate picture of life in Virginia City such as we have been enabled to do for Michigan, Wisconsin, Illinois, California. But we have the journalism of Mark Twain in *Roughing It* and of Dan De Quille. We have, too, the autobiography of a Virginia City journalist, who arrived there at the peak of its prosperity in 1874: Wells Drury's *An Editor on the Comstock Lode*. He himself speaks of Nevada's early history as merely a continuation of California's. The speed and intensity of the Comstock's development meant that the twin towns soon ceased to be a mere mining camp and exhibited, in its joint population of some twenty thousand, a curious mixture of sophisticated vulgarity, extreme extravagance and squalor, a lit-up street night-life in bitter winter-weather, shooting affrays more frequent than ever, hold-ups of the Wells and Fargo stage-coaches, opera and theatre, frequent visits of the best stage-companies and popular celebrities, churches and libraries, a good deal of winter reading and money thrown away on every side.

It is curious to think that in a town where one fool announced that he had "money to throw at the birds"—and he had—no less than 194 volumes of the ever-popular Dickens were sold in one year and, more strangely, twenty-three sets of Froude's *History of England*—an historian to envy.[13] (He was much envied, by those who sold—and wrote—less well.) The peak of extravagance was reached with the Bowers Mansion, built twenty miles away at Reno, costing $300,000, with door-knobs and hinges of silver. The builders ultimately died in penury. When one thinks what might have been achieved for education and culture in the state, the libraries and picture galleries that might have been founded, the treasures that might have been brought to Nevada! . . . Instead of that its treasures were taken away, the territory raped and gutted and left empty. Talk about colonialism! . . . Nevada offers a notorious case in point.

Wells Drury is very conscious of the Cornish element in the place, who as usual stood out by their names and their speech, no less than by their temperament. "The payrolls of the mines bristled with names like Trevillian, Trelease, Trezona, Tregillis, Treglown, Trewhella, Trewartha, Trezise, Tremayne, Treloar, Trevethan, Polmear, Pengilly, Penaluna and Penrose."[14] He has got them right—"I was always on good terms with the hearty Cornish folk"—and he records their turns of speech correctly. Here is a Cornishwoman expressing lack of sympathy for someone else: "What's it to we, us don't care for she!" This is correct in dialect, if not in ethics. When General Grant visited Virginia City, a Cornishwoman, who was a widow, was heard to say with approval, "Isn't he a *fitty* little chap!" This also is correct usage: "fitty" means proper.

Drury notices the old Cornish addiction to wrestling, and "fierce were the contests in which they struggled—wrestling in canvas jackets, in accordance with the usage of their native county."[15] He remembered an evening when some famed Irish patriot lectured to empty benches at Piper's Opera House, because there was a Cornish wrestling-match in Miners' Union Hall that night. Then there was "a whole series of fights between Jimmy Trevillian and Patsey Hogan, both weighing in around 140 lb. In the third of these, in 1874, Trevillian had Hogan bested in the seventh round when a spectator bellowed that Jimmy had a piece of iron in his glove."[16] Actually his seconds had placed a wad of oakum in his hand because it had swollen; the referee gave the fight to Hogan on a foul. At that pandemonium broke out and the mob stormed the ring; pistols were drawn, but the referee failed to get killed. "A couple of years later, local Jimmy worsted Two-handed Sullivan from Australia." The goriest battle Drury witnessed was that when Dublin Pete Lawlor beat Jack Askew. "It was Ireland against Cornwall, and the big crowd yelled itself hoarse throughout the sixty-five rounds."

The greatest of these contests was that when Bob Fitzsimmons won the championship from the Irishman, Jim Corbett —the father of an Irish-American friend of mine never forgave him for doing it. Bob Fitzsimmons was a hero to my father still in my boyhood, a name in our household —Fighting Bob, Freckled Bob, Ruby Robert, in short, The Cornishman. He was a blacksmith by trade, following his father, and there was something of strokes upon an anvil in his terrific pounding punches. He was described as "a cannon-ball on a pair of pipe-stems," for he had very thin legs with the shoulders and immensely long arms of a gorilla. He weighed about 160 pounds. "In action he preferred to stand still, with his left foot advanced and his body weaving around on his hips. His powerful torso was crowned by a small head scantily covered with ragged wisps of sandy hair, beneath which two quizzical blue eyes blinked innocently amid a mass of freckles. He was easy-going, good-natured, and rather sen-

L

timental. He lost most of his money to various fleecers and sharpers; he liked to sing old-fashioned hymns in his high falsetto voice." He had been brought up in a very religious home—"my mother believed everything in the bible," he once said, "and the old man was worse than mother about religion" —but he grew up to prefer fighting to those delights.[17]

He was born at Helston in 1862, but was brought up in New Zealand to which his parents emigrated, and where he won his reputation as a pugilist. He came to San Francisco in 1890, and sprang into fame by winning the world's middleweight championship from Jack Dempsey, the "Nonpareil," at New Orleans next year. His great victory came on March 17, 1897, when he won the heavyweight championship of the world from Gentleman Jim Corbett—some twenty pounds heavier—in a memorable fight at Carson City that lasted fourteen rounds. "Until the last round Corbett seemed to be winning with ease; but in that round Fitzsimmons suddenly drove a terrific left-hand blow to the pit of Corbett's stomach and then smashed the same fist against Corbett's jaw. In less than three seconds Fitzsimmons had accomplished three epochal feats: he had knocked out an Irishman on St. Patrick's Day, he had won the heavyweight championship of the world, and he had invented the terrible 'solar plexus punch' that will always be associated with his name."

Mrs. Mabel Lee has a breathless account of the event in her *Cripple Creek Days*—for special trains were run from that Colorado mining-town to its sister in Nevada.

> The Cornishman's red hair is slicked back, his step is buoyant . . . weighs in at one hundred sixty six and a half . . . not quite six feet tall . . . shoulders broad, arms long and dangling like twisted cables. Odds six and a half to ten on Corbett . . . weighs in at a hundred and eighty five . . . handsome, confident . . . the crowd's favourite.[18]

Of course: he would be. Nevertheless, the Cornishman won. We need not go into the somewhat hysterical account of it all—the fight was memorable also for the appearance of

Nevada, Idaho, Utah: Miners and Mormons

Mrs. Fitzsimmons at the ringside, whose encouraging endearments to her husband were by no means lady-like. In the fourteenth round, when Gentleman Jim was knocked out and his supporters were gamely turning their pockets inside out, "Mrs. Fitz is wringing her hands and crying for joy . . . band strikes up 'There's Only One Girl in the World for Me!' as new world's heavyweight champion leans over ropes and smacks her on the kisser."

However, Bob Fitzsimmons was getting on in years, for a prize fighter: he held his title only two years, when he was laid low by a new champion in James Jeffries. Fighting Bob won more fights, however, even in his forties and went on fighting up to 1914, when he was fifty-two. Three years later he died; though he had fought in over 360 contests, he was without a scar. His biography has been written, and his own book, *Physical Culture and Self-Defence*, was introduced by one of the Philadelphia Biddles, close relations of the Penroses.

There were more agreeable amenities, however. Shakespeare plays were often performed, *Hamlet* most often. The famous Edwin Booth demanded a really practicable grave for the last act. "A section was sawed out of the stage-floor, a couple of Cornish miners did valiant pick-work, and that night the gravediggers shovelled some interesting specimens of ore on to the stage."[19] Later on, "we loved to hear the sweet voice of Dick Jose, a big-hearted Cornish lad who left a Reno blacksmith's forge to go on the stage as a ballad-singer, beloved by all the world." It seems that Dick was immensely popular all over the West, and equally unspoiled. One night, years later, when singing before thousands in Los Angeles he caught sight of Drury in the crowd, and came forward to the footlights to hail his old Nevada acquaintance. No doubt it was good theatre, too.

In the end Drury has a kindly summing up of the Cornish miners he knew in Nevada. "They possess a strain of religious fervor, and even in rough surroundings display a fondness for books, as witness their patronage of the well-stocked Miners'

Library in Virginia City." I find this a little surprising, but this is a generation later than the early folk in Wisconsin and Michigan. The characteristics remain the same: "independence, thrift, geniality, excitability, contempt for familiar dangers—these are characteristic of them. And with what zest they can sing their fellowship song, 'One and All,' and their old patriotic ballad, 'And Shall Trelawny Die?' After the decline of the Comstock, many of the Cornish went to Grass Valley and Nevada City ... some wandered to Australia and South Africa; others went back to Cornwall, and many are the pleasant messages I have had from old cronies, postmarked Redruth and Penzance."

"Some of the old boys died there, but a majority sought new fields to conquer, scattering in all directions. Butte, Montana; Leadville, Colorado; Tombstone, Arizona; Brodie, California—these mining-camps were on the rise at the time the Nevada camps were on the steep skids."[20] Here we shall follow them. "San Francisco received its returning horde with open arms." As for Nevada—"Virginia City now lies stricken and old—yet not dead. The mountainside which shook and echoed once with the stamps of a score of mills is silent. Gold Hill has well-nigh vanished into the thin air of the sierra. Only six families dwell in Slippery Gulch, where once thousands of miners milled around in the streets on Saturday nights. American Flat is almost deserted, Silver City is little more than a memory. Over to the north, about a score of miles away, is Reno—not much more than a hamlet when the Comstock was in its glory; now a populous, flourishing city."

Even so, in the small population of Nevada, there is a considerable sprinkling of Cornish. Even in the dereliction of Virginia City we still find Spargo, Rule, Paynter, Hosking, Berry, Best, Blake, several Bennetts; there are still two Kendall families up on windy Divide. The Cornish who remained have moved out and increased, along with the rest of the population, in larger centers. In Carson City and Reno we find Ede (5), Penrose (4), Couch (4), Crase (4), Rickard (4),

Nevada, Idaho, Utah: Miners and Mormons

Curnow (2), Spargo (2), Rodda (2), Penberthy (2), Hoskins (2 and one Hosking), Trelease (2), Oates (2), along with Tregellas, Tremewan, Trezise, Tonkin, Truscott, Tippett, Kellow, Polkinghorne, Hocking, Nancarrow, Edgecomb. In the largest city of Nevada today, Las Vegas, we find a larger spread: Trelease (4), Couch (5), Kendall (5), Tregaskis, Tregillis, Trezona, Trovillion, Tremaine, Tresilian, Treweek, Trudgeon, Pascoe, Rodda, Rosevear (2), Rouse (5, with one Rowse), Chenowith, Dungey (2), Grose, Gribble, Grenfell, Keast, Lanyon (2), Oates (2), Kello (for Kellow), Hocking.

The point is made: though some hundreds left and moved to other areas, those who remained increased and, with those who came in later, there are many hundreds of Cornish descent in Nevada still.

Almost contemporaneously with the Virginia City excitement, also in the 1860's, but on a much smaller scale, were the gold-rushes to the placer-diggings of Idaho and Montana. They were far more difficult of approach, the latter particularly inaccessible; but by 1870 there was a population of some fifteen thousand in Idaho, twenty thousand in Montana.[21] The peak of gold-production in the latter was in 1863, after that it fell off rapidly—it was no California. As one walks up the main street of Helena, the capital, one is following the gulch where gold was found; the Placer Hotel is on the site of old diggings. Montana's fortune was destined to be made by copper in this century, not by gold in the last, though this gave the state its original fillip. Then, in the 1870's, came the rush to the gold-diggings in the Black Hills of Dakota—we have already noticed examples of Cornish miners trekking there, as to Montana and Idaho, from Wisconsin and Illinois. Here is one who did not make it: Henry Trevarthan, from Guilford Township, drowned in the Platte River near Fort Laramie in 1864, on his way to Idaho.[22]

The way to Idaho—north of Nevada and Utah—followed

the Oregon Trail along the Platte and then kept to the Snake River to get around the difficult mountains running north and south, with the escarpments of lava beds running some hundreds of miles to astonish the traveller from Idaho Falls westward. The Boise Basin—with its settlements at Idaho City and Centerville—just north and east of the Snake River in the southwest of the state, was the first area of placer-activity. It was settled as the result of the gold-rush; the farming in the Basin came later, with the irrigation. Today one sees from the air some of the most beautifully farmed country in America—emerald-green patterned fields around the prosperous farmsteads in their groves of trees—along the course of the ribboned river snaking away below: all the result of irrigation.

To this building of a new state the Cornish made their contribution; we can follow out the pattern in their lives.

One of the first pioneers to become prominent in making the state was Edward S. Jewell. He had been left an orphan and was brought up by an uncle on a Wisconsin farm. A blacksmith by trade, he made the trip overland by ox-team in the earliest days, to go placer-mining, reverting to his trade when mining did not "pan" out. He did well enough to embark on stock-raising in the Salubria Valley, where the Snake River forms the western boundary with Oregon. He was the seventh settler to locate in that area, and "to him must be given the credit for introducing the first thoroughbred horses, cattle and hogs that were found in this section of the State."[23] Building up a fine tract of 850 acres, and prospering, he was able to serve in various county offices and to emerge as an active politician, Republican and Methodist. He was one of the drafters of the state constitution, when Idaho graduated from territory to state, and became one of the first state senators from Washington County. He ultimately retired to end his days in San Diego, California, but with a family of twelve there were plenty of Jewells to decorate the life of Idaho subsequently. One sees him in his photograph, a handsome elderly man, very much the gentleman—the Honorable Edward S. Jewell.

One of his sons became a mining engineer, served in the Spanish-American War, and ended up in the Forestry Service of the state. *His* son became manager of the Farmer Oil Company in Boise and actively interested in the pioneer historical background. His grandfather's brother, Albert, followed him to Idaho, bringing with him a nephew, Eddie E. Edwards, a boy from Mineral Point.[24] In Idaho new prospects opened out—the nephew took to merchandizing in a new area of the state, right across on the eastern boundary with Montana, at Gibbonsville. Here he branched out into banking, made a comfortable fortune and was able to retire to the "palatial old" Logan house in the capital, Boise. On the western boundary the Jewell interests continued in the next generation with the Jewell Store in Cambridge, Washington County.

Another pioneer was a Tregaskis who came on from California placer-mining in 1863.[25] His son, George Thomas Tregaskis, also began mining, then became a cattleman. He purchased a ranch in the Emmett section not far from Boise, but it was seven years before he could secure water for it from the Last Chance Ditch. With that he was able to make an excellent farm of it. That there were Tregaskises early in the territory we can see from one of the first photographs from Silver City: there beside the bare hillside we see a raw stone shack, with painted sign: "R. Tregaskis and Son. Storage. Commission"—evidently for silver.[26]

Charles Berryman made his way west from Wisconsin about 1859 and took to freighting between Corinne, Utah and Butte, Montana, through that difficult mountainous country.[27] The drivers of the stage-coaches were a deservedly famous set of men—and they are celebrated in the books, if not in literature—but the freighters of those days are hardly less deserving of remembrance. After some years Berryman was able to take up a ranch in Bingham County, then to become one of the organizers of the Standrod Bank, ultimately its president. He brought his son into the bank with him; the son served various public offices, and became president of the city council of Blackfoot, near Idaho Falls in the southeastern part of the state. So there are Berrymans about in Idaho.

Northern Idaho running up into the panhandle between Washington and Montana—so that Lewiston on the Snake River is, improbably for this inland state, an ocean-going port—is rather different country. In these earlier years it was supposed to be reserved to its native inhabitants, the Nez Percés Indians. But in the 1860's there was a rush from the placer-mines of the south to the lead and silver finds of northern Idaho. White settlement was already prohibited by government decree, but nothing ever had been able to hold white settlers back from colonial days; the country was disturbed and dangerous, and there followed the mutual scuffles and killings that grew into the Nez Percé War, in which the Indians fought very well. This did not prevent them from having to evacuate their lands to the newcomers.

Among these, a foremost pioneer, was Matthew H. Truscott.[28] He was in Chile and California in the early 1860's, then came to Elk City, in the Nez Percé country, where he ran a sawmill for a dozen years. He served as a volunteer in the war, and was rewarded with the post-mastership of Mount Idaho. To this he added a general store, and the honor of being a pioneer in this country that had been dangerous earlier. We have seen that a number of settlers into this new country were from Iowa. We cannot follow them further here. Coming into southern Idaho over the boundary from Utah, the Mormon element was very prominent. We must turn to Utah.

In the highly idiosyncratic community of the Great Salt Lake Valley the Cornish were represented both among the miners and the Mormons—more numerously among the former, more powerfully among the latter. For it happens

Nevada, Idaho, Utah: Miners and Mormons

that, though very few Cornish folk were Mormons, one of them—Charles W. Penrose—was a figure of the first importance, while one of the leading Mormon families, the Moyles, are also of Cornish descent.

John Rowe Moyle, born of good old yeoman stock in Wendron in 1808, was a stonecutter.[29] Employed at Devonport, he signalized his independence of mind by refusing to join in a strike, and his stand was successful. He won some public notice by his courage—unlike what would have happened to him today. He was no less courageous in his stand for Mormonism, to which he was an early convert and became an elder in the little branch at Plymouth. There were ten children in his family, of whom James at nineteen preceded them in the trek to the new Zion in the West. (The appeal of Mormonism was not only religious but to the desire of the poor to emigrate to America, to a land of better opportunities.) James Moyle linked up with a Penryn friend, John Tripp, and together they came via Liverpool and New Orleans, then up the Mississippi to Kansas City in 1854. There were some four hundred Mormons on board the overcrowded ship; cholera broke out, James tended the sick and helped to bury the dead. "I can remember that we got quite hardened to it, and thought little of people dying. We buried nearly one-third of the passengers."[30] At Kansas City there was sickness in the camp and still more died. One had to be tough, or lucky, to survive.

Within a few days of his arrival James was set on work by Brigham Young in building the Lion House—Brigham was the Lion of the Lord—and in a couple of years James was able to marry the girl of his choice, a maid of seventeen. In the same year, 1856, the family followed in the famous handcart trek across the continent—eleven hundred miles of pushing and pulling their handcarts with their pathetic belongings in them. Again there were many deaths—"one of the most tragic journeys of the entire Mormon trek."[31] Each tent of twenty-five had a captain: John Moyle was captain of the

L*

fourth tent in the first division. Two of his brothers came with him, for Henry Moyle kept a journal: one June day, "my brother Stephen and I helped Job Welling to bury his little son, who had died only that day." We do not know of any further members of the family in the party: they seem all to have come safely through to Zion.

John Moyle worked at his trade cutting stone on Temple Square for a couple of years, and then moved up into the hills to Alpine to break in virgin land, because the country there reminded him of Cornwall. For protection against Indians in that wild country he built a kind of peel-tower—as it might be little Pengersick Castle on Praa Sands at home. There the boys were brought up—Indians, bears, deer in the mountains, gun-dogs, cattle, horses: what better?

Eldest son James took full part in the gathering life of Salt Lake City. In the crisis of 1857–58 when President Buchanan sent armed forces under General Johnston to overawe the Mormons, James was on military service in Echo Canyon. He returned to keep guard on Zion and to set fire to it, if General Johnston should seek to take possession. The Mormons had been abominably persecuted in Missouri and Illinois, their prophet, Joseph Smith—a man of extreme charm and magnetic power, with the charismatic gifts of a leader—murdered with his apostle of a brother in Carthage jail. The atmosphere of fanatical devotion and dedicated hysteria of these years cannot easily be imagined—and the Mormons certainly took a terrible Old Testament revenge in the Mountain Meadows massacre.

After the crisis had passed James Moyle returned to his trade and became a leading builder and contractor. He built a number of stores, the city jail—in which he was subsequently to serve a term—and put in a good deal of the rock-work on the bridges of the Union Pacific Railroad through the region. In 1875 he was called to take charge of the stone-cutters on the Temple Block, and in 1886 he became general superintendent of the works, with some 150 men under his control.

He was a natural arbitrator and there were seldom any disputes. Building the Temple was a prodigious work, with its foundations of vast granite blocks that created a problem to haul from the mountains, until the coming of the railroad. As one looks at the finished fane today, the silver granite glistening in the Salt Lake sun as if built only yesterday, one remembers James Moyle who supervised its erection.

Having prospered, he took to himself a second wife, in accordance with the prophet Smith's "revelation"; James built a home for each of his families, and altogether the children totted up to twenty-four Moyles. This became something of a burden on his resources, so that—in spite of his keenness for the education of his able and ambitious son, James Henry—the boy had to keep himself at the university by stone-cutting under his father on the Temple buildings. In the renewed persecution of the Mormons in the 1880's, for polygamy, the respected Moyle was fined and sentenced for "unlawful cohabitation." He served his sentence, characteristically, reading improving works on geology, chemistry, mineralogy. Over a thousand Mormon men served sentences in these harassing years—until the sainted President of the Church Woodruff had a "revelation" contrary to that of the prophet Smith, that Mormons were *not* to undergo the chore of polygamy. And all was well in Zion; henceforth it blossomed, if not precisely like the rose, at any rate like mad.

The Moyle family was to have a distinguished future through the ability and industry of the son, James Henry. As a boy he was a stout boxer and wrestler. "In these activities he received a little training from Jimmy Hall, a native of Cornwall, where every boy knew how to wrestle."[32] It was a very interesting group of young fellows that worked on Temple Square. Another Cornishman there was William Stockdale, "grandfather of the former United States Senator from Utah, Elbert D. Thomas"; William Britton, the "most belligerent member" of the party, had a Cornish name—and the temperament.

Young James Henry, who had the honor of serving in the guard upon the Lion House, Brigham Young's city-residence, and in the bodyguard upon his portly person, was a serious-minded and ambitious youth. He was called to the deaconship and early given a difficult assignment as missionary in the Southern States. He felt no particular vocation, but at the farewell meeting to speed his departure Charles W. Penrose, with his native eloquence and intuitive perception, promised the young man that he would find it in the course of his work. He did. After this he went, more usefully, to the university. He was bent on becoming a lawyer, but this was contrary to the prejudices of the Church, which had suffered greatly from the predatory activities of such persons in early days. Young Moyle overcame the resistance of the authorities with the argument that in these wicked latter days the Saints needed their own lawyers to look after their growing interests. The point was conceded, and James Henry went off to Ann Arbor, to work like a beaver and emerge with the highest honors.

He returned to Salt Lake City to an official post as assistant city attorney, along with that of deputy county attorney shortly after. It fell to him to advise his own father when assailed for polygamy; he was so fortunate as to be able to rescue the famous Penrose—one good turn deserves another—from the penitentiary. Penrose had often defended polygamy and, being a Cornishman, aggressively; he based his case on Old Testament teaching. Unfortunately he also exemplified it: he made altogether three marriages, though only two that were concurrent. This was sufficient to incriminate him. When summoned before court, "the district attorney put a personal question which Penrose refused to answer."[33] He was sent to the penitentiary, to stay there as long as he remained contumacious. The court had reckoned without Moyle, who feverishly searched up a precedent to the contrary, called on the judge, law books in arms, and convinced him. With papers of release signed, Moyle rushed round to the penitentiary before Penrose was well settled in.

The law firm that Moyle founded became the base of the family's continuing fortunes. He became an active Democrat, and was nominated Democratic candidate for the United States Senate, being seconded by Richard Kendall Thomas, who "spoke of his friendship with the Moyles in Cornwall"— from which one may assume, as also from his name that here was another Cornishman, father of Senator Elbert D. Thomas.[34] Moyle was, however, defeated by the egregious Smoot, who did his little bit to bring on the world depression by the notorious Smoot-Hawley Tariff under Hoover. Moyle won office later as Assistant Secretary of the Treasury, 1917–20, under Woodrow Wilson and again as Commissioner of Customs, 1933–40, under Roosevelt. He was the first Mormon to hold office in the national administration.

Back in Utah he bought up properties in the Silver Lake district and built up extensive interests there in the Mountain Lake Mining Company. To this he added property interests in Salt Lake City, a farm outside where he created a lake and introduced irrigation, Lakewood; and thence branched out into cattle ranching on a large scale in Utah, Mexico and South America. His years of retirement he devoted to accumulating a mass of information about the Moyle genealogy, where the curious importance attached by the Mormons to the subject joined hands with Cornish sentiment. The old Moyle stock is a very interesting one, having produced five or six figures who appear in the *Dictionary of National Biography*, including a Speaker of the House of Commons, a judge, and a distinguished scholar, antiquarian and political thinker in Walter Moyle, 1672–1721. A home of a cadet branch of the family, the pleasant Jacobean and Queen Anne farmhouse of Trevissick, lies just across the fields from my own home in the parish of St. Austell. There is something appropriate in the old stock at home, contemporaneously with the first generation in Utah, producing a mining doctor, Matthew Paul Moyle, who wrote on meteorology and mining; his mother was one of the remarkable family of the Hornblowers.

James Henry Moyle shared a passion for genealogy with President Roosevelt. On a genealogical trip to Britain one of Moyle's daughters remarked, "we travelled about England dusting off every grave marker that had anything to do with the Moyle ancestors."[35]

In the next generation a younger son carried on his father's civil service interests, corporate law and tax-specialty, in Washington; the eldest son inherited the legal and business interests in Salt Lake City, adding to the livestock concerns, insurance and petroleum. This Henry D. Moyle continued the family service in the Church of Latter Day Saints, becoming one of the twelve apostles, and rising to be one of the two councillors in the first Presidency. But for his premature death at seventy-four, and the exceptional longevity of President Mackay—well on his way to becoming a centenarian—there might have been a Cornish President of the Mormon Church.

An even more influential figure, and a formative influence by his missionary work, his writings and his hymns, was Charles William Penrose.* Born in London in 1832, he lived right up to our own time, dying in 1925 at the age of ninety-three. (The mountain air of Utah, allied to the faith—or abstinence from smoking and stimulants—certainly seems a preservative.) His father was Richard Penrose of Redruth, his mother Matilda Sims of Stratton; but both his paternal and maternal grandmothers were Hornblowers.[36] They were Baptists, and no doubt from that remarkable strain came the fanaticism, the force, the organizing drive and ability. His father died when he was a boy, and Penrose was brought up by his mother, from whom he got such education as he received. In effect, he was self-educated; at the age of eighteen he was captivated by Mormon teaching and cast in his lot with the Saints—"he was the only member of his father's family who ever embraced the faith": is it surprising?[37] What is remark-

---

* There should be a biography of this important figure; there is an abundance of material.

able is the tenacity with which he adhered to his adolescent choice; he embraced the Mormon faith in all its fulness, polygamy, the doctrine of blood-atonement and all. Throughout his immensely long life he never wavered: he poured forth preachings—he had all the Celtic fire and eloquence— arguments, editorials, pamphlets, booklets, verse, hymns; he was a tireless propagandist, he ended as a patriarch, First Councillor to two Presidents, of the Presidency, yet never himself President of the Church. This was disappointing: a Scot beat him to it. However, Penrose's services to the Church were far greater, and he was a much more memorable man.

The young convert's gifts as a speaker set him apart from the first, so that, though he was eager to set eyes on Zion, he was kept in England doing missionary work year after year. "Just serve another year and you will be released to gather to Zion," he was told again and again.[38] "Gather to Zion" was the Mormon phrase for plain emigrating. One day, while walking the dusty roads of Essex to his next meeting, the words of a hymn that became immensely popular with the Mormons came into his mind; that evening he sang them, to an old Scottish tune, to the assembled Saints:

    O ye mountains high, where the clear blue sky
        Arches over the vales of the free,
    Where the pure breezes blow and the clear streamlets flow,
        How I've longed to your bosom to flee . . .

    In thy mountain retreat, God will strengthen thy feet;
        On the necks of thy foes thou shalt tread;
    And their silver and gold, as the Prophets foretold,
        Shall be brought to adorn thy fair head.

Some of these apocalyptic hopes were to be fulfilled in blood, with Penrose defending its effusion.

It was at the end of this period of trial and waiting that he wrote his best-known didactic song. He had been accused by a fellow-Mormon of taking something that belonged to the

Church. Conscious of the sacrifices he had endured for the faith, without thought of remuneration, and a man of a fiery temper with "a sting like that of an adder,"[39] he boiled over with resentment—until, turning it over in his mind, he arrived at:

> School thy feelings, O my brother,
> Train thy warm, impulsive soul;
> Do not its emotions smother,
> But let wisdom's voice control.
>
> School thy feelings: there is power
> In the cool, collected mind;
> Passion shatters reason's tower,
> Makes the clearest vision blind . . .

This has been sung, like all of Penrose's hymns, at thousands of meetings all over the world. The great heart of Brigham Young is said to have found comfort in it in the dark days when it seemed that the assault was intended to the city.

At last, after ten years, Penrose received his release and permission to come over. At the mature age of nineteen he had married, himself baptizing his wife into the faith. In 1861 he and his family, with some of his wife's relatives, crossed the Atlantic in an old sailing-vessel. They had a sick child with them, not expected to live, for whom they had prepared a metal casket in case of need; the child got better, and the casket became the family's bread-bin.[40] On the way across the plains by ox-team Mrs. Penrose had to be left behind in Echo Canyon to give birth—it was no sinecure being his wife—and she then had to catch up with the train by forced marches. The family settled first at Farmington, Davis County, where Penrose set up in trade, afterwards at Logan, where his wife remained on her own in a log-cabin for three and a half years, while Penrose was sent on another mission to England. While he was away another child was born and died. It was at the time of the previous parturition in Echo Canyon that Penrose was inspired to write his more sentimental song, "Blow gently, ye wild winds." He was able to say at last:

> Be gentle in Utah, my loved ones are there!

During his next mission in England, 1865–69, he actively pushed forward the emigration of Mormon converts to fill up the empty spaces of the great valley as rapidly as possible.[41] He was a most effective proselytizer: the Welsh forebears of a well-known Mormon writer on history have the tradition that they came over as the result of Penrose's urging. He wrote a great deal for *The Millenial Star*, the Church's organ in England. On his return to business in 1869 he set on foot the Logan Co-operative Mercantile and Manufacturing Institution, to consist of five hundred members with a subscription of ten dollars each, members to be of good moral character and to pay their tithing.[42] Profits were to be tithed for the Church before any dividend. (There was no dividend.) Penrose reported optimistically to Brigham Young, "notwithstanding the visitation of the grasshoppers [that famous episode in Mormony history, when a cloud of them descended on the chosen valley to eat up the crops] and the decline in the prices of merchandise, if we have the hearty co-operation of our brethren, with the blessing of God we hope to prosper, and believe that our mercantile efforts will be successful and be the means of preparing the way for co-operative manufacturing and finally for that union and order in temporal things which we so earnestly desire."

This passage is of interest in revealing the strain of economic idealism in the early Mormons, the influence of ideas of co-operation upon their thinking. Of course it didn't work, in spite of the frustration of the grasshoppers: God sent a swarm of sea-gulls to eat *them* up. This was a miracle, but all the same the co-operative did not prosper; the economic individualism of the Moyles proved a much better idea than the co-operative idealism of Penrose. He removed to Ogden to take charge of the newspaper, the *Ogden Junction*, for which he was better fitted; later, Brigham Young called him to the *Deseret News*.

In 1880 he became a member of the territorial legislature and at once began a campaign to remove the political disabilities of women; they had been given the vote, but were not eligible for office. With his usual eloquence Penrose held forth:

> Utah is the home of liberty for all, and peculiarly the sanctuary for woman. Here all her rights are popularly acknowledged and accorded; here she is protected and defended; here the conventionalities which have kept her in bondage for ages are thrown aside by the force of an enlightened estimate of her capabilities, and an enlarged view of her claims as an integral part of the body politic ... The power of the suffrage will develop thought, and its responsibilities give occasion for reflection and enlarged capacities of woman, which will be the natural consequence, will be transmitted to her offspring ...[43]

We see what an optimist he was. He managed to push his bill through the territorial legislature, just in time to have the vote withdrawn from all polygamists by the United States Congress, and four years later all the women were disfranchised.

Nothing discouraged, Penrose went off on another three-year mission, 1884–87, to the British Isles, Scandinavia and other European countries. Many are the stories told of his retorts to hecklers, his repartees and effective way of dealing with interruptions—at this he was as effective as John Wesley, Cardinal Manning or General Booth; for, given the assumptions he (like them) had swallowed when young, he had a forceful apparatus of argument and debating dialectic to deploy at will. He was once speaking on the steps of the post office at Belfast when he was constantly interrupted by a heckler on the subject of polygamy, which he regularly defended on Old Testament lines. An inspiration came to him:

fixing the interrupter, he said to him, "You are yourself an adulterer." People in the crowd said, "You are right, Mr. Penrose, he is." The man slunk away. This kind of thing made converts.

He returned to write for the *Deseret News* and to take a leading part in all the agitation of the late 1880's about polygamy and for the achievement of statehood, which had been inequitably held up on that account. He was a member of the constitutional conventions which were held in 1887 and 1894; and meanwhile spent the two winters of 1887 and 1888 lobbying in Washington. "He visited every senator and representative and member of Congress, with the President's cabinet, on the subject of statehood, including the equal suffrage clause."[44] Back in Utah he combined with the women-leaders in a campaign of mass-meetings for statehood with votes for women, during the years 1893-95. Their efforts were rewarded in 1896: Utah became a state, and with equal suffrage.

During all this time Penrose was prolific in journalism and pamphleteering; he was becoming an official spokesman of the Church, who could always be relied on to proclaim the faith in all its fulness and to defend everything the Saints had done. There was his *Mormon Doctrine, Plain and Simple or Leaves from the Tree of Life*; his *Rays of Living Light*; his pamphlets on *What the Mormons Believe*, his defense of *Blood-Atonement*, his exposition of the official view on *The Mountain Meadows Massacre*. During 1892-94 he put the *Salt Lake Herald* on a solid footing, and was appointed Assistant Church Historian. In 1899 he became editor-in-chief of the *Deseret News*, which he made the leading paper in all the mountain region. Within the Church his work received recognition. He passed through all the different branches of the priesthood, becoming at length—though not until he was an old man—First Councillor to the President. He ended up a venerable patriarch. His portraits reveal him as a forceful type, abounding in energy, with ebullient moustache and bright eyes, but a kindly expression in them. Contemporary accounts testify to his tireless activity since he was a boy: "his life has been an aggressive one," "scarcely a moment has been spent in idleness"—even in bed. A modern historian of the Mormons provides me with a critical estimate of him as "the typical zealot of his time, more keen, more perceptive, more articulate than most, with a bearing and attitude that attracted people and a logic that convinced many." This is just.

Though he did not perpetuate himself in a law firm like the Moyles, he was demographically no less effective, by two of his three marriages. By his first wife, who bore with him the trials of the pioneer days, he had eighteen children; she died in 1903. Penrose had married a second wife early, in 1863: a girl with a beautiful voice, whom they called "the nightingale," who had come over on her own at nineteen. By her he had ten children; at his death in 1925 she was eighty-two. His third wife was at that time eighty-six; she was the first doctor in Utah, having practiced as a physician for thirty years. By her he had no children; even so that makes, if my arithmetic is correct, a total of twenty-eight. No wonder there are some fourteen Penrose families in Salt Lake City today. With these wives Penrose had obtained an enviable spread of interests: house-keeping, music, medicine.

It was a very creative life.

Apart from the Moyle and Penrose tribes we come across very few Cornish names among the early Mormons—sufficient for the day was the Methodism thereof. However, on the sailing-ship *Chimborazo*, which left Liverpool in April 1855 with 432 Mormons on board, there was Elder R. Treseder to look after their spiritual wants—marriages, among other things, were celebrated on board.[45] On April 18 Elder Treseder succeeded Elder Sutherland in the Presidency. We do not hear of Treseder again, but it does not appear that he went overboard; at any rate, later we find Treseders in Utah

Nevada, Idaho, Utah: Miners and Mormons 313

—no less than eight entries in Salt Lake City and six in Ogden. From the 1860's we find a Roskelly couple at Smithfield, Utah: Samuel Roskelly and his Welsh wife, with seven children.[46] These proliferated in the Mormon manner: today there are nine Roskelly entries each in Salt Lake City and Ogden, with a company of the name in the former.

The Mormons were reluctant to see the opening up of the mineral wealth of their valley, with the undesirable influx of Gentiles that would inevitably follow; they could not hold up the tide of progress, however. In 1863 some of General Connor's garrison of soldiers scratched the untold mineral wealth of Bingham Canyon, on the west side of the River Jordan, and found gold. Placer-mining inevitably followed, but as yet there was no suspicion that here was one of the world's greatest sources of copper. "At that time Bingham canyon was valued by the Mormons for its fine timber, red pine three feet in diameter being plentiful there."[47] Today, there is not a tree in sight; at the head of the devastated rift of a canyon, the whole side of the mountain is scooped out into a vast red terraced amphitheatre, looking like one of Leonardo's drawings of constructions or a Patinir nightmare-landscape. And what with the sulphurous belchings of the largest of copper-smelters, West Jordan looks like the abomination of desolation. Mormon fears have been fulfilled: progress has taken place.

Connor's men, "having little else to do"—like the angels in Byron's "Vision of Judgment"—lighted on silver in 1864, in Little Cottonwood Canyon on the east side of the valley in the Wasatch Mountains. This did not begin to be exploited until 1868 when the famous—or infamous—Emma Mine was located and at first gave promise of rich resources. This directed attention to the mining potentialities of Utah; by 1870 the mining population was up to four thousand, and there was a flood of interested speculation on the London stock-market.[48] General Schenck, the United States Minister in London, took the lead in promoting a $5,000,000 company to exploit Emma. Brydges Willyams of Carnanton, who had large mining interests in Cornwall and was Member of Parliament for the county, became a director and was generously granted £5000 for a trip of inspection to Utah. He took with him for company an interesting companion, who wrote up their tour in one of the more charming of Victorian travel-books about America, *Silverland*. The author, G. A. Lawrence, was a practiced writer, who had made something of a name with his novel, *Guy Livingstone*, and had already made the acquaintance of the United States, when he tried to join the Confederate Army and had been deported. Lawrence bore no grudge, however, and his account of their American tour is sympathetic as well as informative.

The book begins with an excellent description of his visit to Willyams ("Tresillian") on the uplands of North Cornwall, of the boom of the Atlantic swell on the coast. The two friends crossed the ocean in the *China* in January 1873, when the *Alabama* controversy was at its height. In New York, "at every turn you meet evidences of overweening wealth and luxury," with ladies' dresses straight from the Rue de la Paix. Chicago was just recovering from the great fire. Here they embarked on the Arlington Express, their base for the next two months along the Union Pacific and back. Lawrence has a highly critical account of Salt Lake City and of Brigham Young, supposedly under custody but walking the streets. Willyams made his inspection of the Emma Mine, about the prospects of which Lawrence is discreetly silent. Thence on to California, where Willyams, as a well-known capitalist, had mining speculations pressed upon him.

At the same time other British interests sent out Captain James Nancarrow, who had managed mines in Mexico, Spain and Chile, to report on prospects in Utah.[49] He reported favorably on the silver prospects of Bingham. He spent most of 1871 locating promising claims, and endorsed Silver Hill Mine in Little Cottonwood Canyon. Brydges Willyams visited

Nevada, Idaho, Utah: Miners and Mormons

Camp Floyd with the celebrated Professor Silliman, whose predictions of the ore proved rather silly. At Emma Mine the ore-body suddenly petered out, after yielding $1,500,000 for the investment of $5,000,000. The company had been hopelessly over-capitalized and most of the investors lost all their money. General Schenck fled from London to escape prosecution. Before the final showdown at the company meeting in 1874, Brydges Willyams announced that he would not stand for reelection. In the end the property was sold for a song. "The most recurring theme in the economic history of the American West has been the exploitation of 'outside capital.' "[50] In this instance it was the victims' own fault; but it gave Utah mining a bad name for a period.

Nevertheless, in 1872 a strike was made in the same area which turned out in time to be the most famous of all Utah's silver-mines: the Ontario, around which grew up Park City in a canyon east of Salt Lake City. The claim was sold for a mere $27,000 to George Hearst, who made millions out of it.[51] He brought in miners from Virginia City, Nevada, the "hot-water boys"—at least here in Utah the water was cold. With them came many Cornish, who "found conditions in the Park City mines almost identical with those they had known in Cornwall, with the difference that here they were paid a living wage."[52] Park City was incorporated in 1880 and became a stable community; unlike Nevada the miners stayed on to build homes and send for their families. Mining there continued up to and into the Second World War, only to slump after it. Today Park City is a ghost of its former self.

"The story of Park City in the early days cannot be separated from the story of the Ontario mine and the great Cornish pump."[53] The mine was beset by water and the deeper it went the more of a problem it became. A long and expensive drainage tunnel did not answer; the answer came when "the great pump, which became a famous landmark of the community, was installed." Though of the classic Cornish type, it was designed in San Francisco and built in Philadelphia. It was an enormous creature—"the flywheel alone weighed 70 tons and was 30 feet in diameter; the pump rod was made of Oregon pine and was 1060 feet long"—and it did the job. "Parkites were proud of the Cornish pump." Apparently it acquired almost legendary status in its lifetime, and tales are told of its temperamental performances. Today it has vanished—but there are photographs of it in the Utah Historical Society's museum to remind us of its prowess.

At first the copper deposits of Bingham Canyon, that were to make the fortunes of Utah, were overlooked. They were of low copper-content mixed with sulphides, and it was not until railroad communications were completed and modern methods of smelting introduced that it became profitable to exploit them. In 1870 there were 276 miners in the canyon, mostly Irish.[54] By 1880 there were some 450 Americans (including the children of immigrants), 170 British, of whom the Cornish were the chief element, about 80 Scandinavians and only 50 Irish. Real mining now came to the fore. In the early 1900's Spencer Penrose and his brother, R. A. F. Penrose the geologist, who had already made large fortunes out of Colorado gold, took a leading hand in Utah and organized the Utah Copper Company in 1903.[55] This was the effective start of Bingham's fabulous career. During the decade 1907–17 it yielded nearly 70,000,000 tons of ore, from which over 600,000 tons of copper were extracted, besides much gold and silver. By 1930 its tax-valuation was more than one-eighth that of the entire state.

By then the Cornish had moved out of the canyon—that long narrow winding gulch of six or seven miles, with the houses on top of each other, the liability to land-slides falling in on them. Many of the names once familiar in Bingham—such as Tregaskis—are now to be found in Salt Lake City. The Greeks came in to dominate the canyon, with the modern *sequelae* of labor troubles, strikes, violence and, in the end, evacuation. Nevertheless extraction continues on an immense scale.

The completion of the transcontinental railroad, with the linking of the Union Pacific and Central Pacific lines near Ogden in 1869, ushered in these developments. We find traces of Cornish folk taking part in all of them, as in the Mormon Church itself. A Bolitho family came to settle at Richfield.[56] Henry Bolitho had come over in 1842 to the mines of Greensborough, North Carolina, and then moved to Galena, where he took to landscape gardening and laid out the city cemetery. The family next moved to a farm in Iowa; there were thirteen little Bolithos. One son came to Utah, where *his* son James became a railroad man, a locomotive-driver. He ultimately took to a hardware business, and then was enabled to retire to his own farm of two hundred acres at Richfield.

Several members of the tribe of St. Austell Rowses settled in Utah. Joseph James Rowse first came to New Jersey in 1878 and earned enough money to make the long trip across the continent to Grass Valley to work in the mines.[57] He left his family at home and made two or three return-journeys: "on each trip he organized groups of Cornishmen to go to America with him, thus paying his passage—apparently on a commission-system with the shipping company." Between trips he earned his living in the lead- and copper-mines of Colorado, and the coal-mines at Tintic, Utah. After his last trip home he settled in Terrace, Utah, as an engineer for the Southern Pacific Railroad. He saved enough money to purchase a grocery store, and then sent for his wife and six children. When they arrived on New Year's Eve, 1886, his brothers, Jonathan and Edward, with their wives and families, were on hand to greet the newcomers. Today one finds at Ogden five Rowse families stemming from this group.

John N. Spargo was a leading citizen of Ogden in our time. His father came to Park City in the early 1870's and worked at Ontario Mine in charge of the machine-shops for ten years.[58] In 1887 he moved to Ogden and bought a book and stationery business. He had several children, but, dying at the early age of fifty-two, his son had to give up medicine to take on the family business. To this he added interests in real estate, in mining and oil development. Successful, he became director of the Chamber of Commerce, holding many public offices: a public man.

Taking a cursory glance at the population today, we observe that there is quite a considerable Cornish element in Salt Lake City; and this is understandable—most of them will have moved into the urban area from the mining regions, and from other activities, round about. Perhaps we may venture a general observation: the large coagulations of one name are apt to be of Mormon stock, as we have seen with Moyle (15), Penrose (14), Roskelley (9), Treseder (8). There are other considerable groups, however, which may not belong. There are no less than five of the very rare name Tregeagle, one with a business of consulting engineers—which leads one to surmise that perhaps they had a mining origin. Other rare names appear, one of which has practically died out in Cornwall—Daddow; and there are Bosanko, Chegwidden, Carew, Reseigh, Cargeeg (for Carkeek), Penhallegon, Ennis, Ennor, Tregea, Bottrell, Lampshire. Besides these, not so rare: Kitto, Minear, Ede, Clymo, Varcoe, Pendray, Penhale, Ivey, Easterbrook. Of other groupings we may cite Chenoweth (9), Pascoe (8), Rosevcar (8), Goldsworthy (4), Lobb (4), Retallick (3), Treglown (3), Trelawney (3), Trevithick (3), beside the usual spread of Tre-, Pol-, Pen- names.

At Ogden we are struck by an immense tribe of Hoskins—23 entries; there are Tremaine (4), Tremelling (2), Truscott (2), Rosevear (2), besides the larger Roskelly, Treseder, Rowse groupings mentioned. In both towns there are many more common names under which Cornish folk are hidden.

NOTES

1. R. W. Paul, *Mining Frontiers of the Far West*, 56.
2. T. A. Rickard, *Hist. of American Mining*, 83.
3. *Ibid.*, 97, 98.
4. Paul, 57–58.
5. E. Lord, *Comstock Mining and Miners*, 383.
6. Paul, 101.
7. Rickard, 106, 109.
8. Paul, 86.
9. Rickard, 108, 110.
10. *Ibid.*, 112.
11. Paul, 67.
12. Lord, 404.
13. *Ibid.*, 214.
14. W. Drury, *An Editor on the Comstock Lode*, 70–71.
15. *Ibid.*, 90.
16. *Ibid.*, 88–89.
17. D. A. B., VI, 443–44.
18. M. B. Lee, *Cripple Creek Days*, 116ff.
19. Drury, 55, 60.
20. *Ibid.*, 292–93.
21. Paul, 41.
22. *The History of Jo Daviess County, Illinois*, 706ff.
23. H. T. French, *History of Idaho*, II, 833; *History of Idaho*, (New York, 1959), III, 386–87.
24. J. H. Hawley, ed., *History of Idaho*, III, 660–61.
25. *Ibid.*, 603.
26. T. Donaldson, *Idaho of Yesterday*, facing p. 38.
27. Hawley, 848.
28. *An Illustrated History of Northern Idaho*, (1903), 545.

29. O. F. Whitney, *Hist. of Utah*, IV, 457ff.; G. B. Hinckley, *James Henry Moyle*, 12ff.
30. Hinckley, 21.
31. *Ibid.*, 24, 27.
32. *Ibid.*, 75, 81, 82.
33. *Ibid.*, 201.
34. *Ibid.*, 240; Richard Kendall Thomas married Caroline Stockdale. *Utah: A Centennial History*, (1949), III, 368.
35. *Ibid.*, 357.
36. N. T. Taylor, "Genealogy of Charles W. Penrose and family," *Utah Genealogical and Historical Mag.*, XVI, 138ff., 185ff.
37. "President Charles W. Penrose," *Ibid.*, 97.
38. Elder H. H. Bennett, "Hymns of the Restoration," No. 10.
39. J. H. Evans, *The Story of Utah*, 308.
40. K. B. Carter, *Treasures of Pioneer History*, vol. 5, 464–65.
41. *Biographical Record of Salt Lake City and Vicinity*, (1902), 75ff.
42. J. E. Ricks, *The History of a Valley: Cache Valley, Utah*, 188ff.
43. S. Y. Gates, "President Charles W. Penrose," *The Relief Society Mag.*, IX, 63ff.
44. *Ibid.*
45. K. B. Carter, *Treasures of Pioneer History*, vol. 5, 32.
46. *Utah Genealogical and Historical Mag.*, XVII, 236, 288.
47. Rickard, 185.
48. W. T. Jackson, "The Infamous Emma Mine," *Utah Historical Quarterly*, XXIII, 339ff.
49. W. T. Jackson, "British Impact on the Utah Mining Industry," *Utah Historical Quarterly*, XXXI, 347ff.
50. *Ibid.*, 372.
51. W. M. McPhee, "Vignettes of Park City," *Utah Historical Quarterly*, XXVIII, 137ff.
52. *Ibid.*, 139.
53. *Ibid.*, 146.
54. H. Z. Papanikolas, "Life and Labor among the Immigrants of Bingham Canyon," *Utah Historical Quarterly*, XXXIII, 289ff.

55. Rickard, 197–98.
56. *Portrait, Genealogical and Biographical Record of the State of Utah*, (Chicago, 1902), 365–66.
57. I owe the information in this paragraph to his grandson, Dr. Robert O. Johns.
58. *Utah: A Centennial History*, (1949), III, 317.

12   COLORADO: GOLD AND SILVER

With Colorado we move out of the aura of California into an empire of its own. For one thing, it was a thousand miles away, straddling the slopes of the Rockies, and its ties were with the Middle West and even the eastern coast. For another, there was the extraordinary diversity of its mineral wealth. Beginning in the usual way with the exploitation of surface gold and placer-diggings in 1859—that second *annus mirabilis* in the history of western mining—this was soon followed (far more rapidly than in California) by the transition to mining the quartz lodes. Next, from 1877 onwards came a silver boom with the vast silver and lead deposits of Leadville. When this declined, with the slump in the world-price of silver, unexpected new discoveries of gold at Cripple Creek in 1891 produced a new boom prolonged into this century. Later, Colorado's varied riches in molybdenum, tungsten and uranium have become valuable in our own delightful nuclear age. Altogether this enviable diversity has given Colorado mining a longer life than most, with—when the railways came—a true center of its own in Denver.

Another distinguishing characteristic of Colorado mining has been its far greater reliance on scientific technology.[1] Its fundamental problem, after the collapse of the first little gold boom and the turning to quartz-mining, was a metallurgical one. Colorado gold was not free-milling as in California: it was heavily mixed with sulphides, which could not be got rid of in the ordinary stamp-mills. There was an enormous wastage. Where California mill-men could claim that they were saving 75 per cent of the gold by the ordinary processes of milling and amalgamation, in Colorado the proportion saved was only from 15 per cent to 40 per cent.[2] It was a formidable and an urgent problem. It was solved by Richard Pearce, who was brought over from Swansea—then the chief smelting center in the world—to tackle the problem. Colorado has much reason to keep his memory green—it has been perpetuated in a mineral special to Colorado, a sulphide of silver and arsenic first found there: pearceite.

After the first flush days were over, in the later 1860's Colorado mining came up against its problems and experienced a depression. It surmounted this only slowly, by various means and by directly confronting the difficulties. The original Pike's Peak excitement had proved a deception; of the thousands of light-hearted participants in that gold-rush, with the motto "Pike's Peak or Bust," most had gone back, some with the simple explanation—"Busted." The long-term developments of Colorado mining were to take place notably in Gilpin County. "Here, at an altitude of 8,000 feet and a distance of thirty-five miles (mainly rough, up-hill mountain roads) from the new supply-centre of Denver, developed one of the most notable mining counties in America, Gilpin, and its important neighbours, Clear Creek on the south and Boulder on the north."[3] A contemporary geologist remarked of this region "where so much in mining and metallurgic technique had its beginnings . . . in many respects it holds in this country a position analogous to that of Cornwall in Great Britain."

Professor Paul tells us that among the ways in which Colorado overcame its early disappointments, "at many mines highly professional Cornish or Irish miners took the place of American amateurs . . . In Gilpin county the Cornishmen became an especially notable part of the life of the community. With their long experience in underground work, they contributed much to the improvement of mining technique."[4] Mr. Perrigo specifies the significant contributions the Cornish miners were making to the recovery of mining by their "skilful sinking of shafts and tracing of veins," their "mechanical aids like the Cornish pump for removing water from the underground recesses."[5] In addition they introduced their contract system, by which they worked undeveloped portions of the property for 10 per cent or 15 per cent of the proceeds. They lived well on their $2.50 daily wage; they were hardworking individualists, who seldom joined unions or strikes. They were interested in their work.

Nevertheless the main problem became more and more acute, and it was a metallurgical one. As the miners went deeper the ore-bodies were impregnated with sulphides; the ores refused to amalgamate with mercury and most of the gold was lost in the tailings. This could not go on. Professor N. P. Hill set up a smelter at Black Hawk in 1868, which succeeded in reducing the richest ores at great expense; even so, the rest went to the stamp-mills, with the consequent waste. At last he decided to take a consignment of ores to Swansea for what he could learn there—several tons which he teamed across the plains to Missouri, shipped down the Mississippi to New Orleans and so to Wales.[6] It was there in the famous Copper Works of Swansea, run by the Cornish Vivians, that Hill had his ores successfully treated; he entered into a contract to enable him to use the process at his own smelter at Black Hawk.

It does not appear that Hill made contact with Richard Pearce—with whom he was subsequently to enter into such fruitful association—on this occasion. Pearce was at this time employed by a rival Cornish concern, Williams, Foster and Company. Born in the year of Queen Victoria's accession,

1837, at Barrippa near Camborne, he was the son of Richard Donald Pearce, captain of Dolcoath. From the age of fourteen he was employed in the tin-dressing department, where he became "practically conversant with the different stages of tin-dressing then in vogue," and developed "a fondness for minerals and chemistry."[7] From this he became assistant to his father, especially in assaying ore samples. In 1858 he began taking mining classes at the Royal Institution at Truro, and at mining centers like St. Just. He showed such promise as a teacher that he was sent to the Royal School of Mines in London. In 1865 he was given his first great chance, when he was asked to construct a new smelter for Williams, Foster and Company at Swansea, to deal with the refractory ores from Chile. Pearce, whose mind was not only pragmatic but thoroughly scientific, made a tour of the smelting centers of Germany to learn all that he could learn before building his own smelter. For it he adopted the Ziervogel process—stopping the roasting of silver at the sulphate stage and leaving it soluble for precipitation on copper plates—and then much improved on it with modifications of his own, injecting air and steam together into the silver in contact with water toned up with sulphuric acid. This process he patented and it worked; it solved the problem of the refractory ores at Swansea.

In 1871 Pearce was invited to Colorado by a director of a London company also having difficulty with its ores. Pearce made the journey across the Atlantic on the Cunarder, *Batavia*, in twelve days; west of Kansas City, the prairies were still alive with buffalo, the train actually being stopped on one occasion by a herd. Denver was then a small town of five thousand—just before the silver-lead boom that made the fortunes of Leadville from 1877. Pearce completed his journey into the mountains by horse and buggy, not without misgivings as to the "spider-like vehicle" on such rough roads. Arrived at Black Hawk, Pearce visited Hill's smelter, which suggested to him new ideas as to smelting methods that might be adapted to the ores of Clear Creek for which he was bound.

On his way, examining mines as he went, he made the first discovery of pitchblende (uranium oxide) on the American continent—in Russell Gulch. "In looking over the old dump my attention was drawn to a beautiful canary yellow coating on the surface of several pieces of mineral which had been exposed to the weather for a few years, and I immediately suspected the presence of uranium . . . A piece of this interesting mineral, recently made famous on account of its radio-active properties, which I picked off the dump at the Wood mine thirty-four years ago, still shows radio-active properties to a very high degree." Many years later, shortly after Pearce's eighty-eighth birthday, T. A. Rickard found that "Pearce kept a lump of this very mineral in water in a glass jug and that he drank the radio-active water twice each day . . . Was that why the dear man lived to within a month of his ninetieth birthday?"

On his return to England with his report Pearce was asked to go out to Colorado and build a smelter according to his own ideas. He accepted, and sailed with his family early in 1872. In Colorado difficulties multiplied; freight rates, in particular, proved prohibitive for a small concern. Next year Professor Hill's contract with Vivian and Sons at Swansea expired and Hill proposed to Pearce that he should take charge of the smelter at Black Hawk, in which they should reduce their own minerals on the ground. "In accepting this new position," Pearce wrote later, "I felt that I was assuming a great responsibility. The method which I proposed to adopt was new to American soil. The science of metallurgy was little known at that time, and in the general arrangement and construction of the plant, I was limited to whatever the district itself could afford." However, the new plant was in action by November 1873, when its first shipment of silver bars created much excitement in Colorado. "It was a notable event in the history of the young mining industry of the Rocky Mountain region, for it marked the beginning of the separation and refining of the metals on the ground, and the creation of a self-sustaining metallurgical enterprise, relieving the mines of the heavy toll involved previously in the marketing of their unfinished products in Europe." The success of the new methods at Black Hawk were important not only for Colorado, they gave a new impulse to the mineral industry elsewhere in the Rocky Mountain area, particularly in Montana.

Pearce brought over a band of his own Cornish workmen from Swansea; working together as a team they effected remarkable improvements. He altered the reverberatory furnaces so that their capacity was increased 30 per cent at a saving of one-third of the fuel. For this unqualified success Professor Hill made him a present of $2500. The professor was a good man of business, but "by instinct and training Pearce was much more of a scientist than Hill, and he continued to be for years a dominant figure in Colorado sciences related to mining. His presence, even more than Hill's and Baeger's, symbolised the beginning of Colorado's long and ultimately successful attempt to bring science as well as engineering to bear upon problems presented by the complex nature of its ores."[8]

Next, "he tackled the problem of separating and refining the gold in the matte and other furnace products," which he did in separate stages with entire success. "In the next thirty years, to October 1905, no less than forty-five tons of gold were separated and refined at Black Hawk and later at Argo, by this process as devised by Richard Pearce. Forty-five tons of gold are equivalent to $27 million. The details of the process were kept secret for a long time, because until the electrolytic separation of gold from copper came into vogue it was the method best adapted to the metallurgic conditions of the West." Apparently, like all the best ideas, it was of a simplicity that baffled the experts.

In 1876 the celebrated copper magnate of Montana, W. A. Clark—afterwards senator—visited Black Hawk and, much impressed with what he saw, decided to send the copper-silver ores from his Original Mine at Butte, which had proved refractory, to Pearce for treatment. At the same time the immense resources of Leadville in silver and lead were opening up. In 1878 Hill and Pearce moved the smelter to a more strategic situation at Argo, just outside Denver. Business grew so fast that a branch smelter was built at Butte, Montana, a new company formed, Hill and Pearce subscribing half the capital. He must have been on the way to being a rich man now, but, like so many of the Cornish, Pearce continued to be more interested in the scientific side of the business than the financial—it was Clark in Montana and Penrose in Colorado who made the vast fortunes.

The Butte smelter proved an equal success and worked in with Argo by providing matte for final processing. Meanwhile, Pearce in his intensely creative life never stopped still: he doubled the capacity of the reverberatory furnaces, from twelve to twenty-four tons a day. He managed to solve the problem posed by the rich silver ores of Leadville which were mixed with chloride and so had suffered heavy loss in treatment. "Owing to his knowledge of tin ores he was consulted frequently in regard to supposed finds of tinstone in Colorado, and usually was able not only to recognise the mineral as cassiterite, but also to state the name of the particular mine in Cornwall from which it came, for many of these supposed tin prospects were 'salted' with imported mineral."

Pearce was far too experienced a mineralogist to be taken in in this way, but he maintained a lively interest in the new mineral discoveries being made in Colorado throughout the thirty years of his residence there. He was a friend from early days of the distinguished geologist Emmons, whose epoch-making report on the *Geology and Mining Industry of Leadville* announced the application of scientific geology to mining, and together they founded the Colorado Scientific Society at Denver in 1882. In 1891 occurred the discovery of gold in quantity, but in unfamiliar form as tellurides, at Cripple Creek near Pike's Peak, where there had been such bitter disappointment thirty years earlier. At first there was a good deal of scepticism and the mining industry was genuinely puzzled.

"Cripple Creek became famous for its lustrous tellurides, both of gold and of silver, minerals of a kind previously but rarely known to the miner . . . It is not recorded who was the first to recognise the tellurides of Cripple Creek," but Rickard thought that it was probably Pearce.[9] Certainly he contributed papers on the new Cripple Creek ores to the Colorado Scientific Society and took a leading part in the discussions of the problems they posed. In these there now joined two figures of a younger generation, T. A. Rickard, and Philip Argall, a young Cornish metallurgist of already wide experience, who had come out first to Leadville and was now moving to Cripple Creek. R. A. F. Penrose, the geologist brother of Spencer Penrose, went to study and report on Cripple Creek and shortly his brother, the great capitalist, moved in: it made the foundation of his vast fortune. The Cripple Creek boom was on, its technical problems successfully tackled; by 1894 the original cow-ranch was a town of ten thousand and in ten years some $125,000,000 of gold was taken out.[10]

Pearce himself had mining interests, in addition to his chief concern with smelting: he was a large holder in the Smuggler-Union Mine at Telluride in the San Juan region of Colorado. A prosperous and highly fortunate man—nothing that he touched seems ever to have failed—Richard Pearce was also a kindly and generous one, very helpful to younger men. Nothing ever seems to have gone wrong with him, and this is reflected in the ease and charm of his personality—the more ebullient Rickard refers to him revealingly as "the dear man." Pearce and Rickard had a common bond in their Cornishry no less than in their vocation; the two were combined in a present that the elder made the younger man, of a copy of Pryce's rare *Mineralogia Cornubiensia* of 1778. Pearce seems to have generated confidence and affection around him. In his big, roomy house in Denver, to which he moved from Central

City, he kept open house for the Cousin Jacks. He never became an American citizen; he had always kept up his links with Cornwall and in 1902 he retired there. But he was too active—or possibly too radio-active—to rust in idleness. In 1888 he had joined with his brother to take over a long-established smelter in Cornwall, that of Williams, Harvey and Company; they thought of calling it Harvey, Pearce and Company, but in the end retained the old name for the goodwill.[11] Thus it was with this firm twenty years later, at the age of seventy-one, that he worked to build a tin-smelter at Bootle, for the new ores of Nigeria and Bolivia. In the same year he was made president of the Royal Institution of Cornwall, of which he was a life-member; and at the age of eighty-eight he was awarded the gold medal of the Institution of Mining and Metallurgy. It seems a meager reward for a lifetime of creative activity, for a life filled with useful achievement, when so many useless persons receive public honors. Richard Pearce was of a nature not to mind, probably not even to notice. He had a happy family life, with four sons, all of whom followed in his footsteps as metallurgists or mining engineers, in Colorado, Montana and Mexico.[12] He was nearly ninety when he died in 1927, having "lived so long that he outlived the reputation he had won among his contemporaries." But his life's work is part of the history of Colorado, and it is there that he should have his memorial.

Another characteristic of Colorado mining was that it often took place at dizzy altitudes, placing an added strain on health and temper—a short life and a gay one. Leadville, at the head of the upper valley of the Arkansas River, is situated at over ten thousand feet. A boom began with the silver-lead discoveries of 1877; its heyday was in the 1880's; the collapse came with the fall in the price of silver in 1893. Late in the 1890's there was a partial recovery with the opening up of some gold-mines, and until after the First World War lead, zinc and other minerals continued to be worked.

Colorado: Gold and Silver 331

A Cornish friend, T. H. Clarke of Colorado Springs, whose father left St. Austell in 1887 to work at Leadville for four years, "until the bottom fell out of silver and the mines closed down," writes me that "Leadville and Central City were full of Cornish between 1880 and 1890. Then, when the United States went off silver, nearly all the mines closed down and the men moved on to the copper-mines and many returned to England." His father in effect did both: he went back for a couple of years during which he married a wife, then brought her out with him to Butte, Montana, where he worked for eight or nine years and then went home for good. "They were there [Butte] nine months before my father got a job. So you see everything wasn't easy in those days." This introduces us to a pattern that was to become more frequent in this century. With the increasing ease of communications people went to and fro more frequently; and also they were apt to return home with their savings—life in the old country was not so impoverished as it had been in the previous century. Nevertheless, the vast majority, we shall see, remained in America: opportunities were still wider and better there. They became good American citizens—without forgetting Cornwall, however.

An idiosyncratic figure who has not failed to be commemorated—in fact he left an immense memorial of himself in the Benevolent and Protective Order of Elks—was Charles Algernon Sidney Vivian, who died in Leadville at the height of its garish glories in 1880.* A younger son of a Cornish clergyman, Vivian was born in Exeter in 1846. On his father's early death he went on to the stage and became a popular entertainer with songs, skits, character-sketches. Coming to America he had a great success on the West Coast, particularly in San Francisco where—Vivian was always a dandy —the stores sported Vivian hats, Vivian collars and ties. He

---

* I. H. Vivian, *A Biographical Sketch of Charles Algernon Sidney Vivian, Founder of the Order of Elks*. There is no notice of him in the *Dictionary of American Biography*. There should be.

had married, too early, in England, but got a divorce and married Imogen Holbrook in 1876 at Oakland. Together they played to packed houses "at mining town prices" at Eureka, Nevada and Salt Lake City. They made a stage-coach journey of seven days in winter—across that intractable country!—to Helena, Montana, breakfasting at 3 A.M. to be on the road by four.

Vivian always made a hit with clubs, with men's audiences in the mining camps, or officers in outposts like Fort Shaw on his tour of Montana. Mrs. Vivian recited "All Quiet Along the Potomac Tonight" or read Bret Harte's "Idyll of Battle Hollow," while Vivian brought the house down with his favorite "Ten Thousand Miles Away." They went by boat down the Missouri—where Mrs. Vivian says that they saw the fine specimen of an elk swimming the river and that suggested changing the name of the clubs from the original "Jolly Corks"—and then took the Red River boat into Manitoba. At Winnipeg they performed before the celebrated Lord Dufferin, Governor-General of Canada. During their Chicago season they played at two theatres a night, on East Side and West Side. At St. Louis in 1879 Vivian appeared in "Pinafore" and "Trial by Jury." Thence they toured Kansas City, Lawrence, Fort Leavenworth, Denver, to arrive at Leadville, where Vivian produced "Oliver Twist." Here—at that height and in that winter climate ("Carbonate Camp" they called it)—he caught pneumonia and died, only thirty-three, in 1880.

In his brief life he made a popular impression everywhere he went and, in the end, a prodigiously large and unexpected impact on America. He was a very clubbable personality, gifted and guileless, impetuous and quick to childlike anger, good-looking, with curly hair, inclined to fat, but every ounce a gentleman. He had no sense of money, which ran through his fingers or was always available to his friends or anybody in want. It was this that, in the end, kept the memory of his brief life green. On his first visit to New York in 1867 Vivian had started a convivial dining club for his theatrical friends to mitigate the horrors of Victorian Sunday evenings. These were the "Jolly Corks," with himself as "Imperial Cork." Then, shortly before Christmas, one of the members died, leaving his family in distress. Vivian, only twenty-one, was the spirit of the club, which decided to turn itself into a benevolent society to help its members. This was founded on February 16, 1868, its original organizers describing themselves as "members of the Theatrical, Minstrel, Musical, Equestrian and Literary Professions." The organization grew slowly at first, since a number of the original members wanted to confine it to the theatre. Vivian had been elected its head, and wherever he went he tried to organize a lodge—he founded the one at Salt Lake City, for instance. The Order grew steadily, and had a strong appeal with its benefit performances and social activities. The Elks had another advantage in that their members travelled about in pursuit of their profession, and this brought requests for lodges elsewhere. "In March 1871 the Elks obtained a corporate charter from the New York legislature, under which they created a Grand Lodge with power to establish subordinate lodges anywhere in the country."[13]

Since then the Order has made vast strides—it evidently met and answered very real human needs in a voluntary society long before the age of the Welfare State. Reaching its centennial in 1968, it has a membership of 1,350,000 with two thousand lodges throughout the nation. It spends more than $8,000,000 a year on youth programmes, aid to the physically handicapped, veterans in hospital, scholarships to students. Since Charles Vivian's death in 1880 the Order has contributed some $200,000,000 in welfare work and services to the nation. It is a highly conservative and patriotic body—strange that it should all go back to this young strolling actor!

Charles Vivian was buried on a bitter, snowy day at Leadville, but in 1889 his body was brought to Elks' Rest in Mount Hope Cemetery, Boston, where he has his shrine. This simple little fellow achieved more good by his brief life than thousands of those who have received far more public recognition—particularly, we may say, those public men by profession, politicians.

It was in these years, the 1880's, that T. A. Rickard served his apprenticeship in practical mining. The youngest of his father's four brothers was managing a group of Colorado mines; one at Idaho Springs had John Curnow for captain, and young Rickard started as assayer there in 1885. Next year he went on a visit to Leadville, staying at the La Plata smelter with William Hanson—Rickard's father was consulting engineer to the company. The cheap side to life in the mining camps, written up by popular writers under the name of romance, had no charms for the serious-minded young Rickard. Leadville was one of the roughest camps and, while there, "I would hear of a shooting scrape almost every day, but it did not interest me much."[14] He felt that the real romance was in the work. "The pursuit of wealth was incidental to the scientific search for ore and the application of technical ingenuity both to the mining and the milling of the ore." His *Retrospect* gives us an enjoyable picture of the all-round life he much appreciated there.

That summer Rickard moved from Idaho Springs across the ridge to Central City with his uncle, who was in charge of the California, Kansas, Kent County and other mines on Quartz Hill. "In the Kansas mine the haulage was effected by a bucket and a hemp rope to a depth of 1500 feet"—equipment that a little later would be regarded as suicidal.[15] In 1887 Rickard was left to supervise during his uncle's absence, when Philip Argall came to inspect the mines of Central City. The last time he had met this first-class mining engineer was as a boy, when Argall was managing the Duchy Peru Mine in Cornwall for Rickard's father. Since then Argall had been all over the world accumulating experience, and shortly Rickard was to go on his world-tour. One sees what a cosmopolitan experience these mining experts came to have, and how closely connected they were by their Cornishry —almost a kind of free-masonry. Later on, Rickard and Argall, like Pearce, became residents of Denver. When Rickard returned to Colorado after his world-tour, he went back to visit the mine at Central City of which he had been in temporary charge—and was put through his paces by old Captain John Prouse, to see if he had learned anything on his travels. The young man was put a poser as to the proper price for the stope they were examining, and apparently passed the test. These were the men that Rickard liked best, "the old Cornish miners, of whom there were some to be found at every mine of any size." Rickard hadn't much use for the pathetic and vulgar millionaires the mines made, many of whom ran through their millions as rapidly as they made them, and whose flashy doings made mere copy for the press —and for journalistic books since.

Rickard had a very varied experience of Colorado mining, for in 1893 he was made manager of the Yankee Girl Mine at Red Mountain and of the Enterprise Mine at Rico in the mountains of southwestern Colorado. Life there was full of excitement: his visits to the mines "required long trips on horseback and the crossing of snowy ranges on foot, sometimes by aid of snowshoes, or skis."[16] The snow-slides were dangerous; at the Liberty Bell Mine near Telluride the buildings were buried and eighteen men killed in them. Other excitements were not without their dangers. "While I was at Rico there was a riot at Cripple Creek, and some of the Rico miners captured a train, on which they went to help their comrades." Rickard met obstruction from his own miners' union when he introduced the system of work by contract— with improved results. Rickard told them that "my father and grandfather had been Cornish mining engineers and that I had learned to use the contract system while assistant to my uncle at Central City"—and asked them to give it a fair trial. They did—O *tempora!* O *mores!*

In 1896 Rickard was consulting engineer of the Columbus Mine in the La Plata Mountains, at an altitude of twelve thousand feet, difficult of access in the winter. The Colorado mining region stretched sickle-shaped for over a couple of hundred miles across the Rockies down the western half of the state; Rickard rode all over it, some ten or twelve hours in the saddle a day. One long ride of some four hundred miles he took in the fall of 1902 he describes in his rather technical book, *Across the San Juan Mountains*. Since the aim was to examine various mines, it is full of geological description, though Rickard had a lively appreciation of Colorado's fine mountain scenery. For years he had been searching for the telluride of copper, and at length he had his reward: he found specimens at Cripple Creek (as at Kalgoorlie in Australia) which, when tested and approved, gave Rickard's name to mineralogy with the new mineral "rickardite" to place beside "pearceite."

His services were rewarded by his honorary appointment as State Geologist in 1895, though not an American citizen. He retained it under governors of both parties, for he had no interest in politics. When he gave a public address at the University of Colorado at Boulder in 1898, he devoted himself to exposing "two prevailing delusions: that mines grew richer in depth and that men were born free and equal."[17] This produced protests from two different confraternities, one of which suggested that he should be dismissed from his post of State Geologist. One discerns in Rickard a kindred spirit: he detested humbug. It was not exactly a popular characteristic.

Nothing dissuaded him from telling the truth about mining. "Mines are short-lived. They yield a harvest that is gathered once only. Nine mines out of ten are sold for more than their worth; more money is made by selling than by buying them. Much of the so-called business of mining is based on a scant knowledge of its operations and a profound recognition of the essential foolishness of human nature."[18] However, this did not prevent him from being called in to report on the Cripple Creek mines then in the later 1890's occupying the center of attention. He gives us some examples of a similar turn of humor to his own amongst the miners themselves. An "expert" who did not disdain the name of "professor" was shown in friendly fashion over a mine near Silver Plume and dismayed the miners with a lot of long words for simple objects. Until a little man from St. Just brought up a piece of "gouge," the waste clay along the edge of a vein, with "What do 'ee call'n, you—Professor?" The Professor described it as "the argillaceous remnant of an antediluvian world." The miner placed a hand confidentially on the professorial shoulder, with "That's just what I told me pardner."

Rickard evidently much enjoyed his years in Colorado, from which he was called in 1902 to the editorship of the *Engineering and Mining Journal* in New York.

Philip Argall, in contrast, was a pure specialist, though of exceptionally wide experience. Born in Ireland in 1854 where his father was engaged in the lead- and copper-mines, he used to call himself an Irishman, until he became an American citizen in 1889. In fact his father was "descended from a Cornish mining family, spent his lifetime in the mining business, commencing with tin, lead and copper-mining in Cornwall, leading to lead and coal-mining in Wales," thence to the Isle of Man and finally Ireland.[19] It must have given him a wide acquaintance with the Celtic fringe. On his apprenticeship in Cornwall young Philip patented a handbrake for the horse-whim, while he won the first prize for the best plan and section of any mining district at the Royal Cornwall Polytechnic Society's exhibition in 1878. Next year he took a course in metallurgy at Swansea, after which he was put in charge of the Stannic smelting works, where tin was reduced in old-fashioned Cornish furnaces, with John Uren for his refiner. In this, his first, job Argall made a decisive improvement in reducing the ore. His health suffering from the sulphur-fumes, he accepted an offer from Rickard's father to manage the Duchy Peru Mine near Newquay. After that there followed further mining experience in New Zealand, France and Mexico, until he became manager of the La Plata smelter at Leadville in 1887.

At that time there were too many smelters for the available ore, with intense competition between those up at Leadville and those in the valley, at Denver and Pueblo. Argall made his reputation as a pioneer of the cyanide process in the reduction of the Cripple Creek ores. "The treatment of the telluride gold ores of Cripple Creek gave him a congenial problem, which he attacked with all the intensity of the Celtic temperament, incidentally waging a technical war of considerable vigour with the advocates of both bromination and chlorination in Colorado."[20] Actually Argall devoted years to patient experimentation upon and improving the cyanide process. His efforts resulted at length in the erection of a cyanide mill at Florence, Colorado, in 1895; later he designed a similar mill for the great Independence Mine of which he became manager in 1906. His campaign was crowned with complete success: he was able to tell Rickard that in the twenty years, 1893 to 1913, he had seen the cost of treating Cripple Creek ores fall from $15 per ton to $1.38. "And then, as if to prove his up-to-dateness, Mr. Argall became involved in the use of flotation, achieving a noteworthy technical success so quietly that . . . this interview is the first publication of it." This was the latest "flotation-process" in the reduction of gold ores.

Argall retired from active work at the mines to Denver, where he formed a consulting partnership with two of his five sons. He had married the daughter of Captain George Oates, "a Cornishman with a long ancestry of miners, to whom I am indebted for much of my early training in engineering ethics."[21]* One of the sons was a practicing metallurgist, the

* Yet the standard *History of Colorado*, ed. by J. H. Baker and L. R. Hafen, 'V, 112, describes Argall and his wife as "both natives of Ireland."

Colorado: Gold and Silver 339

other general manager for one of the Leadville mines; the firm were consulting engineers to Stratton's Independence and other mines. A third son, born at Roche, near St. Austell, graduated from the University of Colorado, to become an ear, nose and throat specialist in Denver and to serve as a surgeon in the United States Navy in the First World War.

Philip Argall certainly made his contribution to Colorado, was part of its history.

Colorado's last gold-rush, that to Cripple Creek in the early 1890's, took place in the same Pike's Peak vicinity that had so much disappointed the prospectors of thirty years before. The discovery of a rich gold-field came, fortunately for Colorado, just at the moment to offset the collapse of silver-mining. The effective opening up of these resources was owing to the pertinacity of W. S. Stratton, a carpenter of neighboring Colorado Springs, who had taught himself the elements of mineralogy and for some years spent his spare time prospecting. He certainly received his reward. For the first seven years the output of Stratton's Independence was some $4,000,000, with nearly $2,500,000 profit to himself.[22] When the mine was sold next year to a London company, it "became the sport of reckless promotion," and Stratton received another $11,000,000. He died two years later, in 1901, by which time Cripple Creek had yielded some $125,000,000 in gold. This was to be trebled by the time of the First World War, when its glory ended.[23]

We have already noticed something of the interests of Spencer Penrose and his brother Richard, of the famous Philadelphia family, in Colorado mining. It was in Cripple Creek that Spencer Penrose struck lucky in 1892, his claim coinciding with the apex of one of the district's richest locations.[24] From this he branched out into the smelting and milling business. In 1903 he brought his brothers and his father into organizing the Utah Copper Company to exploit the ores of Bingham Canyon and treat them with the new refining process. This proved so successful that soon he was making $200,000 a month from it. Subsequently these copper interests were sold to the Guggenheims at figures that left Penrose a multimillionaire.

This is not the place to go into his vast interests—there should be a biography of him—which extended into real estate, banking, railroads, pioneering in agriculture, the sugar-beet industry, the tourist industry.[25] Here we should merely note that it all pivoted on Colorado and his vast, gloomy, mountain-shadowed mansion at Colorado Springs where he lived, enjoyed his gargantuan feasts (like his brother, the senator), and where he died. He made Colorado Springs a resort center, he built the lavish Broadmoor hotel, with golf-course, zoo, ice-palace. He built the road to the top of Pike's Peak and inaugurated the annual automobile races up it. A gentleman of old stock, of the seventh generation in the New World, he affected a wide-brimmed cowboy hat and Western habits—though late in life he married a young American widow in London. Though he divided the bulk of his immense fortune between widow and step-daughter, there was still $11,000,000 left over to establish his El Pomar Foundation for charitable purposes. A place in Fremont County, the center of the Beaver Park farming district, is named after him: the little town of Penrose.

A man made in a big mould, grasping and open-handed, immensely extrovert and avid of life, predatory and sensual, swashbuckling and lavish, irreligious but in the end a philanthropist on the grand scale, one recognizes nothing Cornish in him—except his indefeasibly Cornish name and his atavistic instinct for mining.

Smaller people made their contributions, too. Let us take a few examples from different fields.

The Honorable John Frederick Vivian had an important public career.[26] He was born in 1864, at Phoenix Mine, Michigan, where his father was a pioneer and died young.

The widow came to Colorado and married another Cornishman. The boy worked on a farm, took to merchandizing and then cattle-ranching with success. Up until 1895 Jefferson County was controlled by the Democrats.[27] Vivian now interested himself in politics, and, a Republican like nearly all the Cornish, he canvassed and card-indexed the whole county so effectively that in that year the entire Republican ticket was elected, with himself as county clerk and recorder. He proceeded to build up the Republican organization as it still functions today; this provided a base for his own public career and that of his son, who became Republican governor of Colorado, 1943–47. Vivian was thrice mayor of his local town of Golden, where he had a considerable property. He then went into the service of the state as deputy-superintendent of insurance, next surveyor-general and collector of customs at Denver. For eight years he was register of the State Board of Land Commissioners. *Pour comble de tout*, when Prohibition came in with the Republicans, he became Federal Prohibition director for Colorado, 1923–25, and Federal Prohibition administrator of the 18th district until the end of the business in 1933. It was probably a vexatious, if not unrewarding, job, for the mountain-stills of Colorado were among the most inaccessible. However, he must have been a man of great energy to keep going to his ninetieth year: he died in 1954. What a span his life had covered from those early days in the Copper Country of Lake Michigan to ours, to the Korean and Viet Nam wars!

The old gentleman saw out the active career of his son, Governor Vivian. John Charles Vivian, born at Golden in 1887, went to the University of Colorado and became a lawyer, where his father had been a farm-boy. Returning from service with the United States Marines in the First World War, he became Federal Food Administrator. He was city attorney of Golden, then county attorney of Jefferson County, and ultimately governor of the state—one of the few Cornishmen to achieve such a position.

Of older Cornish name and stock, we find, as we might expect, Chenoweths and Trevilians. The Honorable J. Edgar Chenoweth, born 1897, was a Republican congressman from 1940.[28] His parents, from Maryland, were among the pioneer settlers of southern Colorado. Other members of this old and wide-spreading clan gave their name to their large ranch in Elbert County.[29] The grandfather moved from Ohio to Missouri, the son was wounded in the Civil War fighting on the Union side—though most Chenoweths were southerners. The son came to Colorado ranching; *his* son became a doctor in Denver. Another doctor was Edward B. Trovillion of Gold County.[30] His grandfather had changed the spelling of the name from Trevelian, which at least makes sense. This man was of the third generation: his grandfather had come to Massachusetts, the next generation went to Virginia, with a son who was a tobacco planter and served in the Seminole, Florida and Black Hawk wars. So the Colorado doctor was the fifth generation.

Just as Mr. Louis Copeland bicycled round the Blue Mounds country of Wisconsin in the 1890's collecting material about the first generation of Cornish there before it was too late, so Professor Lynn Perrigo gathered material in the 1930's about their life in Central City before all the old folk had gone. The picture is very similar, and by now familiar: it was an extrapolation, four or five thousand miles away, of the life at home, as it might be Camborne and Redruth. The central gold-producing region was a similarly small cramped area, in this case all canyon and gulches, a mile high up in the Rockies. A branch of the refuse-muddied waters of (once) Clear Creek bisected it; these emptied into Gregory Gulch, where the main deposits were found. At the junction was Black Hawk; at the extreme upper end, Nevadaville; extending an arm on either side of the creek was Central City, the county seat of famous Gilpin County. The mining settlements ran into each other, pivoting upon Central City dominated by Quartz Hill.

Among the earliest arrivals were some from California; these were followed by experienced hard-rock miners, as we have seen, from Lake Superior and some from the Blue Mounds region. But from the 1860's miners poured in directly from Cornwall.[31] By 1869, Frank Young, who remembered those days, tells us, "there has been a steady influx of robust, stout-chested, pink-cheeked lads from the tin-mines of Cornwall, and these promise in time to outnumber all but the native element . . . There is very little brawling. For a time, indeed, after the Cornish lads first appeared, they fell into an occasional mix-up with their hereditary enemies, the Celts of Nevada[ville]," i.e. the Irish.[32] Actually, Central City was a rather respectable, stable community, like Grass Valley, and unlike the feverish Leadville. By 1870 15 per cent of the population were immigrants, but by the 1880's they formed one-quarter.[33] The majority of them were Cornish, but they made such a strong impression by their highly marked characteristics that some people fancied that "the majority of the population was Cornish."

As usual, what struck people was their lingo, the mix-up of personal pronouns, the dropped *h*'s and haphazard insertion. "Her 'edn' a-callin we," and " 'Ow art e gettin hon, you?" are familiar forms; a miner thrown off his horse explained why in these terms: "Dam she: I could ride she if it wudn' for the dam dinner pail."* The miners' wives dressed up in their "finery"—purple velvet, feather boas, hats with bright yellow plumes: this was just on the way out in the village of my youth. The Methodist chapel was as important at Central City as at Tregonissey, and the choir was a leading feature—Mrs. Raynolds spent long hours coaching the miners, who had good voices. Nor were they averse to lifting them up in the saloons with "Trafalgar's Bay" or "The Wreck of the Arethusa." In contemporary photographs one sees the naïve young faces against the background of the new stone Method-

---

* I have occasionally corrected the transliteration.

ist church they had built, the women with their leg-of-mutton sleeves, the frocks with the ruches and gathered tucks. Others show the men in working kit outside their wooden shed at the mine, or a smaller group beside a stack of silver bricks at the smelter at Black Hawk—the end-product.

Miss Caroline Bancroft has studied, and given us an authentic report of, their folk-lore.[34] She records the warm, old-fashioned hospitality she received from Carters, Warrens, Williamses still in Central City, from Hancocks, Grenfells, Hugheses of Russell Gulch. Judge W. C. Mathews, who had been born in Cornwall, worked in the mines of Nevadaville, and died at Denver in 1925, wrote a history of Gilpin County, full of Cornish information, which has apparently disappeared. The stories turned as usual on the illiteracy of the early folk, many of whom could neither read nor write but would not confess their ignorance; or there were bawdy stories among the miners, too coarse for reproduction. At Nevadaville Nankervis ran a butcher's shop, which sported a large stuffed owl for decoration on a shelf. "Ow much for the broad-faced chicken," asked a Cousin Jenny. "That edn' no chicken. Tes an owl." "I dunt care 'ow owl 'ee be; ee'll do for my boarders." Or, a miner took his pasty to the hoistman to heat it up for his dinner. When he arrived for it, the hoistman had eaten it. "God damme! I dedn' mean for ee to eat'n up, but *eat'n* up." Edward Rowe got a letter from his girl at home, which he took to his partner to read for him, meanwhile holding his hands over his partner's ears so that he shouldn't hear what was in the letter.

These stories—and there are many such[35]—have the pathos of these simple people's lives. And we learn more about their superstitions, too. For example, women in a mine will bring bad luck to the miners or some disaster to the mine. If a miner's candle goes out three times or falls off ledge or wall, somebody is at home playing with his wife. These associations of ideas may be recommended to the anthropologists. Cornish cooking goes on in Colorado into the third generation, as in Grass Valley and Mineral Point to the fourth and fifth. Miss Bancroft has collected a number of recipes, if less variegated than those of the Old Cornwall Societies at home: there is the almost ubiquitous (and much misrepresented) pasty and saffron cake, in addition she gives us "kiddley broth" (leek soup) and the redoubtable "figgie hobbin."[36] She notes the frequent purchases of saffron at 25 cents a packet, recorded in the daybook of a grocery store for 1894-95.

The Cornish and the Irish, though both Celts, were antipathetic here as elsewhere. With the decreasing prosperity of mining in this area, towards 1900, Italians from the Tyrol came in to work for lower wages. The Cornish began to move out, into business or ranching, increasingly into Denver; those who remained miners were apt to move up to Montana or down into Arizona. Frank Young, returning to Central City in 1903 writes:

> Walk the streets . . . and you will find strange faces and note unfamiliar ways. You may indeed encounter William Williams or Thomas Thomas of Cornwall—but it was their fathers that you knew in the long ago, and you met them underground; while the son of today may be the man who will rent you a store-house on Main Street or a cottage on the hill side. He has become a landed proprietor, or a mine lessee and an employer of men, and his old place below on the tenth level of the Bobtail or the Gunnell is taken by a son of sunny Italy . . . True, you may still hear "Trafalgar's Bay" or "The Wreck of the Arethusa" rolling out in the robust baritone of Cousin Jack about the time of the monthly payday . . . But the old home-brewed beer of Eureka Street has largely given place to the *chianti* of Italy, and strange names ending in *ini* abound on the signboards or on the mine payrolls where John Penglase or Thomas Trelawny once made their marks.[37]

And then, Central City "has finished its career. Its days are done; but its memory lives, and will ever be kept green in the hearts of the survivors of the cycle just completed."

It has entered into history.

But Cornish miners are still about in Colorado. In the 1930's the depression, by lowering costs, made it profitable for some of the gold-mines to start up again. David Lavender's *One Man's West* gives an account of life at Camp Bird in the San Juan Mountains. "Up on our floor we had a couple of Irishmen, some Cornishmen—Cornish miners are called Cousin Jacks—a Frenchman, two Norwegians and a scattering of native Americans." The Scandinavians at the mine were, we are told, almost without exception handsome. But when something went wrong with the inexpert Dave's hoist-brake and, having taken it to pieces, he found that he could not put it together again, it was an old and expert Cousin Jack who came to his rescue. Since David Lavender is a real writer the scene is vividly described. At the bottom of the shaft the bell was ringing madly for the hoist:

> Since the bucket wasn't there, I could only surmise that a man was coming up without it. Sure enough, a few minutes later Tommy Rice's ugly Cornish face [the name is a pseudonym] appeared through the manway hole. He was perhaps fifty years old, brown and wrinkled as a withered apple. One of his upper front teeth was gone, and two of his lower ones were made out of gold. His left leg had been shattered in an explosion, and he walked with a strange hitching, half-hopping gait. Something had also happened to his vocal cords; he talked in a husky whisper that cracked every now and then into a shrill falsetto. He was only five feet tall and thin as a splinter, but none of these infirmities prevented his being one of the best hands in the place and straw boss of our shifts. Like most miners, he chewed snuff perpetually. I don't

know how so big a heart as his came to be in so odd a body.

He eyed my chaos. "Good gracious," he whispered, or words to that effect. Then he picked up a wrench and went to work. While he repaired the damage he taught me the whole mystery of the machine. Not by tone or gesture did he imply that I was anywhere near the fool I really was. I loved that man.[38]

Let that stand as a tribute to the thousands of silent practitioners of his craft, the underground mystery of mining.

We have already noticed what a natural capital Denver was, and is, for all that area and what a magnet for mining folk as mining declined and other industries came up. The Cornish moved into the city in hundreds—today there must be at least a couple of thousand of them there. Even in old days it was Cornish miners who built little St. Peter's Episcopal Church of rough stone.[39] Today a well-known radio announcer has the appropriate name of Yelland.[40] It is pleasant to notice how many names that we have encountered in this chapter are represented there. There are four Argall entries in the telephone directory. There are no less than fifty-five Pearce with one Pearce Drill Steel Corporation; this is the usual Cornish spelling of the name, but I do not know if any are direct representatives of Richard Pearce. We find also Dawe (11), Curnow (8, with a transportation company of the name—is it the same we have mentioned?), Trezise (8, including one in an oil concern), Vivian (8), Chenoweth (8), Penrose (6, though not of Spencer Penrose's family—more recent recruits), Nankervis (4), Trenberth (2), Grenfell (12). There is a very large spread of Tre- names. Among uncommon names we find Bolitho (6), Daddow (5), Reseigh (5), Quintrall (5), Santo (5), Vosper (3), Lanyon (4, with one plumbing and heating concern), Retallack (9), Kitto (5), Prouse (5), Crago (4), Spargo (2, one of them a minister), Wearne, Rescola (for Rescorla, a name practically extinct at home), Rodd, Bosanko, Chegwidden, Otey (5), Carkeek (2), Carew, Rosewarne, Laity, Penhallow, Penhaligen, Polmear, Angove, Combellick (2), Menhenett (2), Kellow, Olver.

Among rather more common names we find Opie (11, with one jeweller), Pascoe (13), Goldsworthy (8), Triplett (14), Davey (11), Minear (3), Faull (5), Rodda (5), Ede (2), Retallack (11, including an optician and a surgeon), Chenoweth (8, under both forms of the name), Polkinghorne (3), Oates (7), Rosevear (2), Nancarrow, Edgecomb, Tamblyn (3), Penberthy (3), Luke (12), Cornish (11), Chubb (4, with Chubb and Son Incorporated, and Chubb's Sixty Six Service), Trudgian (3), Truscott (3, including a physician), Lobb (6). Under Varcoe: Varcoe's Restrainer Jacket, Varcoe Ferne Evans slipcovers, Varco Products Company. There must be hundreds among English names common with Cornish people.

Altogether, including all the Tre- names, Denver offers as fine a feast of Cornish names as any city in the United States. In total Cornish population it would come very high, after Chicago, Detroit, San Francisco, New York, Philadelphia. Since it is a much smaller city the Cornish element is proportionately higher. It reflects, precisely and concisely, the Cornish contribution to Colorado as a whole.

NOTES

1. cf. R. W. Paul, "Colorado as a Pioneer of Science in the Mining West," *Mississippi Valley Historical Review*, XLVII, 34ff.
2. R. W. Paul, *Mining Frontiers of the Far West*, 119.
3. *Ibid.*, 114–45.
4. *Ibid.*, 122.
5. L. I. Perrigo, "The Cornish Miners of Early Gilpin County," *Colorado Mag.*, XIV, 92ff.

Colorado: Gold and Silver 349

6. "N. P. Hill Takes Ore to Swansea, Wales," *Colorado Mag.*, XXXIV, 184ff.
7. For my account of Pearce I am much indebted to T. A. Rickard, "Richard Pearce: The Biographic Sketch of a Pioneer Metallurgist," *Engineering and Mining Journal*, March 10, 1928, 404ff., based on Pearce's own notes, and from which quotations are taken, unless otherwise stated.
8. Paul, 124.
9. T. A. Rickard, *Hist. of American Mining*, 144.
10. *Ibid.*, 146.
11. D. B. Barton, *Hist. of Tin Mining and Smelting in Cornwall*, 203.
12. *Encyclopedia of Biography of Colorado*, (1901), I, 233ff.
13. "Elks Near Century of Service to Nation in War and Peace," a publication of the Order.
14. T. A. Rickard, *Retrospect*, 33.
15. *Ibid.*, 34, 78–79.
16. *Ibid.*, 54–56.
17. *Ibid.*, 68.
18. *Ibid.*, 77, 79–80.
19. T. A. Rickard, *Interviews with Mining Engineers*, 5.
20. *Ibid.*, 36.
21. *Ibid.*, 33.
22. T. A. Rickard, *Hist. of American Mining*, 146.
23. *Colorado*, (American Guide Series), 245.
24. D. A. B., XXII, Supplement 2, 525–26.
25. cf. *Hist. of Colorado, op. cit.*, V, 14–17.
26. *Denver and Vicinity*, 1156–57.
27. *Colorado Mag.*, XX, 37.
28. *Colorado and its People*, IV, 735.
29. *Denver and Vicinity*, 487–89.
30. *Ibid.*, 199–200.
31. L. I. Perrigo, "The Cornish Miners of Early Gilpin County," *Colorado Mag.*, XIV, 92ff.

32. F. C. Young, *Echoes from Arcadia*, 87.
33. Perrigo, *loc. cit.*
34. Caroline Bancroft, "Cousin Jack Stories from Central City," *Colorado Mag.*, XXI, 51ff.
35. cf. J. T. Thomson, "Cousin Jack Stories," *Colorado Mag.*, XXXV, 187ff.
36. cf. Clementine Paddleford, "Cooking in Colorado," *This Week Mag.*, April 12, 1959.
37. Young, 9–10, 207.
38. David Lavender, *One Man's West*, 38.
39. From information of Mrs. Dorothy Mackenzie.
40. From information of Mr. T. H. Clarke.

13 *MONTANA, OREGON, WASHINGTON, DAKOTA*

*M*ontana mining, up in the remote northwestern Rockies, went through a comparable cycle to that of Colorado, though somewhat simpler: from gold in the 1860's to silver in the 1870's, thereafter to copper, where it has rested, today the nation's greatest single source of supply. There is a marked contrast with the diversity of Colorado "the evolution of a new mining community was to centre in one area, the vicinity of Butte. Butte, by itself, was to Montana what Gilpin county and Leadville jointly were to Colorado."[1] Then, too, we are reminded that, "in Montana, as elsewhere, the placer miner blazed the trail for the lode miner; indeed, widening the generalisation, one may say that all over our western domain, as in other parts of the world, the finding of gold has been the first step in the development of a mining industry . . . The extraction of gold from the gravel of the stream is the simplest process used by the miner; it can be performed with an apparatus of the crudest kind; and the results are evident forthwith."[2]

The first discoveries of gold in the gulches of western Montana were made in the early 1860's: "at Bannack in the summer of 1862, at Alder Gulch (where Virginia City was founded) in 1863, Last Chance Gulch (where Helena developed) in 1864, at Butte in the same year," and in some other places.³ At once there ensued something of a rush, though not on the scale of the original gold-rush to California; Montana had a population of only twenty thousand by 1870. Nor were the gold resources comparable to California's; still the placer-diggings yielded altogether some $150,000,000 by 1876, and that was much greater than the first, disappointing phase in Colorado's cycle.

The usual motley bodies of men travelled the long routes to Montana: from Idaho and Utah, from California and Nevada, from the Middle West, particularly from Missouri and Iowa, up the Missouri River by boat. Bishop Tuttle, the first Protestant missionary bishop in the territory, reported that in 1868-69, "among the miners were many Cornishmen and Irishmen."⁴ These became the two dominant elements in the population of Butte. A good many Montana placer-miners confined themselves to summer diggings, and went south in the fall on the home-made raft-like boats—we have already come across several Cornish prospectors from the Middle West making the journey. Later, the steam-boat service to Fort Benton, still more up to the splendid gorge of the Missouri at its nearest point to Helena, was apt to be unsatisfactory and even precarious from the frequently low water. However, it was the main route into the new country, until the Union Pacific linked it up with Ogden in 1881.

By 1870 the yield of gold was rapidly declining and the population falling, as simultaneously in Idaho. Butte was almost deserted—until the discovery and exploitation of silver revived it, and by 1880 it had a population of three thousand. Far more important were the ultimate resources in copper, of prodigious extent—Butte has been described as "the richest hill in the world"—and the development of these was mainly due to two remarkable men, William Andrews Clark and Marcus Daly. They stood out in striking contrast to each other and, at first friends, later their careers were locked in dramatic conflict, which constituted much of the history of Montana in their time.

Clark was a native Pennsylvanian farm-boy of Scotch extraction, shrewd and resourceful, who had at one time been a school-teacher and believed in education.[5] It was much to his credit that, after a varied experience of the trials and hardships of life in the diggings, once he began to be successful and already a man in his thirties, he went back to the Columbia School of Mines to equip himself for his career of conquest in Montana mining. We have already seen him entering into agreement with Professor N. P. Hill and Richard Pearce to organize the Colorado and Montana Smelting Company and set up the first smelter at Butte. Upon the foundation of Butte he built up his empire and ended as United States Senator for Montana. He was a cold, reserved, rather fastidious man, who built up a grand, if somewhat variegated, art-collection in his New York house. (His son, in Los Angeles, had all the fun.)

Marcus Daly was a penniless and uneducated Irish immigrant; he made up for his lack of education by his exceptional flair.[6] Starting as a pick and shovel man in California, he was sent by his firm to Butte. Here he had the hunch that underneath the silver lodes approaching exhaustion there lay immense quantities of ignored, disconsidered copper. He was a thousand times right. He went back to California to impart his belief to George Hearst, who credited him, and they joined to buy the mine that became the great Anaconda. When its riches in copper were proved, Daly quietly closed it to buy up neighboring claims. Anaconda, only a couple of miles away, was the foundation of his empire as Butte was of Clark's. Daly set up a bigger smelter—it ultimately came to have the tallest chimney, 530 feet high; he organized the original Anaconda Copper Mining Company, he added his own coal-mines and vast timber tracts for fuel, power plants, banks, irrigation schemes, and established the best newspaper in the state, the *Anaconda Standard*. What probably pleased him more, he succeeded in thwarting Clark's ambition to sit in the Senate for ten or twelve years. Clark then bought what proved the richest individually-owned copper-mine in its time, the

United Verde Mine in Arizona, proceeded to outlive Daly and become United States Senator after all. Daly had a more popular personality and popular tastes: no art-collection, but race-horses. No wonder he commanded the votes. He had a shorter life, but a merrier one.

Where Daly brought in shiploads of Irish miners, Clark preferred the Cornish.[7] Both of them were Democrats, but it was Republican votes that threw the election to Clark—and the Cornish, as we have seen, were almost always Republican.[8] These affiliations counted. We learn, for example, that "there was a Cornish foreman at the Mountain View or 'Saffron Bun' [evidently named for its predominantly Cornish miners], who would hire none but Cousin Jack miners and always told the Irish rustlers, 'Thee are in the wrong line, my boy!'"[9] No wonder there were fights between them on the streets!

Clark survived right up to our own time, dying at the age of eighty-six in 1925, having lived through the whole cycle of Montana mining to the last phase of the huge combines and violent labor troubles. At home in my childhood Butte was a familiar name to us: it stood for the roughness and toughness of a mining camp still, the latest in time of all those to which the Cornish miners had flocked. They continue there today. The exploitation of immense low-grade reserves by modern methods has, as at Bingham Canyon, laid open a vast amphitheatre to the sky, mechanically scooping the hillside away, a cloud of dust hanging over the operations like a region in Dante's Inferno.[10]

We have examples to hand of Cornish folk taking part in each of these phases. Let us take the Rowe brothers, who came to try their luck in the gold-diggings in 1867. They were the sons of a miner who had settled in Jo Daviess County, Illinois—he was also a carpenter, who built his own home and could make his own clothes.[11] They worked on their farm in summer, in the mines in winter—two of the sons worked the windlass for their father down below. In April 1867 sons William and Charles took the steamer, *Deer Lodge*, from Omaha up the Missouri to Fort Benton, where they landed on June 3 and walked all the way to Helena. The elder, William, had fair success in mining and hauling; he moved about from diggings to diggings—Helena, Pioneer City, Deer Lodge, where he served as sheriff at the jail. He opened and sold a billiard-hall, went into the hotel business, got the contracts for carrying the mail; then sold them profitably, bought horses and started a livery business. In the end he was able to buy a ranch of 340 acres near Fort Benton, breeding Shire horses and Shorthorn cattle to his heart's content. A photograph of him as an old man shows him an adventurous type, well satisfied with life, a spare figure with trim white beard and a shaky signature: a pioneer. A Mason and a Republican, he had sixteen children; his father had had thirteen. It is not surprising that there are so many Rowes among the Cornish. The father at the age of seventy-six started on the long trip to see his sons in Montana, but died on board the steamer *Benton* on the way up the Missouri. William's brother, Charles, left home telling his parents that he would return when he "got rich."[12] He had no luck mining at Helena, so he took to driving a stage-coach, then opened a saloon. This paid and enabled him to purchase a hotel, which he sold in 1876 to buy a ranch of 472 acres. Acquiring other interests in real estate, he was an active Republican and twice mayor of Fort Benton, where he had landed practically penniless years before.

Thomas D. Tregloan was a pioneer cattleman in the development of southern Montana, a well-known figure there for over half a century.[13] His father had operated a smelter at Galena in the early 1850's. Of the children, James had been a Confederate soldier, became an employee on the Santa Fe Railroad, and died in Texas; William was a cavalryman in the Civil War and then a farmer in Iowa; Honor married a Cornish miner in Wisconsin, Hannah a Cornish miner in Colorado, Margaret a Cornish farmer at Hazel Green, where brother John had also settled; Samuel was a fruit-grower in the Yakima Valley, Washington. Thomas came to Gallatin County at nineteen as a cowboy, riding the ranges over a large part of it. He then became a cattleman on his own account, was a hard worker and a good manager. He ended up in partnership with another cattleman, owning five thousand acres, with a fine breed of Shire horses and excellent herds of Shorthorns and Herefords. He went back to Hazel Green for a Cornish wife.

In the 1870's and 1880's came several Cornishmen who made their place in the public life of the new state. William Dyer, born at St. Austell in 1853, worked in the iron-mines of New Jersey for three years, then a couple of years in Colorado and came to Butte in 1878.[14] He invested his savings from mining in city property, and in 1884–85 was able to take a holiday in Cornwall. Reinvigorated, on his return he discovered the famous Ontario Mine, and bought out his partner's half-interest for $60,000. Himself realized $117,000 net profit on ore sold. In 1893 he organized the Ontario Mining Company, with a capital of $300,000. In 1889 he was a delegate to frame the constitution of the new state: the Honorable William Dyer.

In 1883 arrived a man who became one of the leading figures in Butte mining—Captain Thomas Couch.[15] Born in Camborne in 1843, at twenty he left for Michigan. Lured on by California, he was five years mining in Grass Valley. Thence he went over the Sierra into Nevada in 1868, where he became captain of the Hidden Treasure Mine at White Pine. He next went to various mines in Utah, and, as an expert, travelled all over the West examining mines for eastern capital. Coming to Butte, in 1886 he organized the Boston and Montana Consolidated Copper and Silver Mining Company, taking over Mountain View—worked largely by Cornishmen, as we have seen—and other claims. This became one of the largest mining corporations of the day, and paid enormous dividends. He bought Clark's smelter at Meaderville, and on his advice huge new smelters were erected at Great Falls in 1889. In 1896, displeased by a new turn in the company, the captain handed in his resignation. A rich man, he was independent. A couple of years later he began gold-dredging operations on the Feather River, near Oroville, which were a success from the start. He developed his own model ranch, which supplied a good many farm owners with stock from the Couch herds. He was a leader of the Republican party in the state, though he refused the nomination for governor. Someone wrote of him, "an Englishman by birth, Captain Couch seemed always most typically American in mind, heart and manner." But, of course, Couch was not an Englishman, and there was a greater natural affinity between the Cornish and nineteenth-century Americans. Montana was "the state nearest his heart, where every citizen knew his name." Evidently a strong personality, his portrait shows him aggressively bearded, dark intelligent eyes under bushy eyebrows. He had seven children; three sons served in the First World War against Germany. Thomas Couch managed his father's ranch at Great Falls, and after his death formed into a family corporation twenty-five thousand acres in Cascade and Teton counties. An able business head, he organized a number of companies, telephone, life insurance, besides pioneering in flax-growing in which Montana took a foremost place. A rich family, there must be Couches continuing in Montana.

The Honorable A. F. Bray also achieved eminence in the state.[16] Coming over to the Centennial Exhibition in 1876, he spent all his money and decided to stay in the "land of opportunity." First, he was a railroad employee in Texas at $1.25 a day; then he spent nine years constructing levees in Mississippi for the government. In 1885 he came to Butte, and with only $2200 opened a grocery store, which prospered and expanded. Bray sold out and, on account of ill health, spent a year in Oakland. He returned to buy a new business, which soon grew into two establishments with $100,000 worth of stock, and retail trade over three hundred miles. He married a Cornish girl from Illinois, and served two terms in the state legislature, the first term as Republican, the second as Populist.

At the turn of the century Josiah H. Trerise held a responsible position as captain of the Amalgamated Mine for F. A. Heinze, the third leading figure in Montana mining, after Clark and Daly.[17] Heinze was an even more controversial figure, who involved himself in numerous lawsuits. In this case the Amalgamated workmen drilled into the Michael Davitt Mine, whose men attacked with steam and hot water, to which the Amalgamated men replied with powder-smoke and liquid lime. Heinze's forays into disputed ground enriched the Amalgamated: it must have been worth the fine he had to pay. Trerise was fined $1000 for the fun.

In 1919 Malcolm Bowden became superintendent of the Travona Mine, one of the oldest, producing silver and zinc.[18] His father, Josiah, had come out direct to his brother-in-law at Helena and, being a Quaker, made a good bookkeeper and accountant. He had four children, one of whom became a draughtsman for the Anaconda Copper Company. Malcolm took his degree as a mining engineer, was made superintendent of Hecla, then foreman of a gold-mine at Helena.

These examples serve to illustrate the whole cycle of the state's history from the beginnings to today.

We have no such detailed picture of the social life of the Butte Cornish as we have for Mineral Point and Grass Valley, though it could be reconstructed from the local newspapers. Actually the account of Butte brought together under the Writers' Program of the Work Projects Administration during the depression, *Copper Camp*, is based on the newspapers, and it is interesting to see the impression the Cornish made from the outside. Again it is brought home that they got on naturally and easily with native Americans; there was a real affinity of temperament, and the Cornish had no difficulty whatever in fitting into their new environment. They liked it, they were grateful—and frequently expressed it—for the better opportunities their new country gave them, and they were proud to become American citizens. At the same time, it is interesting to note, they never ceased to be loyal to Cornwall, were consciously Cornish. There was no conflict. This stands out in marked contrast with some other groups in the variegated great nation.

In Butte, as elsewhere, the Cornish and the Irish were in some conflict and occasionally collided—though as time went on the contests became friendlier, over sport, prize-fights, wrestling matches. The Cornish belonged to the Sons of St. George and celebrated St. George's day; the Irish, of course, St. Patrick's. Once at Butte, they agreed, in friendly fashion, to swop feasts: "the Irish miners celebrated on St. George's day, and their Cornish friends, the Cousin Jacks, whooped it up on St. Patrick's day."[19] The Irish were Democrats, the Cornish Republicans. "Whether the Irish outnumbered the Cousin Jacks . . . or carried some secret vote-getting power cannot be explained; but the fact remains that the Democrats were winners far more frequently than their Republican rivals." One Cornish miner had his explanation—"Thee robbing Hirish, they not honly 'ave two votes heach on Helection day, but the buggers vote seven years hafter they 'ave been dead hand buried." I suspect he was not far out: the Irish were politicians, the Cornish not.

Occasionally there were street fights. "Bottles, stones, bricks, clubs, were hastily gathered in the rush to the firing line . . . Corktown Irish fought shoulder to shoulder with Anaconda Road Serb. Centerville Cousin Jack battled in hand-to-hand or club-to-club combat with East Granite Street Finn."[20] This at least tells us the localities where the leading elements in the immigrant population lived. Cornish wrestling was introduced by the Cousin Jacks. "Strangler Lewis, Farmer Burns . . . and even Butte's old favourite, Pat Connolly, are relegated to the wrestlers' limbo when Cornishmen recall the early-day champs of the Butte camp. Nick Crewell, Tony Harris . . . the Chapman trio, Charley Vellenweth [an interesting modification of the rare name, Vellanoweth]. Bill Andrews and many others, all had their backers among the clans . . . A thousand dollar side bet was a common wager of the Cornish wrestlers . . . The scene of most of the matches in Butte was the Arena on Talbot Avenue in the rear of Union Hall. In 1900 Tony Harris was the popular champion of the Butte camp, acclaimed by every Cornishman on 'the hill' as 'the best man to ever wear a jacket.' So confident of the prowess of Harris were the Cousin Jacks of Butte that plans were made to bring the English champion, Pierce, to the mining camp and wrest away his hardwon laurels. The Englishman, however, was not to be tempted and refused all offers to show his ability in Butte."

We hear much less of Methodist church-life in Butte than we do earlier in Wisconsin or in Colorado. But we hear quite enough about Cornish cooking, the pasty in particular. The authors of *Copper Camp* seem to think that it is a Butte specialty. "The camp at once adopted the pasty as its own. Today it is as much a part of Butte as the ore dumps. There are few other cities where it may be found. Possibly among the copper mines of Michigan or the Coeur d'Alènes [Idaho]. Elsewhere it is alien."[21] On the contrary: wherever two or three Cornishmen are gathered together, there is the pasty; it is fast becoming ubiquitous. Moreover, I should point out a variation: in the American form of pasty the meat is diced; at home in Cornwall, never: it is always sliced.

Just as Grass Valley had its famous Miners' Choir, so Butte had its no less renowned Miners' Brass Band—an equally characteristic contribution to the gaiety of life. Its start was due to the redoubtable Captain Couch himself.[22] There was precious little in the way of entertainment in Meaderville, where his Boston and Montana Copper and Silver Mining Company operated, when he took charge of the operations there. There were only the saloons and attractions of Butte, drink, gambling, brothels—a long two-mile walk, and often after pay-day the miners were late in turning up for work. Captain Couch noticed the musical talent and enthusiasm of a miner, Sam Treloar, who spent all his spare time in better fashion. He had got together a group of five young enthusiasts who gave up their time to practicing on their instruments in a log-cabin in Meaderville. Captain Couch had a talk with Sam Treloar—this was in 1887, a year after Couch had become manager of the company; Treloar, like himself, had been born in Cornwall and was then a young fellow of twenty. Out of this encounter "the idea of a miners' band was born. Couch arranged for workers who could play instruments to work the day shift so they could rehearse in the evening. Couch's deep interest in the band continued until his death in 1902. Through him the rapport between band and company was initiated and grew. After the Boston and Montana company was absorbed by the mighty Anaconda company in 1913, officials continued prideful co-operation by allowing musicians time off to travel to competitions and appear at concerts."

With Couch's encouragement the little log house was abandoned, numbers were recruited and rehearsals took place at the Knights of Labor Hall; they began to attract the attendance of miners, officials and citizens alike. Sam Treloar proved an inspired leader and his own musical gifts developed with experience. In the end he directed the band for over sixty years, and deposited his reminiscences, its history, with the Montana Historical Society. In a couple of years, with nearly thirty members, it was already in great demand. Within a decade it was beginning to achieve national fame, certainly all over the West, winning awards and prizes wherever it went. It is pleasant to find it competing in a Welsh Eisteddfod in Brigham Young's Salt Lake City Tabernacle, or attending annual conventions of the Elks, serenading William Jennings Bryan on his nomination for the Presidency, celebrating Clark's election to the Senate, playing for Presidents Roosevelt and Truman. In 1922 Sam Treloar appeared at the Salvation Army Congress in Butte with the band of which he was the only survivor. Twenty years later he retired to California, but he returned once more to direct the band for the last time, in a Fourth of July parade in 1949, at the age of eighty-two. "Too feeble now to march, Sam Treloar stood on the rear step of a fire-truck as it moved slowly ahead of the musicians." Two years later he was dead: he, too, no less than Couch, was part of the history of Montana.

When we take a cursory glance at the population of Montana it is at once borne in upon us how strongly concentrated the Cornish are in Butte. There are very few in Anaconda, not many in Great Falls, where the smelters are, and disappointingly few in Helena and Missoula. But Butte still has a large Cornish population, running into many hundreds; names that have been mentioned are represented, and even themes—for instance, there is the Band and there is Carrie's Pasty Shop. We will pass over the usual spread of Tre-, Pol-, Pen- names to note a few rarities: the very rare Anstice (2), Angelly, Angwin, Carkeek (4), Colenso, Chellew, Carne, Jose, Mellow, Pedlar (2), Jobe, Jolly, Laity (4) Nankervis (4), Trueworthy (probably, as we have seen, a form of Treworgy), Vigurs (3, with Vigus 2), Penaluna (4, with a Penaluna construction concern), Polgreba (2), Pentilla (2), Scown, Sara, Sleeman, Kellow (3), Geach (2). Among more common names: Clemo (4), Grenfell, Goldsworthy (5), Nankivell (2), Ivey (4), Sweet (4), Uren, Truscott, Coombe (3), Blewett (4), Barnicoat (4), Eustice (4), Carlyon (4), Liddicoat (2), Symons (3), Varcoe (2), Rosevear, Retallack, Tonkin (3), Trudgeon (2), Pengelly (3), Welch (5), Berry (4), Coon (4), Wedlake (4), Warne (3), Batten (4), Beard (2), Toy (5), Bartlett (4).

We have cited enough to show, even with our omissions, how large the Cornish element continues to be in Butte and how varied the spread of names. It is interesting that there is a Trerise, among the few Cornish names, at Anaconda—perhaps descendants of the original Captain Josiah Trerise of the Amalgamated Mine. At Great Falls we find: Tucker (12, of whom some must be Cornish), Tonkin (3), Crocker (3), Courtney (3), Truscott (2), Triplett (2), Penberthy, Chenoweth (2), Vivian (2), with the rare names, Annear, Bosanco, Carbis, Curnow, Gribble. At Helena there are: Trerise (2), Trewhella, Angove, Clemo, Courtney, Davy, Ivey, Kitto, Foote. There are others among such names as Richards and Hicks; but none of this exhausts the number of Cornish: the Polgooth family of May, for instance, is represented by daughters whose married names are Roddy and Bielman. There are however, six of the name of May in Butte; these may or may not be Cornish.

Gold was discovered in 1874–75 in the Black Hills country of South Dakota—so called because the thick covering of conifers gave a dark appearance to the hills. There ensued the usual rush to the placer-diggings. Next year George Hearst bought a promising claim for $70,000; with his usual luck, it turned out to be one of the richest of mines, the famous Homestake, which produced some $300,000,000 worth of gold up to 1935, and is still producing.[23] Miners moved into the gulches of the area, Deadwood and Gold Run, from older centers like Montana and Idaho; we have already observed the interest displayed among the mining folk of Wisconsin and Michigan, and a number of Cornish prospectors moving thence to the new, and exciting, country of the Black Hills.[24] (This was the region of "Deadwood Dick"—his supposed cabin in the hills now a tourist attraction.) Deadwood lies at the bottom of the gulch, where Lead is at the top, a mile high, spread out over the surrounding hills: it is pronounced Leed, i.e. lode.[25] Cornish miners moved in along with others, though I have little information about them. As early as 1880 a John Trudgin died there, evidently a Trudgeon[26]; while

William Tredwith, born in England, died of a crushed skull—presumably a mining fatality.

That Cornish mining interests were well aware of developments in South Dakota is witnessed by their immediate reaction to the alarming news of the discovery of large resources of tin there in the late 1880's—for by then Cornish mining depended entirely upon tin. The Bolithos in West Cornwall immediately and quietly sent one of their American agents to report, and send samples home for analysis.[27] They followed this up by dispatching one of their mine-agents, Captain Curtis, to report fully and confidentially on the prospects. Mr. Barton comments that "Captain Curtis's adventures in the Black Hills, secretly reporting for Messrs. Bolitho, but posing as a British tourist, would make interesting reading had any record of them been preserved." As if this were not enough, the redoubtable Captain Josiah Thomas of Dolcoath—"reckoned to 'knaw tin' better than any man alive—was called in to make a public report and was paid 1000 guineas to visit the Black Hills. His findings brought a collapse of Dakota's hopes." It was not from thence that the competition came that eventually ruined Cornwall's tin industry—and sent thousands more miners overseas.

Mr. Philip Dyer, who worked for forty-four years with the Homestake, helps me to fill the gap in my knowledge of the Cornish there. He came to Hancock, Michigan, in 1909—following an old trail—to work with the Quincy Mining Company for a couple of years. Thence he went to Lead in 1911 to work for the Homestake. He tells me that at that time "you would think you were in Truro or St. Austell, there were so many Cornish people; but after two wars a lot of them went away and never returned." He himself served in the United States Army in the First World War, but after six months at home at St. Austell returned to the Homestake. It is a gratifying comment on the change from nineteenth-century conditions to the twentieth that he writes with enthusiasm of this company: "when a person *can't* work for the Homestake he

can't work for anyone." For the past seventeen years he has
been president of the Homestake Veterans' Association,
which provides for the welfare of all those who have been
twenty-one years with the company. Mr. Dyer retired from his
job as electrical engineer in 1956, but his son carries on the
family connection with the Homestake.

Cornish neighbors still nearby are Arthur Morcom from
Penwithick, near St. Austell: all five of his sons served in the
Second World War brought on by the Germans. Then there is
Philip Cann from near Truro. We have not noticed these
names so far—Morcom and Cann are both East Cornwall-
West Devon names. A Mrs. Nicholls came from the St. Aus-
tell area—but that is a name we are familiar with in this book.
The fact that there are few Cornish people left in Lead today
serves to bring home to us the increased mobility of the twen-
tieth century, at least between Cornwall and America—yet,
Heaven knows, there was plenty of mobility among the
miners in the nineteenth century!

Two streams of population converged upon the beautiful,
debatable land north of California known as the Oregon
country, which included the present states of Oregon and
Washington. To begin with, it was debated between Great
Britain (on behalf of Canada) and the United States, until
the accord of 1846 along the 49th parallel gave all this territory to the United States. Until then a dominant influence in
the country had been the Hudson's Bay Company. In 1843
had taken place the decisive immigration along the Oregon
Trail that brought nine hundred Americans into the country,
which had only some four hundred Americans and British.
Manifest Destiny pointed the way: next year a provincial
government was organized and the Hudson's Bay Company
significantly withdrew its central office in the Northwest from
Fort Vancouver, just opposite present Portland on the Columbia River, to Victoria Island.[28] By 1846 some six thousand
Americans were in the Oregon country—an irresistible tide.

The California gold-rush depleted these new territories of two-thirds of their population, at first delaying agricultural and pastoral settlement. Shortly, however, it began to exert a powerful influence aiding their development, in addition to the smaller gold discoveries being made in southwest Oregon and Washington. "The rapid settlement of the Pacific coast consequent upon the migration stimulated by the gold discoveries had a quickening effect upon the whole of the Oregon Territory. The exportation of grain and lumber to California enriched the settlers in the North-West. Many of the gold-diggers returned from the south with the capital needed to develop the resources of their home locality; they busied themselves in felling timber for the sawmills that provided the piles for the new wharves of San Francisco and the lumber for the city that was being built on the Golden Gate."[29] Thus these streams converged to create the new state of Oregon, which achieved statehood in 1859, Washington not until thirty years later, along with Montana and the Dakotas. We shall find these various themes illustrated by incoming Cornish folk.

We find a Tremewan, for example, at Champoeg, along the Willamette River just south of Portland: his wife was a daughter of Captain Manson of the Hudson's Bay Company, and she had lived all her youth at the headwaters of the Fraser River in British Columbia.[30] Among the early pioneers came Samuel Coad in 1853.[31] His parents had emigrated to Pennsylvania and had sixteen little Coads. In 1842 they moved to Iowa to farm on the western frontier. Young Samuel was a carpenter by trade, who worked his passage across the plains and got work in Salem. Next year he took off for the Rogue River in southern Oregon, prospecting for gold, but at the big bend was attacked by Indians and forced to give up. In 1855 he took part in the discreditable war waged against the Rogue River Indians and was in the engagement at Snake River. Meanwhile, he continued at carpentering and building, adding to it contracting. He built one of the first woollen factories in the state. This enabled him to purchase a farm and let it, purchase a drug-store and sell it, then buy a sheep ranch. Having "quietly and steadily prospered," he ended as a considerable stockholder in and director of Dallas City Bank, with five children. That was the way in Oregon: quiet and steady prosperity.

Several members of the old Chenoweth clan take a leading part in building up Oregon in these early decades. Justin Chenoweth, born in Illinois, went to California in 1849, via New Orleans and Panama.[32] After a short time he started back east overland, met with the 1st United States Mounted Rifles, joined the party and reached The Dalles in the fall of 1849. Later he settled on a claim to the west and carried the mail between it and the Cascades in a small boat. Prior to this he taught school in the Willamette Valley and was clerk to the territorial legislature. He was actively engaged in surveying the public lands and retired to Portland. Chenoweth Creek rising in the hills west of The Dalles and Chenoweth Flat across which it flowed to the Columbia River, were named for him.

Justin Chenoweth had two brothers; one of them, Francis, was a leading organizer of the territory, was named for the House of Representatives in 1854 and was its Speaker 1866–68.[33] In 1872 he became district attorney. In the same year James Chenoweth rented a large holding of thirteen thousand acres.[34] Born in Missouri, he had been brought to Oregon in 1852, and became a member of the legislature in 1878. They located around Roseburg in the southwest. To Union County in the northeast there came a group of Quakers in 1884, among them William and Wesley Chenoweth.[35] These may have been more recent arrivals in America, to judge from the first name Wesley. On September 18, 1879, John R. Trewavas—a very rare name from the Penzance area—a Cornish mason experienced in building light-houses, was drowned in the attempt to land on Tillamook Rock, in the surges of the Pacific.[36] He was making a preliminary survey for a light-house there, on the coast due west of Portland.

We see in most of these men, Cornishmen of the second

generation, born in America, builders of their new state in the far Northwest.

With the twentieth century, we come to a better known name, since it was that of a politician: William Simon U'Ren was known in his day in Oregon and beyond as a leading Progressive, the originator of the "Oregon system," of the popular Initiative and Referendum, for what that was worth. He has his place in the political tradition of his state.*

He was born in Grant County, Wisconsin, in 1859; his father was William Richard Uren (of that old name in its proper form), a blacksmith who took to farming, moved on to Wyoming and finally Nebraska. A recent student of U'Ren's career tells us that "for generations the Urens had been blacksmiths and preachers. They had been French Huguenots, Dutch Dissenters."[37] They were of course plain Cornish folk, devout Wesleyans, given to Bible reading. Young U'Ren declared himself "especially fond of the Old Testament leaders, Moses and the rest; I suppose it's because they were never satisfied with things as they were, but were always kicking."

At seventeen U'Ren left home to work in the mines of Colorado; at nineteen he was a blacksmith in Denver, studying at a business school at night. He read law, was admitted to the bar in 1881, went to practice at Tin Cup and to edit the local newspaper. Here he read Henry George and was converted to his nostrum of single-tax as a cure for all social ills, as so many people of good will in England and America were at the time. The young fellow was consumptive and, the doctor telling him he had only a few months to live, U'Ren went to Honolulu. In 1889 he came to Oregon, where he spent the rest of a long life, feverishly engaged in politics. At first, very poor, he moved into a deserted cabin not far from Portland, and practiced as a spiritualist medium. Then, more fruitfully,

* There is no biography of him in D. A. B. This should be rectified in an expanded edition.

he became a partner on a fruit-farm. But he read a pamphlet on the Initiative and Referendum, was converted and saw his life's work open before him. "The one important thing was to restore the law-making power where it belonged—into the hands of the people. Once give us that, we could get anything we wanted—single-tax; anything."[38] Or so he supposed. This was soon after the Panic of 1893. Next year he began his well-considered campaign to bring pressure to bear on both parties, to get the legislation he wanted, with the ultimate objective of freeing Oregon from the domination of special interests, especially the railroads, which controlled the legislature and the state.

He proved a remarkable backstairs organizer, a kind of Francis Place or Sidney Webb, pulling the strings from the background. "Never be president. Never be conspicuous. Get a president and a committee, and let them get to the front. The worker must work behind them out of sight. Be secretary." He brought together a joint committee of the Portland Federated Trades, the Chamber of Commerce, the Oregon Knights of Labor to form a Direct Legislation League. He became secretary. He joined the Populist Party, talking "incessantly, quietly, convincingly" to get the Initiative and Referendum plank accepted. He became secretary of the state committee. He then travelled round pledging political candidates to support the proposal. When the conservatives went back on their promises he published the names of the defaulters. Elected to the legislature in 1896, he held up the session, forcing both parties to carry out their pledges, and no business could be transacted. "The Prince of Hold-ups," he was evidently a man to be reckoned with.

In 1898 he was defeated for the state senate by the railroads' candidate; but he continued his campaign undaunted, and next year his proposal for a constitutional amendment passed both houses. (Away in South Africa in 1899 to settle the estate of a relative, he was convinced that the British were fighting for equal rights in the Boer War, and this made him anti-Boer.) On his return he continued his propaganda to hold the legislature to its promises, and the people of Oregon approved the amendment by 11 to 1. But U'Ren had not forgotten the wider objectives for which the Initiative and Referendum had been won—in order to secure single-tax reform (a tax on land-values) and to break the power of the monopolies, against which Theodore Roosevelt was campaigning simultaneously. U'Ren became organizer and secretary of the Oregon Direct Primary Nominations League in 1904, of the People's Power League in 1906, a member of the Proportional Representation League, the Civil Liberties Union, the National Popular Government League, the Anti-Monopoly League. He was the secretary of the Oregon Single-Tax League from 1909 to 1917.[39] What a life!

From 1904 to 1910 he and his Leaguers pushed forward in the elections for local option liquor laws, prohibiting free passes on railways, for a gross earnings tax on telephone companies, for employers' liability laws, a corrupt practices act, for women's suffrage, additional normal schools, single-tax, state prohibition—the whole progressive program.[40] Roosevelt thought U'Ren was a mere "muckraker"; but when Lincoln Steffens visited the reformer's home he found a soft-spoken country lawyer living in simplicity on $1800 a year. The United States Senators for Oregon would not support Roosevelt in his campaign against Standard Oil and other monopolies; so U'Ren decided to run against them for the Senate, with only $1100 in his pocket. "I want to show the voters of Oregon that they may safely trust themselves with power," he said. His private circumstances were cruelly caricatured in the *Oregonian*—apparently he continued to be a spiritualist, as he certainly was an idealist. He withdrew from the Senate race, so as not to endanger his reform program: it seems that four of his measures got through. The success of his campaign had a marked influence in the neighboring state of Washington, which also adopted the Initiative and Referendum.

Montana, Oregon, Washington, Dakota

U'Ren's objective was the doctrinaire one of direct control of the state government by the voters, as later he wished to see subordination of the executive to the legislative. Like Woodrow Wilson he preferred the idea of the Ministerial system as in Britain. Wilson, another doctrinaire, appeared to be impressed with Oregon's adoption of the Initiative and the Referendum, and paid U'Ren the compliment that Oregon had two legislatures, one at the capitol and "one under W. S. U'Ren's hat." This rather shook U'Ren's Republicanism, though he supported Roosevelt, the Progressive Republican, in the election of 1912. From then to 1914 he campaigned to educate the electorate into abolishing the state senate, tackling unemployment and introducing prohibition. The electorate turned him down by immense majorities. Nor did he have any better luck with his campaign for a workmen's compensation bill, which was lost at the polls in 1924. At seventy-three, in 1932, he was a candidate for the state legislature, but was defeated, and again in 1934. In 1932 he supported Franklin Roosevelt, but regretted his apostasy and became a bitter critic of the New Deal (like his fellow-Cornishman, John Spargo): he was too high-principled to approve of government handouts, and put forward the doctrinaire proposal of labor-colonies. In 1949 he died, full of disappointments. His biographer says of him, "America never became really aware of U'Ren." Nevertheless, he made his impression, an unexpected one, considering his unpromising start; he was an element in forming and handing on the Progressive Republican tradition in Oregon: Senator Neuberger in our time paid tribute to him as "the father of governmental reforms."

Mrs. Keith Powell of Salem, Oregon, of the third generation in the United States, has given me particulars of her family's movements which illustrate the main drive to the West. Descended from an old line of Menhinnicks, her great-grandmother married Charles Hicks of Pengenna Manor in the parish of St. Kew. Of their children, well-to-do farming folk, four daughters married and came to America, and two sons. One of the daughters, Mrs. Powell's grandmother, married Adam Oliver, who followed his brother, Nicoll Oliver to America about 1859. Nicoll Oliver settled in Ottawa, Illinois, "where he later became a prominent magistrate. Of those following his lead some remained in Illinois. One branch is today in Lawrence, Kansas; one is in Berkeley, California; one in Connecticut. There seems no indication of mining interests. They seem mostly to have been gentry-farmers." Mrs. Powell's grandparents were those who were at Lawrence, Kansas, at the time of Quantrill's Raid. She herself moved west to Oregon, where her own family is. "My husband and I have been three times in these later years to Cornwall and have driven over much of it, my own personal, family records in hand. We have visited the three churches associated with the family, [St. Kew, St. Eval, Egloshayle] and I have taken many pictures." She has kept in touch with the old family manor of Pengenna going back to Elizabethan times and with its modern occupants.

Let this devotion in the third generation, a century after her grandparents left Cornwall, stand as a record of what many unnamed folk feel about the place they come from.

A stalwart of Willamette University at Salem for over half a century was Professor James T. Matthews—evidently an endearing figure: for the university's centennial the president suggested that "I write my autobiography, dealing chiefly with my fifty years at Willamette. What would Mother say to this?"[41] His mother had always been set on a college education for her children, but the father was a poor carpenter in a village not far from Penzance: not a prospect of it in those days. But a friend of his was doing well in Portland, Oregon, wrote enticingly of "high wages there, and cheap lands, and free schools." In 1872 the parents decided to take the plunge, piled their precious possessions on to a donkey-cart, drove away along the country road through green stone hedges, down the zigzag streets of Penzance to the quay and the steamship taking them to Liverpool.

Actually Matthews' father never made much more in the way of wages in the New World than the Old; for, a devout Methodist, he became an itinerant preacher on a small salary all his life. "However, as a preacher's wife Mother was a parsonage queen," and there were open opportunities for the children to work their way to college—which they did.[42] Their first pastorate was in the Coos Bay region, the lively seaport of Empire their home, where Father would struggle with the Greek Testament in the evenings. They next moved into Washington Territory, then back to a charge in Oregon at Dallas, then in Oregon City. When young James began to teach school and took his wages to Father, "he was deeply impressed, for my monthly pay was a little more than twice what he had ever earned as a carpenter in England." Next, James made the university, working in the vacations to pay his way. "Father came to this opportunity-giving land a humble carpenter. Already he had risen to be the Methodist pastor at McMinnville, Oregon. My sister Emma was attending McMinnville college (now Linfield) and I was on my way to Williamette university. Mother's plans for college for her children were expanding into reality."

Then came the day in 1893 when young James, who had already proved himself as a teacher and had a gift for mathematics, was unexpectedly promoted professor. Still, it was not until fifteen years later—with marriage and a growing family —that he was able to make his first trip abroad and, of course, his chief longing was to go back to Cornwall and the scenes of his childhood. It is all described—the narrow streets of Penzance, the hedges on either side the country road "with soil in the crevices, and flowers and grass and honeysuckle growing ... Now I am come to the graveyard where we spent many a sunny afternoon with Mother, she sewing seated on a flat gravestone, we children playing quietly in the aisles between the tombstones. . . ."[43] Then the church, where his parents were married—James Matthews and Emma Jane Peters—a solid, settled old granite church with chancel, rood screen, aisles, square tower, all as he had remembered them. Lastly, to the cottage where he had been born, "a tiny flower-garden running up to the front steps," and he is invited within by the stranger: he is home again, with all the early memories that come flooding on.

How often has that scene been enacted by Cornish folk returning across the seven seas to their early homes, or the places where their people came from yet earlier!

The next time he made a trip abroad, in 1927, he went to Australia to see his cousins, with whom the family had kept touch through the years. For himself, "why, I had not seen a cousin of my very own in fifty years. And these cousins none of our family had ever met."[44] There was equal excitement with the Australian cousins at meeting him; when he arrived at the door in Melbourne, the good wife flew to the telephone: "Come home. Cousin James is here from America." The professor noticed that his cousin Edgar "spoke *my* English"; the rest of the family Australian English. "With Edgar's help I met all the cousins except the one in Perth. These Australian relatives were children of my mother's sister and brother who went to Australia in an early day."

Thus we Cornish keep together.

Salem has a sprinkling of Cornish names today: Tremaine (4), Tresidder (2), Trahan (3), Minear (2), Treleaven, Trezise, Trudgeon, Pengelly, Angove. A rare name is Vosper: there is a Methodist minister of the name. Behanna may be a form of Behenna; it would be amusing if Trojan were a form of Trudgeon. Much the same holds good for Eugene, where we find a whole Luke clan (13); besides Lanyon (3), Hoskins (8), Kendall (12, of whom some will be Cornish), Chenoweth (3), Tippett (2), Julian (3), Rouse (3), besides Curnow, Grenfell, Hocking, Jobe, Roche, Rhoda, Pender, Penrose, Tremaine.

Montana, Oregon, Washington, Dakota

When we come to Portland we find quite a large Cornish population, several hundred, reflecting the drift into a large industrial city from a considerable area, as well as those who came there direct—like friends of mine of the name Brckenshire (6). One of the largest groups is that of Chenoweth (21): these will represent both old American stock of Cornish name as well as newcomers. We find the following rarer names: Penhalurick, Penketh, Penwarden (2), Penkert, Jagow, Gover (2), Pellow (2), Cardew, Spargo (2), Santo, Penquite, Nankervis, Nankivell, Chegwidden (2), Chirgwin (4), Hender, Ede (5), Trezona, Trefry, Trelawny (2), Trehearne, Tregemba, Pender (2), Tregea, Tregidga, Treloggen, Dungey (2), Wedlake. There is a considerable spread of more familiar names: Treleaven, Treloar, Tremaine (4), Trembath, Trenerry (3), Trethewey (2), Trevarrow, Trevathan, Truscott, Trewhella. We find Pascoe (5), Penrose (5), Penberthy (3), Curnow (5), Lobb (5), Kellow (3), Berryman (2), Daw (3), Oates (4), Kitto (4), Goldsworthy (3), Hocking (8), Rundell (3). It is pleasant to note, among the names of people who have contributed to the building of Oregon, that there is still a U'Ren in Portland today.

This is by no means exhaustive: enough to show that Portland is one of the main centers of Cornish folk on the West Coast, as Seattle is another.

Since accounts of Cornish folk moving along the Oregon Trail must be very rare, we are fortunate to have that of Samuel James, who left Wisconsin for the Far West as early as 1850. The moving spirit was his forceful Foxwell wife, who concluded from Frémont's experiences of the mud there in winter that the climate would be more like the West Country in England. The Jameses made their start in October and wintered in Iowa, making their preparations, overhauling wagons, yoke, etc. for the long trek of over two thousand miles to the Pacific. From Iowa they set out in the spring, with another family; they had three wagons, a number of cows and a few oxen. "Before going to bed Grandma James often dug a shallow hole near the fire; she then kneaded a loaf of bread, placed it in the baking kettle with a heavy lid on top, and put this in the hole which she covered with hot coals and ashes. In the morning, behold a loaf of fine brown bread."[45] I conclude from this that at home she had been accustomed to baking out of doors in the old-fashioned cloam (i.e. earthenware) oven.

Along with their household goods they carried a collection of books, and the astronomical instruments to determine the latitude and longitude at various points. Apparently they made some thirteen miles a day. Early in May they came up with some Pawnee Indians, who surrounded them and demanded pay for passing through their territory. In Nebraska, they united with a train making for California, thirty-six wagons in all, for greater security. Just before Kainsville they passed through a valley where a company of Mormons had wintered in the caves. Godly Samuel James always observed Sunday if possible as a day of rest, and so kept his cattle in good condition. This particular Sunday he and his wife called on the Mormon elder who was leading his flock to their promised land. They were duly shocked by what they saw. (The mutually exclusive prejudices of simple people exist to provide amusement to the intelligent.)

At Fort Laramie they came up with an encampment of Sioux hunting the buffalo, large herds of which thundered across the plains. Hundreds of whitened buffalo skulls were strewn along the Trail: people pencilled messages on them for their friends following on behind. At Independence Rock, scrawled all over with names and dates, son Samuel took a bucket of tar and inscribed some of the family names. His mother commented, with Foxwell spirit: "Fools' names, like their faces, are always found in public places." The son replied with equal spirit that no fool would venture so far from civilization. As they trundled along the high ground of the Continental Divide, the jolting of her wagon was so bad that

Mrs. James got out and walked. The Little Sandy was their first river on the Pacific slope and here they camped comfortably, son Johnny taking his test as ox-driver at eleven years old. Passing Emigrant Springs, they forded the John Day River, and hired some Indians to swim the cattle across the Deschutes River. James and his eldest son drove the wagon with their precious books to The Dalles to be freighted on a flat boat down the Columbia River to Portland, while the other two wagons went round the south side of Mount Hood. This trail had been opened only a few years previously with the opening up of the Willamette Valley, and here they stuck in the corroborative mud. It took eight oxen to pull each wagon out and over the summit to the west side of the Cascades. At the home of the first settler here they got their first fresh vegetables after months of hardtack and strong sausage. From here James and son William went scouting towards Puget Sound country, but on their return they moved to settle at Grand Mound Prairie, which they reached on October 12, 1851, a twelvemonth after departing from Wisconsin. Their wagon-meter registered 2,453 miles from leaving Yorkville.

On surveying her new home, Mrs. James broke into Cowper, her favorite poet:

> I am monarch of all I survey,
> My right there is none to dispute:
> From the center all round to the sea
> I am lord of the fowl and the brute.

As for brute creation, the Jameses found their claim close to a lot of Indians who were far from the idealized picture of James Fenimore Cooper's *Leather Stocking Tales*. They found themselves "the first Indian missionaries (without salary) in the Oregon Territory. Grandmother James taught them the use of soap, soft soap, realizing that cleanliness is next to godliness. They became apt pupils and would steal it whenever they got a chance."

Samuel James and his Foxwell wife had eight children. By

the time of Pearl Harbor there were over one hundred living descendants of the fourth son alone. In July of that year, 1941, there was a reunion of the Foxwell and Shepherd tribe at the old Hannibal Shepherd home at Yorkville, Wisconsin—it took the local Methodist Church the family had founded to feed the multitude. The days passed pleasantly listening to the reading of ancient diaries and letters, collecting and re-telling anecdotes of the early pioneers. There were representatives from no less than thirteen states by now. A grandson of Samuel James, a Shepherd of Wenatchee, Washington, who contributed a paper, has compiled a history of this particular family "whose descendants are scattered throughout the Pacific Northwest."

The northern part of the original Oregon country, that north of the Columbia River to the 49th parallel, became the Territory of Washington in 1853 and achieved statehood in 1889. This magnificent lumbering country on either side of the Cascades, a continuation of Oregon, exhibited similar characteristics and was subject to much the same conditions. The needs of San Francisco dominated its lumber market and that for provisions; there naturally followed ship-building along the deep-water inlets of Puget Sound. There was a widespread scattering of gold-finds across the territory on much the same scale as Oregon, nothing comparable to California. Various tribes of Indians inland held out in what they regarded as their country; this made things dangerous for early settlers and prospectors. In the 1850's there was a series of campaigns; not until the 1860's and later were the Indians penned into the reservations allotted them. In this century the gold-rush to Alaska and its subsequent development turned Seattle, its base, into a great international port.

We can observe something of all these themes in the incoming Cornish. There are those of the second generation coming on from Wisconsin, Illinois, Colorado, as well as those coming in directly. With these newer lands opening up we move into the twentieth century.

R. J. Berryman was born in Wisconsin, then his parents came west to Montana.[46] In 1871, after the Indians were settled, they moved to what had been the exposed country of Walla Walla in southeastern Washington on the Oregon border. The Berrymans bought land at an outpost that came to be known as Berryman Post Office; the son built up a large holding of 480 acres, renting up to a couple of hundred more, under wheat and barley. Pioneering in this neighborhood, he took on public duties as school director and road supervisor. J. E. Berryman had been in the gold-rush to California in 1854, went off to Australia in the next gold-rush for a couple of years, then back to California.[47] In 1861 he made an early trip to Walla Walla, going in the summer to the placer-diggings of Idaho. Next year he made a trip back to Wisconsin and home to Cornwall. On his return to Wisconsin he married a Cornish girl, Mary Berryman: they had twelve children—there should be quite a clutch of Berrymans in Washington. For the next five years he was mining in Montana and, "not yet ready to give up the search for nature's hidden treasures," he made trips to the Powder River country, to Butte and Florence, Arizona. At last he settled in Walla Walla, built a homestead and raised wheat, cattle and horses. Among the first to locate in the neighborhood, he had to make his own dirt roads and with two others built the first school-house. Though well settled on the land, he never lost his interest in mining.

John James Tregoning was a pioneer of Denver who retired to Seattle.[48] (The Cornish take very much to the climate of the mild and damp Northwest Coast—it is similar to that of Cornwall.) His son, Frank, born at Clear Creek, Colorado, came to Seattle in 1894. Apprenticed to the metal trade, he struck out on his own with the Tregoning Boat Company, building life-boats for ocean-liners. From this developed the Tregoning Manufacturing Company, making doors, window-sashes, general mill-work, and coming to employ several hundred operatives: one of the larger concerns of its kind in the Northwest. Tregoning also ran the Bainbridge Fisheries Company of Alaska.

The Yakima runs southeast through central southern Washington to join the Columbia River, opening up a splendid valley which was formerly a sage-brush desert: with the Indians confined to their reservation in the hills, and with plentiful irrigation, now half-a-million acres of cultivated land. Robert C. Trenbath emigrated at twenty-one and took to farming.[49] His son, Edwin—a favorite first name with the Cornish—joined with a partner in real estate and insurance business, which grew with the development of the valley to become one of its foremost. Henry Hicks emigrated, to farm in Jo Daviess County, Illinois.[50] His son, Alfred, farmed and then took to grain and livestock at Scales Mound. He was then caught by the gold-rush to Alaska—one used to hear the mysterious word Klondike in the village at home—and for the ten years 1896 to 1906 was making trips up and down the Yukon, winning and losing money. John Verran was a Michigan miner, who married Marjorie Trevena.[51] Their son was apprenticed printer; he went to British Columbia for four years, where he became part owner of a paper. In 1903 he came to the Yakima Valley, and after some years was able to buy the languishing *Wapato Independent,* give it new equipment and turn it into a fine weekly paper. He made a Cornish marriage to an Ishpeming girl: four children, himself Oddfellow and Republican.

With these people we are well into the twentieth century and can observe the increasing variety of their contribution with the times.

We find these names well represented in Seattle, which has a considerable Cornish element, if not as large as Portland. Of those mentioned we find Pascoe (16, with 3 Pasco), Tregoning (5), Trezise (2), Trenbath and Trenbeath. There is a fair spread of the usual Tre- names, such as Treffry (3), Treglown (3), Trengove (3), and, more rarely, Treloggen, Tregellas, Tremelling. Among rarities we find, at last, the rare name Hobba, spelt Hoba; also Menheniott, usually found in the form Menhennitt; both Kellow and Kelloway, Anstiss and Annear; Penna, Penfold, Penhalurick (a minister), Penglase, Penhollow, Petherick (2), Golley, Nankervis (2); Hender (2) and Hendra; Carne and perhaps Dusto, for Dustow, that very rare name. And along with these a good many more with which we have become familiar.

Altogether Seattle offers a wide variety of names in its Cornish population, and with its large industrial development is a powerful magnet drawing people from a wide area in the Northwest and beyond.

NOTES

1. R. W. Paul, *Mining Frontiers of the Far West*, 146.
2. T. A. Rickard, *History of American Mining*, 344.
3. Paul, 140.
4. *Ibid.*
5. D. A. B., IV, 144–46.
6. D. A. B., V, 45–46.
7. C. B. Glasscock, *War of the Copper Kings*, 74.
8. *Ibid.*, 114.
9. *Copper Camp*, (Work Projects Administration), 210.
10. cf. I. F. Marcosson, *Anaconda*, Ch. 12.
11. T. Stout, ed., *Montana: its Story and Biography*, III, 680.
12. J. Miller, *An Illustrated History of Montana*, II, 682.
13. Stout, II, 404.
14. Miller, I, 88.

15. Stout, II, 498.
16. Miller, II, 561.
17. R. G. Raymer, *Montana. The Land and the People*, I, 495.
18. Stout, III, 1176.
19. *Copper Camp*, 7, 49.
20. *Ibid.*, 140, 225–26.
21. *Ibid.*, 243–44.
22. *Montana Historical Society, Official Newsletter*, May, 1966.
23. H. S. Schell, *History of South Dakota*, 147–48.
24. See above, pp. 363–65.
25. *South Dakota*, (American Guide Series), 118.
26. *South Dakota Historical Collections*, X, 461.
27. D. B. Barton, *Hist. of Tin Mining and Smelting in Cornwall*, 208.
28. S. B. L. Penrose, "The Wagon-Train of 1843—Its Dual Significance," *Oregon Hist. Quarterly*, vol. 44, 361ff.
29. T. A. Rickard, *Hist. of American Mining*, 316–17.
30. *Oregon Hist. Quarterly*, vol. 4, 261.
31. H. K. Hines, *An Illustrated History of the State of Oregon*, 677.
32. *Oregon Hist. Quarterly*, vol. 44, 342–43; vol. 26, 388.
33. *Ibid.*, vol. 2, 332, 345; vol. 6, 156–57.
34. *Ibid.*, vol. 31, 378.
35. *Ibid.*, vol. 45, 202.
36. *Ibid.*, vol. 28, 184.
37. I am much indebted for my account of U'Ren to R. C. Woodward, "William Simon U'Ren: In an Age of Protest," (M.A. thesis, University of Oregon).
38. *Pacific Northwest Quarterly*, vol. 35, 292ff.
39. cf. *Who's Who in America*, 1928, under W. S. U'Ren.
40. cf. C. O. Johnson, "The Adoption of the Initiative and Referendum in Washington," *Pacific Northwest Quarterly*, vol. 35, 294.
41. J. T. Matthews, *Turn Right to Paradise*, 9, 18.
42. *Ibid.*, 23, 30–31, 39.

43. Ibid., 114–15.
44. Ibid., 158, 168.
45. H. C. Duckett, *The Generations of the Children of William Foxwell and Ann Harris*, 10–13.
46. W. D. Lyman, *An Illustrated History of Walla Walla*, 506.
47. Ibid., 500–01.
48. *Seattle and Environs, 1852–1924*, (1924), III, 189.
49. *History of the Yakima Valley, Washington*, (1919), II, 266.
50. Ibid., II, 645.
51. Ibid., II, 509.

14 ARIZONA

The last area of significant Cornish penetration, and where their contribution was a considerable one, was Arizona. Here again mining was of the first importance—indeed in this century, from about 1907, Arizona took the place of Montana as the leading state in the production of copper. Moreover, Arizona had several copper districts, not just one as with her rivals. Her copper was often mixed with silver and gold, production of which was by no means unimportant. (I recall the chunk of raw Arizona copper in a glass case, which stood on the mantelpiece in the Cornish home of a mining uncle there, Joe Anstis, and which as a child I took for gold.)

The development of Arizona's vast mineral resources was retarded by two main considerations. There was its remoteness before the railways came through it—the last frontier away there on the Mexican border. Even New Mexico was more accessible from the Middle West and from Colorado—and we have already noticed Cornish miners and mining engineers going into it. Then, too, Arizona had an Indian population that was prepared to fight for its rights, particularly the aggressive Apaches, who fought back with gun and tomahawk and met massacre with massacre. The country was for long hostile and dangerous; lawless elements from other areas took advantage of its unsettled state. Campaigns against the Indians went on into the 1880's: it was not until 1886 that Geronimo, the last fighting Apache chief, surrendered and was moved out of his country for the rest of his life. Then the Indians were settled on their reservations: for them it was indeed the end of the long trail, reaching back to those first white settlements in Virginia and New England. Geronimo died in Oklahoma in 1909; three years later Arizona and New Mexico achieved statehood together—the last for a long time to come.

The Mormons were early into the country, under the delusion that the Hopi might be descendants of the Welsh Madoc —that old medieval mare's nest transmitted by Hakluyt—and hoping to convert them.[1] But the Indians knew better: they knew that at the back of the Mormon mind was colonization. The Indians killed some of them under the delusion that they were miners, or perhaps it was that they were whites anyway. There were individual prospectors braving it in the wild country, some of them, as in Utah, regular soldiers with time on their hands. In 1874 an important discovery of silver was made with the Silver King Mine at Globe, east of Phoenix, below the San Carlos Mountains in Apache country. "A good supply of water, obtained from Pinal creek, served to make Globe a distributing point for mining operations in the vicinity. For a decade the district produced silver and gold, rather than copper."[2] Then it was discovered how rich in copper content these ores were; "the Old Dominion smelter was built at Globe, this event marking the beginning of important copper-mining operations in the district. By 1886 there were six furnaces at work . . . In 1888 the Old Dominion company was reorganised, starting forthwith on a long and successful career. In 1892 Phelps, Dodge and Company purchased the United Globe mines," and became the dominant influence in the area, which was launched at last on its long and immensely productive career.

Into the district Cornish miners at once began to come, keeping together, as elsewhere, and gradually forming their own section of the town. Up to the Second World War it was possible to say that "the different residential sections of Globe used to be an index to the many nationalities living in the camp, but today only two groups—the English from Cornwall, and the Mexicans—still have particular neighbourhoods . . . The three hills—Noftgers, Pascoe, and School, are said to be Cornish territory. Pascoe Hill is separated from Noftgers Hill by a deep steep-sided canyon approximately a block wide and crossed by long bridges. Noftgers and School Hills share the nickname of Cousin Jack Hill . . . The Cornishmen have been known as Cousin Jacks so long that they are also known as 'Cuzzie' . . . Pascoe Hill has been corrupted to 'Pasty' Hill, in honour of the Cornish delicacy, meat and potato pie."[3]

We are told that until Geronimo's surrender in 1886 "the trails to the mining camp were so dangerous as to discourage all but the most adventurous, and development of the district's copper mines proceeded very slowly."[4] It was not until the coming of the railroads, and the purchase of the Old Dominion by the Lewisohn interests in 1895 that development became rapid. "For the next twenty-five years the Old Dominion was one of the greatest copper mines in the world." Globe boomed along with this and other mines in the neighborhood for which it was the natural center, with countless cattle in the fine grazing country of Gila County in the hills all round. "The Cousin Jacks and other hard-rock miners brought to Globe the idea of collective bargaining for working men, and the union they formed was the strongest and most militant miners' local in Arizona." In 1917 this union struck against the Old Dominion Company for a closed shop. This was war-time: martial law was proclaimed and the strike was defeated. "The grip of the powerful trade-unions in Globe was completely broken, and a large number of skilled hard-rock miners left the town for ever." Still more so when the great depression clamped down in 1931, and the Old Dominion and other mines closed for good.

We can observe something of the Cornish participation in

all this from the beginnings through the careers of a few typical individuals.

A couple of strong personalities were the Pascoe brothers. The elder, Benjamin, was born in England in 1838, but had only "a dim remembrance of his native land."[5] The parents emigrated in 1844; in 1852 the father went to California via the Isthmus. He mined for two or three years, then settled on a farm near Marysville; there were eleven children in the family. During the Civil War Benjamin enlisted in the 1st California Cavalry, stationed at Fort Goodwin. In 1878 he came to Globe, adventurously driving ox-teams into the mountain country. At Globe he served as a night-watchman: "the position in those days required iron nerve and fearlessness. Under his jurisdiction were some of the toughest and most lawless scamps that ever invaded a mining camp." An ex-soldier, he was United States marshal in those parts for four years in the warlike early 1880's, but was particularly successful in his relations with the Indians, having an Apache as his deputy when he became sheriff. He thought himself lucky in keeping order without shooting anyone. He next went lumbering until 1898, when he purchased a livery business and traded in grain and hay. One has a picture of him as a bearded old man, with honest eyes and high cheek-bones.

His brother Thomas had a more important career and is portrayed at the end a fine old uniformed gentleman in all the fur and feather of high Masonic rank.[6] He was a speculator and promoter of projects for the good of Globe. (Was Pascoe Hill named perhaps for him?) He was born at Galena in 1846, but he grew up in California, went lumbering for four years in the redwood district, and had a varied experience ranching, stockraising and butchering. He came after his brother to Globe in 1881, when the "now famous settlement contained but a few hardy and venturesome miners and prospectors, who were willing to brave the dangers of life in the immediate shadow of the ever-upraised Indian tomahawk. . . ." He was four years mining, then served as under-sheriff to his brother, and became sheriff of Gila County 1882–86. He next ran a livery stable for some years, and then sold out to his brother, purchasing a large ranch, with an extensive hay and grain business. Much of this was wiped out by a flood; so, by a not unnatural turn of thought, he sold his business interests to establish the Globe waterworks system. He became the chief stockholder in the construction of a reservoir to hold 140,000 gallons. He sold out, to organize the Miners and Merchants Bank, of which he became president. He combined this with stock-farming in the Salt River Valley, until the Roosevelt Dam was built, when he sold out well to the government, and went in for the latest demand—for ice and cold storage. By this time he had acquired various properties, and was recognized as one of the leading pioneers of Globe and of Gila County.

James P. Faull first worked for the celebrated Dr. James Douglas—the leading intellectual influence in early Arizona mining—in Gila County in 1883, and put the first pick in the ground for the Phelps, Dodge Company at Hoosier Mine, of which he became foreman.[7] In 1896 a treaty with the San Carlos Indians opened up the San Carlos strip for exploitation. Faull became a large stockholder in the Copper Reef Company, and himself owned a group of four small mines almost surrounded by the United Globe Mines of Phelps, Dodge, which became "the Company" *par excellence* hereabouts and at Bisbee. A couple of Kingdon brothers were well-known mining engineers there, right down south on the Mexican border. The younger, George, came to Arizona in 1883 and was altogether twenty-five years with the Old Dominion and United Globe companies, with some three years divided between Tombstone and Bisbee.[8] After twelve years at Globe, the Phelps, Dodge interests sent him to Silver City, New Mexico, to operate a copper concern; thence into Mexico to run a gold-mine in Sonora. He was called back to direct the mine-work for the Old Dominion and United Globe companies for the rest of his career. Harold Gribble, one of the best known engineers in eastern Arizona and county-engineer of Gila County was born there: the son of a mining engineer who installed the machinery for the Contention Mine at Tombstone, erected mills on the San Pedro River, and ran the Contention stamp-mill.[9] Dr. C. S. Vivian was born at Denver, and became chief surgeon of the Consolidated Copper Company at Humboldt.[10] He settled at Phoenix, where he researched into urology, publishing many articles in leading medical journals. Though he died young, he was an important figure in the life of the state.

With these figures we are over the divide into the second and third generations in America, and well into the twentieth century.

The next area to attract attention and ultimately prove one of the richest copper regions in the United States was around Bisbee. By 1877 two promising mines were started in close proximity, the Atlanta and the Copper Queen. With the aim of selling the latter in London a report on its prospects was asked from the old firm of John Taylor and Sons, which had been active in the Cornish mines from early in the century. The firm sent out Percivale Taylor and Captain W. R. Toms who reported favorably, but the price asked of the English was, as usual, excessive.[11] In 1881 James Douglas went over the ground, himself took an option on the Atlanta claim and interested the Phelps, Dodge people in New York, then quite a small concern. By 1884 the ore-bodies in the two mines seemed to be petering out. The explorations underground were not guided by scientific method, but by rule of thumb and old-fashioned know-how.

The foreman of the Atlanta was a Cornishman, John Prout, who had had considerable experience but was obstinate and aggressive. Prout drove a tunnel into the Copper Queen ground, but since it found no ore there was no trouble. Nevertheless, "between the officials of the Queen and John Prout, our foreman, there was undisguised dislike and hostility," wrote Douglas.[12] Prout's methods were not answering, and the prospects were discouraging. He had had experience at the Ore Knob Mine in North Carolina, and "had his own notions of prospecting, being a chlorider, a term derived from the fact that silver chloride is a mineral found in the outcrops of this desert region. His idea was therefore to follow little streaks and stringers of the oxides of iron and manganese into the limestone with the hope of finding the larger masses of copper ore. By such methods he frittered away $70,000 without finding anything. Phelps, Dodge and Company were disheartened and wished to stop the work, but Douglas had not lost heart and urged them successfully to spend $15,000 more. He returned to Bisbee and compelled Prout to sink a shaft, which broke into a big body of malachite, or carbonate ore. Indeed, later it was shown that the entire area of the Atlanta claim covered ore."

The old-fashioned hand-to-mouth methods were on their way out; the future was with the application of scientific method to mining. All his life T. A. Rickard was a vocal propagandist for the latter, and he had a marked admiration for Dr. Douglas who exemplified it. As politic as he was scientifically acute, Douglas saw that the way to the future was to amalgamate the two mines and buy in the claims around. He persuaded the Phelps, Dodge Company to follow his policy; the ore reserves at Bisbee proved immense. He made the fortune of the great concern that came to control one-half of Arizona's copper, gold and silver. He has his memorial in the town of Douglas, not far from Bisbee.

In bare and treeless Bisbee, clinging by the eyebrows to its hill—like so many mining sites all over the West—the Cornish were a distinctive element, as old inhabitants have told me. The town covers the upper end of a steep-sided gulch, "its houses clinging to the slopes of two long narrow canyons, terraced tier upon tier. Flights of stone and wooden stairs, dirt trails and casual uneven streets reach the uppermost dwellings, their foundations often level with the roofs of the houses below.¹³ But though a rough community, it was a stable one: "Bisbee is a town in which many families have lived more than thirty years; it has good schools and churches, and almost as many solid, brightly painted houses as mining-camp shacks."

Here the Cornish miners lived contentedly, and still do. There is more than a sprinkling of them left today: Trestrail (3), Vivian (2), Warne (2), Gregory (2), Rowe (2), Rowland (2), Rosewarne, Clemo, Visick—a rare name; while there must be a considerable number among such popular names as Allen (13), Williams (15), Thomas (9), Harris (8), Phillips (7), Hancock, Tucker. At Douglas George Dawe was superintendent of the smelting department of the Calumet and Arizona Mining Company.¹⁴ His parents had emigrated to Wisconsin, and moved to Santa Barbara, California, where the father did well in a hardware business and took his part in public affairs, serving six years as city assessor. Today Douglas also has a Visick family, Vivian, Stanaway, Hicks, Hickman (3), Gregory (3), Tremaine, Sanders (3).

A third area, very important in its day, but a shadow of its former self now, is Jerome in central Arizona, between Prescott and Flagstaff. There it is, or was, "hanging precariously on the side of Mingus Mountain in the Black Hills, its frame-houses a jumble on stilts."¹⁵ Most of them are empty now, tottering down the precipitous hill-side, the place depopulated; as one goes gingerly down the steep main street of this ghostliest of ghost-towns, the view opens out from its natural amphitheatre across the Verde Valley to Clarkdale, where the smelters are, or were. Up to the Second World War the place was still working: there were still "a few Italians and Cornishmen through the various districts [to] complete the town's racial mixture."

The United Verde Company was organized by Eugene Jerome to exploit the copper here in 1883. He employed a

Welshman, William Thomas, who had got his training at smelting with the Vivians at Swansea, to erect a furnace. But it was not until William A. Clark of Montana bought the property in 1888 that its full development was undertaken and its tremendous riches revealed. Clark certainly had luck as well as *nous:* "the United Verde is probably the richest mine that was ever worked under individual ownership."[16] Between 1888 and 1930 it produced, in copper, gold and silver, over $350,000,000. By then it, too, had come under the control of Phelps, Dodge and Company.

In the early years of this century further discoveries of ore led to the formation of the United Verde Extension Mine. George Kingdon, an early associate of Dr. Douglas, became general manager of this company.[17] Born in Cornwall, he emigrated to the iron-mines of New Jersey for a year, moved on to Michigan for a couple of years, and came to Arizona, to Tombstone first, in 1883. For some half a century he was associated with the copper industry, most of the time with the United Verde. He ended up prosperous, vice-president of the Clemenceau Bank at Clemenceau, where the smelters were—the mine closed down in 1938—and director of the Valley Bank at Phoenix. His portrait shows a frog-like, intelligent face.

The discovery of the Commonwealth Lode in Cochise County near the Mexican border—not far from Sulphur Spring Valley, a favorite hunting ground of the Apaches—is, as Rickard says, one of the romances of Arizona. It happened in 1895, and was the prize of a Cornish family of the name of Pearce, who had a small ranch on the outskirts of the Dragoon Mountains, not far from Tombstone. James Pearce had been a miner all his life; born in Cornwall in 1844, he married Maria Curnow at twenty, and came to the eastern states in 1868.[18] In 1870 he went west to Colorado, after three years he moved on to Idaho, another three years to Grass Valley, next Montana, then Nevada. They ultimately settled in Arizona, near Sulphur Springs; they had saved quite a bit of money, he from his mining, his wife from running a miners' boarding-house. The two sons were keener on cattle, and a ranch was bought in the valley where they built up a small herd.

It seems that one of the sons, John, got into a spot of trouble with the family when, entrusted with the shipment of some cattle to Kansas City, he proceeded to blow the money and was called over the coals on his return. If so, he recouped the family dramatically; for, leaving home to go prospecting, he came upon an outcrop of quartz on the old trail to Tombstone, broke off some pieces of it and returned home with them. The family put no faith in his ventures, but at length his mother was persuaded to advance the money to have the specimens assayed at Tombstone. They proved to be extremely rich in silver. All was forgiven, and the whole family joined in staking a claim for each member of it. This was obvious good sense, as was the family's decision to sell their joint claims for a really large bid; for, as Rickard says, "the sale of a mine, to people living in a mining region, is usually the simplest way of making quick money out of it."[19] The history of mining is full of discoverers of rich mines—notoriously of the Comstock Lode—who reaped little benefit from their discovery. Not so the Pearces.

At the end of the year Professor Richard A. F. Penrose came to the district, tested the ores and, with a couple of partners, purchased the property for some $275,000.[20] I cannot but think that there is an additional element of romance in this seventh-generation Cornish-American coming to terms with this old Cornish couple on the far away Mexican border of Arizona. It was Mrs. Pearce, formerly Maria Curnow, who was the hard-headed woman of business, as Penrose told the story to Judge Sloan. She was the unchallenged head of the family, and whatever she said went with the others: "in negotiating for the property they had to deal with Mrs. Pearce."[21] In addition to the cash she insisted on being conceded the sole privilege of "running the boarding-'ouse": evidently re-insurance, in case their luck was too good to be true.

There was a sequel when Penrose got back to Philadelphia and asked one of his Drexel relations in the Drexel Bank to put up the money. He received the reply: "Dick, you know we won't let you have the money. We are bankers, not miners." So Penrose turned to his father and his own family to raise the cash. When the Commonwealth Mine was shortly depositing $300,000 a month with the Drexel Bank, Mr. Drexel reproached his kinsman: "Dick, when you came to me for that money, you didn't tell me that you had a rich mine like the Commonwealth has turned out to be." "No," said Penrose; "there was no occasion: you were a banker, not a miner." That is a completely characteristic Penrose turn of humor—it is also quite Cornish.

The purchase of the mine had been put through in 1896; by 1899 it had already yielded $4,000,000, of which over $2,500,000 was pure profit. It is said that the mine yielded altogether some $15,000,000 in silver and gold, the district some $30,000,000.

One wonders what became of the Pearces and their money. Some of it went into other mining ventures, for one learns that they owned the Horn Spoon and the Blue Bell mines, in which the sons-in-law were also interested. What became of the tough old lady in her new circumstances of affluence? Did she continue to run her boarding-'ouse long? All that remains today is the Cornish name they bequeathed to a ghost-town where once the Apaches hunted.[22]

An area of more recent development, to which the Cornish went, is Ray, east of Phoenix. To this place migrated neighbors of mine, Sidney and Ernest Jenkin, from Carn Grey—a favorite haunt from childhood, a tor high up above St. Austell Bay, the bracken- and heather-covered slopes, wine-red in autumn, tin-streamed through the ages by our ancestors.[23] My friend, Harry Clarke, who comes from that nostalgic spot—

Home of the silent, vanished races—

tells me that Ernest Jenkin "came from Carn Grey in 1907, did quite well out there in Arizona and became manager of a large copper mine in Ray. His four daughters all graduated from college. Sidney Jenkin's son has been principal of a good-size school down that way for years. I could mention many others who have done well since coming from Cornwall." But, for those who did well, there were those who found an early grave, like my cousin, Percy Anstis. William Treloar, of Marquette, Michigan, tells me that his grandfather went to mine in Arizona. In 1905 he wrote home to his wife and family to get their things together to come over, he would meet them in New York. He never did; there was no further word, until a letter came—from the company, to say that he had died of pneumonia. There was an orphaned family to bring up. Harry Clarke writes of "the very deep and hot copper mines of Arizona: Globe, Jerome, Ray, Bisbee, Douglas." Today, however, at Ray—as at Butte and Bingham—"it is interesting to see how they mine the copper now, large open pits instead of underground." There is no longer need for the old inherited miner's skill that filled so large a place in the nineteenth century and helped to populate America with useful citizens.

An early pioneer, who was not a miner but did a great deal towards building up the territory and state, was George J. Roskruge, who came to Arizona as early as 1872.[24] Born at Roskruge near Helston in 1845, he had his start as a messenger boy in the old firm of Grylls. From 1860 to 1870 he served in the Duke of Cornwall's Rifle Volunteers and became a first-class shot, champion of his county—a skill he put to good use in Arizona. In 1870 he emigrated to Colorado, and in 1872 formed one of a party of sixteen determined to see Arizona; "overcoming the perils of flood, drouth, famine and the hostility of the Apaches, the little band reached Prescott in June 1872." Roskruge traversed the whole territory to Tucson, not far from the Mexican border, where he settled.

A survey was being made, running along the 5th parallel to the Colorado River, and Roskruge assisted the United States surveyor as cook and packer, then as chainman; he ultimately helped to prepare the maps and notes for the surveyor-general. Having proved his usefulness, he became chief draftsman in the state-office, and in 1880 deputy land and mineral surveyor. He was for four years surveyor for Pima County, and for three years city engineer of Tucson. He ended as United States surveyor-general of Arizona in 1896, president of the civil engineers of the territory next year. Meanwhile he concerned himself with many aspects of its growing life. He carried on his lifelong interest in rifle-shooting and marksmanship, organizing groups of *aficionados* and serving as secretary of the National Rifle Association for Arizona. He pushed forward the founding of schools, planning the first school in Tucson, which was named Roskruge School after him. He served as regent of the University of Arizona and president of the board of education. An active member of the Archaeological Association, he gathered together an important prehistoric collection. Becoming a Master Mason before leaving Cornwall, he carried his enthusiasm into new country; secretary of the Grand Lodge of Arizona from 1882 to the end of his career, he was regarded as the father of Masonry in Arizona. His photograph shows him an ancient whitebeard, plastered with Masonic emblems and honors.

But, indeed, he had had a good life; the opening up of the last new territory meant *la carrière ouverte aux talents* and he, like so many others, made the most of his opportunities. One of the best known pioneers in building the territory and the state, his biography records: "he was proud of his state, as it was proud of him." Arizona, even more than most of the West, must have been wonderfully romantic and exciting in those pioneering days.

One finds not many Cornish in Tucson today—and I do not know if there are any of the rare name Roskruge. There are Pascoe (4), Tremaine (3), Penrose (2— one of the name Tremaine Penrose, so there can be no doubt about him), Rouse (3, and one of the rare form, Rous); but there are large numbers of people with names like Harris (over 50), and Rowe (20), among whom there must be a good proportion of Cornish.

It is in Phoenix that we find the main concentration, and in sum it is quite considerable; as with Denver in Colorado, as the mines have declined the mining population has moved into the largest industrial city of the state. Of the Foote clan there are no less than 28; I know that some of these must belong, for my old friend, John M. Foote, who was an official of the state Department of Agriculture, was Cornish by descent. Of the Chenoweth name we find 9—Dr. W. F. Chenowith was a pioneer physician of the border town of Nogales, and county superintendent of health.[25] We notice the following: Triplett (11), Trezise (6, including a minister), Tippitt (5, including another minister), Trethewey (3, and Treadway 3, if that is another form), Trevillian (2), Trehearne (2), Trenberth (2), Tredennick, Trefry, Tregaskes, Trembath, Tretinick, Trevey, Trevethan, Trewartha, and Trebil (2—if that is a shortened form of Trebilcock). We find Pellow (3), Penberthy (2), Penrose (3, including a doctor), Pentecost (4), Pascoe (5), Pender (2). There are 18 Rouse, of whom some must be Cornish, and 4 Rowse; Nancarrow (5), Menhennet (6), Minear (2), Uren (2, and 2 U'Ren), Vivian (5), Westlake (4), Merrifield (7), and a rarity in Beswetherick, an East Cornwall name. There are Hoskins (14, in various forms), Jolly (21, of whom some belong), Gear (9, and Geare 9—some will be Cornish), Grose (7), Gover (2),

Goldsworthy, Furse (2), Jobe (6), Jose, Joliff (a minister), Hambley (4, including a minister), Jago (4), Carlyon (2), Curnow (2), Dungy (2), Cardew, Carne, Chubb. We notice Honey (2), Searle (2), Stocker (5), Stickland, Rodda, Rosevear. There are large groups within which many Cornish are certainly to be found. There were Prouts in Phoenix, for a daughter of John Prout and Ada Chenoweth, who had moved from Michigan, married there.[26] We have learned that there are Cornish Jenkins there, and that there are plenty of Cornish blood under English names we may illustrate by the fact that descendants of Bishop Restarick, of the name of Withington, live in Phoenix—his grandson in the male line carries on the name in Rome, Georgia.

NOTES

1. *History of Arizona*, (1930), II, 88.
2. T. A. Rickard, *History of American Mining*, 292.
3. *Arizona*, (American Guide Series), 194–95.
4. *Ibid.*, 196, 198, 199.
5. *Portrait and Biographical Record of Arizona*, (1901), 289; J. H. McClintock, *Arizona*, III, 628.
6. *Portrait and Biographical Record*, 54.
7. *Who's Who in Arizona* (1913), 658.
8. *Ibid.*, 475.
9. *Hist. of Arizona*, (1930), IV, 287.
10. *Ibid.*, III, 366.
11. T. A. Rickard, *The Romance of Mining*, 261.
12. *Ibid.*, 263–64.
13. *Arizona*, (American Guide Series), 171–72.
14. *History of Arizona*, (1930), IV, 40.
15. *Arizona*, (American Guide Series), 333.

16. T. A. Rickard, *Hist. of American Mining*, 291.
17. *Hist. of Arizona*, (1930), III, 164.
18. *Portrait and Biographical Record*, 754.
19. Rickard, 274.
20. The figure given varies between $250,000 and $300,000: I have adopted that given in *Portrait and Biographical Record* as being closer to the family.
21. R. E. Sloan, *Memories of an Arizona Judge*, 101–2.
22. W. C. Barnes, *Arizona Place Names*, 323.
23. It is described in my book, *A Cornish Childhood*.
24. *Hist. of Arizona*, (1930), III, 609; J. H. McClintock, *Arizona*, III, 200–01.
25. *Who's Who in Arizona* (1913), 196.
26. *Hist. of Arizona*, (1958), III, 123.

15   FROM NINETEENTH TO TWENTIETH CENTURY

The vast majority of miners moved out of mining into other callings—even in the first generation we have seen how many of them put their savings into a farm or business of their own. Not many of them made the change with such dramatic suddenness as the father of my informant, William Treloar. Cornish miners worked, as we have seen, in pairs; one day Treloar's partner was killed beside him by a fall of rock, himself miraculously escaped. The mine closed, as usual, the day after the fatality. Treloar never went down the mine again; he went out and got a job as an insurance agent. It was a very uncertain and uphill assignment. The son remembered his mother sitting on a trunk with all their belongings in a strange town, crying—for there were three children and not a cent in the world. The father was out, looking for a commission. Successful, with his first $3 commission, he came back with two big bags of groceries, one in each arm, provisions for half the week: one could get a lot in those days for $2.50. He had to walk the roads in all weathers, in iron winter, to get insurance business. Today the son—the grandson of the Arizona miner—is the prosperous commercial editor of the three papers of Marquette, Michigan.

Even in unlikely Oklahoma, where there cannot be many Cornish, it happens that a group of quarry-men and stone-cutters went from my native St. Austell to Granite, where the main streets of the town end abruptly against a towering cliff of granite. This is very familiar material to us at home, and it is appropriate that the first Pellow to meet it should have written home to his father and brothers to come to Oklahoma and "see this granite sticking up out of the ground."[1] John Henry Harris Pellow, who had served his apprenticeship at St. Austell, came to the United States and landed with 25 cents in his pocket. His first job was cutting stone for Grant's Tomb, above the Hudson, in New York. By 1905 he was able to send for his father to work as foreman in the quarry, which furnished the stone for the state reformatory. In subsequent years the younger sons—Simon, Paul and Joe—came out to join their father and eldest brother. Together they were able to run their own concern, the "Pellow Brothers Monument Works." A sister married Joseph Thomas Penhall of St. Austell, who came to Granite to work for Pellow Brothers, as a stone polisher.

In the next generation, two sons of John Henry Harris Pellow operate the "Jack H. Pellow Monument Works" at Enid, Oklahoma, which was started by their father in 1911, when trade was evidently flourishing. Of the Penhall children, Joseph Arthur Penhall bought the quarry at Granite from his uncles upon their retirement, and operated it until his early death in 1951. After that it was sold; though the family no longer has any connection with it, the name was retained "because it was so well known in that part of the state." When old John Henry Pellow married a second time, in America, he married a Cornishwoman whom he had known in the old country, Eliza Opie: she was a nurse in Vermont, but came on the train to marry John—"all arranged by John Henry Harris, his son." One sees what a managing sort he was, the real leader of the family, through whom they all came out, a spreading connection now in several states. At the same time, one sees in their lifelong craft of quarrying and stone-cutting the granite uplands, grey and rock-ribbed, above St. Austell.

The truth is that wherever one moves about the States one will find some Cornish, even in unlikely places. We have already seen that Oklahoma City has a respectable complement of Cornish.[2] Perhaps one is in Wilmington, Delaware; what does one find?—no less than five Penrose families, six Oates, two Trescott, a Chenoweth, Lanyon, Pasco, Tonkin, Trebilcock, Treleaven, Tremaine, Trembath, Trevorrow. At Houston, Texas, we notice the following: Pendarvis (9), Nettle (8), Hocking (7), Pascoe (6, with typical Cornish occupations: a machine works, an instrument company, a packing concern), Chenoweth (5), Estabrook (5), Trevathan (5), Penrice (4), Penrose (4), Tremaine (4), Pender (4), Trevillion (3), Pengelly (3), Trevena (2), Polkinghorne (2), Annear, Edgecomb, Kitto, Nancarrow, Trelawny, Treleaven, Trevenen. There must be many others.

Even in Anchorage, Alaska, we find that there have penetrated a couple of Chenoweths, one of them a doctor, a couple of Hoskens, a Tonkin and a Spargo.

With Alaska, alas, it is time to call a halt.

A meteor that flashed across the darkened firmament of the Civil War and sputtered out to a tragic end was Lieutenant-Colonel George St. Leger Grenfell. "No Confederate soldier other than officers of the first rank enjoyed greater notoriety in his lifetime or has had a greater measure of posthumous fame than this British soldier of fortune"—so an authority tells us.[3] "In a seven-month tour of duty from June to December 1862, as John Hunt Morgan's adjutant-general, Grenfell established a great reputation by his outstanding bravery. His many eccentricities added to his fame. His habit of making himself conspicuous in battle by wearing a British cavalry forage cap of bright scarlet was greatly admired. His custom of bathing in every stream crossed by Morgan's men in the course of their raids caused astonishment rather than imitation." (It may be added that Grenfell was very much a gentleman.) "But it was Grenfell's pre-Civil War adventures, even more than his achievements as a Confederate cavalryman, that caused Fremantle [of the Coldstream Guards, who wrote up his experiences in the Southern States] to describe him as 'one of the most extraordinary characters I ever met.'"

Actually Grenfell was not only a romantic figure but an inveterate romancer—in that like his compatriot, Edward John Trelawny—and it is hard to come at the truth about his adventures. What we can be sure of about them is sufficiently romantic, without embroidering: a figure out of Rider Haggard or Henty. And though he was already an elderly man of sixty-four when he won fame as Morgan's right-hand man in his dashing raids, his character, no less than his appeal, has the aroma of adolescence.

Grenfell belonged to the celebrated clan that descends from Hercules Grenfell of St. Just near Land's End and has produced so many remarkable men, soldiers, financiers, explorers, missionaries.[4] Such men were Field-Marshal Lord Grenfell; Lord Desborough with his fighting sons, Julian and Billy Grenfell, killed in the First World War; George Grenfell, missionary and explorer of the Congo; the sainted Wilfred Grenfell, of Labrador, heroic doctor of the Eskimos. One branch of the Grenfells, led by Pascoe Grenfell, went in for high finance, beginning in Amsterdam; it may be said that the exalted firm of Morgan, Grenfell and Company was a very different kettle of fish from the Morgan, Grenfell and company who executed the raids into Kentucky and Tennessee.

The Grenfells were no doubt an offshoot of the Norman aristocratic clan of Grenville (or Granville), and this was asserted by the names given to both St. Leger Grenfell and his father Bevil Granville Grenfell. The boy, born in 1808, was brought up at Penzance, then sent to the family's business connections in Holland for his schooling. After a continental tour he settled in Paris in 1830, where he joined the Royal

Guard and took part in the three days' street-fighting that brought down the Bourbon monarchy and made the July Revolution. After that he served five years in the National Guard; in 1833 he married a girl who was half-English, half-French. But his employment was with a branch of the family firm, banking and dealing in metals. Anything more unsuitable can hardly be imagined for one of his reckless, adventurous temperament, and in 1837 he committed some financial misdemeanor that led to his father's ruin. In 1840 he absconded from France to avoid prosecution. His eccentricity was such that he was hardly held responsible for his misdoings: "no-one ever bore him malice or refused to forgive him."[5] At any rate, he was now free—he regarded no home-ties—to follow the vagaries of his disposition.

He had a taste for hare-brained speculations and he made for Morocco. In the 1840's he entertained the fantastic notion of farming in a madly xenophobic country, distracted by the campaigns of Abd-el-Kader and his national resistance to the French. No point in going into the eccentricities of Grenfell's life, the dangers to which he deliberately exposed himself —he never knew what fear was. He certainly made the acquaintance of Abd-el-Kader, paid him a visit, formed a high admiration for him—were they not both *condottieri* of a type?—and wrote a lofty commendation of him to Lord Palmerston. (Was he not himself a Grenfell?) It is more than probable that the basis of his activities in the Western Mediterranean was illicit trade, in other words, smuggling—if so, a very Cornish inflection.

The outbreak of the Crimean War gave him an opening. A fellow-Cornishman, Major-General Hussey Vivian commanded the "Anglo-Turkish Contingent": Grenfell was given a captaincy and sailed happily off to Constantinople. With the end of the war Grenfell emigrated to South America, ranching and taking a hand in the local revolutions. The outbreak of the American Civil War was, for such a man, the chance of a lifetime. He returned to Europe and got in touch with the Confederate envoy, Slidell, in Paris, who sent him over with an introduction to General Robert E. Lee. Lee, with excellent judgment, handed him on to Morgan, about to begin his marauding campaign in Kentucky. A good cavalryman, hard as steel, tough as leather, though white-haired, he was just the man for the job: Morgan made him his adjutant-general. General Basil W. Duke testified that he was "of great assistance to him [Morgan], but sometimes gave trouble by his impracticable temper; he persisted, among other things, in making out all papers in the style he had learned in the English service, the regulations and orders of the War Department 'to the contrary notwithstanding.' He was always in a good temper when matters were active—I never saw him hilarious but once and that was the day after the battle of Hartsville; he had just thrashed his landlord and doubled up a brother Englishman [sic], in a set-to about a mule, and was contemplating an expedition on the morrow with General Morgan to Nashville. He was the only gentleman I ever knew who liked to fight with his fists, and was always cheerful and contented when he could shoot and be shot at."[6]

All through that summer and autumn Morgan and Grenfell pursued their devastating raids in and around Kentucky—where there were many Confederate supporters—making a compass of a thousand miles about the state. They harassed the Federals by penetrating their lines, threatening communications, capturing trains and hundreds of prisoners, destroying enormous supplies and returning safely to base. General Duke gives us a close-up of the old boy in action in the raid on Cynthiana: "Grenfell headed a charge upon the depot, in which some of them [the Federals] took refuge. He received eleven bullets through his horse, person and clothes, but was only slightly wounded. A curious little scarlet skull-cap, which he used to wear, was perforated. It fitted so tight upon his head that I previously thought a ball could not have gone through it without blowing his brains out."[7]

In December 1862 he resigned from Morgan's command,

and in the spring of 1863 was made inspector-general of cavalry in Bragg's Army of Tennessee. Duke says that he "became the terror of the entire front. He would have been invaluable as commander of a brigade of cavalry, composed of men who (unlike our volunteers) appreciated the military necessity of occasionally having an officer knock them in the head. If permitted to form, discipline and drill such a brigade of regular cavalry after his own fashion, he would have made gaps in many lines of battle, or have gotten his blackguards well-peppered in trying."[8] This is a handsome tribute, coming from a brother-officer who knew him. That autumn there followed a brief period of service as assistant inspector-general of cavalry in the Army of Northern Virginia under General "Jeb" Stuart. Evidently Grenfell's services were appreciated.

After two years of hard labor and fighting he left the Confederate Army to visit in the North—he was free to do this, since he was neither an American citizen nor an enlisted man. It may have been at this time that he sent home to his family the fine silk flag of the Kentucky Guards, made by the ladies of Leesburg, which has recently come back to Kentucky into the collection of the Filson Club.[9] He ran the blockade to New York, where he casually called on the commander of the area for clearance as having "retired" from the Confederate Army. That officer sent him on to Washington, where the Secretary of War, Stanton, who knew of his exploits and his reputation, interviewed him. Stanton asked him about the strength of the Confederate armies. Grenfell, loyal to his Confederate comrades, thought that Stanton had no right to ask him such questions and told him tall tales of the strength of Lee's army, of southern reserves and rolling stock. Stanton gave him a pass on condition that he would not take up arms against the Union.

It is probable that Grenfell was already involved in the preliminaries of the wide-ranging Northwestern Conspiracy, that was timed to create havoc and destruction along with the

Presidential election—particularly in Chicago and New York. He went first to Canada, whence he wrote to his daughter at home:

> I am well, but nervous. Two years and a half of excitement and hard work have told on me. I shall rusticate a month or so, I hope, before I again get into the saddle. I passed through New York, was sent up to Washington, reported to Mr. Seward, was released and allowed to continue my journey through Canada. It is impossible to give a safe opinion upon what may take place in the South within the next three months, but they cannot subjugate it, never, never![10]

His next letter was from Chicago, August 31, 1864: "Tell the girls [his daughters] I am alive and well, although engaged in rather dangerous speculations, which you will know more of, probably, bye and bye."[11] It shows how completely he had identified himself with the southern cause—he was a Confederate type, out of *Gone With the Wind*—and also how hopelessly his judgment was at variance with the objective facts of the situation. We need not go into his fantasies —and the Northwestern Conspiracy would do no good to the southern cause. Grenfell's part in it was to have raided Rock Island Prison and release the Confederates held there. No more open conspirator walked the earth. "Dressed in hunting tweeds, carrying a fowling piece and followed by a large hunting dog, Grenfell arrived in Chicago. He registered at the Richmond House, using his own name"—by this time a well-known one.[12] Every day he went out "for birds," really to reconnoitre Rock Island Prison and report to the Confederate agent, Hines. The conspirators were betrayed by an informer, and Grenfell was the first to be caught—a sitting bird. He was a familiar figure to the hotel clerk, whom he had told, with typical bravado, that he had come to the Richmond House, "because it was the favourite hotel of my friend, His Royal Highness, the Prince of Wales." There he was at the fireside sipping his brandy, dog at his feet, when the patrol came to get him. "A veteran of a hundred such encounters, he surrendered gallantly. 'I am your prisoner, gentlemen,' he told the lieutenant."

He had written his daughter, "I have been too long used to discomfort to consider comfort as being at all necessary . . . We have all got to live a certain time and, when the end comes, what difference will it make whether I lived in London or Illinois, and whether I died in a four-post bedstead, with a nurse and phials on the bedtable, or whether I died in a ditch?"[13] But he did not know the fate that was in store for him.

Grenfell's trial took place in the New Year, 1865, and received international attention; the London *Times* ran a daily story on the court-martial proceedings. There was no doubt of Grenfell's involvement, but the government failed to get conclusive evidence of his part in the conspiracy. Their witnesses were shoddy unreliable characters, chief of whom was a sergeant whom Grenfell had arrested for stealing his horse during the raid on Gallatin, Tennessee. Nevertheless, it was wartime, and Grenfell was condemned to death. In Parliament there were demands that the English government should intercede, and President Andrew Johnson commuted the sentence to life-imprisonment on the Dry Tortugas, the swampy islets running south from the Florida coast beyond Key West. "I am a soldier, I can bear my fate," wrote Grenfell.

It turned out far worse than he could have imagined: he was kept working a twelve-hour day in a chain-gang under the burning sun; food was inadequate, "in fact I am dying by inches from inanition," he wrote in the summer of 1867.[14] Yet the tough old boy's only serious complaint was rheumatism, which disabled him from bending his back. When he insisted that he could not load bricks from the ground, he was tied to an iron grating and left all day in the sun. On still persisting, an Irish Lieutenant Robinson had Grenfell thrown into the water, with wrists tied behind his back; the old fellow had no difficulty in floating, so the operation was repeated until he was hauled in more dead than alive. It seems that Robinson was a brutal type, and several of the prisoners fainted under his treatment. We need not go into it all, or into the efforts that were made from England on Grenfell's behalf by his relations: they all came up against Stanton's opposition, who had not forgiven Grenfell's misleading him as to southern strength back in 1863.

Then came Grenfell's chance for real heroism, to show the best that was in him. Yellow fever swept through the garrison, the men were dying like flies. The celebrated Dr. Mudd, who had set Booth's leg—Lincoln's assassin—and been condemned to life imprisonment for it, was a fellow-prisoner. He and Grenfell now took charge of the sick and dying soldiers; they turned the gun-room into a hospital, Mudd as doctor, Grenfell as chief nurse. "In three months not a boat or a schooner touched the fortress. Once a small boat made the journey from Key West to deliver medicine and some supplies."[15] At night the burial-parties rowed the dead bodies to the tiny cemetery on Bird Key—some forty died. The surgeon-general at Key West officially reported that during the first month, when the epidemic was at its height, Grenfell "scarcely slept or rested during that time. He administered the medicine made by Dr. Mudd, washed men burning with fever, wrote their letters, their wills and wiped the black vomit from their cracked lips."

Major Valentine Stone died; Grenfell had to report the ill news to the family. "I write only a few lines, I am tired and grieved, having been now twenty-one days and nights by the bedside of the sick. Last night was my first night passed in bed—grieved on account of your brother's death, who was the only officer that has ever shown me any kindness since I first came here ... We have had some one hundred and eighty yellow fever cases and upward of thirty deaths."[16] Before the epidemic died down Dr. Mudd himself was stricken; not so Grenfell. But when the three-months' nightmare was over he emerged from the pesthole gaunt and emaciated, bearded and completely exhausted. No more chains for him: the grateful commander said, "I will immediately communicate with the Secretary of War and with the President to inform him of your heroic conduct."[17]

Communications flew to and fro; Grenfell's conduct was highly commended to the President; his relations at home sent him money and clothes, pulled every string they could for his release; Jefferson Davis's wife sent him shirts and $20. The old fellow was allowed the freedom to cultivate a garden: in January 1868, "I have tomatoes, peppers, and melons in full bloom, salad, radishes, peas and beans at maturity, in the open air of course, for be it known to you they have turned my sword into a shovel and rake, and I am at the head of my profession here. What I say or do (horticulturally) is law."[18] There really was something irresistible about him. His thoughts began to turn homewards, to the little garden beside the Thames he had always neglected, found too constricting. News of home came through to him now—when earlier he had been shut in a dungeon for ten months, without light, books or papers, for publishing to the outside world the punishments inflicted on soldiers and prisoners alike at Fort Jefferson. Now, "I do not see any harm in the old maids, my sisters, becoming Roman Catholics. It is the fashion to do so nowadays, and, after all, one religion is as good as another, provided one is sincere. I am nothing at all at present, or, if anything, a follower of the Devil, for he reigns here supreme."

Sanguine as ever, he thought he would be released. He asked President Johnson "only for a fair inquiry to be made as to facts, one in which I may be heard."[19] But influences at Washington against him were still too strong: his appeal for clemency was denied. Irrepressible as ever, though now approaching seventy, Grenfell resolved to take his fate into his own hands. On March 7, 1868, during a night of terrific storm, Grenfell and a couple of companions made their escape from the prison on a lowered rope, to a row-boat on the shore. Here they were joined by two "desperate characters," one with a thirty-pound iron ball chained to his leg. The five men rowed away into the storm, and nothing was ever heard of them again.

For Grenfell it was a far cry from those early quiet days beside Mount's Bay.

With the twentieth century we come to a personality in marked contrast: John Spargo, for some years a leading figure in the American Socialist Party. Take him all round, he was one of the most remarkable Cornishmen of this century, along with Wilfred Grenfell of Labrador, Field-Marshal Blamey of Australia, and Quiller-Couch at home. Born at Stithians in 1876, he came to America in 1901 and died, just over ninety, in 1966.* Most of his long career, then, was spent in the United States and it was to its life that his rich and varied contributions were made. Nevertheless, it was in Cornwall that he was formed.

The son of Thomas Spargo and Mary Hocking, he was brought up in the granite-quarrying district of Stithians, Mabe and Penryn—those high moorlands with the grey rock outcrops and russet bracken in autumn: an Andrew Wyeth coloration, chaste and severe. He went to school at Penryn until he was ten, worked half-time till he was thirteen, then full-time as a granite cutter. (We recall that James Dyer, a Cornishman, was for many years secretary of the Granite Cutters' Union in America.) Young Spargo took every opportunity to educate himself, joining mutual improvement societies (forerunners of adult education classes) and Methodist discussion circles. The Methodists wanted to put him on their regular plan leading to the ministry; he rejected the belief in the doctrine of eternal damnation. That avenue was blocked.

---

* The outline of Spargo's life and work is given in both the American and British *Who's Who*, many editions; but much of my information in the above section is based on notes that I took from his conversation.

His wages were 18s. a week (then worth $4.50), so he went to South Wales, where he earned £2 5s., and interested himself in the trade union movement. Once, at Cambridge, he heard Gladstone speak, standing on a low curb with a railing, Spargo sitting on the outside, the great man's toes touching his behind. Something of the inspiration entered into him: he was impelled with the desire to speak and move masses like that. From Sir George O. Trevelyan he derived the aim to speak with a mastery of the language—"his diction was perfection," Spargo said—and took every opportunity to practice. He became an accomplished orator in the Victorian manner, much sought after later as a lecturer in America: I have heard it said that, in his heyday, when he rose to speak "you could hear a pin drop." There was the Celtic gift of eloquence; he was black-haired and dark, with fine eyes.

At an early age, poor and full of generous instincts, he was converted to socialism, and became an early member of the Social Democratic Federation. He knew many of those figures now historic: H. M. Hyndman, its affluent, gentlemanly leader; Keir Hardie, the first Labour Member of Parliament. In London he became acquainted with some of Karl Marx's circle: Marx's protégé, faithful Wilhelm Liebknecht; Lästner, who brought the manuscript of the *Communist Manifesto* to the printer; Marx's daughter, Eleanor (a "beautiful and wonderful woman," Spargo said), who, when the odious Aveling deserted her, poisoned herself. And Spargo knew both Longuet, Marx's son-in-law, and also Lafargue. He was well-acquainted with John Burns, the trade-union leader, and the young Ramsay Macdonald, who was then attracted by Enid Stacey, a university girl much in love with him; but he made a better marriage for himself to Margaret Gladstone (another "wonderful woman," Spargo gallantly repeated).

Spargo took an active part in the agitation against the Boer War. At a meeting at Gloucester he was badly beaten up and had to be smuggled out of the hall disguised as a woman through the mob waiting for him. In 1901, before the end of the war, he decided to try America; his mother was already there. Just before leaving, her companion wrote that she had died but that Spargo and his wife were to come all the same. When they arrived in New York, on a bitter February day, they went up Amsterdam Avenue to the address, to find that her friend had died too, and the people who had taken over wouldn't let them in. Spargo had the address of the Socialist Club, to which his luggage was to be sent, and went up to a forlorn locked-up room above a saloon: no luck there, and they had no money for a hotel. He remembered the name of a Russian socialist, Walter Winchensky, who took them in for the night.

When Spargo went to look for work as a granite-cutter, the affable Irish trade-union boss, O'Brien, froze at the request and wouldn't recognize Spargo's membership-card of the British Trade Union: he demanded $250 entrance fee and a six months' wait. However, the socialist comrades asked Spargo to speak at $5 a time, and shortly he got a regular job on the *Jewish Encyclopedia*, correcting its English, or putting it into English. Spargo's determination to speak and write good English served him well: he was next employed on Funk and Wagnall's *Standard Dictionary*. After that he gradually built up a position, as lecturer, orator, prolific pamphleteer, propagandist of democratic socialism. By 1906 he had written his famous book, *The Bitter Cry of the Children*, which was not a sentimental tract but a serious work of research into the sweated conditions of work among children in the New York slums. This book had a nationwide response, it became known internationally; it had a widespread influence on legislation and improving conditions of children's employment, it made John Spargo a national figure overnight, it made him a lot of money. Henceforth he was known everywhere, and financially independent.

This success spurred him on to work all the harder: he was an immensely industrious Cornishman, quick-working and prolific. He poured forth a large number of books on every aspect of socialism, democratic and idealistic, which need not detain us. But one book may: he wrote the first biography of Karl Marx to appear in English (1909), and this was valuable, for in London he had been close to Marx's circle. He was also very active lecturing all over the country, and not only in talk. While he lived at Yonkers he took a leading part in founding the Prospect House Social Settlement there; he was a member of the New York Milk Commission—he had gone into the question of its proper distribution, public inspection of its quality, hygiene, etc. (This was the great age for exposing scandals, the floruit of Upton Sinclair, Lincoln Steffens, Ida Tarbell and others.) At the same time as he pushed forward active philanthropy and social betterment, he was for several years a leading member of the executive of the Socialist Party, sent as United States delegate to the International Socialist and Trade Union Congress at Copenhagen, in 1910.

Then came the First World War—the first crest in the two mounting waves of the German attempt to achieve ascendancy in the twentieth century—which shattered our hopes and made the kind of world we live in. One of the first and most fateful casualties was the international socialist movement. Spargo was not surprised by the collapse of the German socialist party—the largest in number—in 1914. "Personally I had not expected anything else," he wrote. "In 1910 I wrote from Germany to my friend and comrade, George D. Heron, telling him that, so far as I could see, the German socialist movement had lost its soul and that it could never be relied upon to stand any severe test."[20] This was the simple truth— as Jaurès found, and as Lenin concluded.

The American Socialist Party was dominated by Germans —working-class socialism had been brought to America by Wilhelm Weitling and Joseph Weydemeyer, Marx's early associates. "When I came to America, early in 1901," Spargo wrote, "and joined in the creation of the Socialist Party—it was then known as the Social-Democratic Party—there was not a branch to which I could belong at which the business was wholly transacted in English. Business was transacted in German, records were kept in German. Only those specially fond of associating with Germans, and those who possessed an unlimited amount of patience, stayed in the movement for long."[21] No wonder the American Socialist Party was a failure—it lost numerous officials and devoted workers from sheer bureaucratism.

At the St. Louis convention in April 1917 the Socialist Party accepted Lenin's thesis that the war was unjustified in defense of democratic institutions; what it came to was that international socialism was not concerned, that one side was as bad as the other and it did not matter which side won. Spargo, who believed in democracy, dissented. Victor Berger of Milwaukee, a strong pro-German member of the executive, demanded an embargo on the export of food and munitions to Europe and said that, if there had been an embargo, Germany would have won the war two years before. This clumsily gave their game away, and enabled Spargo to point out that the policy of the party, under their direction, uniformly coincided with the views and interests of the German Foreign Office. But he was profoundly shocked at a National Peace Congress, when the whole gathering cheered the sinking of an American passenger ship by a German submarine—"perhaps the most despicable episode in all the dirty and sinister propaganda movement of the German sympathisers in this country."[22]

The American Socialist Party had no representation of French or Italian workers in the party membership, no reflection of their views; it was overwhelmingly German. There was never any condemnation of the worst of Germany's conduct, even in the sector in which they might have been expected to be interested—the deportation of workers in conquered territories to slave in Germany. Morris Hillquit joined with Victor Berger in contending that no compensation was necessary by Germany for the destruction she had inflicted on the northeastern departments of France. Very much in the minority, Spargo argued that the defeat of the militarist Central Empires was necessary for the well-being of the proletariat of all lands, including their own, Germany and Austria. For himself he was perfectly candid: he did not claim that his British birth and background had no influence on his views; "all the same, never once have I asked myself, 'How will England's cause be best served?' Always I have asked myself, 'How will the international socialist movement be best served?' Answer—by the defeat of the Central Empires."[23] And when America came into the war in 1917, he could say with a clear conscience: "the decision of the United States to enter the great war accords with the highest and best interests of all mankind."[24]

Nor was he taken in by German peace-proposals when faced by the prospect of America's unfolding power. "She wants a peace, now that she cannot have a triumph, which will leave the seeds of future wars; a peace which will leave her full-armed and ready to fight again at a not far-off future."[25] Who, with any knowledge of what happened after the first war, can say that he was wrong? So far from that, events all too tragically bore out his foresight. The Stockholm Conference in 1917 marked a decisive turning point for the international socialist movement. In the American Socialist Party he was alone in demanding that delegates to Stockholm should oppose a separate Russian peace with Germany; when he pressed for German compensation to Belgium, he was completely isolated, with only his own vote for it. On the issue of America's entering the war, he was left in a minority of one out of fifteen members of the executive.

By now he was through with the party. He realized that it was not only in regard to the war that the party was "entirely out of touch with American life and American needs . . . The same fact was apparent throughout."[26] He regarded the executive as quite unrepresentative of the membership; and, with so ossified a leadership, there were no more Socialist

Party workers in the large centers than there had been ten years before. He thought a supreme opportunity to move into the mainstream of American life had been missed, but that the decadence of the party had been manifest before the war. Himself its most effective propagandist with the public at large, both by tongue and pen—who was there to compare with him?—he withdrew from both executive and party with a dignified statement: "of all the good my life has known I count highest and best the comradeship of the men and women of the Socialist Party during these many years." It had indeed been his life. Privately his conviction was, "for a long time it has been painfully clear to my mind that the Socialist Party is probably the greatest single obstacle to the progress of socialism in America."

One cannot go on making bricks without straw forever. He had better things to do. With the trade union leader, Sam Gompers, he founded the Alliance for Labor and Democracy, in support of President Wilson and the war. Wilson put the funds behind the Alliance, and the campaign in the Middle West, waged from Chicago, was a success. In 1918 Spargo, now in close consultation with Wilson on this front, was sent over to Europe to counteract the defeatism of the French Socialists. Spargo was convinced that they could be divided— as they effectively were. He went on to London, where, of the two leaders of the Independent Labour Party, Macdonald was co-operative but Snowden refused to meet him. He renewed his old friendship with John Burns, who showed him the treasures he had collected: his third copy of More's *Utopia*, then the first edition, now worth a fortune. There was the cap he was wearing at the time of the Trafalgar Square riots of 1887 and the policeman's truncheon that broke his head—afterwards presented to him. Next, the closet containing the robes of his honorary degrees: "it has been a long way," said the old Labour leader.

For six months Spargo was attached to the United States Commission on Public Information in Italy, a listening post for the international working-class movement. The Bolshevik Revolution in Russia had not only split it from top to bottom but made the breach permanent with the setting up of the Communist International. Spargo was anti-Bolshevik from the first; he was a democrat and he saw where the suppression of all freedom would lead. In quick succession he produced a number of books right on the target: *Bolshevism, the Enemy of Political and Industrial Democracy*, in 1919; next year, *The Psychology of Bolshevism, The Greatest Failure in All History, Russia as the American Problem*. These books also are evidences of Spargo's insight, and early foresight: it is odd that he should have been neglected, when more hare-brained prognosticators have been awarded Nobel Peace prizes.

By this time he must have become thoroughly disillusioned with politics—ploughing the sand—though he may not have realized that his earlier idealism was based on an unreal psychology: an untrue view of human nature. However, it had given him a career, perhaps the most that can be said for it. He continued to be consulted by Presidents privately in regard to those issues, and he formed a lasting friendship, oddly enough, with Hoover. Like William S. U'Ren, he could not abide Franklin Roosevelt and the New Deal. From politics, where he had been so much to the fore, he faded out in the 1920's; he turned to an alternative life, a worthier cause: local history and antiquities. "I had to have something else," he said to me.

At one point he had had a complete nervous breakdown, from the strain of incessant lecturing and campaigning. The doctor gave him a year to live, and he betook himself to beautiful Bennington in the hills of Vermont. Here he created the Bennington Museum, his best monument; it was founded on nothing: there was no money, his wife used to lend her own cleaner, by the end of his days it had an endowment of $400,000. (His portrait should be there.) For twelve years he was president of the Vermont State Historical Society:

it began with $500 endowment, now $240,000. He turned to the delights of historical research, than which there is nothing more rewarding, when so much else is dust—and ashes. Active-minded, hardworking as ever, in addition to building up the museum and running the Historical Society, he wrote a number of books on pleasant Vermont subjects. President Coolidge made him president of the Vermont Sesquicentennial Commission: it was a modest reward. He even made a contribution to Cornish local history with his *Notes on the Name and Family of Spargo of Mabe, Cornwall*. He produced a work of original research on *History of the Potters and Pottery of Bennington*, and followed this with a standard work, for its time, *Early American Pottery and China*.

With these works Spargo showed a thorough mastery of the subject—ceramics were better than politics. He had absorbed the authorities in English and French, reaping the rewards of his determined self-education; and there was the aesthetic sensitivity of his Celtic temperament. I like to think that behind this was an inherited aptitude, perhaps an elective affinity; for Cornwall is china-clay country, and Spargo's strange and fascinating career comes full circle with this. China-clay is in part a deposit of decomposed granite; Spargo was born and reared in granite country, not far from where Cookworthy made his original discovery of kaolin (china-clay) and china felspar. Spargo tells us that "the discovery of an abundant supply of china-clay of superior quality in Cornwall, in 1768, gave the manufacture of porcelain its greatest impetus."[27] Both Cookworthy and Wedgwood had at first used clays from America, while America provided a leading market for chinaware of the best quality.

It must have given Spargo pleasure thus to draw together the two ends of his long, full life. Of the many books that he wrote, he left it too late to write the best that was in him: with that rich and crowded career, full of accomplishment and significant experience, he could have written one of the best autobiographies of our time. Striking as is the contrast between those two Cornishman, St. Leger Grenfell and John Spargo, both in social background and in character and temperament, they yet had qualities in common: courage, independence, high adventurousness. The working-man was the more honest of the two, yet each had an element of idealism, of fantasy of a kind. Spargo came to terms with reality in the end, Grenfell never did; yet each exemplified the individualism of the Cornish. Perhaps Spargo would have been a more successful politician if he had been prepared to sacrifice his own convictions; but could he have accomplished more than he did? A famous name in his heyday, forgotten before the end of his long life, he deserves to be remembered and even commemorated.*

The Cornish have not ceased to come to America in the twentieth century, though their numbers must have varied greatly in different decades. In the first three decades large numbers came, reaching a peak in the 1920's, after the First World War. Then came the world depression in the 1930's, when the United States was hit as badly as Britain, and a number of Cornish folk returned home. With the Second World War and after, fewer emigrated, though more might have done with advantage. Conditions tended to approximate in the two countries, and the welfare-state meant less incentive to emigrate, indeed less initiative all round.

Harry Clarke writes me about the attitude of mind in those more interesting, early decades. His parents returned home after eight or nine years in Butte, Montana. "One of the main topics of conversation at meal times was America. Mother and Father always talked about it, how different things were, how the houses were built and how people lived. Father talked for many an hour over the hedge with our next neighbour, Tom Nichols, about America: he had also lived in Butte, Montana. We would listen and hope some day we

* There should be a biography of him, and certainly notices of him in D. A. B., and D. N. B.

would be able to go and see for ourselves. It was an understood fact that, as soon as we were old enough, we would all go abroad. During the first world-war my oldest brother, Will, joined the United States Army in England, went to France and came back to the United States while still in the army. He went to Butte, Montana, and stayed there until 1925, when he returned to Cornwall." Two other brothers went to New Zealand in 1921. Indeed, in those immediate post-war years, there was an out-pouring from the old seed-bed to America, Canada, Australia. (My brother went to Australia.)

Harry Clarke himself came first to British Columbia; he left home with three young men from Foxhole, near St. Austell. Thence he moved to Washington, to "a nice town on Puget Sound called Bellingham, about a hundred miles north of Seattle. I lived there two years, working in several different lumber mills. Nearly every winter I went to night-school in the evenings, taking different courses: which, I'm sure, helped me a great deal." There was the good old motive of self-improvement at work: "I would say those who came after the first war came with the idea of finding better conditions for themselves and their families. Most of them have done very well, much better than if they had stayed in England. Many of the third generation have college educations. At the moment I'm thinking of the Warricks in South Bend, Indiana (nephews of Ernest Warrick, grocer at Slades), five brothers went there before and after World War I: nearly all their sons went through college." As we come to the end of this long story, our perspective is narrowing: some of the brothers were at Carclaze Elementary School with me. Harry Clarke tells me that, when he was living in Detroit, at a party given for some visitors from home, out of the fifty who came "about forty had attended Carclaze school. They all lived in and near Detroit: that shows how many Cornish people have settled in Detroit and Highland Park."

Detroit—then a boom-town in the rapid expansion of the

automobile industry—was a great magnet to the Cornish in those years. Harry Clarke writes, "I first went to Detroit in 1928, but I was told by some of the fellows from home that a few years before then, about 1923 or 1924, a large group of Cornishmen used to gather down on Detroit's main square, Cadillac Square, every Saturday evening—where they used to meet their friends, just the same as they used to meet in the towns and villages in Cornwall on Saturday nights. The crowd was finally broken up by the City Police. I suppose they wondered what kind of organization was gathering there. [I expect that the police were Irish anyway.] When we lived in Detroit we used to have several of the men from Tregonissey and Carclaze and their wives come to our house on Christmas Eve and sing many of the old Cornish carols. I'll mention a few who used to come—Passmore Edwards, Bill Trethewey, Jim and Jack Andrew, Walter Bawden, Clifford Hick from Charlestown, Dick Lagor from St. Stephen's." To these Detroit names I may add that of a cousin, Sid Courtney.

Those years were the heyday of the Cornish Arms Hotel in New York. Sid Blake, who ran it, was a cousin of my friend (and gardener), Jack Blake. He tells me that Sid's father had married the hotel-keeper's daughter, succeeded to the hotel, which had previously been called the Star, and changed its name to the Cornish Arms. This underlined its connection with Cornish folk, and the Blakes ran a travel-agency for their benefit. (At St. Austell the auctioneer, King Daniel—a name in my youth—was their local agent.) Harry Clarke writes: "It was used mostly by Cornish folk coming and going to England; it was a sort of home away from home. They were also shipping agents and met any boats and trains. I think it was a rather small and old hotel, so Sid Blake decided to tear it down and build a large high-storey new hotel, which he did. He sold shares of stock to raise the money to build, and many Cornish people bought shares in it. It was finished in 1927. I stayed there myself early in July 1927 on my way to England. On that trip I went on the *Majestic*; Sid

Blake sailed on the same ship, and there were around 150 Cornish people on that ship." Not long after that happy voyage "the depression came on and the hotel went bankrupt." So now we know the end of that story.

Narrowing the focus at the end to my native village and my earliest memories, how many of the working people who lived there, and whose children went to the elementary school with me, left home for America! About 1910 my earliest school chum, Ernest Brokenshire—he was eight and I six—left home for Portland, Oregon: I still remember the sense of desolation when he went away. We have managed to keep in touch for over half a century now, and he has written me a few notes on leaving home. He still remembers St. Austell railway station: "often there were returning miners from America. You could always tell them, they wore broad-brimmed hats, ill-fitting light grey suits, and tremendous watch-chains with gold nuggets hanging heavily on them." Then the day came when his father, a remote figure, five years away mining in Oregon, sent for his family. "The same kind of thing was happening around the neighbourhood, and several families we knew had said farewell." The Sunday before leaving it was the regular thing, at Carclaze Methodist Chapel—rising abruptly on the hill and dominating the long straggling village—to read out the names of those leaving and sing 'God be with you till we meet again.' " All this was a closed book to me, going to the parish church in the town below, and that much removed from the inner life of the people; however, I am glad to learn about it now, and to have kept touch across the century, filled with so many happenings and so many estrangements.

For all that the twentieth century is America's century of power and pride, there is a charm upon the nineteenth, a romantic appeal, that this can never touch. Some sense of this comes through in the cult of westerns, of films of the Wild West. For then all was yet to make: it was the really creative period in America's history, when the country was filling up, with a continent to lick into shape. Anything might happen in it, anything could be expected of it: it opened the western gates of the imagination to the Old World, to people in remote Cornish hamlets, as much as to the eastern seaboard, to Horace Greeley and Francis Parkman. It was, indeed, the age of the Oregon Trail, of the trails to California and how many others; of the gold-rushes, sputtering hither and thither, scattering people to California, Nevada, Montana, Colorado, Arizona. The Indians still hunted the immense herds of buffalo that roamed the great plains, and warred against the frontiersmen, the incoming migrants—in how short a time it was all over, twenty-five years and the buffalo, the warring tribes that lived on them, the Wild West, had all vanished!

It was the age of the fabulous trek of the Mormons, with the strange (and true) stories that clustered about them; of the Civil War, with its romantic as well as its harrowing aspects, of Lee and Stonewall Jackson and the tragic Lincoln, with lesser men like Morgan and St. Leger Grenfell skirmishing around them; of the opening up of the West, the mining camps with their excitements, the shootings and the hold-ups in the mountain passes, the stage-coaches like those described by Bret Harte in his mining stories; the age of *The Luck of Roaring Camp,* of "The Jumping Frog of Calaveras County," of *Huckleberry Finn* and the heyday of the Mississippi, rolling its story down to the waters of the Gulf; of the headwaters of the Missouri and the home-made rafts bringing the miners down in the brilliant colors of the fall, or Charlie Vivian spotting a splendid elk swimming the river and changing the name of his club accordingly; of Deadwood Dick and Buffalo Bill, who meant so much to the boys in our village at home, still playing "cowboys and Red Indians" in the early years of the century; of Bob Fitzsimmons' defeat of Gentleman Jim Corbett; of Robert Louis Stevenson on his way to California sharing a railway compartment with Cornish miners, to him a closed book, and never asking them a question; of T. A. Rickard riding across the mountains of Colorado, the men making their way up those gulches, snow or sheen, teaming across the plains, inscribing their now vanished names upon Independence Rock, crossing the Isthmus or rounding Cape Horn to come in at the Golden Gate; or coming up the Great Lakes and in upon the coast of the Upper Peninsula of Michigan, where so many of them now lie in their quiet graves, lulled by the mingled sound of wind in the pines and surf on the shore.

In all this movement, in all the creation and construction, in all the swirling human tides and currents out of which has emerged the greatest of modern nations, the Cornish have been a distinctive element and made their contribution not without significance.

NOTES

1. I owe the above information to the kindness of Mrs. Norman Penhall, of Oklahoma City.
2. See above, p. 155.
3. S. Z. Starr, "Colonel George St. Leger Grenfell: His Pre-Civil War Career," *The Journal of Southern History*, XXX, 278ff.
4. cf. my *Sir Richard Grenville of the Revenge*.
5. Starr, *loc. cit.*, 283.
6. B. W. Duke, *Morgan's Cavalry*, 113–14.
7. *Ibid.*, 132.
8. *Ibid.*, 114.
9. M. C. Weaks, "Colonel George St. Leger Grenfell," *The Filson Club History Quarterly*, vol. 34, 5ff.
10. *Ibid.*, 9–10.
11. *Ibid.*, 11.
12. J. D. Horan, *Confederate Agent*, 184, 191.
13. Weaks, *loc. cit.*, 12.
14. *Ibid.*, 13.

15. Horan, 281.
16. Weaks, 16.
17. Horan, 281.
18. Weaks, 18, 19–20.
19. Horan, 282.
20. J. Spargo, *Americanism and Social Democracy*, 143.
21. *Ibid.*, 165.
22. *Ibid.*, 181.
23. *Ibid.*, 323.
24. *Ibid.*, 150.
25. *Ibid.*, 154.
26. *Ibid.*, 299, 315, 317.
27. J. Spargo, *Early American Pottery and China*, 62.

APPENDIX

Cornish Surnames

The great majority of Cornish people all over the world bear, as I have said, English surnames and in much the same order of popularity as English people—Williams, Johns, Thomas. But a minority bear Cornish names from the old Celtic language by which they are immediately recognizable—Trevelyan, Polglase, Penrose. Interpreting these names is a subject of great difficulty, for they have never been fully studied by qualified Celtic scholars, and there is very little published on the subject that is of any value or reliability. I should never have been able to tackle this subject if it had not been for the generous help that I have received from three scholars: Professor Idris Foster, Professor of Celtic at Oxford, Professor Charles Thomas, Professor of Archaeology at Leicester, and Mr. Richard R. Blewett of St. Day.

Mr. Blewett tells us (*Western Morning News*, April 29, 1967), on the basis of his complete analysis of Cornish names from the Voters' Lists of 1953, that there are still some 750 Celtic names in use, covering some 7700 of the population in Cornwall. This gives us an average of 10 people to an old Celtic name, compared with over 6500 of the name of Williams and its related names. In the course of the last few centuries a number of Celtic names, some of them famous ones like Killigrew, have died out; others have died out in Cornwall, but are represented in America, such as Penhallow, Keigwin and Restarick. In 1953 among names dying out in Cornwall were Trerise (the homestead by the ford) and Pencover (the head of the stream), of whom only one bearer of each name was left.

Some of these names are personally descriptive, e.g. Couch, red-head, but the great bulk of them are descriptive of the places which gave the original bearers their names, e.g. Penrose, head of the heath or hill-spur or promontory. A glimpse at the meanings of these names will show how true they are to the landscape and its simple peasant way of life at the end of the Middle Ages, when these surnames took their rise. It is a poor country of hills and slopes, rocks, heaths, marshes, thornbrakes, thickets, withies, broom, elders; of cliffs, earthworks, hill-forts, longstones, wayside crosses, church-enclosures, hollygroves, woods and copses, broken by patches of cultivation, isolated hamlets, single homesteads by pool, or arable, ford or furze-bushes. Very little of any urban life appears, if at all —in this completely true to Celtic societies everywhere. The comparative popularity of the name Kitto, Christopher's children, or a pet-name for Christopher, opens a door to the imagination—as one entered the door of one's parish church to see the image of the saint painted on the wall opposite the porch.

The most frequent prefix to these names is Tre-, which means homestead, farm, hamlet, village, town (as in Truro or Tréguier in Brittany), or even tribe or clan. The next most frequent is Pen-, which means head, chief, top, end or beginning. Next come Bos-, dwelling place; Pol-, pool or pit; Ros-, heath, moor, promontory or peninsula; Car-, hill-fort or earthwork; Lan-, church enclosure; Nan-, valley; Res-, ford; Hen-, old; Kil-, grove; An-, the definite article, the. With these one has clues to the meaning of the first element in most of these names. There are many difficulties, however; in some cases the original Ros- (heath) has become Res- (ford). The name

Polmear, for example, which means big pool, was originally Porthmear, big beach or cove; Carveth, which one would suppose to mean the earthwork of the grave, was originally Carvergh, and so actually means the earthwork of the horses. And so on. In these problematical cases one needs to know earlier forms of the name, and for these Mr. Blewett has based himself on those collected by Charles Henderson, R. Morton Nance and J. E. B. Gover, whose materials are in the County Museum at Truro.

In the following list my aim has been to reduce the matter to its simplest and most practical: simply to give the meanings of the names for those people interested, and to accent them as a guide to their proper pronunciation.

Andéan, Endéan, the man (i.e. leading man)

Andrewártha (pronounced *an-dre-wártha*), the upper homestead (cf. English "Upton")

Angéar, the fort, earthwork, camp

Angílley, the grove

Angóve, the smith

Angwín, the white or fair man (cf. English "White")

Annéar, the tall, or long, man (cf. English "Long")

Árgall, retreat, shelter

Báragwánath, wheaten bread (cf. English "Whitbread")

Bárnicoat, top of the wood

Behénna, dwelling of Hanna

Bennállick, broom-brake

Bennétto, Bennet's, or Benedict's, children

Beswárrick, dwelling of the cattle-man

Beswétherick, dwelling by the little thicket

Bíddick, personal name Budic

Blámey, ? Cornish form of Bellamy, fair friend

Bóase, dwelling
Bolítho, dwelling in a damp place
Bonýthon, dwelling of Nighton, or Nectan
Borláse, green bank
Bosánko, (originally *Bosánketh*), dwelling in the wood
Boscáwen, dwelling by the elder-tree
Bosústow, dwelling of Ustou, or Ustoc
Boswárva, upper dwelling or end-house
Bray, hill
Búllock, (if Cornish), hare-lipped man
Búzza, dwellings

Cárbis, up to the hill-fort, or earthwork
Cardéw, dark earthwork
Cargéeg, Carkéek, Carkéet, hedged earthwork
Carlýon, earthwork of slate or shale
Cárne, pile of rocks
Carnséw, dark pile of rocks
Carvéth, earthwork of the horses
Chegwín, Chegwídden (*ch* is pronounced *sh*) white, or light-colored, house
Chelléw, house by the pool, or house of Lew
Chenháll, house on the moor
Chenhálls, house on the cliff
Chenóweth, Chynóweth, new house
Chirgwín, house of the fair man
Clémo, Clímo, Clýma, dweller on the slopes
Cloke, Clook, cliff
Coad, Coode, wood
Colénso, enclosure of the pool
Colquíte, narrow wood

Combéllack, originally *Carnebéllack*, pile of rocks among willows
Cónnock, Cúnnack, Cúnnick, personal name
Coombe, Coombes, little valley
Coon, ? dog-man
Couch (pronounced *Cooch*), red, red-haired
Craze, middle of a place
Créba, Crébo, ridges of rocks
Crówgey, hut
Cúndy, house of the dog-man
Curgénven, mound of old rocks
Cúrnow, Cornishman

Dáddow, ? good fellow (cf. English "Goodman")
Dówrick, wet place
Dúngey, field or enclosure by the hill-fort
Dústow (pronounced *Déwstow*), parish name from Davidstow

Édyvéan, house of little ? Edward
Énnis, island, peninsula, isolated place
Énnor, the boundary
Éva, personal name

Fénton, spring or well

Géach, Géake, ? personal name
Géar, hill-fort, earthwork
Godólphin (originally *Gothólgan*), rounded hill, hillock; or ? stream for washing(tin)
Góldsworthy (if Cornish), field of the fair or feast
Gúmmow, little valleys
Gúndry, homestead on the down
Gwávas, winter dwelling

Hénder, Héndra, old homestead
Hóbba, horseman
Hócking (if Cornish), little fellow
Hósken, Hósking, Hóskins, (if Cornish), sedge-marsh

Inch, island

Jágo, (? Jacka), James
Jélbart, Jélbert, Gilbert

Keigwín, light-colored field (cf. English "Whitfield")
Kéllow, groves
Kelýnack, holly-grove
Kent, ? people of the corner
Kérnick, little corner
Késtle, earthwork, castle
Kílligrew, grove of the ? flock or herd
Kítto, Kit's children, pet-name for Christopher
Knúckey, reed-bed, or boggy place

Laíty, milk-house
Lánder, churchyard or enclosure
Lanyón, bleak enclosure or pool
Léah, flat stone
Lean, stitch of land, or pool
Lewárne, enclosure by the marsh
Líddicoat, wood and personal name
Lugg, calf (plural, *Lídgey,* calves)
Lútey, calf-house

Máddern, parish name from Madron
Mágor, ruin, old walls

Ménadúe, dark hill

Menhénick, Menhénitt, Menhínick, parish name from Menheniot, or ? little old rocks

Minéar, Mennéar, Manhíre, long stone, menhir

Moyle, bald

Nancárrow, valley of the deer or stag

Nance, valley

Nancóllas, valley of the hazel-trees

Nankérvis, valley of the deer (plural)

Nankívell, valley of the horse

Nanscáwen, valley of the elder-tree

Noon, the downland, moor

Páscoe, Easter children

Péllow, nickname for round (figure or head)

Pellymóunter, Polmóunter, pool by mineral land

Pelméar (originally *Pórthmear*), big beach

Pénalúna, end or head of the groves or pools

Penbérthy, end of the thickets or bushes

Pendárvis, end of the oak-trees

Pénder, Pénter, Paynter, end of the land

Pendráy, end of the homestead

Penfóund, end of the beech-trees

Pengélly, Pengílly, end of the copse

Pengláse, green top

Penhále, Penháll, end or top of the marsh, or moor

Penháligon, end or head of the willow-trees

Penhállow, end of the marshes

Penhálurick, Penlérick, top of cultivated ground on the moor

Pénna, hill-tops, summits

Pénneck, top of the hillock
Penpráse, end of the meadow
Penríce, end of the ford
Penróse, top of the heath or hill-spur or promontory
Pentréath, top of the beach, end of the sand
Pénver, big hill-top
Penwárden, Penwárne, end of the marsh or alder-grove
Pétherick, Pédrick, Péthick, little Peter or Petroc
Pézzack, decayed, broken-down
Polgláse, green pool
Polgréen, gravel pit
Pólkinghórne, Pólkinhórn, pool of Kynhern (iron chief)
Polméar, big pool
Polsúe, dark pool
Polwhéle, pool in the open field
Praed, meadow
Prídeaux, clay, clay-ground
Prout, proud, puffed-up

Quick, wood or village
Quíntrell, personal name

Rescórla (originally *Roscórla*), heath of the sheepfold
Reséigh, dry ford
Reskélly, ford by the copse
Restárick, watery place
Retállack, steep hill-spur
Ródda, ? personal name
Roscárrock, rocky heathland or hill-spur
Rosdéw, dark heath

Rosemérgy, Rosemúrgy, heath of the horses
Rosevéar, big heath or moor
Rosewárne, swampy heath
Roskílly, heath or hill-spur with copse
Roskrów, moor or heath of the hut
Roskrúge, heath with the mound or barrow
Rule, ? furrow, cleft

Sándry, Sáundry, holy place
Scawn, Scown, elder-tree
Skéwes, sheltered place
Spárgo, thorn-brake

Tállack, steep place
Teague (if Cornish), fair, beautiful
Tóllick, place with holes or pits
Tráthen, ? the sandy place
Trays, Trease, house by the ford
Trebílcock, homestead and personal name? Bill Cock
Tredínnick, homestead at the little fort, or in the bracken
Treffrý, homestead on the hill or slope
Tréganówan, homestead at the mouth, or hollow
Tregárthen, homestead with garden
Tregáskes, Tregáskis, homestead in sheltered place
Tregéa, homestead by the bank or hedge
Tregéagle, Tregágle, homestead of the dunghill
Tregéar, homestead of the earthwork
Tregélles, hidden homestead
Tregémbo, homestead where streams meet
Tregénna, Tregúnna, homestead on the down

Tregénza, foremost, first homestead
Tregídgo, homestead by ? kennels
Tregílgas, homestead and personal name
Treglówn, homestead of the hedged pool
Treháne, homestead of John
Treláwny, homestead of the grove
Treléase, homestead of the court
Treléaven, homestead of the elm-tree
Trelóar, homestead with the garden
Tremáine, Tremáyne, homestead by the stone
Trembáth, homestead in the nook
Trembéth, homestead by the grave or burial
Trembérth, Trenbérth, homestead by the bush
Treméer, homestead by the wall
Tremélling, homestead of the mill
Trémenheére, homestead by the long stone, menhir
Treméwan, homestead and personal name
Trenéar, long homestead, or of the tall man
Trenérry, Trenáry, homestead in the field, or homestead and ? personal name
Trengóve, homestead of the smith
Trengróuse, homestead by the cross
Trenwíth, homestead and personal name
Treríse, homestead by the ford
Tresáwna, Trezóna, homestead at the cleft in the cliff
Treséder, Tresídder (pronounced *Tre-sídder*), homestead and personal name Seder, Sider
Tresíse, Tresíze, homestead of the Englishman
Trestáin, homestead at the tin-place
Trestraíl, homestead of mat- or carpet-maker

Trethéwey, homestead of David (Dewi)
Trethówan, homestead and personal name
Trevaíl, homestead and personal name Mael
Treván, the homestead up above
Trevánion, homestead and personal name Enion
Trevárthen, homestead and personal name Arthien
Trepáskis, homestead and personal name
Trevéan, little homestead
Trevéllick, homestead by the little mill
Trevélyan, *Trevílian*, homestead and personal name Milian
Trevéna, *Trevénna*, homestead on the hill
Trevénen, homestead of the white stone
Trevéthan, homestead by the meadow
Trevíthick, homestead and personal name
Trevórrow, *Trevérrow*, *Trevárrow*, homestead and personal name
Trewártha, upper homestead
Trewávas, winter homestead
Trewéek, homestead at or in the wood
Trewérn (pronounced *Tre-wérn*), *Trewren*, homestead by the marsh
Trewhélla (pronounced *Tre-whélla*), homestead by the stream
Trewín (pronounced *Tre-wín*), fair or white homestead
Trewórgie (pronounced *Tre-wórgie*), homestead and personal name
Trúdgian, *Trúdgeon*, *Trégian*, homestead and personal name
Trúscott (if Cornish), across the wood
Trýthall, homestead and personal name
Tyack, farmer, peasant
Týzzer, (pronounced *Tízzer*) personal name Teuder

Úglow, upper people, ? yeomen
Úren (pronounced Your'n), swamp or marsh; or ? personal name
Ústick (pronounced Yóustick), personal name, or people of St. Just

Várcoe, Vércoe, Mark's children
Veale, personal name Mael
Véllanóweth, the new mill
Vérran, Vérrin, the short man
Vían, the little man
Vísick, finger, finger of land
Vívian, Vývyan, personal name
Vósper, pasture by ditch or rampart

Wállis, Walsh, Welch, stranger (applied by Saxons to Celts)
Warne, Wearn, swamp
Whear, Wheare, green

INDEX

Abd-el-Kader, 404
Abercarn mine disaster, S. Wales, 178
Akron, Ohio, 144–5
Alabama, 133
Alaska, 241, 266, 282, 283, 378, 380, 402
Albright, William Foxwell, 236
Alleghenies, 140, 144
America, South, 33, 77, 150, 162, 211, 268, 404
American Revolution, 64, 73–4, 89, 92, 95, 98, 119, 127, 128, 129–30, 140, 141; —— Socialist Party, 414–7
Anaconda, Mont., 353, 363; — Copper Mining Company, 353, 358, 361
Andersonville, 213, 214
Andrewartha, 29
Andros, Sir Edmund, 50–1
Angel's Camp, Cal., 266
Anglo-Saxons, 3, 15, 16, 18
Anstis, Joe, miner, 384; —, Percy, 395
Apple River, Ill., 214, 227, 250
Argall, 184; —, Philip, 329, 334–5, 337–9
Argo, Colo., smelter at, 327, 328
Arizona, 35, 384–98; —, University of, 396
Arkansas, 99
Arnold, Matthew, 4
Arthur, Thomas, 221
Arundell family, Va., 38–40
Aspinwall, 151, 218.
Atlanta, Ga., 133, 215
Auchincloss, Louis, 76
Australia, 6, 8, 17, 44, 77, 102, 150, 163, 165, 188, 243–4, 249, 374, 379, 421

Bakersfield, Cal., 274
Baltimore family, 123–4; —, Md., 128, 140
Bancroft, Caroline, 344–5
Baragwanath, 33; —, John, 33; —, William, 33
Barrett, Robert, 37–8
Beach Lake Colony, Pa., 110–3
Belfast, N. Ireland, 310–1
Beloit, Wis., 11, 229
Bellingham, Wash., 421
Bennett, Captain Dick, 9; —, James, 209–10; —, Hon. Joseph, 223
Bennington, Vt., 418–9
Berger, Victor, 415
Berkeley, Cal., 281, 282, 372
Berkeley, John, Lord, 62
Berryman brothers, 20, 167; — fam-

439

Index

Berryman brothers (continued)
ily, Cal., 268; ——, Idaho, 299–300; ——, Wash., 379; —, William, 270
Bethlehem, Pa., 113
Bice, William, 177
Bickford, George, 270; —, William, 270
Bilkey, Charles, 204
Billing, Edward, founder of New Jersey, 60–9; Billingsport, 69
Bingham Canyon, Utah, 313, 314, 316
Birmingham, Ala., 133
Bisbee, Ariz., 10, 388, 389–91
Black Hawk, Colo., smelter at, 324, 325, 326, 327, 344; —— War, 197, 202, 203
Blake, Sid, 79, 422–3
Blewett, W. H., 249
Blue Ridge Mountains, Va., 201–2
Boer War, 260, 369, 412
Boise, Idaho, 299; — Basin, 298
Bolitho, 29; — family, Cornwall, 364; ——, Utah, 317; ——, Va., 41, 117–8; —, Hector, 29; —, Captain John, 103
Bonython, 8, 29, 38, 42; — family, Mass., 43–5; —, Sir Langdon, 44, 45
Booth, Edwin, 295
Bootle, Eng., smelter at, 330
Boscawen, Admiral Edward, 4, 29; —, N.H., 29, 35
Boston, Mass., 47, 51, 169, 175, 189, 333
Boulder, Colo., 336
Bowden family, Mont., 358
Bray, 177; —, Hon. A. F., 357–8
Brazil, 210, 211
Bree, John, 261
Bristol, Eng., 91, 97, 101, 102
British Columbia, 190, 268, 273, 282, 380
Brittany, 5, 102; Bretons, 16, 28, 183 270
Brokenshire, A. E., 423; —, J. R.,

Brontes, the, 4
Brooklyn, N.Y., 82, 151
Buckingham, Thomas, 210
Buffalo, N.Y., 76, 165
Burlington, N.J., 65, 67, 72
Burns, John, 412, 417
Burrell, Paul, 104–6
Butte, Mont., 10, 22, 174, 328, 331, 351–62, 363, 420; —, Cornish in, 362, 363; — Miners' Brass Band, 360–2
Buzza, Captain, 172

California, 12–3, 21, 135, 142, 166, 178, 208–11, 216, 241–83, 287, 289–90, 323, 353, 387; Southern —, 272–9; —, University of, 283; Californian mining stamps, 164
Calumet, Mich., 182, 183; — and Hecla Mine, 166, 171, 174
Camborne, Cornwall, 161, 163, 165, 166, 189, 201, 202, 245, 325, 356
Cambridge, Eng., 46; —, Mass., 48
Camden, N.J., 71, 72, 109
Canada, 51, 76, 77, 171, 180, 274, 332, 365, 380, 407
Cape Cod, Mass., 34
Carbondale, Ill., 148
Carclaze Methodist Church, St. Austell, Cornwall, 423; —, school, 421, 422
Carleton College, Minn., 157–8
Carson City, Nev., 294–5, 296–7; — Valley, 287, 288
Carveth, Thomas, 72
Casco, Me., 43, 52
Catchfrench, Cornwall, 94
Celtic languages, 3
Central City, Colo., 11, 334, 335, 343; — Mine, Mich., 20, 174, 186
Chancellorsville, battle of, 135
Chapin Mine, Mich., 177, 178
Charleston, S.C., 107, 129–31
Charlestown, Mass., 51–2, 53

Charlotte, N.C., 129
Chattanooga, battle of, 75
Chenoweth, 7, 29, 72, 128, 148; — family, Ariz., 397; ——, Colo., 342; ——, Ky., 140–1; ——, Ore., 367; — Massacre, 141; —, J. E., 342; —, Lemuel, 142; —, Richard, 140–2
Chicago, 151, 205, 216, 223, 227, 237, 332, 407–9; —, University of, 100
Chickamauga, battle of, 17, 213–4, 215, 250
Chile, 33, 162
China, 248, 266; Chinese miners, 248, 259
China clay industry, 165, 419
Chynoweth, 141–2, 175, 270
Civil War, American, 17, 75, 120–1, 135, 223, 235, 242, 342, 387, 404–6, 424; —, Cornish in, 211–6; English ——, 45, 49
Clark, George Rogers, 141; —, Senator William A., 327–8, 352–4, 361–2, 392
Clarke, T. H., 331, 395, 420–2
Cleveland, Ohio, 144
Cliff Mine, Mich., 78, 174, 180; —, Captain John, 174
Clyma, 82; —, Francis, 202
Coad, Samuel, 366–7
Cock family, Va., 117–8
Cocking, Stephen, lighthouse keeper, 179
Colenso, 33; —, Bishop J. W., 8; ––, William, 8
Colorado, 35, 100, 282, 317, 322–48, 356, 368, 379, 392; —, University of, 339, 341; — Springs, 100, 331, 339, 340
Columbia University, N.Y.C., 146; — School of Mines, 353
Commonwealth Mine, Ariz., 13, 35, 100
Comstock Lode, Nev., 267, 387, 389–91
Connecticut, 46, 48

Coode family, Md., 127; —, Col. John, 122–7
Coon, Professor Carleton S., 8, 15
Cooperation, 152, 153
Copeland, Louis J., 198, 201, 216, 221–23
Copper Harbor, Mich., 171, 179
Copper Mining, 161–2, 166–76, 243, 316, 351–4, 356–8, 384–95
Corbett, "Gentleman Jim," prize-fighter, 294–5
Cornell University, N.Y., 146
Cornish Arms Hotel, N.Y.C., 79, 422–3
Cornish brass bands, 78–9, 207, 220, 360–2; — characteristics, 16–20, 186–7, 221–3, 258; — cooking, 11, 220, 230, 258, 263, 344–5, 360; — dialect, 186–7, 222, 343, 344, 359; — language, 25; — place-names in U.S., 34–5; — pumping engine, 13, 78, 162–5, 315–6; — societies, 185–6; — temperament, 15, 186–7; — wrestling, 16, 293, 360
Cornish, 52, 274; — family, Cal., 261; —, T. J., 274
Cornwall, 5, 24–5, 49, 61, 86, 90, 112, 161–6, 189, 190–2, 236, 267, 330, 356, 365, 372, 373–4, 411
Cornwall, Conn.; —, N.Y.; —, Pa.; —, Vt., 35; — Ironworks, Pa., 95–6
Couch, 26; —, Captain Thomas, 26, 356–7
Council Bluffs, Iowa, 250, 278
Cowling, Donald J., 157–8
Cox, Phil, murdered miner, 206
Crimean War, 404
Cripple Creek, Colo., 322, 328–9, 335, 336, 337, 338, 339–40
Cromwell, Oliver, 49
Cuba, 178, 208
Curnow, 77, 178, 392, 393; —, Alan, 8
Cutt, John, 54; —, Mary, 54, 55
Cynthiana, Ky., raid on, 405

Index

Dakota, *see* South Dakota
Dale, Edward, 244–5
Daly, Marcus, 352–4
Daniell, Captain John, 174–5
Davey family, 113
Davies, Joe, 210
Davis, Jefferson, 119–20
Davy, Sir Humphrey, 6, 142
Dawe family, 391
Dayton, Ohio, 142
Deadwood, S.D., 363
Debs, Eugene, 152
Delaware, 402; — River, 59, 96, 97, 103, 104
Democratic Party, 136, 305, 309
Denver, Colo., 282, 322, 325, 328, 329–30, 335, 338, 339, 379; —, Cornish in, 347–8
Des Moines, Iowa, 143–4
Detroit, 167, 421–2; —, Cornish in, 180–2; — Trades Assembly, 151
Devon, Eng., 161, 163
Devonport, Eng., 106, 190, 301
Dickens, Charles, 232, 292
Dimmick, George, 214
Dodge, Governor Henry, 197–8, 202, 207
Dodgeville, Mich., 198, 200, 207, 210, 217–8, 220
Dolcoath Mine, Cornwall, 325, 364
Donner Party, 253–4
Douglas, Ariz., 391; —, Dr. James, 388, 389
Drexel Bank, Philadelphia, 394
Drury, Wells, 291–3
Duke, General Basil W., 405–6
Dunstan, Hon. T. B., 173
Durham Ironworks, Pa., 89
Dutch Flat, Cal., 248, 259
Dyer, Hon. W., 356; —, James, 411; —, Philip, 364–5

Eagle Harbor, Mich., 166, 179, 180; — River, 168, 169, 172, 173, 185, 188
Echo Canyon, 308
Edgcumbe, John, 42; —, Nicholas, 42; Sir Richard, 43; —, Lord Mount, 43
Edwards family, 172; —, Captain Richard, 172, 188–9
Elizabeth City, Va., 40
Elks, Order of, 17, 331, 333
Emma Mine, Utah, 313–4, 315
Empire Mine, Cal., 11, 246, 260, 262, 263
Erie Canal, 148, 202, 227, 231
Esterbrook, Richard, 108–9
Eugene, Oregon, 374
Eureka Mine, Cal., 261, 263
Eustice, Richard, 199
Exmouth, Admiral, 1st Viscount, 127; —, 6th Viscount, 127–8; *see also* Pellew

Falmouth, Cornwall, 39, 67, 80–1, 106, 226, 231, 232, 251; —, Me., 34–5; —, Mass., 35
Farmers' Guard, Wis., 212
Faull, J. P., 388
Featherstonhaugh, G. W., 205–6
Fendall, Governor J., 123
Fenwick, John, 62–3, 67
Figg-Hoblyn, Mrs., 273–4
Fitzsimmons, Bob, prize-fighter, 16, 293–5
Florida, 37, 135, 136–7
Foote family, Ariz., 397; ——, Va., 119; —, Senator H. S., 119–21; —, J. M., 397
Fort Benton, Mont., 352, 355
Forty-Niners, 208–11, 241, 243–6, 249–55
Fowey, Cornwall, 45, 50, 86
Fox family, Cornwall, 94, 163; —, George, 61, 67, 68; —, James, 94; —, Joseph, 94–5; —, Josiah, naval designer, 106–8
Foxwell colony, Wis., 231–6; — family, Wash., 375, 378; —, John, 231–4; —, William, 231
France, 270, 403–4, 415–6
Franklin, Benjamin, 91, 92
Freighting, 264, 266, 387

Index 443

Frémont, General J. C., 257, 281
Froude, J. A., 292
Funk and Wagnall's *Dictionary*, 413

Galena, Ill., 148, 178, 196–7, 202, 205–6, 214, 215, 216, 227, 387
Gallatin, Tenn., 408
Galloway, Grace Growden, 89–90, 103–4; —, Joseph, 21, 89
George family, 235; —, Harold, 257–8; —, Henry, 368
Georgia, 132–3
Geronimo, Apache chief, 384–5, 386
Gettysburg, battle of, 212
Giles family, Cal., 258
Gladstone, W. E., 412
Glanville, John, 149
Globe, Ariz., 385–8
Godolphin, 33, 39; Lord Treasurer —, 16; —, Professor F. R. B., 33
Gold Mining, 241–6, 256–7, 259, 263, 272, 287–8, 297, 322–4, 329, 351–2, 363, 366
Gold Rush to California, 203, 208–11, 216, 241–55, 366
Goldsworthy, J. C., 274; —, Thomas, 213
Gorges, Sir Ferdinando, 20, 41
Graeme Park, Pa., 91, 101
Granite, Okla., 401–2
Grant, President U.S., 77, 154, 196, 225, 292
Grass Valley, Cal., 9, 11, 246–9, 256–8, 260, 261, 262–3, 276, 289, 356, 392; —— Choir, 11–2, 257–8
Great Falls, Mont., 363
Greeley, Horace, 169
Greenback Party, 153
Grenfell family, Cornwall, 403; —, George, 8, 403; —, Col. G. St. L., 402–11, 420; —, Sir Wilfred, 8, 403
Grenville, Sir Richard, 4, 38
Gribbel, James, 109; —, John, 109–10
Gribble, Harold, 388–9

Growden, Grace, 89–90; —, Joseph, 87–8; —, Joseph, Jr., 88; —, Lawrence, 21, 86–7; —, Lawrence, Jr., 88–9
Grubb family, Pa., 95–6; —, Henry, 97
Grylls, 395; —, H. M. M., architect, 180
Guadalupe-Hidalgo, Treaty of, 267
Guggenheims, the, 340

Haarlem Meer, 163
Halifax, Nova Scotia, 76
Hall, Captain Josiah, 173
Hallam, Judge Oscar, 219–21, 223–6
Hambley, E. B. C., 128–9
Hambly family, Cal., 265; —, Loveday, 61
Hancock, Mich., 166–7, 173, 178, 182, 183, 364
Hardy, Thomas, 5, 90
Harper, Captain R. B., 268–9
Harris, Hon. W., 173
Harrisburg, Pa., 114
Harry, Captain James, 267–8; —, John, 163
Harte, Bret, 248, 332, 424
Harvard College, 47–8, 53, 136, 229
Harvey Foundry, Cornwall, 163, 164; —, John, 163; —, Len, boxer, 16
Hawkins, Sir John, 37
Hayle, Cornwall, 163
Hazel Green, Wis., 198, 199, 218, 219, 230, 356
Hearst, George, 257, 315, 353, 363; —, W. R., 257, 282
Heinze, F. A., 358
Helena, Mont., 297, 332, 351, 352, 355, 363
Hendra, Christopher, 229–30
Herrin, Ill., 228
Hicks, 51, 229; —, Obadiah, 151
Hill, Professor N. P., 324, 326, 327
Hillquitt, Morris, 415–6
Hoar family, 171; —, Captain John, 171
Hocking, Henry, 170; —, Professor

Hocking, Henry (*continued*)
  W. E., 229
Holland, 47, 163
Holman Foundry, Cornwall, 163
Homestake Mine, S.D., 363–5
Honolulu, 142, 277, 278–9
Hooper, F. W., 262
Hoover, President Herbert, 257, 280–1, 305, 418
Hornblower family, 164, 305, 306
Hosken (Hoskin, Hosking, Hoskins), 80, 218, 277; Henry Hosking, 274
Houghton, Mich., 166–7, 172, 180, 182, 183; — Technological University, 168; —, Douglass, 167–8
Houston, Tex., 402
Howe, Helen, 14
Hudson's Bay Company, 365
Humboldt Sink, 244–5
Humphreys, Joshua, 106–8
Hutchinson, Mrs., 48

Idaho, 297–300, 379, 392
Illinois, 148, 149, 209, 302, 372, 380; —, Cornish in, 218–9, 249–50; — Volunteer Infantry, 213–5; —, University of, 146
Independence Rock, 253, 376
Indiana, 142, 143–4, 264, 421; —, University of, 228
Indianapolis, Ind., 143
Indians, American, 39, 44, 45, 55, 70, 140, 248, 424; Apaches, 384–6, 387; Creek, 132; Narragansetts, 54; Nez Percés, 300; Pawnees, 376; Pequots, 47; Sioux, 253, 376; Winnebagos, 197
International, First, 151
Iowa, 143, 155–7, 231, 235, 236, 300, 375
Iron Mining, 176–9
Iron Mountain, Mich., 176, 177, 182, 184
Irish miners, 169–70, 248, 343, 345, 354, 359–60

Isbell, David, 213; —, Jason, 213
Ishpeming, Mich., 176–7, 182–3, 184
Italian miners, 168, 169, 345, 391
Ivey, Henry, 266

Jackson, John, 218–9; —, General "Stonewall," 13, 212
James family, Cal., 262; — —, Wash., 375–8; —, Edward, 202; —, Samuel, 234–5, 375–8
James II, 50; *see also* York, Duke of
Jamestown, Va., 39, 343
Jefferson, President Thomas, 107
Jehovah's Witnesses, 236
Jenkin, 395, 398
Jenkins, Thomas, 211
Jennings, Samuel, 67
Jerome, Ariz., 391–2
Jewell family, Cal., 250–2; — —, Idaho, 298–9; —, Hon. E. S., 298–9; —, William, 250–2
Johnson, President Andrew, 408, 410
Johnston, General A. S., 302
Johnsville, Cal., 263
Joinville, Prince de, 197, 206
Jose, 32; —, Dick, ballad singer, 295

Kansas, 100, 146–7; —, University of, 147; — City, 301, 393
Keats, John, 4
Keigwin, 33
Kennedy, President J. F., 3
Kentucky, 119, 140–3, 214; —, Morgan's Raids in, 405
Kern County Land Company, 274
Keweenaw Peninsula, Mich., 166–7, 176, 190
Key West, Fla., 409
Killigrew, 33, 39, 143
Kimber, 102–3; —, Richard, 102
Kingdon brothers, 388–9; —, George, 392
Kittery, Me., 42
Kitto, 11, 229; —, Captain Richard, 78
Kittoe, Surgeon General Edward, 215–6

Klondike, 380
Knights of Labor, 153, 369
Knoxville, Tenn., 133

Lake Champlain, 78, 113, 127
Lake Erie, 135, 144
Lake Superior, 20, 96, 148, 166, 167, 207
Land's End, Cornwall, 4, 161, 226
Langhorne, Jeremiah, 89
Lanyon, 237; — family, Wis., 203–4; —, Henry, 203–4
Laramie, Fort, 244, 376
Las Vegas, Nev., 297
Laurel Hill, Philadelphia, 92
Lavender, David, 346–7
Lawrence, Kan., 147; —, G. A., novelist, 314
Laxey Methodist Church, Wis., 219–20
Lead, S.D., 363, 365
Lead Mining, 196–207, 223
Leadville, Colo., 322, 325, 328, 330–1, 332
Lean, William, 174
Lee, General Robert E., 405
Lenin, V. I., 414, 415
Lexington, Ky., 252, 253
Lincoln, President Abraham, 120, 121, 148, 197, 207, 211, 213, 409
Linden, Wis., 199–200, 203, 213, 220, 221
Lizard Peninsula, Cornwall, 231, 234; — Point, 226, 232
Logan, Utah, 307, 308
London, Eng., 52, 165, 306, 325, 339, 340, 412, 417
Longfellow, H. W., 45, 169
Look Out Mountain, battle of, 214
Lord, Eliot, 289, 291
Los Angeles, Cal., 274–7, 295, 353
Louisiana, 134–6; — Purchase, 98–9
Louisville, Ky., 141, 215
Luke, William, 262
Lutey, Captain John, 231
Luxulyan, Cornwall, 80, 263–4

Lynnhaven, Va., 41

Macdonald, J. R., 412, 417
Madoc, legendary Welsh prince, 385
Maine, 20, 34–5, 41–5
Manning, Bishop W. T., 278
Marblehead, Mass., 44, 47, 50
Marquette, Mich., 168, 176, 182, 183, 268, 400
Maryland, 122–8
Marx, Karl, 151, 412, 414; — family, 412
Masons, Order of, 185, 387, 396
Massachusetts, 41–53, 73–4, 97
Matthews, Professor J. T., 372–4; —, Thomas, 67; —, Judge W. C., 344
Maurier, Daphne du, 230
May family, Mont., 363
Melville, Herman, 197
Menhennick, 29; Menhinnick family, 146–7
Methodism, Cornish, 9, 148–9, 157, 184–5, 191, 192, 207, 218, 219–21, 230, 232–4, 259–60, 268, 411, 423
Mexico, 10, 37, 149, 269, 388
Michigan, 21, 149, 166–93, 218, 340, 392, 425; — Volunteers, 179; —, University of, at Ann Arbor, 172, 173, 304
Milwaukee, Wis., 178
Minear, 29, 155
Mineral Point, Wis., 10, 12, 199–200, 202–8, 217, 220, 224, 230
Miners, *see* individual nationalities
Miners' Guard, Wis., 207, 211–3
Minneapolis, Minn., 157, 158
Minnesota, 35, 157–8
Mississippi, 119–20, 357; — River, 147–8, 196, 203, 208, 215, 301, 424
Missouri, 145–6, 252, 302; — River, 209, 332, 352, 355, 424
Montana, 210, 211, 227, 297, 327, 328, 332, 351–63, 379, 384, 392, 420, 421

Index

Montez, Lola, 248–9
Morcom, 365
Morgan, General J. H., 405
Morgan, Grenfell and Company, 403
Mormons, 278, 287–8, 301–19, 376, 385, 424
Morocco, 404
Morton, Charles, 52–3
Mount Vernon, Va., 118
Moyle, 26; — family, Utah, 301–6; —, Henry, 302; —, Henry D., 306; —, James, 301–3; —, James H., 303–6; —, John R., 301–2; — family, Wis., 235–6; —, Thomas, 231–4; —, Walter, 305
Mudd, Dr. Samuel, 409–10
Mullion, Cornwall, 235

Nancarrow, 30, 207; —, Captain James, 314–5; —, John, 103–4
Nankivell, 30, 237
Napoleon, 219, 235
Nashville, Tenn., 214, 215
National Labor Union, 151, 152
Neal, Robert, 12, 230
Nebraska, 158–9, 251–2, 368
Negaunee, Mich., 176, 183, 184
Negro Slavery, 65, 107–8
Netherlands, 46
Nevada, 166, 218, 287–97, 356, 392; — City, Cal., 246–9, 256–8
New Almadén, Cal., 12, 242, 266–9
Newark, N.J., 71, 72
New Castle, Delaware, 86
New England, 39, 41–56; —, Dominion of, 50–1
Newfoundland, 42
New Hampshire, 41, 44, 54–6
New Harmony, Ind., 264
New Jersey, 59–72, 96–7, 218, 392; — Concessions and Agreements, 63–5
New Mexico, 385
New Orleans, La., 134–5, 136, 151, 214, 215
Newquay, Cornwall, 189, 338

New York, 72–82; — City, 72–3, 104, 188, 252, 332–3, 413, 414, 422–3
New Zealand, 8, 29, 150, 165, 294, 338, 421
Nicaragua route to California, 209, 210, 244, 251
Nicholls, Nichols, 420; — family, Cal., 259; — —, La., 134–6; —, General F. T., 134–6; —, "Uncle Ab," 205–6, 207
Nicholson, Governor F., 126
Norfolk, Va., 107, 122
Normal, Ill., 230
North Carolina, 128–9, 317, 390
North Western Conspiracy, 406–8
Nova Scotia, Can., 35, 76

Oakland, Cal., 271, 332, 357.
Oates, Captain George, 338
Ogden, Utah, 309, 317, 318, 352
Ohio, 108, 142, 144–5, 146; — River, 140–1
Oklahoma, 155, 401–2; — City, 155
Old Dominion smelter, Ariz., 385–6
Olver family, Pa., 110–3
Omaha, Neb., 158–9
Ontario Mine, Utah, 315–6
Ontonagon River, Mich., 166, 169–70
Opie, 401
Oregon, 147, 214, 231, 253, 365–75, 423; — Trail, 297–8, 375
Oxford, Eng., 52

Pachuca, Mex., 10, 149
Padstow, Cornwall, 39, 81, 132
Palamountain, 32
Panama route to California, 150, 244, 261
Paris, Fr., 403–4, 405
Park City, Utah, 315–6
Parnall, Captain William, 175
Pasadena, Cal., 276, 277
Pasco, Senator Samuel, 136–7
Pascoe, 32, 34, 178, 190, 276, 402;

Pascoe (continued)
— family, Ariz., 387–8; — —,
Cal., 275; — —, Mich., 180–1;
—, Richard, song writer, 180;
—, William, portrait painter,
180
Paul, Professor R. W., 246, 289–90,
323–4
Paynter, Thomas, 217
Pearce, 200, 276, 277, 347; —, Ariz.,
13, 392–4; —, James, 13, 392–
4; —, Richard, 10, 323, 324–30
Pellew family, 127–8; see also Exmouth
Pelleymounter, 32
Pellow family, Okla., 401–2
Penberthy, 11, 28, 180; —, John, 210–1
Pendarvis (Pendarves), 28, 82; — family, S.C., 8, 28, 129–31
Pender, W. R., 270
Pengelly (Pengilly), 28, 52, 72, 275; Pengilly, Minn., 35; —, W. G., 145
Penhall family, Okla., 401–2; —, Bennet, a Cornish character, 260
Penhallow, 8, 28; — family, N.H., 52–6; —, Pearce W., 56; —, Chief Justice Samuel, 52–6
Penn, Admiral Sir William, 85; —, William, 60, 62, 63–4, 66, 67, 85–8; —, —, Jr., 88
Pennsylvania, 20–1, 59–60, 85–114, 165, 171; —, Cornish in, 113–4; — Historical Society, 93, 100–1, 110; —, University of, 100
Penrice family, N.C., 128; —, John, 40
Penrose, 8, 27, 71, 101, 276; — family, Georgia, 132; — —, Pa., 8, 20–1, 97–101, 106; —, Bartholomew, 21, 97–8; —, Senator Boies, 21, 99; —, Boies, 15, 100; —, Charles B., 99, 100; —, Clement B., 98–9; —, Col. Joseph, 98; —, Richard A. F., 99–100, 316, 329, 393–4; —, Spencer, 99, 100, 316, 329, 339–40; — family, Utah, 306–12; —, Charles W., Mormon leader, 27, 304, 306–12
Penryn, Cornwall, 122, 127, 411
Penzance, Cornwall, 118, 190, 372–4, 403
Perkiomen, Pa., 164–5, 188
Perranzabulo, Cornwall, 201, 203
Perrigo, Lynn, 324, 342
Perth Amboy, N.J., 69–71
Peru, 33, 150, 162
Peter, Hugh, 27, 45–50; —, Robert, 142–3; —, Thomas, 49
Petherick (Pedrick, Pidrick), 63, 69, 71
Phelps, Dodge, Company, 385, 388, 390
Philadelphia, Pa., 90, 93–4, 95, 97–8, 100, 101, 102, 104–7, 109, 113–4, 165
Phoenix, Ariz., 389, 392, 397–8
Pidrick, William, 77
Pike's Peak, Colo., 100, 225, 323
Piscataqua, Me., 42, 48, 56
Pittsburgh, Pa., 104, 142, 165
Placer Mining, 245, 250, 351–2
Placerville, Cal., 209, 250, 251
Platte River, 244, 253, 297–8
Platteville, Wis., 199, 203, 211
Plymouth, Eng., 39, 41, 90, 94, 301; — Company, 20, 38–9; — Meeting, Pa., 90, 94
Polkinghorn (Polkinghorne), 16, 28, 224, 277; —, W. A., 274–5
Polygamy in Utah, 303–4, 310–11, 312
Pomeroy, 214
Populist Party, 369
Portage Lake, Mich., 166, 167, 170, 171
Portland, Me., 34–5; —, Ore., 365, 367, 375, 423
Portsmouth, N.H., 54
Potomac River, 203–4

Pottsville, Pa., 85
Powell, Mrs. Keith, 371-2
Price, Judge Rose, 150
Prideaux, 38; —, Benjamin, 213
Princeton, N.J., 71
Prisk, C. H., 276; —, W. F., 276
Prouse, William, 287-8
Prout, 398; —, John, 389-90
Pryor, Rev. J. T., 221

Quakers, 59-69, 85-94, 123; Cornish —, 21, 67, 86-90, 94, 101, 103-4, 106-8, 109, 163
Quantrill's Raid, Kan., 147, 372
Quebec, Can., 81, 113, 179
Quicksilver Mining, 266-9
Quiller-Couch, Sir Arthur, 26, 411
Quincy Mine, Mich., 166, 364

Rablin, William, 204
Ralegh, Sir Walter, 38, 288
Raleigh, N.C., 129
Rawle family, Pa., 21, 90-4; —, Francis I, 90, 94; —, Francis II, 90-1; —, Francis III, 92; —, Francis IV, 93; —, William, 92-3, 99; —, W. B., 93; —, W. H., 93
Ray, Ariz., 394-5
Reconstruction (after Civil War), 136, 137
Redruth, Cornwall, 161, 166, 225
Read, Charles, 97
Red Jacket, Mich., 180
Reed, Thomas, 226-7
Reno, Nev., 292, 296-7
Republican Party, 173, 180, 203, 223, 341, 357, 359
Rescarrick family, N.J., 69-71
Restarick, Bishop H. B., 277-9, 398
Revolution of 1688, 51, 124
Richards, 214
Richmond, Va., 75, 122, 214
Rickard, Captain James, 281; —, Donald S., 187-90; —, Edgar, 280, 283; —, R. H., 187-90; —, Tom, 383; —, T. A., 242, 279-83, 290-1, 326, 329, 334-7,

390, 393
Roanoke Colony, (1585-6), 38
Roberts, James, 218; —, John, 243, 245-6; —, William, 167
Rochester, N.Y., 76, 77
Rock Island Prison, 407
Rockland, Mich., 170
Rocky Mountains, 244, 322, 326, 336
Roosevelt, President F. D., 305, 306, 362, 418; —, — Theodore, 278-9, 370, 371
Roscarrock, 39
Rosevear, 28
Roskelly family, Utah, 313
Roskruge, George J., Ariz. pioneer, 395-7
Rouse, Nicholas, 52
Rowe family, Mont., 354-5; —, Wis., 199; —, Samuel, 149
Rowse, 237; — family, Utah, 317; —, J. J., 317; —, Sir Anthony, 38
Rule, John, 163
Rundle, 177
Russian Revolution, 418

Saco, Me., 43, 44
Sacramento, Cal., 243, 250-1, 271-2
Safety Fuses in mines, 173, 198, 270
St. Austell, Cornwall, 30, 87, 101, 110, 161, 163, 166, 259, 356, 394, 401, 423
St. Juliot, Cornwall, 90
St. Just, Cornwall, 161, 166, 325, 337, 403
St. Louis, Mo., 145, 196, 415; —, Washington University at, 146
Salem, Mass., 47, 48, 53; —, N.J., 63, 71; —, Ore., 147, 371, 372, 374; —, Willamette University at, 372
Salt Lake City, Utah, 209, 210, 301-3, 304-5, 312, 333; —, Cornish in, 318; —, building the Temple at, 302-3
San Bernardino, Cal., 279
San Diego, Cal., 277, 278, 279, 298

Index   449

San Francisco, Cal., 190, 244, 245, 247, 252, 254, 255, 265, 268, 282–3, 287, 294, 331, 366, 378; —, Cornish in, 271
San José, Cal., 12–3, 265
Santa Barbara, Cal., 273, 391
Santa Fé Trail, 254, 278
Saroyan, William, 7
Sawle, 10
Scales Mound, Ill., 209, 230, 250, 251, 380
Scandinavian miners, 168, 346
Schenck, General R. C., 313–4, 315
Schuylkill River, Pa., 92, 102
Scilly Isles, Cornwall, 5, 149–50, 151, 228
Scots, 6, 16, 17, 327
Scripps College, Cal., 278; —, George, 278
Seattle, Wash., 378, 380–1
Seville, Spain, 37
Seward, Secretary W. H., 407
Shaddick, "the Scotch giant," 206
Shepherd family, Wash. and Wis. pioneers, 234
Sherman, General W. T., 215
Ships: *Abigail*, 40; *Adelaide*, 80–1; *Alabama*, 314; *Annie Wilson*, 235; *Anson*, 231; *Batavia*, 325; *Benton*, 365; *Bona Nova*, 39; *Chesapeake*, 107; *Chimborazo*, 312; *China*, 314; *Clio*, 81; *Cornwall*, 80–1; *Deer Lodge*, 365; *Desire* (I), 47; *Desire* (II), 90, 94; *Diligence*, 98; *Illinois*, 170; *Ivanhoe*, 171; *Kent*, 65; *Lady of the Lake*, 235; *London*, 226; *Majestic*, 422–3; *Orient*, 231–3; *Philadelphia*, 107; *Siddons*, 218; *Speedwell*, 41–2; *Springflower*, 111; *Titanic*, 30; *Trent*, 270; *True Love*, 40
Shoemaker, Samuel, 92
Shullsburg, Wis., 12
Silver Mining, 288–91, 314–6, 322, 325, 326, 328, 330–1
Skewes, 235
Slidell, John, 405

Smelting, 323–8, 337
Smith, Joseph, Mormon leader, 302
Snake River, Idaho, 298, 300
South Africa, 8, 260, 369, 412
South Bend, Ind., 143
South Carolina, 129–30
South Dakota, 172, 173, 297, 363–5
Southern Pacific Railroad, 264, 317
Spain, 37–8, 242; Spanish Armada, 111
Spargo family, Utah, 317–8; —, John, socialist writer, 8, 411–20; —, J. N., 317–8; —, J. W., 229
Spettigue family, Pa., 110–3
Spokane, Wash., 231
Staging, 205, 264
Stamp Act, 95
Stanford University, 103
Stanton, Secretary E. M., 406, 409
State-in-Schuylkill, Pa., 95
Staten Island, 72
Stephens Colony, Wis., 203
Stevenson, R. L., 255–6
Stockdale, William, 303
Stockholm Conference (1917), 416
Stockton, Cal., 264–5
Stone, Major Valentine, 410
Stratton, W. S., 339
Sutter's Fort, Cal., 252, 254
Swansea, S. Wales, 323, 324, 325, 326, 327, 337, 392
Syracuse, N.Y., 76

Tamar River, Eng., 5, 38, 112, 161
Tamarack Mine, Mich., 175
Tamblyn family, 259–60; — —, Pa., 110–3
Taylor, John, and Sons, 389
Tennessee, 133–4, 215; —, Army of the, 215, 245
Terrell, 170, 203
Texas, 99, 402
Thomas, Captain Josiah, 364; —, Newton G., 161, 191–3
Thompson, Hon. Philip, 119
Tippett, 214
Tombstone, Ariz., 13, 388, 389, 392.

450 Index

Tombstone, Ariz. (*continued*) 393
Tonkin (Tonkyn), 180, 274
Toronto, Can., 274
Tortugas, Dry, 408–11
Traver, Robert, (Judge Voelcker), 187
Trebilcock, 30; —, Paul, portrait painter, 8, 81
Tredinnick, 200; —, Nicholas, 218
Treffry, 27, 45, 50; — brothers, 50
Treganowan, 82
Tregangeeves, Cornwall, 87, 101
Tregaskis, 127; — family, Idaho, 299; —, Richard, war-correspondent, 8
Tregeagle family, S.C., 131; — —, Utah, 318
Tregear, 127; —, Edwin, 8
Tregenza, 199
Tregidgo, Nicholas, 71
Tregloan family, Mont., 355–6
Treglown, 230; — family, Cal., 270; — and Sons, Wis., 200
Tregoning, J. J., 379–80
Tregonissey, St. Austell, Cornwall, 22, 224, 422
Treherne brothers, 40
Trelawny, Robert, 20, 41–3, 45
Trelease, 8, 229; Mount —, Colo., 8, 146; —, Professor William, botanist, 145–6; —, S. F., 146
Treleaven, 179; —, Thomas, 263–4
Treloar family, Iowa, 155–6; —, Mich., 201; —, Sam, 361–2; —, William, 395, 400
Tremain (Tremaine), 8, 28, 81, 144; — family, N.Y., 73–6; —, Ben, 223; —, H. B., 75; —, I. H., 155; —, John, 72–3; —, Jonathan, 75–6; —, Lyman, 75
Tremaine's Village, N.Y., 35
Tremayne, 73
Tremewan family, Oregon pioneers, 366
Trenbath family, Washington pioneers, 380

Trengrouse, Henry, 6
Trenouth family, 265
Trenton, N.J., 71, 72
Trerice, H. O. Company, 237; —, Nicholas, 51–2
Trerise, Captain J. H., 358
Treseder, 30; — family, Utah, 312–3
Tresize, 179, 229
Trestrail, 178
Tretheway family, 264–5
Trevaskis, 12
Trevellick, Richard F., labor leader, 149–54
Trevelyan, 7; —, Sir George O., 7, 412
Trevethan, 41, 118; — family, Mich., 179–80
Trevilians, Va., 8
Trevillian, 7, 118, 122; —, Jimmy, prize-fighter, 293
Trevithick, Richard, 6, 16, 33, 162
Trevorrow, 82
Trevose, Cornwall, 86; —, Pa., 21, 86
Trewartha, 20, 229
Trewavas, J. R. 367
Treweek, 30, 131
Trewin family, Ga., 132; — —, S.C., 131; —, J. H., 156
Treworgy (Treworgie), 27, 42–3
Triplett family, Va., 118–9; —, William, 118
Trovillion, Hal W., 228
Trubody, W. A., 252–5
Truro, Cornwall, 23, 38, 228, 243, 325; —, Mass., 34; —, Va., 34, 118
Truscott, M. H., 300
Trythall, John, 266
Tuckingmill, Cornwall, 10, 230
Tucson, Ariz., 396, 397
Tuttle, Bishop D. S., 352
Twain, Mark, 266, 291

Uglow, 26
Union Pacific Railroad, 302, 314,

Index 451

Union Pacific Railroad (continued) 317, 352
United States Army, Cornish in, 17, 211–6, 235, 342, 387, 421; —— Navy, 98, 107–8
United Verde Mine, Colo., 391–2
Uren, 30, 368; —, Harriet, 167; —, Captain Richard, 172–3; —, Stephen, 264
U'Ren, W. S., 368–71
Utah, 301–19, 356; — Copper Company, 100, 316

Vanderbilt Line, 209
Ventura, Cal., 269, 273
Vermont, 418–9; — Historical Society, 418–9
Verran family, Wash., 380
Viall (Vyell), 184
Vicksburg, fall of, 207–8
Victoria, Queen, 112
Vincent, John, 214; —, Major W., 215
Virginia, 7, 35, 39–41, 117–22, 123, 126, 140, 164, 218; —, Army of Northern, 406; — Company, 38–9
Virginia City, Nev., 268, 274, 287, 288, 289–92, 295–6, 315
Vivian, 51, 131, 165, 199; — and Sons, Swansea, 324, 326, 392; —, Charles A. S., 17, 331–4; —, Dr. C. S., 388; —, Francis, 202–3, 206, 207; —, Governor J. C., 341–2; —, J. F., 340–1; —, Dr. John H., 207, 212
Vosper, 374
Vyvyan family, Cornwall, 234; —, Wis., 235

Wales, 178, 337; Welsh, 119, 392; — miners, 290
War of 1812, 108, 135, 204
Washington, 204, 231, 235, 366, 378–81, 421; —, D.C., 122, 127, 152, 204, 311, 410; —,

President George, 74, 92, 118, 119
Watt, James, 162
Wayne, General Anthony, 74, 98
Wearne, Edward, 213; —, Richard, 211
Weequohela, Indian chief, 70
West, John, 165
West Indies, 47
West Virginia, 142
Westminster, Eng., 61
Whirly Thunder, Indian chief, 204
White, John, cartographer, 38; —, of Dorchester, 46
Whitman, Walt, 151
Whittier, J. G., 45
Wilderness campaign, 93, 212
William III, 124
Williams, James, 261; —, R. B., 11; —, Roger, 48; —, Samuel, 101–2; —, Thomas, 101
Willyams, Brydges, 314–5
Wilson, President Woodrow, 371, 417
Winnipeg, Can., 332
Winter, John, 42, 45
Winthrop, Governor John, (I), 46, 47; —, —— (II), 49, 50
Wisconsin, 12, 196–236, 245, 368, 379; — Cavalry, 235; —, Cornish in, 216–7; — Volunteer Infantry, 207, 211–3
World War I, 103, 137, 262–3, 270, 283, 339, 357, 364; —— II, 23, 365

Yellowstone River, 209, 210
Yonkers, N.Y. 414
York, James, Duke of, 66; see also James II
Yorktown, Va., 119
Yorkville, Wis., 231, 236
Young, Brigham, 209, 288, 301, 304, 310; —, Frank, 342–3, 345–6

Zennor, Cornwall, 102
Ziervogel process of smelting, 325